MARCEL PROUST IN CONTEXT

This volume sets Marcel Proust's masterwork, *À la recherche du temps perdu* (*In Search of Lost Time*, 1913–27), in its cultural and socio-historical contexts. Essays by the leading scholars in the field attend to Proust's biography, his huge correspondence, and the genesis and protracted evolution of his masterpiece. Light is cast on Proust's relation to thinkers and artists of his time, and to those of the great French and European traditions of which he is now so centrally a part. There is vivid exploration of Proust's reading; his attitudes towards contemporary social and political issues; his relation to journalism, religion, sexuality, science and travel, and how these figure in the *Recherche*. The volume closes with a comprehensive survey of Proust's critical reception, from reviews during his lifetime to the present day, including assessments of Proust in translation and the broader assimilation of his work into twentieth- and twenty-first-century culture.

ADAM WATT is Associate Professor in French at the University of Exeter and is a member of the Équipe Proust at the ITEM/ENS in Paris. He is author of *Reading in Proust's 'À la recherche': 'le délire de la lecture'* (2009), *The Cambridge Introduction to Marcel Proust* (Cambridge, 2011) and an illustrated biography of the author, *Marcel Proust* (2013).

MARCEL PROUST IN CONTEXT

EDITED BY
ADAM WATT

CAMBRIDGE
UNIVERSITY PRESS

CAMBRIDGE
UNIVERSITY PRESS

University Printing House, Cambridge CB2 8BS, United Kingdom

Published in the United States of America by Cambridge University Press, New York

Cambridge University Press is part of the University of Cambridge.

It furthers the University's mission by disseminating knowledge in the pursuit of education, learning and research at the highest international levels of excellence.

www.cambridge.org
Information on this title: www.cambridge.org/9781107021891

© Cambridge University Press 2013

First published 2013

Printed by CPI Group (UK) Ltd, Croydon CR0 4YY

A catalogue record for this publication is available from the British Library

Library of Congress Cataloging-in-Publication Data
Marcel Proust in context / [edited by] Adam Watt.
pages cm. – (Literature in context)
ISBN 978-1-107-02189-1 (Hardback)   1. Proust, Marcel, 1871–1922 – Criticism and interpretation.
2. Proust, Marcel, 1871–1922. À la recherche du temps perdu.   3. Proust, Marcel, 1871–1922 – Knowledge.
4. Proust, Marcel, 1871–1922 – Appreciation.   I. Watt, Adam A. (Adam Andrew), 1979–
PQ2631.R63Z7225 2013
843'.912–dc23   2013021437

ISBN 978-1-107-02189-1 Hardback

Contents

v

Illustrations

Notes on contributors

NATHALIE AUBERT is Professor of French Literature at Oxford Brookes University. She has written a range of chapters and articles on European modernism and avant-garde movements, with a special emphasis on the 'visual'; she has published two books (2001 and 2003) and a number of articles and chapters on Proust. Her latest book is dedicated to Belgian poet and painter Christian Dotremont: *Christian Dotremont: la conquête du monde par l'image* (2012).

HUGUES AZÉRAD is Fellow in French at Magdalene College, Cambridge. He is the author of *L'Univers constellé de Proust, Faulkner et Joyce* (2002). He is co-editor (with Peter Collier) of *Twentieth-Century French Poetry: A Critical Anthology* (Cambridge University Press, 2010); he also co-edited (with Emma Wagstaff, Michael G. Kelly and Nina Parish) a special issue of *French Forum*, 'Poetic Practice and the Practice of Poetics in French since 1945' (2012), and *Chantiers du poème* (2012). He has written articles on Reverdy, Proust, Glissant, Faulkner, Nerval and Joyce and is an editor for *The Literary Encyclopedia*.

THOMAS BALDWIN is Senior Lecturer in French and Co-Director of the Centre for Modern European Literature at the University of Kent. His publications include *The Material Object in the Work of Marcel Proust* (2005), *The Flesh in the Text* (co-edited with James Fowler and Shane Weller, 2007), *The Picture as Spectre in Diderot, Proust, and Deleuze* (2011) and *Text and Image in Modern European Culture* (co-edited with Natasha Grigorian and Margaret Rigaud-Drayton, 2012).

CHRISTINE M. CANO is Associate Professor of French at Case Western Reserve University in Cleveland, Ohio, where she teaches French language, literature and cinema. She is the author of *Proust's Deadline*

(2006) and has published articles on various topics in twentieth-century book and media history.

WILLIAM C. CARTER is Distinguished Professor Emeritus at the University of Alabama at Birmingham. His biography *Marcel Proust: A Life* was named a 'Notable Book of 2000' by the *New York Times*, 'Best Book of 2000' by the *Los Angeles Times*, and 'Best Biography of 2000' by the *Sunday Times* of London. Harold Bloom has written that Carter is 'Proust's definitive biographer' and that his most recent book, *Proust in Love* is 'a marvellous study of the comic splendour of the great novelist's vision of human eros and its discontents'. He co-produced the award-winning documentary *Marcel Proust: A Writer's Life*. His website is www.proust-ink.com.

DAVID ELLISON is Distinguished Professor in the Humanities at the University of Miami, Florida. He is the author of three books on Proust – *The Reading of Proust* (1984), *A Reader's Guide to Proust's 'In Search of Lost Time'* (Cambridge University Press, 2010), and *Proust et la tradition littéraire européenne* (2012) – as well as studies on Albert Camus, the experimental French novel, literature and philosophy, literature and psychoanalysis, and Franco-German literary relations.

ANNA MAGDALENA ELSNER is a Leverhulme Early Career Fellow at King's College London and a member of the Équipe Proust at the ITEM/ENS in Paris. After completing her doctoral thesis at Cambridge University in 2011, she held the Joanna Randall McIver Research Fellowship at St Hugh's College, Oxford. Her current research investigates the clinical encounter in twentieth-century French literature and film. She is co-editor of *Anamnesia: Private and Public Memory in Modern French Culture* (2010) and author of articles on Proust and documentary cinema. Her book on mourning and creativity in Proust is forthcoming in 2014.

VINCENT FERRÉ is Professor in Comparative Literature and Theory, Université Paris Est-Créteil (UPEC, LIS) and a member of Fabula.org. His scholarship centres on the European and American novel, especially on Proust and Tolkien: on genres, the essay, philosophy; on medievalism. He is author and editor of *Sur les rivages de la Terre du milieu* (2001), *Tolkien, trente ans après* (2004), *Médiévalisme: modernité du Moyen Âge* (2010) and *Dictionnaire Tolkien* (2012); and co-editor of *Proust, l'étranger* (2010), *Cycle et collection* (2008) and *Littérature,* *politique et histoire au XXe siècle* (2010). Forthcoming: *L'essai fictionnel: roman et essai chez Proust, Broch et Dos Passos* (2013) and, co-edited: *Cross-Cultural Medievalisms* (2013) and *Proust: dialogues critiques.*

MICHAEL R. FINN is Adjunct Professor of French at Ryerson University, Toronto. His main research focus is the interaction between late-nineteenth-century medico-psychological theory and fiction. His articles have addressed fin-de-siècle subjects such as feminists and vivisection, the Naturalist movement and sexology, and French novels of sterilization and artificial insemination. He is the author of *Proust, the Body and Literary Form* (Cambridge University Press, 1999) and *Hysteria, Hypnosis, the Spirits and Pornography* (2009), a study of the decadent novelist Rachilde. His current book project examines figures of the pre-Freudian unconscious in the works of French writers including Flaubert, Maupassant and Proust.

LUC FRAISSE, Professor of French Literature at the University of Strasbourg, co-directs the Bibliothèque Proustienne collection for Classiques Garnier. He has published numerous books on Proust, including *Lire 'Du côté de chez Swann'* (1993), *L'Œuvre cathédrale: Proust et l'architecture médiévale* (1990, Grand prix de l'Académie française) and, recently, *L'Eclectisme philosophique de Marcel Proust* (2013). He has just submitted a new edition, with commentary, of *La Prisonnière* to Classiques Garnier, which is the first part of a re-edition of Proust's work.

CYNTHIA GAMBLE is Vice-Chairman of the Ruskin Society, a visiting Fellow of the Ruskin Library and Research Centre, Lancaster University, and a contributor to the online American University course www.proust-ink.com. Her publications include *Proust as Interpreter of Ruskin: The Seven Lamps of Translation* (2002); *'A Perpetual Paradise': Ruskin's Northern France*, co-authored with Stephen Wildman (2002); *Ruskin–Turner: dessins et voyages en Picardie romantique*, co-authored with Matthieu Pinette (2003); and fourteen entries to the *Dictionnaire Marcel Proust* (2004). Her most recent books are *John Ruskin, Henry James and the Shropshire Lads* (2008), and, with Matthieu Pinette, *L'Œil de Ruskin: l'exemple de la Bourgogne* (2011).

MARGARET E. GRAY is Associate Professor in the Department of French and Italian at Indiana University, Bloomington. She has published on Proust (*Postmodern Proust*, 1992, as well as additional articles and book chapters) and such authors as Sand, Colette, Camus,

Beauvoir, Beckett, Belgian writer Jean-Philippe Toussaint, Parisian immigrant Calixthe Beyala and Swiss novelist Noémi Lefebvre. Her current manuscript, *Stolen Limelight: Gender, Display, and Displacement in Twentieth-Century French and Francophone Narrative* comprises chapters devoted to novels by Gide, Colette, Mauriac, Duras, Japrisot and Oyono. Her research interests involve narrative dynamics of display, and the ways in which they work across a range of novels towards politicized purposes of struggle, resistance or repression.

EDWARD J. HUGHES is Professor of French in the School of Languages, Linguistics and Film at Queen Mary, University of London and is a former President of the Society for French Studies. He is the author of *Marcel Proust: A Study in the Quality of Awareness* (Cambridge University Press, 1983), *Albert Camus: 'Le Premier Homme'/'La Peste'* (1995), *Writing Marginality in Modern French Literature: From Loti to Genet* (Cambridge University Press, 2001) and *Proust, Class, and Nation* (2011). He edited *The Cambridge Companion to Camus* (2007).

JULIAN JOHNSON is Professor of Music at Royal Holloway, University of London. He has published widely on music from Beethoven to contemporary music, but with a particular focus on modernism, musical aesthetics and the wider idea of musical modernity. He has written four books, including *Webern and the Transformation of Nature* (Cambridge University Press, 1999), *Who Needs Classical Music?* (2002) and *Mahler's Voices: Expression and Irony in the Songs and Symphonies* (2009), and has contributed chapters to twenty edited volumes and articles to journals including *Nineteenth-Century Music*, *Music Analysis*, *Music and Letters* and *Austrian Studies*.

ELISABETH LADENSON is the author of *Proust's Lesbianism* (1999) and *Dirt for Art's Sake: Books on Trial from 'Madame Bovary' to 'Lolita'* (2007). She teaches at Columbia University.

ÁINE LARKIN is Lecturer in French at the University of Aberdeen, and the author of *Proust Writing Photography: Fixing the Fugitive in 'À la recherche du temps perdu'* (2011). A graduate of Trinity College, Dublin and the Université de la Sorbonne Nouvelle – Paris III, in 2008 she was awarded a Postdoctoral Research Fellowship by the Irish Research Council for the Humanities and Social Sciences. Together with text/image relations and Proust studies, her research interests include literature and medicine, the literary representation of music and dance, and contemporary women's writing in French.

BRIGITTE MAHUZIER is Professor of French at Bryn Mawr College. She edited special issues on Proust (*Littérature*) and queer French literature (*Yale French Studies*). Her book, *Proust et la guerre*, is forthcoming.

NATHALIE MAURIAC DYER is Directeur de Recherche at the CNRS (ITEM/ENS, Paris). Her work initially focused on the history of the posthumous part of *À la recherche* (*Proust inachevé: le dossier 'Albertine disparue'*, 2005). She is editor of the *Bulletin d'informations proustiennes*, and Director of the publication of Proust's *Cahiers 1 à 75 de la Bibliothèque nationale de France* (Brepols-BnF), of which she has co-edited *Cahier 54* (2008), *Cahier 71* (2009) and *Cahier 53* (2012). Recent edited volumes include *Proust aux brouillons* (2011) and *Proust face à l'héritage du xixᵉ siècle: tradition et métamorphose* (2012).

MARION SCHMID is Professor of French Literature and Film at the University of Edinburgh. She is the author of *Chantal Akerman* (2010), *Proust dans la décadence* (2008), *Proust at the Movies* (2005, co-authored with Martine Beugnet) and *Processes of Literary Creation: Flaubert and Proust* (1998). She co-edited (with Nigel Harkness) *Au seuil de la modernité: Proust, la littérature et les arts. Essays in Honour of Richard Bales* (2011) and (with Paul Gifford) *La Création en acte: devenir de la critique génétique* (2007). She is a member of the Équipe Proust at the Institut des Textes et Manuscrits Modernes, Paris (CNRS/ENS).

CÉLINE SURPRENANT is currently a post-doctoral research assistant to Professor Antoine Compagnon at the Collège de France, and Visiting Senior Lecturer in French in the School of English, University of Sussex, where she was Lecturer, then Senior Lecturer (1996–2010). She is the author of *Freud's Mass Psychology: Questions of Scale* (2003) and *Freud: A Guide for the Perplexed* (2008), and of articles on Freud, Proust, Proust and Darwin, and Samuel Beckett. She is currently writing a monograph entitled *Figures of Quantity*, on the paradigm of quantification in late-nineteenth- and early-twentieth-century literature and thought.

CAROLINE SZYLOWICZ is Associate Professor, Kolb-Proust Librarian and Curator of Rare Books and Manuscripts at the University of Illinois at Urbana-Champaign Library. She oversees the digitization of Philip Kolb's research notes held in the Kolb-Proust Archive for Research (www.library.illinois.edu/kolbp). She has published several articles related to Proust's drawings, his correspondence and an inventory of the Proust collection of manuscripts held at the University of Illinois Library.

MARGARET TOPPING is Professor of French at Queen's University Belfast. Her research spans a number of key areas: the work of Marcel Proust with a particular focus on its metaphorical construction; textual and visual narratives of travel and migration; intermediality; and street art. She is the author of *Proust's Gods* (2000) and *Supernatural Proust* (2007), the editor of *Eastern Voyages, Western Visions: French Writing and Painting of the Orient* (2004) and co-editor of *Beckett's Proust/ Deleuze's Proust* (2009). She is currently completing a book on *Photo-textual Journeys: Francophone Travel Literature and Photography* and developing a project on transcultural identities and music.

GABRIELLE TOWNSEND is a writer, editor and translator. After a career in publishing she completed a DPhil on Proust at Oxford under the supervision of Malcolm Bowie. Her book *Proust's Imaginary Museum: Reproductions and Reproduction in 'À la recherche du temps perdu'* was published in 2008, and she also contributed to *'When familiar meanings dissolve . . .': Essays in French Studies in Memory of Malcolm Bowie* (2011). She was for several years Assistant Editor and Reviews Editor of the *Journal of Romance Studies*.

SARAH TRIBOUT-JOSEPH is Lecturer in French at the University of Edinburgh. She is the author of *Proust and Joyce in Dialogue* (2008) and numerous articles on Proust.

ADAM WATT is Associate Professor in French at the University of Exeter. He is the author of *Reading in Proust's 'À la recherche': 'le délire de la lecture'* (2009), *The Cambridge Introduction to Marcel Proust* (2011) and *Marcel Proust* (2013). He edited *'Le Temps retrouvé' Eighty Years After* (2009). After studying at Oxford he taught at Trinity College, Dublin (2005–6) and Royal Holloway, University of London (2006–12) before joining the University of Exeter. He is a member of the Équipe Proust at the ITEM/ENS, Paris.

MICHAEL WOOD is Professor of English and Comparative Literature at Princeton University. His most recent books are *Literature and the Taste of Knowledge* (Cambridge University Press, 2005) and *Yeats and Violence* (2010). His selection of the letters of Italo Calvino, translated by Martin McLaughlin, is forthcoming.

Figure 1. Marcel Proust, portrait in oils by Jacques-Émile Blanche, 1892

Preface

What unique place might we allot to his work? Between philosophy, science, epic poetry, satire, memoirs and all hitherto recorded forms of the novel?[1]

Readers of Proust are still asking these questions today, posed by the society painter Jacques-Émile Blanche in a memoir that appeared in 1928, the year after the publication of *À la recherche du temps perdu* was completed. Proust was dead only six years but the myth of the man was already alive and strong. It had been growing, in fact, since the time of Blanche's portrait of the author, in oils, in 1892, some thirty years before (see Fig. 1). The plurality of Proust's writing – prose that shifts effortlessly from cool logic to impassioned bluster, from the observational noting of the laboratory to spinning the fine and delicate thread of metaphor – invites multiple modes of interpretation, multiple frames of reference through which we might read. Such writing is singular, provocative, demanding. The chapters that follow offer a succession of approaches to individual aspects of this plurality; they provide spaces in which we might think about Proust, his work and the conditions of its creation: in its own way each chapter contributes an answer, or part of an answer to Blanche's question.

Proust's lifetime (1871–1922) spanned an exceptional period of accelerated world-historical change and development in every sphere of human activity. To explore the 'contexts' of Proust's work, then, is to step into rapidly flowing waters, to seek to capture the dynamic rush and thrust of socio-cultural shifts that stretch from the Paris Commune and its fall, via the bold display of industrial and colonial force at the World's Fair of 1889 and the rarefied whirl of the Belle Époque, to the cold, violent reality of a world war and its aftermath. At no other time in history has experiment in literature, music and visual art been more radical or revolutionary than during Proust's short life.

xvii

Part I of *Marcel Proust in Context* approaches the author's biography, his extraordinary correspondence, the faltering journey that led towards the construction of *À la recherche* and the intriguing story of its evolution from two to three to (eventually) seven substantial volumes. The first section of Part II offers an account of Proust's relations to the arts most broadly understood: how does his reading offer a context for understanding his writing practice? In what ways did Proust assimilate or resist the artistic and intellectual currents of his own time and those of the longer tradition of which he is now a part? How did the artistic energies that pulsed and surged through Paris in the early years of the twentieth century feed into Proust's project?

À la recherche is at once a sustained exploration of the nature of the self and a study of a whole social world in a state of flux. The second section of Part II takes 'Self and Society' as its focus and considers a range of frames of reference: the writings of Freud and the development of psychoanalysis; contemporary thinking on sexuality and medical matters; science, religion, travel and journalism. The French socio-political landscape of Proust's time is treated in three complementary chapters that close this section, exploring Proust's relation to questions of politics and class, his attitude towards the Dreyfus Affair and the ways in which the First World War had an impact on the shape, substance and reception of *À la recherche du temps perdu*.

Part III tackles the critical reception of Proust's work in two ways. A first group of four chapters explores the responses *À la recherche* has elicited since the publication began in 1913, up to the present day, mapping trends and assessing the fortunes of the novel through the past century. Three final chapters conclude the volume with discussions of Proust's reception in more specifically defined terms: first within the sometimes troubling category of modernism; then within contemporary media culture; and finally in translation, that medium which has broadened the reach of this most plural of novels further still.

In preparing this volume I have been fortunate to work with a terrific team at Cambridge University Press: I would like to thank Linda Bree for suggesting the project in the first place and Anna Bond and Abi Jones for their support and hugely efficient assistance in the final stages. Thanks also to Lesley Lawn for providing the translation of the chapter by Luc Fraisse and to Catherine Terk at Rue des Archives for her help in sourcing the illustrations. Thanks too for her love and support, as always, to Stace. It has been an honour to work with the distinguished scholars from institutions in France, Canada, the US and the UK whose work fills the pages that follow. Writing a short piece about a big subject is always a challenge and a multiplier effect seems to take hold whenever Proust is involved. Fortunately (and for this I am very grateful) my contributors managed to resist the swell rather better than Proust ever did.

ADAM WATT

Notes

1 Jacques-Émile Blanche, *Mes modèles: Barrès, Hardy, Proust, James, Gide, Moore* (Paris: Stock, 1928), p. 118.

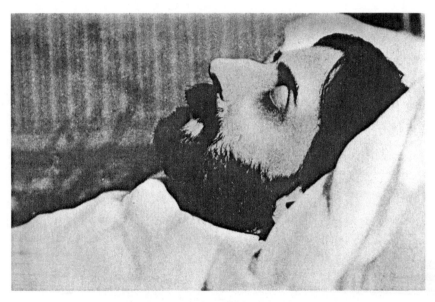

Figure 2. Proust photographed on his death-bed by Man Ray, 1922

Note on the text

All quotations are taken from the Vintage Classics six-volume edition of *In Search of Lost Time*, translated by C. K. Scott Moncrieff (except for *Time Regained*, translated by Andreas Mayor and Terence Kilmartin), revised by Terence Kilmartin and D. J. Enright (London: Vintage, 2000–2). References are given in the form (3: 456), i.e. volume number, followed by page reference. These are followed in the text by volume and page references to the four-volume 'Pléiade' edition of *À la recherche du temps perdu*, produced under the general editorship of Jean-Yves Tadié (Paris: Gallimard, 1987–9). References to the French text take the form (IV, 321).

References to Proust's essays and shorter writings are taken from *Against Sainte-Beuve and Other Essays*, translated by John Sturrock (Harmondsworth: Penguin, 1988) and *Contre Sainte-Beuve précédé de Pastiches et mélanges et suivi de Essais et articles*, edited by Pierre Clarac and Yves Sandre (Paris: Gallimard, 1971) and are incorporated in the text in the form *ASB* or *CSB*, each followed by page numbers. Where no reference to *ASB* is given, the passage in question is not included by Sturrock.

References to Proust's early, unfinished novel *Jean Santeuil* are identified with the abbreviation *JS*, followed by page references first to *Jean Santeuil*, translated by Gerard Hopkins (Harmondsworth: Penguin, 1985 [Weidenfeld & Nicolson, 1955]), then to *Jean Santeuil précédé de Les Plaisirs et les jours*, edited by Pierre Clarac and Yves Sandre (Paris: Gallimard, 1971). Where only one page reference is given, this is to untranslated material from the French text.

All references to Proust's correspondence (abbreviated to *Corr*, followed by a volume number and page reference) are to the *Correspondance de Marcel Proust*, edited by Philip Kolb, 21 vols. (Paris: Plon, 1970–93); translations from the correspondence, and from all other works in French, unless otherwise stated, are by the author of the chapter in question.

Chronology

1871	10 July: Marcel Proust is born to Jeanne Proust née Weil and Dr Adrien Proust in the village of Auteuil, to the west of Paris. He is very weak in infancy.
1872	The Proust family moves to an apartment on the boulevard Malesherbes in the 8th arrondissement of Paris.
1873	24 May: Robert Proust, Marcel's brother, is born.
1878–86	Family vacations at Illiers (renamed Illiers-Combray in 1971) in the Eure-et-Loir.
1881	Proust's first, and near-fatal, asthma attack. Respiratory and other health problems will henceforth be a permanent part of his life.
1882–9	Proust attends the Lycée Fontanes (renamed Condorcet in 1883); attendance poor due to ill health, but various friendships formed.
1889	Proust turns eighteen. *Classe de philosophie*. Inauguration of the Eiffel Tower as the entrance arch to the World's Fair. November: Proust signs up for one year's voluntary military service.
1890	3 January: Death of Proust's maternal grandmother, Adèle Weil. Enrols at the Faculty of Law and the School of Political Science.
1891	Journalism appears in *Le Mensuel*. Thomas Hardy, *Tess of the D'Urbervilles*.
1892	Proust and friends from Condorcet found a review, *Le Banquet*. Increased socializing.
1893	Publications in the important journal, *La Revue blanche*. Completes Licence en droit.
1894	President Carnot assassinated in Lyon by an anarchist. December: court martial judges Captain Albert Dreyfus guilty.

1895	Completes Licence ès lettres. Unpaid position at the Bibliothèque Mazarine. Scarcely attends due to 'ill health'. Stays in Brittany with Reynaldo Hahn. Begins notes towards *Jean Santeuil*. Trial of Oscar Wilde.
1896	March: Publication of *Les Plaisirs et les jours.*
1897	Duels with journalist Jean Lorrain over Lorrain's public insinuations of Proust's homosexual relation with Lucien Daudet. Henry James, *What Maisie Knew.*
1898	13 January: Zola's 'J'accuse' in *L'Aurore*. Later in the year Proust attends Zola's trial.
1899	*Jean Santeuil* abandoned, Proust starts work on a translation of Ruskin's *The Bible of Amiens*. Freud, *Die Traudeutung* (*The Interpretation of Dreams*). Conrad, *Heart of Darkness.*
1900	Ruskin's death. Proust publishes a series of articles on the Englishman. Travels to Venice with his mother and friends in April; returns, alone, in October. Death of Nietzsche.
1901	Thomas Mann, four years Proust's junior, publishes *Buddenbrooks.*
1902	Travels to Belgium and Holland with Hahn, visits Bruges and Amsterdam amongst other places. Sees Vermeer's *View of Delft* and many old Dutch masters.
1903	February: Marriage of Robert Proust. Society pieces published in *Le Figaro*. Gertrude Stein moves to Paris from the United States. November: sudden death of Proust's father.
1904	*La Bible d'Amiens* published. Translation of Ruskin's *Sesame and Lilies* begun. Society journalism continues.
1905	June: Proust's important essay on reading, the preface to *Sésame et les lys*, is published. July: French government passes a law separating the Church from the State. Mme Proust is taken ill in Évian and rushed back to Paris by Robert. 26 September: death of Mme Proust. December: Proust checks in to the clinic of Dr Sollier, something he had promised his mother he would do.
1906	Sollier's treatment having made little difference to Proust's health, he spends August to December in the Hôtel des Réservoirs in Versailles, unwilling to be alone in the family home. Dreyfus reinstated in the Army. *Sésame et les lys* is published. Proust resolves to move into what was his great-uncle Georges Weil's Paris residence, 102 boulevard Haussmann.

1907	Picasso's *Demoiselles d'Avignon* completed in Paris. Various articles and stories published. Summer in Cabourg on the Normandy coast. Proust meets Alfred Agostinelli, a young taxi driver. Proust will return to Cabourg every year between 1907 and 1914.
1908	Proust plans a project 'Against Sainte-Beuve', part critical essay, part dialogue. Features of what will become *À la recherche du temps perdu* take shape. Succession of brilliant pastiches, around the Lemoine Affair, appear in *Le Figaro*.
1909	*Contre Sainte-Beuve* amounts to around 400 pages; publishers show no interest. Marinetti's first *Manifesto of Futurism* in Paris; Gustav Mahler's Symphony No. 9.
1910–11	Proust develops the core sequences of his novel that will become *Du côté de chez Swann*, *Le Temps retrouvé*, part of *Le Côté de Guermantes* and, latterly, parts of *À l'ombre des jeunes filles en fleurs*.
1912–13	Successive rejections from publishers.
1913	In the spring, Agostinelli moves into Proust's apartment as a secretary. *Du côté de chez Swann* is accepted for publication at the author's expense by Grasset. Stravinsky's *Rite of Spring*, Lawrence's *Sons and Lovers*, Duchamp's *Bicycle Wheel*. 14 November: publication of *Du côté de chez Swann*.
1914	May: Agostinelli dies, drowned in the Mediterranean as a result of a flying accident. August: French forces mobilized. Printing presses cease activity during the war. Céleste Albaret officially enters Proust's service. James Joyce, *Dubliners*.
1915	Proust develops *Sodome et Gomorrhe* and the 'Albertine cycle', *La Prisonnière* and *Albertine disparue*.
1916	Negotiations with the Nouvelle Revue française who wish to take over publication of *À la recherche* from Grasset. May: Proust reports suffering a seventy-hour period of insomnia. July: first Dada manifesto proclaimed in Zurich.
1917	February and October: revolution in Russia. 18 May: in Paris, Proust attends the première of *Parade*, performed by the Ballets Russes, with a scenario by Cocteau, score by Satie, set and costumes by Picasso and programme notes by Apollinaire.
1918	Proust's health, always fragile, becomes a near-constant preoccupation as he devotes longer and longer hours to correcting his novel.

1919	June: NRF reissues *Du côté de chez Swann*, publishes *Pastiches et mélanges* and *À l'ombre des jeunes filles en fleurs*. The relative who owned 102 boulevard Haussmann decides to sell and Proust has to move, twice, eventually settling at 44 rue Hamelin in October. December: *À l'ombre* awarded the Prix Goncourt.
1920	André Breton employed by Gallimard as proofreader for *Le Côté de Guermantes*. May: Breton and Soupault's *Les Champs magnétiques*, the first work of surrealist (or proto-surrealist) 'automatic writing'. October: *Le Côté de Guermantes I* published.
1921	May: Proust sees Vermeer's *View of Delft* once more, at an exhibition at the Jeu de Paume. *Le Côté de Guermantes II* and *Sodome et Gomorrhe I* are published together.
1922	Increasing doses of self-medication. February: Joyce's *Ulysses* published in Paris. April: *Sodome et Gomorrhe II* published. October: T. S. Eliot's *The Waste Land* appears in *The Criterion*. 18 November: Proust dies after developing pneumonia. Gaston Gallimard and Robert Proust undertake to publish the remaining volumes of the *Recherche*.
1923	Publication of *La Prisonnière*.
1925	Publication of *Albertine disparue*; Virginia Woolf, *Mrs Dalloway*.
1927	Publication of *Le Temps retrouvé*.

PART I
Life and works

CHAPTER 1

Life

William C. Carter

On 10 July 1901, Marcel Proust called on his friend Léon Yeatman in his law office and announced: 'Today I'm thirty years old, and I've achieved nothing!' (*Corr*, 11, 32). Yeatman must have protested, but Marcel had good reason to be discouraged. Nearly all his friends had established themselves as writers or launched other successful careers. Although he held university degrees in literature, philosophy and law, he had never entered a profession. He had stubbornly rejected the advice of his father, Dr Adrien Proust, one of France's most distinguished physicians and scientists. After one of their heated discussions about his failure to choose a career, Marcel wrote: 'My dearest papa . . . I still believe that anything I do other than literature and philosophy will be just so much wasted time' (*Corr*, 1, 237).

Dr Proust was a self-made man from the little town of Illiers. His fortune had greatly increased when he married Jeanne Weil, the daughter of a wealthy Jewish family. Proust adored his mother, who, though modest and discreet, quoted with ease from the classics in several languages. Her influence was the strongest in Proust's life. From the age of ten, he suffered from asthma and other ailments and was regarded by his parents as neurasthenic if not neurotic. In the *Recherche*, Proust has a physician say: 'Everything we think of as great has come to us from neurotics. It is they and they alone who found religions and create great works of art' (3: 350; 11, 601). But neither he nor his parents had such confidence; his childhood ailments prevented him from enjoying many activities and even caused him to miss an entire school year.

Proust's *lycée* professors and classmates, many of whom later became writers themselves, recognized his talent early. Jacques Bizet gave his cousin Daniel Halévy a letter from Marcel describing the scene that had erupted when his father caught him masturbating: 'this morning, dearest . . . my father . . . begged me to stop masturbating for at least four days'. He goes on to say that if his parents refuse him permission to invite Jacques, then he will 'love' him 'outside the walls' of the family prison.

3

This letter amazed Daniel not only because of the glimpse into Marcel's private life and the revelation of his homosexual proclivities, but also as a text. Halévy recorded that Proust had written it without crossing out a single word: 'This deranged creature is extremely talented, and I know NOTHING that is sadder and more marvellously written than these two pages.'[1] Years later, when asked if any of Proust's schoolmates had a premonition of his genius, Halévy answered that no one believed he had 'the will power ever to achieve a masterpiece'.[2]

In 1896, Proust published his first book, *Pleasures and Days*, consisting of stories and poems written in his early twenties. He persuaded a society hostess, Madeleine Lemaire, to illustrate the volume, which was prefaced by Anatole France. Prior to publication, *Le Gaulois* and *Le Figaro* carried on their front pages France's preface that praised Proust's 'marvelous spirit of observation, a supple, penetrating and truly subtle intelligence'.[3] Although the book received several laudatory reviews, few took Proust seriously as a writer.

A year earlier, Proust had vacationed in the seaside village of Beg-Meil in Britanny, where he began writing *Jean Santeuil*. Despite its fragmentary state, this manuscript is, after the *Recherche*, his most important work, because it represents his first attempt to write a novel and contains many themes and characters that he was to refashion for his masterpiece. One finds in *Jean Santeuil* episodes of memory ignited by a physical sensation, a phenomenon that he was to call involuntary memory in the madeleine scene in *Swann's Way*. He recognized the potential of such experiences, but was years away from discovering how to make them serve a plot. In *Jean Santeuil*, Proust indicates his uncertainty about the genre of the work he was struggling to create: 'Should I call this book a novel? It is something less, perhaps, and yet much more, the very essence of my life' (*JS*, 2; 181). Proust saw what he wished to achieve, but did not yet know how to transpose the essence of his life into a work of fiction.

In October 1899, Proust went to the Bibliothèque nationale to consult the works of John Ruskin. A short time later he wrote to a friend, informing her of his failure at novel-writing and announcing his new project: 'For the last fortnight I have been busy with a little piece completely different from what I usually do, about Ruskin and certain cathedrals' (*Corr*, III, 377).

After Ruskin's death in early 1900, Proust decided to expand the 'little piece' into a more ambitious undertaking. He devoted most of the following five years to translating and annotating works by Ruskin. As was typical of him during this period, he often stalled and became frustrated. But when his father died suddenly in 1903, his mother urged him to finish translating *The Bible of Amiens*. Proust took her advice and, in 1904, published the work, dedicated to Adrien Proust.

In June 1905, the *Renaissance latine* printed the preface to his translation of *Sesame and Lilies*, which begins:

> There are no days of my childhood which I have lived so fully perhaps as those I thought I had left behind without living them, those I spent with a favourite book. . . . If still, today, I chance to leaf through these books from the past, it is simply as the only calendars I have preserved of those bygone days, and in the hope of finding reflected in their pages the houses and the ponds which no longer exist. (*ASB*, 195; *CSB*, 160)

The readers of the *Renaissance latine* did not know – nor did Proust himself – that they were receiving a foretaste of Combray.

In the preface, Proust gives the different meanings of *sesame* employed by Ruskin that create not only a structure but also layers of meaning, a method that will be characteristic of Proust's style. He describes Ruskin as passing

> from one idea to another without any apparent order. But in reality the fancy that leads him follows his profound affinities that in spite of himself impose on him a superior logic. So that in the end he happens to have obeyed a kind of secret plan which, unveiled at the end, imposes retrospectively on the whole a sort of order and makes it appear magnificently arranged up to this final apotheosis.[4]

Although Proust had not yet begun *In Search of Lost Time*, his method of composing was to be similar to Ruskin's.

On 26 September 1905, Proust's mother died. For the next two years, depressed and ill, he seldom rose from his bed. His 1907 summer vacation in Cabourg marks his resumption of an active schedule. He wrote an article for *Le Figaro*, 'Impressions de route en automobile' ['Impressions of riding in an automobile'], that related an excursion to Caen, where, as Alfred Agostinelli's red taxi sped along, the writer observed the rapidly shifting positions of the church steeples of Saint-Étienne and Saint-Pierre. One aspect of this article is remarkable: Proust twice mentions wanting to arrive before nightfall at the home of his parents, who were deceased. Here, as in the preface to *Sésame*, he is transposing his life into a fictional work, but remains uncertain as to its exact nature and content.

On New Year's Day 1908, Mme Geneviève Straus gave Proust five little notebooks. On thanking her, he said that he had a new project in mind and was eager 'to begin a fairly long piece of work' (*Corr*, VIII, 39). He chose the largest notebook (now referred to as *Le Carnet de 1908*), and began jotting down ideas and sketches that were to converge and lead to the *Recherche*. One scene described the anger of his little brother Robert when forced to part with his pet goat. The locale is inspired by childhood memories used to create Combray. Eventually, Proust dropped Robert and reduced this scene to twenty-five lines in which the Narrator bids farewell to his beloved hawthorns. He made entries about themes and characters in the notebook for several years and listed sensations capable of reviving the past.

Having written the poems, sketches and short stories published in *Les Plaisirs*, drafted over a thousand pages for *Jean Santeuil*, translated Ruskin, and written society articles and parodies for *Le Figaro*, Proust had completed his long apprenticeship. Yet he still found it impossible to focus on one topic or genre. In May 1908, he listed his projects:

> a study of the nobility
> a Parisian novel
> an essay on Sainte-Beuve and Flaubert
> an essay on Women
> an essay on homosexuality (not easy to publish)
> a study of stained-glass windows
> a study of tombstones
> a study of the novel. (*Corr*, VIII, 112–13)

These are the topics that interested him when he began the earliest drafts of his novel, which contain many of the same elements as *Jean Santeuil* and his early stories: the child's nervous dependency on his mother, obsessive jealousy, snobbery in the world of high society, and meditations on the arts, especially literature and music. The essay on homosexuality will form part of the beginning of *Sodom and Gomorrah* and be linked to the novel's themes of sexual obsession and jealousy, elaborated in the loves of Swann and Odette, the Narrator and Albertine, and Charlus and Morel.

In July 1908, Proust listed the six parts already written. Among these was 'the Villebon Way and the Méséglise Way'. He soon changed 'Villebon' to the more euphonious Guermantes. The two place names, the first from a chateau near Illiers and another from a nearby village, indicate he had found the 'two ways', one of the major unifying elements of his novel, destined to become Swann's way and the Guermantes way. Another key episode was the drama of the goodnight kiss, in which the child Narrator, unable to sleep, places his mother in the position of making concessions and spending the night in his room. This primal scene of all Proustian narration, sketched in a story in *Les Plaisirs et les jours* and reprised in the drafts of *Jean Santeuil*, became the scene in the *Recherche* where the

Narrator as a child loses his will. He will spend the rest of his life trying to regain the independence and strength in order to become a writer. The last episode on the list indicates the story's conclusion: 'What I learned from the Villebon Way and the Méséglise Way.'[5] He had conceived an apprentice novel, in which the Narrator becomes neurotically dependent as a child, grows up to explore the two ways of his world, that of the landed gentry and Paris salons, and fails to find happiness in erotic love. But soon he stalled again, unable to see that he had found the 'sesame' that would open the doors to a new world of fiction.

In late 1908 Proust began an essay attacking Charles-Augustin Sainte-Beuve. Some of the drafts of *Contre Sainte-Beuve* constitute parts of the first version of the future novel. In the passages containing the early versions of the madeleine scene, Proust describes the past resurrected through involuntary memory, summoned by toast and tea, and follows with another involuntary memory evoking Venice. These rare moments are triggered by the chance encounter with an object unconsciously connected to a past impression. The draft continues with a series of such experiences. In the novel, he places the toast and tea episode, replacing the mundane toast with a madeleine, in *Combray I*, where it serves as an example of the 'true life' and the type of vivid recollection the Narrator needs to capture in his writing, when he feels such joy at being outside time. All the other involuntary memory experiences from *Contre Sainte-Beuve* were placed near the story's end, where these felicitous moments create a crescendo effect as the Narrator, after many years of idleness, reclaims his will, forfeited long ago in childhood, and finds his vocation:

> And I understood that all these materials for a work of literature were simply my past life; I understood that they had come to me, in frivolous pleasures, in indolence, in tenderness, in unhappiness, and that I had stored them up without divining the purpose for which they were destined or even their continued existence any more than a seed does when it forms within itself a reserve of all the nutritious substances from which it will feed a plant ... And thus my whole life up to the present day might and yet might not have been summed up under the title: A Vocation. (6: 258–9; IV, 478)

In spring 1909, Proust abandoned the critical essay and devoted himself entirely to the novel. If he had had such difficulty in finding his genre, it was because ultimately he had to reinvent it. By the time he finished, Proust had created what is perhaps the richest narrative voice in literature, a voice that speaks both as child and as man, as actor and as subject, and weaves effortlessly between the present, past and future.

In 1912, after receiving rejection notices from Fasquelle, Ollendorff, and the *Nouvelle Revue française* (Gallimard), Proust signed a contract with Bernard Grasset and agreed to pay all the publishing costs. On 8 November 1913, one week before publication, Proust received a reporter from *Le Temps* and explained his views on time, characters and style. During the interview, he quoted from passages from *Swann* and future volumes, perhaps hoping to thwart criticisms about the lack of a plot by showing some of the lessons the Narrator learns at the end of his quest. And he insisted on the importance of time: 'I have attempted to isolate the invisible substance of time, but to do that the experiment had to be able to be long-lasting' (*ASB*, 234; *CSB*, 557).

The year 1914 proved to be a terrible one for Europe and especially for Proust. Gaston Calmette, editor of *Le Figaro*, to whom *Swann* is dedicated, was assassinated in March. In May, Proust's beloved secretary, Alfred Agostinelli, perished in an aeroplane crash. Then in August, came the outbreak of the First World War. Welcome news arrived in a letter from André Gide: 'My dear Proust, for several days I have not put down your book; I am supersaturating myself in it, with delight, I am wallowing in it.' Then Gide confessed: 'The rejection of this book will remain the gravest mistake of the NRF – and (for I have the shame of being largely responsible for it) one of the bitterest, most remorseful regrets of my life.' Gide had been prejudiced by the image of Proust, based on a few social encounters years earlier: 'I thought you – shall I confess it? – were from the "Verdurin way," a snob, a dilettante socialite – the worst possible thing for our review.' Gide admitted that he had only glanced at a few sentences before tossing the manuscript aside. Saying that he would never forgive himself, he begged Proust 'to be more indulgent towards me than I am myself' (*Corr*, XIII, 50–1).

Proust replied immediately: 'My dear Gide, I have often felt that certain great joys are conditional on our having first been deprived of a lesser one, which we deserved, but without the denial of which we could never have known the other, greater joy.'[6] He told Gide to feel no remorse, 'for you have given me a thousand times more pleasure than pain' (*Corr*, XIII, 57). Proust now had what he had always wanted: to be read and respected by the group of men at the *NRF* whom he considered his peers. Gide and Gaston Gallimard began planning, with Proust's aid, to secure his release from the contract with Grasset.

Proust followed the progress of the war by reading seven daily newspapers. Given the circular structure of the *Recherche*, it was relatively easy to incorporate the war years into his story. As a result of Agostinelli's death,

Proust greatly expanded the part known as the Albertine cycle. When peace came in November 1918, Proust worried that readers would not remember or even care about the long, meditative story he had begun in *Swann* five years earlier. He received the answer on 10 December 1919, when *Within a Budding Grove* won the Goncourt Prize, France's most prestigious literary award.

As his health worsened, Proust worked to complete the remaining volumes. Although he lived to see *The Guermantes Way* and *Sodom and Gomorrah* in print, he had revised only the first hundred pages of *The Captive* when he died on 18 November 1922. The final volumes appeared posthumously: *The Captive* (1923); *The Fugitive* (1925); *Time Regained* (1927).

In *Time Regained*, the Narrator gives a pessimistic forecast about the fate of the book that he at long last intends to write:

> No doubt my books too, like my fleshly being, would in the end one day die. But death is a thing that we must resign ourselves to. We accept the thought that in ten years we ourselves, in a hundred years our books, will have ceased to exist. Eternal duration is promised no more to men's works than to men. (6: 445; IV, 620–1)

Now nearly a century after the publication of *Swann*, we know the fate of Proust's book. *In Search of Lost Time* has not merely survived, it has triumphed and continues to provide its readers with the rejuvenating energy and joy that resides in great works of genius.

Notes

1 *Marcel Proust: Correspondance avec Daniel Halévy*, ed. Anne Borrel and Jean-Pierre Halévy (Paris: Éditions de Fallois, 1992), pp. 42–4.
2 *Letters of Marcel Proust*, trans. and ed., with notes, by Mina Curtiss, with an introduction by Harry Levin (New York: Vintage, 1966), p. 4.
3 See *Pleasures and Days*, trans. by Andrew Brown (London: Hesperus, 2004), p. 3; *Les Plaisirs et les jours* in *Jean Santeuil précédé de Les Plaisirs et les jours*, ed. by Pierre Clarac and Yves Sandre (Paris: Gallimard, 1971), p. 3.
4 John Ruskin, *Sésame et les Lys*, preceded by *Sur la lecture*, trans. with notes by Marcel Proust, ed. Antoine Compagnon (Paris: Éditions Complexe, 'Le Regard littéraire', 1987), p. 104, n. 1.
5 *Le Carnet de 1908*, transcribed and edited by Philip Kolb, *Cahiers Marcel Proust*, n. s., 8, (Paris: Gallimard, 1976), p. 141 and n. 61.
6 Proust, *Selected Letters*, trans. by Terence Kilmartin, ed. Philip Kolb (London: HarperCollins, 1992), p. 226. Translation slightly altered.

CHAPTER 2

Correspondence

Luc Fraisse, translated by Lesley Lawn

When readers of *À la recherche* come to examine Proust's correspondence, they are struck by two contradictory facts: on one hand, the considerable size of the task taken on by the editors of the letters and, on the other, the perplexing issue of the importance that might be attributed to these documents. The most extensive edition of the correspondence, completed by Philip Kolb, consists of more than five thousand letters written between 1879 and 1922 by an author who, in the last years of his life, was a total recluse and capable of writing up to eighteen letters in one day. Thanks to this outstanding editorial achievement, the importance of Proust as a letter-writer has been proven beyond doubt. Although more letters or collections of letters come to light quite regularly from various sources (Kolb was of the opinion that he had discovered perhaps only one letter in twenty) the general basis for their publication is henceforth firmly established. On the other hand, the interpretation of the letters is an area that remains largely unexplored, representing for criticism as-yet-uncharted waters.

The publication of Proust's letters

To some extent, the publication of the letters is partly called into question by a ban imposed by the author himself. On one occasion in January 1921, Proust was returning a letter to one of his female correspondents, and expressed in the broadest terms the wish that his letters should not be preserved: 'I insist ... that no correspondence written by me should be preserved, let alone published' (*Corr*, XX, 35). Such a statement would have carried significant implications if the novelist had followed through his decision. When questioned by myself on the subject, Philip Kolb alluded to the account given by Proust's governess, Céleste Albaret, according to whom a lawyer who was consulted on the matter said that the novelist did

10

not have the right to dispose as he wished of any letters he had written. Kolb challenged this account:

> no lawyer would ever maintain that the owner, the recipient of a letter, was free to do with it what he pleased. He could do what he wished with the paper and the ink but not with the text. We can be certain that if Proust had wanted to prohibit the publication of his letters, he had every means at his disposal. However, he must have changed his mind, realizing primarily that it would be impossible to get all his letters returned, because he had written thousands and thousands. He regretted having written so many letters but it was too late to do anything about it.[1]

Such assumptions are particularly significant, both from the legal and the psychological perspective, since some of Proust's letters were indeed published during his lifetime, having been included in works written by friends of the author: in *Le Chancelier des fleurs* by Robert de Montesquiou (1908) and in *Dates* by Jacques-Émile Blanche (1921).[2]

After Proust's death however, several of his correspondents judged that, as regards the letters, they were sometimes in possession of documents of prime importance, which would contribute to a wider knowledge and understanding of an author already considered to be one of the key figures of his generation. In a special edition of the *Nouvelle Revue française* paying homage to the late author in January 1923, under the title 'Les clefs de l'œuvre de Proust' ['The Keys of Proust's Work'], Jacques de Lacretelle made public a letter from 1918, which revealed a variety of sources relating to the monocle episode and more importantly that of the Vinteuil sonata in *Un amour de Swann*. From then on, Proust's closest and more astute friends realized that their own accounts and memoirs concerning the author ought to be centred around the letters that they had preserved, their own narrative being the thread that would weave them all together. Robert Dreyfus paved the way with his *Souvenirs sur Marcel Proust* (1926), followed by the Princess Bibesco with *Au bal avec Marcel Proust* (1928), Lucien Daudet's *Autour de soixante lettres de Marcel Proust* (1929) and subsequently the invaluable *Marcel Proust – lettres et conversations* by Robert de Billy (1930). Since there was sometimes a considerable delay before the writer's friends decided to pass on their letters, such books continued to appear throughout the twentieth century (for example, *Proust connu et inconnu* by Louis Gautier-Vignal (1976) and Jacques Benoist-Méchin's *Avec Marcel Proust* (1977).

Others among Proust's old friends would choose a different option, which was to publish a collection of those letters in their possession with a substantial preface in lieu of a souvenir portrait, notably Marie

Riefstahl-Nordlinger's *Lettres à une amie* (1942) and Georges de Lauris's *À un ami* (1948). Meanwhile, Proust's brother Robert, who oversaw the publication by Gallimard of the remaining volumes of *À la recherche*, noted the fragmented way in which his brother's letters were being published and persuaded the publisher Plon to accept his proposed *Correspondance générale*, a collection organized not yet chronologically but according to the recipients. His reasons for going from Gallimard over to Plon, solely in order to publish the letters, have recently been brought to light by Nathalie Mauriac Dyer in a collection of documents published in 1999 entitled *Robert Proust et la Nouvelle Revue française: les années perdues de la 'Recherche' (1922–1931)*. Clearly, any plan to publish a more extensive edition of Proust's letters is inextricably linked to the extraordinary personal endeavour of his brother, who was the jealous guardian of the writer's posthumous fame. The first volume published in 1930, *Lettres à Robert de Montesquiou*, brings together 252 letters, which, in spite of the dates mentioned (1893–1921), are not organized in any precise order, since Proust did not date his letters. Nineteen thirty-one saw the publication of *Lettres à Anna de Noailles* with a preface by the poet herself, and by 1936 six volumes had been published.[3] Even though these letters were not dated or annotated, the project as a whole marked an important step in assuring the posterity of the correspondence.

Meanwhile, however, a young researcher had arrived in Paris from Chicago where he had studied under Robert Vigneron, who since the 1930s had himself been studying the correspondence of both Proust and Stendhal with the aim of establishing the chronology of their life and works.[4] At the end of one seminar, Vigneron declared 'What I have done for Stendhal, should also be done for Proust.' This statement determined the vocation of Philip Kolb and, in the long term, has led to the extensive knowledge of Proust's correspondence that we have today.[5] Kolb had published the results of his doctoral thesis, a work of seminal importance, in 1949 and had the intention of setting the already daunting mass of letters in order.[6] Then, in 1950, on the recommendation of Suzy Mante-Proust, the Plon publishing house entrusted him with the huge task of assembling all the Proust letters that could be found into one edition, with a preface, fully annotated and in chronological order. Taking into account his worldwide quest for these letters, the extensive archive that he set up at his home institution, the University of Illinois at Urbana, enabling all the documents to be dated and annotated, and the fact that for the first time ever it was possible to establish a chronological record of Proust's life and activity week by week, Kolb's undertaking should be seen as a major achievement. It has increased our understanding of Proust while also allowing full consideration to be given to this collection of letters and its relevance to one of the major literary works of the twentieth century. The twenty-one volumes published between 1970 and 1993, covering over 10,000 pages, represent an inexhaustible mine of information, since they establish thousands of facts and because most of Proust's allusions to a particular person, book or journal can be identified immediately, backed up by an exact quotation.

Before examining the influence of this monumental collection on the study of Proust as a letter-writer, it is necessary to mention some works published elsewhere, relating to specific correspondents, and which have more recently come to complement the existing body of publications, namely *Mon cher petit*, additional letters to Lucien Daudet, and a supplement to the correspondence with Daniel Halévy.[7] The overriding question now is whether the correspondence should be republished, and if so, how this should be done. In 2004, Françoise Leriche published a large volume of selected letters, which were re-annotated and re-dated where necessary.[8] A proposed digital edition of the complete correspondence is underway at the ITEM (Institut des textes et manuscrits modernes) in Paris, in collaboration with the Kolb-Proust Archive at the University of Illinois, set up in 1994 as a centre for research.

Critical study of Proust's letters

Critical study of the correspondence began as early as the appearance of the first letters, setting out some very high-flown objectives in order to justify the publication of supposedly private documents. In 1923, Jacques de Lacretelle published the letter on the Vinteuil sonata with a view to determining the inspiration for the episode. When Robert Proust published the *Lettres à Robert de Montesquiou* in 1930, he stated in his preface that he did so in order to bring to light the 'constant exchange of ideas that went on between Montesquiou and my brother over a period of nearly thirty years, which allows us to witness the beginnings of a great work and not least to learn more about Marcel's views on the composition of his characters'.[9] The most distinguished pioneer of the sort was Louis de Robert, who first took steps to get *Du côté de chez Swann* published and as a result of the very interesting exchange of letters on this subject, he compiled his *Comment débuta Marcel Proust*, published in 1925. Nevertheless this is an avenue which to the present day remains largely unexplored.

The first to seek out the letters were the biographers. Having conducted his research among the closest sources, Léon-Pierre Quint published his *Marcel Proust – sa vie, son œuvre* (1925), which became a bestseller with over 80,000 copies sold. The letters again play a significant role in André Maurois's seminal work *À la recherche de Marcel Proust* (1949). According to circumstance, the letters serve both to document and to bear witness, but it is only after Robert Vigneron's detailed examination of the documents and the enormous amount of work done by George Painter that the correspondence truly enables researchers to establish a chronological record of episodes in Proust's life.[10] In this respect our knowledge of the subject has been revolutionized by Kolb's prefaces to each of the volumes of the correspondence, which retrace a year in Proust's life and give a chronological account of his daily activities. Indeed, the editing of Proust's work, notably in the Bibliothèque de la Pléiade, is considerably enriched by Kolb's contribution. By the same token, in the 1990s, three biographies appeared in close succession, which drew in various ways on existing letters published in chronological order. Ghislain de Diesbach's biography offers for the first time a running commentary of Proust's life based on his reading of the letters.[11] Meanwhile Roger Duchêne, aware of the problems involved in dealing with a writer's correspondence, presents the subject complete with detailed background information.[12] Finally, Jean-Yves Tadié takes a decisive and qualified approach, introducing his biography with the following caution:

> The inner life of a person might well be revealed in the correspondence – but not in the case of Proust, who does not give himself up to confession, or at least ceases to do so as soon as he leaves the *lycée* ... To reveal [the letters], with all their omissions, their lies, their misunderstood humour, is not the same as revealing a life.

In spite of the cautionary notice however, Tadié's work is based on a perceptive reading of the letters, which is borne out by the following remark: 'Marcel's correspondence is ... studded with allusions to his novel, of which only he can know the secret.'[13]

Others have made a more selective use of the correspondence in order to present a monograph on a precise subject. René de Chantal paved the way in 1967 with his two-volume *Marcel Proust critique littéraire*, in which he compared all the theoretical passages in the work to all the letters accessible at the time. Denise Meyer took the same approach but from a different angle with an extensive study, *Marcel Proust et la musique d'après sa correspondance* (1978). Christian Péchenard has since established himself as an expert on the subject, having published *Proust et son père* and *Proust à Cabourg* (1993 and 1994). Equally, research carried out by journalists Alain Coelho and Franck Lhomeau, devoted to *Proust à la recherche d'un éditeur* (1988), was largely based on study of the letters and in fact their book is dedicated to Philip Kolb. Even more recently, Patrick Brunel's *Le Rire de Proust* (1997) begins with a detailed analysis of the writer's comments on the subject of humour in his letters, which itself gives rise to a whole range of topics for discussion.

Besides these monographs, the correspondence has fuelled a multitude of assorted publications, especially in the area of literary history. Thanks to Kolb's annotations, it can be seen that the letters cover a period of forty years of literary, cultural and artistic life in France and Europe: we know that Proust, a recluse but ever curious, related to the outside world by reading widely on all subjects and, consequently, through his correspondence: exhibitions, concerts, publications, newspapers, literary controversies, nothing escapes him and every detail fuels his desire to put pen to paper. The critics gradually became accustomed to drawing on the revelations made possible by Kolb's edition. Fortunately the huge mass of data has been made easy to consult by the immensely helpful *Index général de la correspondance de Marcel Proust*, published under the direction of Kazuyoshi Yoshikawa (1998).

The question of how to interpret the correspondence is one that presented itself very early on, but these initial documents are more or less impossible to find, for example, 'Le roman et la correspondance' by Gaston Rageot in *Le Gaulois* dated 29 September 1938, and above all *L'Introduction aux lettres de Marcel Proust* by Pierre Raphaël (1938) which offers an interpretation of the writer's personality and, even at this stage, contains an index.[14] Then there are the prefaces, which provide the opportunity for a profusion of comments and reflections on the whole subject, notably Thierry Maulnier's preface to *Lettres de Marcel Proust à Bibesco* (1949); that of Emmanuel Berl for his *Lettres à Reynaldo Hahn* (1956); and Philip Kolb's introductions to *Choix de lettres*, *Lettres retrouvées* and the *Correspondance*. The way then opens for a more psychoanalytical approach. In *Marcel Proust du côté de la médecine* (1967), Robert Soupault had already put forward a study based on the handwriting in selected letters written at different periods. Then, of course, there is the question of Proust's relationship with his mother; these letters had previously been grouped together in a separate collection by Philip Kolb. Subsequently Viviane Forrester examines 'Le texte et la mère';[15] and, above all, Alain Buisine in his pioneering work *Proust et ses lettres*, in which he explores the connection between the role of the letters in the fictional world of $\grave{A}$ *la recherche* and the letters to the mother.[16] (It must be said that although the critics tend to focus on this one aspect, this study does contain many other equally interesting observations.) In 1990, Vincent Kaufmann's *L'Équivoque épistolaire* looks at Proust's correspondence from a similar angle, situating it amongst others from the nineteenth and twentieth centuries. Martin Robitaille's interpretation is that, as many of the letters demonstrate, Proust's relationship with his mother places him in a position of *repli*, withdrawal, in reaction to which his correspondence with other correspondents takes on the role of a *transfert* or transference.[17] To understand the connection between the biographical and psychological studies and views concerning the importance of the letters, Roger Duchêne's study 'L'homosexualité dans les lettres de Marcel Proust' is essential reading.[18]

The fact that there is a striking difference between the style and content of the letters and that of $\grave{A}$ *la recherche* poses an extremely interesting dilemma for anyone wishing to understand the nature of literary creation. Therefore, by way of conclusion, I shall explore some ways in which one might approach the subject.

Reading Proust's letters undeniably contributes a good deal to our understanding of the writer's psyche, as long as we read the correspondence in the same way that Jean-Pierre Richard teaches us to read the fictional works: allowing the more original and compelling themes to emerge and at the same time taking into account the *voisinage*, the context, in which these elements occur, just as carefully as an archaeologist makes an inventory of an excavation. One of Robitaille's theories, in the study mentioned above, is that a writer's correspondence should be read as a work of fiction in which the subject, the writer, gradually builds up a picture of himself. Thus certain psychological patterns emerge, which then readily throw light on the more general patterns found in the author's work.[19] Moreover, since Proust only conceived and developed his ideas for $\grave{A}$ *la recherche* during the last years of his life and after a long period of anticipation, the older letters are found to harbour a strange phenomenon: they contain characters, episodes, phrases which will become famous, and which we see briefly skimming the surface of a phrase in a letter, at a time when everything points to the fact that Proust is still years away from his first idea for a great novel. Quite often, the dates enable us to trace the parallel curves of the conscious and the unconscious and measure the changing distances between them. Surely this is an example of the most far-reaching and significant objectives that can be achieved by a detailed study of a writer's correspondence and, as we have seen, the findings of that study extend beyond Proust alone, and indeed might well provide material for future research into the process of literary creation. The critical establishment does not seem to be aware of, or yet to have explored this particular avenue.

More specifically, through Proust's letters we accompany him into several areas of prime importance, since no other kind of document allows us to determine in such a nuanced way his position on religion or homosexuality.[20] The vast number of letters exchanged with his correspondents at the *Nouvelle Revue française* represents an important page in the history of publishing at the beginning of the twentieth century. Furthermore, since Proust was relatively secretive about the composition and the meaning of his work, only the dates of the correspondence can reveal the order in which the episodes in *À la recherche* were written; even those who had read the manuscripts would recognize that they were to some extent kept at bay by the author. Only the correspondence can reveal the secret sources from which the writer was able to draw inspiration, and better still, how at different stages of the creative process, a succession of different *époques* in the novels are drawn from one same source. Moreover, it can be seen that every meticulously placed idea that goes into the creation of *À la recherche* can be traced back to the very moment it was conceived by the author himself.[21] The last years of the letters even enable us to guess at ideas for works that were never brought into existence. Conversely, any specific episode in *À la recherche* will stem from a whole range of sources, accumulated over a period of twenty or more years. In the long term, the letters provide an insight into the way various works are positioned both in the author's memory and in the overall creative process. Whenever a writer's correspondence is as prolific as that of Proust, the rich poetics of the epistolary art are thus revealed.[22] These 5,000 letters, apparently so distinct from the fictional works and to which their author was inclined to attach no importance whatsoever, provide innumerable links between Proust's personality, contemporaneous society and the genesis of *À la recherche*.

Notes

1 Philip Kolb's account retracing sixty years of research was recorded during the summer before his death. A full transcript can be found in my book: Luc Fraisse, *La Correspondance de Proust: son statut dans l'œuvre, l'histoire de son édition* (Paris: Les Belles Lettres, 1998). Here, see p. 144.
2 See Fraisse, *La Correspondance de Proust*, pp. 118–23.

3 Robert Proust had enlisted the help of Paul Brach; on his death, in 1935, Robert's daughter, Suzy Mante-Proust, the writer's niece, prepared the final volume, assisted by a young researcher with a great future ahead of him, Philip Kolb.

4 The results of Vigneron's research were published posthumously as *Études sur Stendhal et sur Proust* (Paris: Nizet, 1978).

5 On the remarkable story of Kolb's sixty-year undertaking, see 'Philip Kolb à la recherche des lettres de Proust', in Fraisse, *La Correspondance de Proust*, pp. 133–89.

6 Philip Kolb, *La Correspondance de Marcel Proust: chronologie et commentaire critique* (Urbana: University of Illinois Press, 1949).

7 *Mon cher petit*, ed. Michel Bonduelle (Paris: Gallimard, 1991); Daniel Halévy, *Correspondance*, ed. Anne Borrel and Jean-Pierre Halévy (Paris: Fallois, 1992).

8 Marcel Proust, *Lettres (1879–1922)*, ed. F. Leriche, C. Szylowicz, K. Kolb and V. Greene (Paris: Plon, 2004).

9 *Correspondance générale de Marcel Proust*, vol. 1 (Paris: Plon, 1930), p. iv.

10 George Painter, *Marcel Proust*, 2 vols. (London: Chatto & Windus, 1959–66).

11 Ghislain de Diesbach, *Proust* (Paris: Perrin, 1991).

12 Roger Duchêne, *L'impossible Marcel Proust* (Paris: Robert Laffont, 1994).

13 Jean-Yves Tadié, *Marcel Proust: biographie* (Paris: Gallimard, 1996), pp. 10 and 628, n. 6.

14 A lengthy investigation by another unrecognized critic, Jean Frétet, can be found in *L'Aliénation poétique* (Paris: J. B. Janin, 1946) and contains a relevant chapter on Proust (pp. 207–311). For an overview of the subject, see Martin Robitaille's 'Études sur la correspondance de Marcel Proust: une synthèse', *Bulletin Marcel Proust*, 46 (1996), 109–27.

15 *Tel Quel*, 78 (1978), pp. 70–81.

16 Alain Buisine, *Proust et ses lettres* (Presses universitaires de Lille, 1983).

17 Martin Robitaille, *Proust épistolier* (Presses de l'Université de Montréal, 2003).

18 In André Magnan, ed., *Expériences limites de l'épistolaire* (Paris: Champion, 1993), pp. 59–73.

19 See Luc Fraisse, *Marcel Proust au miroir de sa correspondance* (Paris: SEDES, 1996), ch. 4, 'Les prédispositions à créer', pp. 169–212.

20 For an overview, see Karin Westerwelle, ed., *Marcel Proust und die Korrespondenz*, Proceedings of the Symposium of the Marcel Proust Gesellschaft in Munich, June 2007 (Berlin: Insel Verlag, 2010).

21 In Luc Fraisse, *L'Œuvre cathédrale: Proust et l'architecture médiévale* (Paris: Corti, 1990), I consider the descriptions in Proust's novel in relation to the sketches and the letters, a comparison which naturally elicits a whole host of conclusions.

22 See Fraisse, *La Correspondance de Proust*, pp. 87–133.

CHAPTER 3

Finding a form: Les Plaisirs et les jours *to* Contre Sainte-Beuve

Nathalie Aubert

It has long been acknowledged that during his 'supposedly idle and unproductive years',[1] the young Proust was in fact extremely actively engaged in writing: journalism, the draft of a novel (later abandoned) and short fictions, translations, pastiches, critical essays ... Varied in their themes (ranging from pure society events and fashion to aesthetic analyses of writers, painters and musicians) and forms (critical essays, pastiches) his articles are usually considered as preparatory stages of *À la recherche du temps perdu*. Genette considered them as 'no more' than 'sketches', 'drafts' of certain episodes, settings, themes or characters of the 'definitive' work.[2] Indeed, the fascination that *À la recherche* exerts on its readers is so strong that one of the most interesting aspects of this period of Proust's life are the ways in which these 'disorderly fragments', as Jérôme Picon has put it, contribute to the 'incubation of the novel', to how the man turned himself into an artist.[3] Thierry Laget goes as far as writing: 'in their varied form, Marcel Proust's *Essais et articles* are no more than one single day of reading, a day of reading that lasts over half a century and which imperceptibly transforms itself into a day of writing'.[4] 'Imperceptible' though it may be, it is clear that the novel did not emerge out of nowhere but can be viewed as the endpoint of a creative cycle chosen after a number of different approaches and processes were tried out.

Proust journalist

Proust belongs to a long line of creative individuals who, spanning the nineteenth century from Barbey d'Aurevilly to Gautier, Vallès and Zola, embody the complex figure that is the 'journalist-writer'. If we are to believe his Narrator, Proust was proud of his contribution to the various newspapers and reviews where his texts appeared as they are the 'spiritual bread of life ... a miraculous, self-multiplying bread which is at the same time one and thousand, which remains the same for each person while

19

penetrating innumerably into every house at once' (6: 579; IV, 148). Spread across a wide range of periodicals (*Le Mensuel, Le Banquet, La Revue blanche*) and daily newspapers such as *Le Figaro* and *Le Gaulois*, most of Proust's early texts were destined for publication in the press. This critical activity and his desire to see his texts published in reviews and newspapers continued into the years when he had started on *À la recherche*.

More than anything else, Proust's contribution to these various publications shows that he was part of a group of young men who had a very clear conscience about taking part in contemporary literary and artistic debates. Neither naturalist nor decadent, their ambition was to be open to all movements and all forms of art of the time. Proust's contribution to various reviews, as well as the articles and chronicles that he gave to the daily newspapers reveal early on his wide interest in literature as well as theatre criticism, music, painting, politics, alongside women's fashion and society events. Thus Proust's criticism and polygraphic production allowed him to accompany his development as a would-be novelist, and express ideas that would be essential for his conception of literature.

The creative search: *Les Plaisirs et les jours*

The 1893 merger of *Le Banquet* with *La Revue blanche* coincided with a rise in Proust's literary production (on 1 December, the *Revue blanche* published six 'studies' by Proust, just as he began his literature degree).[5] In addition to these publications, he started an epistolary novel with his friends, wrote a short story entitled *L'Indifférent*, and began to think about the publication of *Les Plaisirs et les jours*. Composed of texts previously published in different outlets, thus confirming the pre-eminence of a journalistic, more fragmentary model to which he was trying to give a unity, *Les Plaisirs et les jours* was published in June 1896. The 'mise en livre'[6] was thus used by the young Proust trying to make a name for himself on the literary scene and as a way to legitimize disparate texts comprising a collection of short stories, poems, fragments of an 'Italian Comedy' and occasional pieces. His texts are short, but thematically important 'fictions', semi-confessions of fictional characters in the third person, the most important of them women.

In some of the short stories Proust wrote about the power of the imagination, and the deadening effect of habit and laziness on once-fresh perceptions. In 'Mélancolique villégiature de Madame de Breyves', Françoise, the main character (who has a lot in common with Madame de Beauséant in Balzac's *La Femme abandonnée*), is obsessed with longing for an undistinguished young man she hardly knows – showing that she has no control over her imagination. Unsatisfied desire is also at the centre of 'Violante ou la mondanité' (written in 1892) where the title character, giving up her solitary life on her country estate for the corrupting pleasures of fashionable society, realizes too late that she cannot give herself entirely to what Proust describes as 'the joy of being alone and being able to dream'.[7] Love – and sensuality – are usually depicted as a torment, associated with guilt, as in 'La confession d'une jeune fille'. Very often too, love is overshadowed by the suspicion of imagined infidelities as is the case in both 'La mort de Baldassare Silvande' and 'La fin de la jalousie' which tell the story of two male protagonists who, like their female counterparts, already embody some of Proust's preoccupations and anxieties. They both end with a lingering death-bed scene. In 'La fin de la jalousie' Honoré, fatally injured in an accident with a runaway horse, remembers, as Baldassare had done, his mother's tenderness to him at bedtime.

The decadent settings and unhappy love affairs, the luxury edition with facsimiles of Reynaldo Hahn's music for the poems on musicians which follow them, the 'Portraits de peintres', accompanied by several full-page illustrations by Madeleine Lemaire, all this gives an overall fin-de-siècle feel, noted by Anatole France in his preface, underlining the 'greenhouse atmosphere … amid wild orchids that do not draw the nourishment for their strange and unhealthy beauty from this earth … At a stroke the poet has penetrated secret thoughts and hidden desires.'[8] Published by Calmann-Lévy at the author's expense, sales were meagre and Proust was disappointed.

Jean Santeuil

But Proust was really 'out to write a novel'[9] and in 1895, while on holiday in Brittany with Reynaldo Hahn, he had already started to work on what was to be posthumously published as *Jean Santeuil* following the name of the main character.[10] Searching his memory for the impressions which lie at the root of his aesthetic preferences, Jean has a sense that the past is the repository of deep human truths, that the experience of revelation through memory is essential, but, although ordinary novelistic material (the observation and invention of social situations and manners, the psychology of sexual passion and snobbery, and historical events – such as the Dreyfus Affair) is in place, Proust consciously seeks to avoid building the unity of the story. Thus the formlessness of *Jean Santeuil* comes from the lack of coherence of an aesthetic sensibility unable to construct experience into a philosophical drama:

> Should I call this book a novel? It is something less, perhaps, and yet much more, the very essence of my life, with nothing extraneous added, as it developed through a long period of wretchedness. This book of mine has not been manufactured: it has been garnered. (*JS*, xxv; 181)

Having sought to make us sensitive to 'instants' Proust portrayed them as scenes and, instead of surprising beings as they appear, he made something quite the opposite: 'formal portraits'.[11] Scenes, characters, general observations, remain somehow disconnected, fragments of moments are as much a testimony to his aesthetic sensitivity as they are to his perceptive sense of observation but, at this stage, they seem to be the product of a man still accustomed to perceiving the sensuous beauty of the world through the imagination of a great century of poetry, and the vision of an astute reader of novelists and moralists. The tendency to poeticize the real without integrating it into the dynamics of a narrative, resulting from Proust's desire at the time to write only to respond to inspiration, was what was hindering his aspiration to write a novel. The incapacity to build the narrative as a narrative thus resulted in the failure of *Jean Santeuil*, which Proust abandoned in 1899.

The translations

It is widely acknowledged that it was in order to overcome the impasse of *Jean Santeuil* that Proust, who between 1895 and 1897 had become aware of John Ruskin's writings,[12] turned away from the unfinished novel to dedicate himself to the study and then translation of both *The Bible of Amiens* (published in 1904) and *Sesame and Lilies* (published in 1906) as a kind of 'askesis'.[13] The years spent translating the Victorian critic helped him find his own voice and broaden considerably his cultural knowledge, since commenting on Ruskin required an immense volume of research which supplemented his already voracious reading. When *Sésame et les lys* was eventually published,[14] it was accompanied by an important preface devoted to reading, 'Sur la lecture'. With this text,[15] Proust really bade farewell to Ruskin, eclipsing him by contesting his conception of reading. For Ruskin – in this lecture at least – reading is conceived as an edifying task: the main purpose of books and libraries is to bring knowledge to men. For Proust, however, reading can lead us to the threshold of spiritual life, but is not a substitute for it.

If by 1906 Proust had grown more and more frustrated with Ruskin, having absorbed his lesson and even appropriated some of his stylistic traits, there is no doubt however that the Victorian opened his eyes, providing him with a new vision of the world around him. He made him aware of the integration of time through the details of buildings, statues and paintings. It was a valuable lesson: if Proust was ever to write another novel, it should not be made of *pure* impressions, but would convey a sense of the enduring combined with the evanescent, and express the perspective of history alongside that of the precariousness of the moment. Both 'actively and reactively' Ruskin provided Proust with 'the opportunity to clarify the aesthetic philosophy that he lacked',[16] and helped him realize that 'the only true book ... does not have to be "invented" by a great writer for it already exists in each one of us, it has to be translated. The function and the task of a writer are those of a translator' (6: 247; IV, 469).

Pastiches and *Contre Sainte-Beuve*

Still expressing doubts about his ability ('Should it be a novel or a philosophical essay, am I a novelist?')[17] ever to achieve *real work*,[18] it is in the context of the criticism of reading, and of critical reading, that Proust's writing activity started in 1908. He produced a series of pastiches, all based on the Lemoine Affair, news of which broke on 9 January.[19] The majority of these pastiches were published in *Le Figaro* between 22 February and 21 March. Their role, coming as they did after the six years he dedicated to the translation of Ruskin's two texts, was to liberate him from the writers who obsessed him (not without first having appropriated their secrets),[20] just as the translations had done before.

From April 1908, that is to say soon after the publication of his pastiches in *Le Figaro*, Proust's letters to friends and potential publishers started mentioning that he was to begin 'a very important piece of work'.[21] A year later he wrote to Alfred Vallette, the head of the *Mercure de France*:

> I am finishing a book which, despite its provisional title: 'Contre Sainte-Beuve. Souvenir d'une matinée', is a genuine novel and an extremely indecent one in places. One of the main characters is a homosexual ... The name of Sainte-Beuve is not there by chance. The book does end with a long conversation about Sainte-Beuve and about aesthetics ... and when one has finished the book, one will see (I hope) that the entire novel is nothing but the implementation of the artistic principles expressed in this final part, a sort of introduction, if you like, inserted at the end. (*Corr*, IX, 155–7)

The *Contre Sainte-Beuve* material is made of various sets of documents, *cahiers* that the writer bought towards the end of 1908 and where can be traced his aesthetics contradicting Sainte-Beuve's own approach to literature.[22] None of these exercise books forms a whole: the essay and the story are still made of juxtaposed fragments where numerous episodes and structural features (such as the two ways), sketches of characters and the central theme of homosexuality are present. 'When he wrote in the pages of these *cahiers*, whether the content was fictional or critical, he was rarely sure whether he would be able to continue, whether he had a lot to say, or how to organize his material', but all we know, as Tadié continues, is that 'in November 1908 ... Proust began to write *Contre Sainte-Beuve* and thereafter he did not stop'.[23] Although Vallette rejected the book (without having read it) Proust continued working on the beginning of what was to be his novel; the 'essay' in itself vanished, his views on Sainte-Beuve shared among several of the characters of *À la recherche*.

Coming after years of intense critical activity, after years spent researching and translating Ruskin, Sainte-Beuve was to serve as a short-lived intermediary, a trigger to make Proust's own conception of literature and art, his own style, his own voice, heard. Fighting Sainte-Beuve, he then eclipsed him as he had done with Ruskin,[24] and the many important figures of French literature with whom he had grappled in his pastiches before that. The path towards writing his own novel, which would incorporate the essayistic and the fictional, now lay open ahead of him.

Notes

1 J. M. Cocking, *Proust: Collected Essays on the Writer and His Art* (Cambridge University Press, 1982), p. xiv.

2 Gérard Genette, 'Proust Palimpsest', in *Figures of Literary Discourse*, trans. by Alan Sheridan (New York: Columbia University Press, 1982), p. 223.

3 Jérôme Picon, *Marcel Proust: écrits sur l'art* (Paris: Flammarion, 1999), p. 13.

4 Introduction to *Essais et articles* (Paris: Gallimard, 1994), p. i.

5 Jean-Yves Tadié, *Marcel Proust*, trans. by Euan Cameron (London: Penguin, 2000), p. 177.

6 Marie-Françoise Melmoux-Montaubin, *L'Écrivain-journaliste au XIXe siècle, un mutant des lettres* (Saint-Étienne: Éditions des Cahiers intempestifs, 2003), p. 261.

7 *Pleasures and Days*, trans. by Andrew Brown (London: Hesperus, 2004), p. 37.

8 *Pleasures and Days*, pp. 3–4.

9 Cocking, *Proust*, p. 27.

10 Proust never uses this title; it was Bernard de Fallois, who first published it in 1952, who, having organized the manuscript notes into chapters according to their subject matter, titled it thus.

11 Maurice Blanchot, *The Book to Come*, trans. by Charlotte Mandell (Stanford University Press, 2003), p. 21.

12 Very little of Ruskin's work had been translated into French before 1895. Brief extracts had appeared in the *Bulletin pour l'action morale*, a publication to which Proust subscribed because it was edited by a family friend, Paul Desjardins, a lecturer in literature and philosophy at the Sorbonne. Between December 1895 and April 1897, *La Revue des Deux Mondes* published a series of articles on Ruskin's life and work by Robert de la Sizeranne, for which he translated long extracts from Ruskin's autobiography, *Praeterita*, also from his first great work *Modern Painters*; from his most popular one, *Sesame and Lilies*; from *Lectures on Art* and *The Queen of the Air*, as well as shorter passages from *The Seven Lamps of Architecture*, *Val d'Arno* and *Mornings in Florence*, *The Stones of Venice* and *St Mark's Rest*. In 1897, La Sizeranne's articles were published as a book with the title *Ruskin et la religion de la beauté*.

13 Cocking, *Proust*, p. 37.

14 He completed his translation of *Sésame et les lys* in June 1905, just before his mother's death; it was published in 1906.

15 Later republished on 20 March 1907 in *Le Figaro* as 'Journées de lecture' (and then again 1919 in *Pastiches et mélanges* under the same title), although the newspaper had then cut the text, precisely where he extends his reflections on his feelings for the past, which irritated him. This shows the importance the author attached to it. Adam Watt has demonstrated how this highly revealing activity is central to Proust's novel in *Reading in Proust's 'À la recherche': 'le délire de la lecture'* (Oxford University Press, 2009).

16 Tadié, trans. Cameron, *Marcel Proust*, p. 456.

17 *Le Carnet de 1908*, ed. Philip Kolb, *Cahiers Marcel Proust*, n. s., 8, (Paris: Gallimard, 1976), pp. 60–1.

18 Cf. his letter to Antoine Bibesco to whom, as early as 1902, he had written: 'What I am doing at the moment is not real work, but merely research, translation, etc.' (*Corr*, III, 196).

19 In 1905, Henri Lemoine claimed he had discovered a process to produce diamonds from coal. He managed to convince both a British banker and one of the governors of De Beers Diamond Mines to buy his invention. Three years later, the fraud was discovered and he was tried in Paris (but he absconded). Proust himself lost money on the scheme.

20 See Jean Milly, *Les Pastiches de Proust* (Paris: Armand Colin, 1970).

21 Letter to Louis d'Albufera (*Corr*, VIII, 99). He also talks of a 'Parisian novel' (*Corr*, VIII, 112).

22 Filed under the title 'Carnet I' or, following its publication, *Le Carnet de 1908*. A work plan mentioning as work in progress both a novel and a study of Sainte-Beuve as well as reading notes, principally on Balzac, Chateaubriand, Barbey d'Aurevilly and Nerval, and finally actual drafts and written paragraphs, constitute the bulk of the *Carnet de 1908*. The list, made by Proust, of 'written pages' (drawn up some time in July 1908) gives a hint of a novel about childhood, aristocracy, sexuality, and about 'pederasty' and sadism, as well as

the division into the two ways which would later run through the whole of *À la recherche*. A plan for a 'second part' projected a love liaison (see Tadié, trans. Cameron, *Marcel Proust*, p. 512). In addition, there were some seventy-five loose-leaf pages (now lost) of which, according to Bernard de Fallois who had seen them, twenty or so constituted the essay on Sainte-Beuve.

23 Tadié, trans. Cameron, *Marcel Proust*, pp. 520; 519.

24 See Tadié, trans. Cameron, *Marcel Proust*, p. 524.

CHAPTER 4

Finding a voice: from Ruskin to the pastiches

Cynthia Gamble

> His voice contains many voices. He is a magpie and a mimic. He veers this way and that, and takes the colouring of the company he keeps. Proust's narrator is both chorus and soloist.[1]

As well as searching for a form and structure for his writing, Proust was also seeking a voice. Or, rather, he sought affirmation of his own originality, a confidence to experiment found through his engagement with the works of the polymath John Ruskin (1819–1900).

Marcel Proust possessed a keen ear and the gift of detecting inner rhythms, together with a highly developed visual, musical memory. He was acutely aware of this and jotted down in one of his exercise books:

> As soon as I was reading an author, I could very soon make out the melody of the song underneath the words, different in one author from what it is in every other, and as I read, without realizing it, I would be humming it, hurrying the words, slowing them down or breaking off altogether, as one does when singing, when, depending on the tempo of the melody, one often waits a long time before saying the end of a word. (*ASB*, 92; *CSB*, 303)

His prodigious memory enabled him to absorb and retain content, style, nuances, make endless interconnections and comparisons, and excel at writing pastiches. Proust's English friend Marie Nordlinger (1876–1961) remarked that 'a page read aloud evoked many, many others'.[2]

Proust's serious literary life was starting when that of John Ruskin was drawing to a close. Twenty-eight-year-old Proust was on vacation in 1899 in the fashionable French spa town of Évian-les-Bains, on the shores of Lake Geneva, where he was spending most of his time with aristocratic friends and acquaintances, and enjoying an active, but intellectually superficial, social life. Not surprisingly, his writing stagnated: 'his inkwell and his pocketbook had both nearly run dry'.[3]

Suddenly, emotionally stirred by the backcloth of the majestic, snow-capped Alpine ranges and imprecise recollections of Ruskin's descriptions

27

of them, he felt an imperative need to re-read Robert de La Sizeranne's *Ruskin et la religion de la beauté*[4] in order 'to see the mountains through the eyes of that great man' (*Corr*, II, 357). Proust asked his mother to send him the book. It did not arrive in time to satisfy his desires and precipitously he decided to return to Paris to re-read with fresh eyes Ruskin's evocations of, and responses to, mountain scenery in sensitive renderings by La Sizeranne.[5]

In the Bibliothèque nationale, Proust discovered a translation in French by the Belgian poet and critic Olivier Georges Destrée (1867–1919), of 'The Lamp of Memory', a chapter in Ruskin's *The Seven Lamps of Architecture* (1849). This seminal piece of writing, born out of his recollections of mountain scenery in the Jura, explores philosophically and aesthetically themes of memory, time, nature, architecture, of which we find resonances in *À la recherche du temps perdu*. A key element is the theory of the transmission of cultural heritage through the protection and conservation of buildings and the restoration of the stonemason's personality and skills, vulnerable and sometimes effaced in the nineteenth-century climate of neglect and destruction: 'let us think, as we lay stone on stone, that a time is to come when those stones will be held sacred because our hands have touched them, and that men will say as they look upon the labour and wrought substance of them, "See! This our fathers did for us."'[6] The energetic cadence on which this appeal ends is a missionary, zealous voice emanating from Biblical teaching that became, in a slightly modified form and in the very words of the Psalmist, 'Our Fathers Have Told Us',[7] the overarching title of Ruskin's last monumental, but unfinished project of which the first book is *The Bible of Amiens*. Ruskin's mighty patriarchal footprint with a strong authoritative voice emerges as Proust studies this chapter. Destrée conveyed the magnificent prose, poetry and range of Ruskin's thought, sweeping from intense observations of the clusters of early white May flowers, anthropomorphized, intent on remaining close together like lovers, even crushing their leaves in their desire for intimacy, to the thundering voice of a prophet proclaiming doom.[8]

It is difficult, in the twenty-first century, to comprehend the enormous importance of Ruskin in his day. He was a towering figure and the moral, reverential authority in Victorian Britain and beyond those shores. He passed judgments with fervour on almost every aspect of life – art, religion, animal welfare, transport, housing, politics, economics and education. There were Ruskin Clubs in the USA, Ruskin Societies and organizations actively promoting his aims during his lifetime.[9] His death on 20 January 1900 resulted in an outburst of grief and national mourning.

Proust had already commenced his immersion in Ruskin. By November and December 1899 (*Corr*, II, 377) he was working in particular on cathedrals and translating the fourth chapter of *The Bible of Amiens*,[10] soon to be followed by the entire book. Ruskin's death acted as a catalyst and gave Proust the impetus he needed to apply himself seriously to work and focus his energies and talents. He expressed his optimism to Nordlinger:

> So when I heard about Ruskin's death, I wanted to tell you before anybody else about my sadness, a healthy sadness nevertheless and very consoling, for I realise how unimportant death is when I see how vigorously alive that dead man is, how much I admire him, listen to him, try and understand him and obey him more than I do a great many of the living. (*Corr*, II, 384)

Proust decided to act swiftly, positively and creatively, and explain to the world the universality and greatness of Ruskin as a 'homme de génie' ['man of genius'] (*ASB*, 161, 167; *CSB*, 106, 112) – there is also the secondary meaning of 'génie' as a genie or spirit with special or mythical powers –, as 'one of the greatest writers of all times and all countries' (*ASB*, 187; *CSB*, 134), and create a 'true reconstitution' (*Corr*, III, 220) of 'la singulière vie spirituelle d'un écrivain' ['the distinct and unusual nature of the mind of a writer'].[11] This he did by engaging in multiple overlapping non-linear activities of reading, listening, seeing, translation work, Ruskinian pilgrimages, critical writing and discourse, to such an extent that he became 'intoxicated' by Ruskin (*Corr*, III, 25). By early February 1900, Proust claimed to know 'by heart' (*Corr*, II, 387) *The Seven Lamps of Architecture*, *The Bible of Amiens*, *Val d'Arno*, *Lectures on Architecture and Painting* and *Praeterita* – a truly remarkable feat and an understatement.

He wrote in rapid succession five obituary articles about Ruskin in French newspapers and magazines.[12] The first two were short, heralding the theme of pilgrimage to places of Ruskinian significance in France and Italy that would be developed, with others, in a crescendo-like manner in the subsequent articles. The essays, at times self-referential and personal, even confessional – 'I will confess that rereading this passage at the time of Ruskin's death I was seized with a desire to see the little man he speaks of' (*ASB*, 178; *CSB*, 125) – address and involve the reader directly, adopting a method frequently used by Ruskin, whose writings are often oral-based, developed from impassioned lectures he had given. Proust's use of the nominative first-person pronoun 'I' is an amalgam of Proust–Ruskin–Artist, for the degree of fusion is so great that it is difficult to differentiate between them. Yves-Michel Ergal goes even further and suggests that the 'je' of the Narrator in *À la recherche du temps perdu* is Ruskin himself, to whom Proust has theatrically lent his voice, postulating that 'Proust's voice has always harboured faithfully the inflections of John Ruskin's voice, even if they are imperceptible to the ear' (*BA*, xxix).

These homages of 1900, plus a post-scriptum of 1903, encrusted with echoes of Ruskin and a multiplicity of quotations and references from a dozen of Ruskin's works, form the essence of Proust's preface to his translation of *La Bible d'Amiens* (1904). This was followed two years later by Proust's interpretation of *Sésame et les lys*, with an important preface 'Sur la lecture' in which he engages in a discussion with Ruskin on the theme of reading. This essay, an intertextual monument to Ruskin, is a bridge that links directly to 'Combray' and to the Narrator's *rêverie* on reading.

As the unnamed inheritor and executor in Ruskin's will, Proust felt he had a duty and obligation to him, to transmit to future generations his intellectual wealth, or soul, found in, for instance, 'Pisa, Florence, Venice, the National Gallery, Rouen, Amiens, the mountains of Switzerland' (*ASB*, 191; *CSB*, 138). Propelled and accompanied by the spirit of his Virgil, he went on pilgrimages to Rouen, Amiens, Venice and Burgundy, seeking the places of spiritual significance to Ruskin, seeing and absorbing religious and domestic Gothic architecture through his eyes. He felt a special, protective responsibility towards Ruskin, as he explained to the French historian Georges Goyau in December 1904:

> You know how much I admire Ruskin. And since I believe that each one of us has a responsibility for the souls he particularly loves, a responsibility to make them known and loved, to protect them from the pain of misunderstandings and the darkness, the obscurity as we say, of oblivion, you know with what scrupulous hands – but pious too and as gentle as I could be – I handled that one. (*Corr*, IV, 399)

In short, it was Proust's undertaking to ensure the transmission of Ruskin's voice. Equally, it was through his journey among Ruskin's writings and his pilgrimages to the tangible sources of these that Proust came to the reward of finding the solid and sincere ground of his own voice.

In his early exposure to Ruskin, Proust realized that the great man held the key of sesame to a world of treasures that would be revealed to him if he immersed himself in and submitted to his thought:

> sensing the power and attraction of the very first pages I read, I made an effort not to resist them, not to argue too much with myself, because I felt that if one day the attraction of Ruskin's thought should extend for me over

everything he had touched, in short if I became completely enamoured of his thought, the world would be enriched by everything of which I had hitherto been ignorant. (*ASB*, 191; *CSB*, 138)

Ruskin opened Proust's eyes and mind to such an extent that he wrote: 'the universe suddenly took on for me again an infinite value. And my admiration for Ruskin lent to the things which he had brought me to love so great an importance that they seemed to me charged with a value higher than that of life itself' (*ASB*, 191; *CSB*, 139). Realizing that Ruskin's universe was tangible, Proust went to Venice not only to see but to touch its very stones.

In explaining Ruskin's greatness, Proust stripped away preconceived, compartmentalized notions of him as 'a prophet, a seer, a Protestant and other things which mean very little' (*ASB*, 173, note; *CSB*, 119, note). Ruskin's thought could not be contained or summarized simplistically, for he operated on a higher or discursive plane. Proust recognized this originality and wrote:

> Ruskin lives in a sort of brotherhood with all the great minds of every age, and since he is interested in them only to the extent that they are able to answer the eternal questions, for him there are no ancients or moderns and he can talk of Herodotus as he would of a contemporary. (*ASB*, 173, note; *CSB*, 119, note)

Ruskin knew that he went deliberately and defiantly against the grain: 'I am alone, as I believe, in thinking still with Herodotus' (*ASB*, 173, note; CSB, 119, note).

This comprehension of the existence of Ruskin's realm of discourse enabled Proust to appreciate better the potential of his own writing: he was now a man no longer confined within the salons and chambers of amusement, but one able to step further and over the threshold into a higher plane.

Proust, at the time of his encounter with Ruskin, had nobody of this calibre in his circle with whom he could debate at this level. Anatole France (1844–1924), who at most consented to write a supportive preface to Proust's *Les Plaisirs et les jours* (1896), was at a distance of age and otherwise creatively occupied. Hence Ruskin through his writings was Proust's sole mentor – but this was to prove more than adequate. Ruskin and Proust both had sufficient rebelliousness and self-confidence each to challenge the prevailing orthodoxy and to advance his own respective discourse. The topics are limitless, embracing anything the human mind can consider. And in furthering his own discursive assignment Proust's gift for the pastiche became a remarkable working tool. Pastiche was his way to a bold and thorough familiarization with the ideas of others – to a fearless intimate joking relationship with the writers he tackled. This activity reached its zenith in 1908, the year of pastiches, triggered by the Lemoine Affair, the scandal of a fraudster who claimed to have discovered the secret of creating diamonds. Proust used this as a focus for a series of pastiches, presenting different perspectives on the daring deceit in the styles of well-known writers such as Balzac, Flaubert, Renan, Ruskin and many others. The Ruskin pastiche, entitled 'La bénédiction du sanglier: études des fresques de Giotto représentant l'Affaire Lemoine à l'usage des jeunes étudiants et étudiantes de Corpus Christi qui se soucient encore d'*elle*. par John Ruskin',[13] (*CSB*, 201–5; [not in *ASB*]) ['Blessing the wild boar: Study of Giotto's frescoes representing the Lemoine Affair for the use of young male and female students of Corpus Christi who still care about *it*. by John Ruskin'], is the most humorous, most convincing and sparkling of all. It combines Proust's self-pastiching and self-deprecation of his own translations and displays his total self-confidence, certitude and belief in himself, ability to mock himself and his own work, as well as Ruskin's. It is a manifestation of Proust's mastery of the sheer complexity of Ruskin's style.

But in employing pastiche Proust was very aware of its nature and limitations. While at the Lycée Condorcet, he criticized a poem by his young friend Daniel Halévy on the grounds that its style was decadent and insincere. He advised him to 'practise Latin discourses',[14] and learn through reading particular authors: 'si votre esprit est original et puissant, vos œuvres ne le seront que si vous êtes d'une sincérité absolue' (*EJ*, 167) ['if your mind is original and strong, your works will be so only if you are absolutely sincere']. In this same commentary, Proust also advised Halévy that the pastiche was a form of insincerity (*EJ*, 167).

'The more Ruskin lost his voice, the more he was heard, mediated by language.'[15] The main voice that spoke to Proust was Ruskin's,[16] and so it continued after Ruskin's death. For when a discursive voice ceases, it nevertheless continues to be heard because it is comprehended and carried forth into the world. This is a theme – transmogrified into the shape of fire and light – that underpins the symbolism behind Gustave Moreau's painting *Les Muses quittant Apollon leur père pour aller éclairer le monde* ['The Muses leaving their father Apollo to go and bring light to the world'] (*CSB*, 105; *ASB*, 161). It is this mythological allusion that Proust presents at the very beginning of his obituary essay of 1 April 1900. And the theme of light is further pursued with reference to Ruskin's 1871 preface to *Sesame and Lilies* in the Biblical exhortation 'Work while you have light', and to which he added, 'especially while you have the light of morning'.[17] The initial force of this command had so moved Proust that he thereafter applied the philosophy of this work ethic to himself and urged friends to conduct themselves likewise (*Corr*, VIII, 285–6). For underlying the entreaty is the suggestion that men must be labouring continuously in the light that they are given further to create light in the world and for the world.

Notes

1 Malcolm Bowie, *Proust among the Stars* (London: HarperCollins, 1998), p. xvi.
2 Marie Nordlinger-Riefstahl, ed., *Marcel Proust: lettres à une amie* (Manchester: Éditions du Calame, 1942), p. vii.
3 William C. Carter, *Marcel Proust: A Life* (New Haven and London: Yale University Press, 2000), p. 275.
4 Robert de La Sizeranne, *Ruskin et la religion de la beauté* (Paris: Hachette, 1897).
5 See Cynthia Gamble, *Proust as Interpreter of Ruskin: The Seven Lamps of Translation* (Birmingham, AL: Summa Publications, 2002), pp. 43–4.
6 *The Works of John Ruskin*, ed. E. T. Cook and Alexander Wedderburn, 39 vols. (London: George Allen, 1903–1912), vol. VIII, 233.
7 Psalms 44. 1; 78. 3.
8 For a full analysis of the importance of this chapter, see Gamble, *Proust as Interpreter of Ruskin*, pp. 45–58.
9 See Stuart Eagles, *After Ruskin: The Social and Political Legacies of a Victorian Prophet, 1870–1920* (Oxford University Press, 2011), pp. 148–96.
10 Marie Nordlinger-Riefstahl, 'Proust and Ruskin', exhibition catalogue *Marcel Proust 1871–1922* (Manchester: Whitworth Art Gallery, 1956), p. 7.
11 John Ruskin, *La Bible d'Amiens*, preface, translation and notes by Marcel Proust, ed. Y.-M. Ergal (Paris: Bartillat, 2007), p. 12. Hereafter *BA*, translations mine.
12 'John Ruskin', *La Chronique des arts et de la curiosité* (27 January 1900); 'Pèlerinages ruskiniens en France', *Le Figaro* (13 February 1900); 'Ruskin à Notre-Dame d'Amiens', *Le Mercure de France* (April 1900); 'John Ruskin', *La Gazette des Beaux-Arts* (1 April and 1 August 1900).
13 This is a transcription of the original title in Proust's manuscript NAF 16642, folio 10v (http://gallica.bnf.fr accessed 24 June 2013). The printed version is inappropriately presented.
14 Anne Borrel, ed., *Marcel Proust: Écrits de jeunesse 1887–1895* (Illiers-Combray: Institut Marcel Proust international, 1991), p. 159. Hereafter *EJ*, translations mine.
15 I am grateful to Robert Hewison for this comment and for a lively discussion about Proust, Berenson and Ruskin at the Architectural Association, London, on 29 November 2011.
16 Other voices included those of Balzac, Baudelaire, Flaubert, Hugo and Racine: see for example Annick Bouillaguet, *Proust lecteur de Balzac et de Flaubert: l'imitation cryptée* (Paris: Champion, 2000).
17 *The Works of John Ruskin*, XVIII, 37.

CHAPTER 5

Composition and publication of À la recherche du temps perdu

Nathalie Mauriac Dyer

Proust's manuscripts and his correspondence, together with some of his contemporaries' accounts, are our sources for understanding the composition and publication of his monumental novel. Although some are missing – either destroyed by Proust himself or still in private hands – and a few are dispersed (the corrected galleys of *Du côté de chez Swann*, for instance, are at the Fondation Martin Bodmer), the bulk of the manuscript evidence is held in Paris at the Bibliothèque nationale de France. The Fonds Proust includes, for *À la recherche* alone, over 100 notebooks – four *carnets* and up to ninety-eight *cahiers* – as well as numerous corrected typescripts, galleys and proofs. Despite Proust's own scepticism relating to the ability of posterity to understand his 'manner of working' and the 'evolution of [his] thought' (*Corr*, XXI, 373), these manuscripts have been the object of intense scrutiny since the 1960s at least: how did Proust compose *À la recherche* in the years from 1908 to his death in November 1922? For the years 1909 to 1914, at least, there exists a scholarly summa[1] that collects, critiques and completes with unprecedented scope and detail all previous research, while an international team has embarked (2008) on the exhaustive diplomatic edition of the seventy-five core *cahiers* of this extraordinary genesis.[2] All ninety-eight have now been digitized, and most are already available online (gallica.bnf.fr), allowing the general public to appraise their complexity.[3]

Unlike Flaubert's more 'programmatic' practice, Proust's writing does not develop in a linear, systematic and predictable fashion from an initial basis of documentary notes and detailed scenarios. Within a given *cahier*, the relevant genetic unit is the fully textualized sequence (or *unité textuelle*) which can be identified already at the draft stage (*cahiers de brouillon*). These initial, often 'compact' units frequently 'explode' at later stages to be disseminated and 'mounted' with other fragments in so-called *cahiers de montage*. They form new and much expanded sequences, which Proust enriches further in the margins, on facing verso pages and on long,

34

pasted-on papers (*paperoles*). This process goes on at the fair copy stage (*cahiers de la mise au net*), where previously assembled textual units may explode again, their parts be moved around or disappear, in a combination of expansion and condensation. This tireless reworking goes on even at the typescript and galley-proofs stages, making it one of the most defining and remarkable traits of Proust's genetic 'style'. Another defining trait is, conversely, a striking continuity and permanence of some 'core' content. Anyone who has read *Jean Santeuil*, Proust's first abandoned novel, or 'Sur la lecture', the preface to his translation of Ruskin's *Sesame and Lilies*, easily identifies scenes and themes present in *À la recherche*.

There is general agreement today that *À la recherche* emerged from the *Contre Sainte-Beuve* project on which Proust embarked in 1908. *Contre Sainte-Beuve* – today an heterogeneous ensemble of manuscripts[4] – was never completed (although it has been the object of several editions).[5] It began on loose sheets (*Proust 45*), as various attempts towards a conventional essay in literary criticism, which numerous notes on re-reading Sainte-Beuve (*Carnet* 1) would have nourished. At the end of 1908 or beginning of 1909 Proust chose for it a semi-fictional setting. According to *Cahier* 3, one morning, before 'Marcel Proust' went to bed ('already I would only sleep during the daytime'[6]), his mother would surprise him with *Le Figaro* where his article had finally appeared; he would start a conversation with her about a new article, this time on Sainte-Beuve's method (*Cahier* 2). Essays against the critic and in defence of Balzac (*Cahiers* 1, 4), Nerval (*Cahiers* 5, 6) and Baudelaire (*Cahiers* 7, 6), later Leconte de Lisle (*Cahier* 64), must have prepared this 'conversation with *Maman*'. Yet the critique of Sainte-Beuve is far from being the only focus of these early notebooks. In *Cahiers* 3 and 2, the 'je' experiences sensations and impressions that, depending on the weather and season, awaken various memories of travel and/or desires (e.g. of Venice, of girls passing in the street). In *Cahier* 1 a characteristic layering of voices in the first person appears: the protagonist (the one who is supposed to converse with his mother during this memorable morning) is an intermediary instance between the Narrator and a hero who would still sleep at night, experience dreams, awakenings and disorientation, followed by memories of various bedrooms he had lived in: this 'dormeur éveillé' structure allowed for the introduction of multiple narrative threads. In *Cahier* 5, numerous fictional characters suddenly appear – Françoise, a count and countess, later named Guermantes, Mme de Villeparisis, Montargis, Mlle de Quimperlé; in *Cahier* 4, we find Swann and Combray, and even the 'Villebon' and 'Méséglise' ways,[7] which in *Carnet* 1 were listed among other items from seventy-five folios of (now lost) *Pages écrites*.[8] It is very likely, then, that from *Cahier* 5 on Proust used the newly found *Contre Sainte-Beuve* narrative frame to recycle previously elaborated material. By August 1909, after five more *cahiers* had been filled (*Cahiers* 31, 36, 7, 6, 51) – some of which introduce M. de Guercy (the future Charlus) and the theme of inversion, the last one already sketching the 'Bal de têtes' –, Proust felt confident enough to offer *Contre Sainte-Beuve, Souvenir d'une Matinée*, now 'a true novel', for publication to Alfred Vallette of the *Mercure de France*, then, after his refusal, to Gaston Calmette and André Beaunier for instalments in *Le Figaro* (*Corr*, IX, 155–6; xviii–xxv). The conversation with the mother on Sainte-Beuve and aesthetics had been postponed to the conclusion, leaving room for the more fictional parts to develop. Fragments were stitched together to create the first continuous narrative of 'Combray' (*Cahiers* 8, 12), whose fair copy, dictated and enriched (*Cahiers* 9, 10, 63), Proust then had typed (156 pages) and, in December 1909, sent to his would-be editors. *Le Figaro* would (fortunately) never publish it, allowing for new episodes of the novelistic side of *Contre Sainte-Beuve* to appear and expand from 1910 on: 'Un amour de Swann', the story with Gilberte, the girls at Querqueville (Andrée, Maria), the illness and death of the grandmother, the discovery of the Guermantes' social circles, visits to Padua and Venice, erotic pursuits with a chambermaid, all these came to life. In *Cahier* 50, an ill and insomniac Narrator would revel in his morning perceptions, making the novel come full circle with its opening from the first *cahiers*.

Although it is impossible to pinpoint the precise moment when Proust abandoned *Contre Sainte-Beuve* as such, it must have coincided with the invention of *Le Temps retrouvé* in the winter of 1910. Replacing the conversation with the mother at the end of the book, it comprised the epiphanies of involuntary memory ('L'Adoration perpétuelle') which had been sketched on loose sheets at the beginning of the *Contre Sainte-Beuve* project,[9] followed by the revised 'Bal de têtes', which, revealing the passing of Time to the protagonist, urged him to start writing (*Cahiers* 58, 57).[10] The novel about an apprentice journalist and literary critic had become the history of a writer's vocation. In a revealing gesture that took place, perhaps, in the winter of 1910–11, Proust split the 'petite madeleine' episode on the 1909 typescript of 'Combray', leaving the experience of reminiscence at the end of 'Combray 1', and postponing its philosophic import to *Cahier* 57. The years 1911 and 1912 were spent revising and expanding this typescript and having the sequel ('Un amour de Swann' and then 'Noms de pays') reach a similar state;[11] Proust also wrote the fair copy of the first part of *Guermantes*. In October 1912 began the difficult task of finding a publisher for *Le Temps perdu*, the first volume of a novel provisionally called *Les Intermittences du cœur*. Turned down by Fasquelle, the Éditions de la Nouvelle Revue française and Ollendorff, Proust resorted to being published at his own expense by the young Bernard Grasset. The general title *À la recherche du temps perdu* appeared in the spring of 1913 on the first galley, together with *Du côté de chez Swann* (replacing *Charles Swann*). These proofs were so heavily corrected, with suppressions, episodes moved around, *paperole* additions, and even the creation of a new major character, the composer Vinteuil (from the fusion of the naturalist Vington and the musician Berget), that Proust could say that 'not one line out of twenty of the primitive text is saved' (*Corr*, XII, 132). Eventually, because Grasset demanded a reasonably sized volume, he had to cut the greater part of 'Noms de pays' (the end of the Gilberte story and all of the first Balbec stay) and to concoct an alternative ending. When *Du côté de chez Swann* was published in November 1913, it contained a list of chapters for the next two volumes. However, this plan was about to be deeply modified.

While Proust was engaged in the correction of the *Swann* proofs, he was also involved with his ex-chauffeur and secretary Alfred Agostinelli, whom he had first met at Cabourg in 1907. The events that took place from early August 1913 to June 1914 were crucial for the rest of the genesis of *À la recherche* and are well known thanks to Proust's correspondence: the sudden (and still enigmatic) return from Normandy with Agostinelli in August 1913, his flight from the writer's home a few months later, Proust's frantic efforts to have him return, his drowning after a plane crash in May 1914, Proust's immense grief and mourning, followed by a process of forgetting. The *Cahier* 71 titled *Dux* (1913) and *Cahier* 54 titled *Vénusté* (1914) are clear transpositions of this chain of events. Even though the Albertine character who succeeded Maria in the spring of 1913 (*Cahier* 34) owes a lot to her, the Agostinelli story brought to the numerous seaside flirtations sketched in earlier *cahiers* what they lacked: a clearly designed dramatic structure. Proust was well aware of it, calling the Albertine story, as in a Greek tragedy, the 'Episode', and said that her character brought about the 'peripeteia' (*Corr*, XIV, 281). The following summer, the start of the First World War interrupted the publication of the second volume already in proofs, and, not unlike the refusal of *Contre Sainte-Beuve* in 1909, this turned into an opportunity. Proust could now develop the 'Episode' at length, and bring the necessary changes to the overall structure. One was the reduction of the number of stays in Balbec from three to two, the previous first and second (when the hero met the 'little gang') coalescing: 'À l'ombre des jeunes filles en fleurs', formerly the opening chapter in the third volume, grew considerably. The illness and death of the grandmother, once also a chapter in the last volume, was anticipated before Albertine's re-appearing at the hero's Parisian home, drafted in *Cahier* 46. The second and now last stay in Balbec was then developed (*Cahiers* 46, 72), followed by the first amplified, continuous version of the 'Episode', from Albertine's captivity to her death and forgetting (*Cahiers* 53, 73, 55, 56). Proust organized the story of the 'captive' along days, either iterative or singulative, whose mornings filled for the protagonist with climatic sensations and impressions were based on those of *Cahier* 50, themselves borrowing from the first *cahiers* of *Contre Sainte-Beuve*. The literary conversation with Albertine may also be considered as the transposition of the once intended 'conversation with *Maman*'. In 1916, Proust could write to Gallimard, his new publisher-to-be, that his book, 'longer than [he himself] had realized' (*Corr*, XIX, 733), would not comprise three, but four volumes: *Du côté de chez Swann, Le Côté de Guermantes, Sodome et Gomorrhe, Le Temps retrouvé*. The addition of *Sodome et Gomorrhe* is a key compositional moment, creating a third structural opposition after *Temps perdu* and *Temps retrouvé*, Swann and Guermantes, and placing Albertine (Gomorrhe) on a par with no less than Charlus (Sodome). Proust had embarked on a new series of, eventually, twenty notebooks known as *cahiers de la mise au net* and titled 'Sodome et Gomorrhe I' (*Cahiers* 1–7) and 'Sodome et Gomorrhe II – Le Temps retrouvé' (*Cahiers* 8–20). Thickened with *paperoles* and fragments cut and pasted from earlier *cahiers*, they would accompany him until the end of his life and also serve as copytext, after his death, for the publication of two of the three posthumous volumes, *Albertine disparue* (*Cahiers* 12–15) and *Le Temps retrouvé* (*Cahiers* 15–20). It is likely that the last chapter and famous word *Fin* had been written when, in May 1919, Proust informed Gallimard that, if necessary, his *cahiers* were available for 'complete publication' (*Corr*, XVIII, 226).

The publication process had resumed as early as 1917 with the preparation of the second volume, *À l'ombre des jeunes filles en fleurs*. Proust recycled some of his 1914 Grasset proofs, and at least two *cahiers* were dismantled to help typesetting (eventually their fragments adorned the 1920 edition for bibliophiles). With *À l'ombre* (1919), *À la recherche* was now to comprise neither three (1913), nor four (1916), but five volumes. Proust, who had once dreamt of publishing 'all at once' (*ASB*, 234, trans. mod.; *CSB*, 557), opted for a refined subdivision of his manuscript material, as *Le Côté de Guermantes I* (1920), *Le Côté de Guermantes II–Sodome et*

Gomorrhe I (1921), *Sodome et Gomorrhe II* (May 1922). But the rhythm of publication was rushed by his sense of rapidly declining health, and the whole process was laborious. Proust expressed several times his dissatisfaction with the *NRF* secretaries and proofreaders; Gallimard complained about his many last-minute changes (extra *cahiers* were filled with additions for incoming proofs: *Cahiers* 59–62, 75), while he replied that this 'surnourriture' was precisely what gave *À la recherche* its special quality (*Corr*, XVIII, 226). However, condensation also happened in remarkable ways: for instance, the 'soirée chez la princesse de Guermantes' at the beginning of *Sodome et Gomorrhe II* was sharply reduced from its version in *Cahier 2* (now a fifty-page, small-print, variant in the Pléiade edition).[12] The most striking curtailment occurred with the next volume, *Sodome et Gomorrhe III*, whose 1,000 pages were typed from *Cahiers 12–15* in the spring of 1922. Though the first part (finally titled *La Prisonnière* and sent to Gallimard in the beginning of November) was much developed, the second (first titled *La Fugitive* and eventually *Albertine disparue*) was reduced from 450 to 150 pages on the typescript, making it a brief, dramatic ending to the heroine's episode of captivity. Proust would have recycled the greater part of the withdrawn pages, as some last-minute notes suggest.[13] But this sharp revision process interrupted by death marked the end of the composition of *À la recherche*, leaving it cruelly unfinished, not at the end, but *in medias res*.

Yet it was not the end of its publication. An advertisement posthumously published by the *NRF* in December 1922 had announced 'in press' *Sodome et Gomorrhe III* (comprising both *La Prisonnière* and *Albertine disparue*), then, 'in several volumes', '*Sodome et Gomorrhe*, suite' before *Le Temps retrouvé*. This expansion was consistent with an earlier letter to Gallimard promising up to six instalments of *Sodome et Gomorrhe* (*Corr*, XXI, 39). However, the corresponding material was not to be found by the posthumous editors. Besides, the cut of almost all of *Cahiers* 13 and 14 from the *Albertine disparue* typescript, and of some of *Cahier* 15, was hardly compensated by the audacious move of Albertine's death to 'the bank of the river Vivonne', i.e. near the dreaded Montjouvain, home of Mlle Vinteuil and her lesbian friend.[14] Proust's brother, Dr Robert Proust, and his collaborator Jacques Rivière saw no alternative but to come back to the longer, *cahiers de la mise au net* version, which, at least, allowed for *À la recherche* to be published to its end. The two parts of the intended *Sodome et Gomorrhe III* came out as separate volumes in 1923 and 1925, and in 1927 *Le Temps retrouvé* included chapters that had clearly been destined to the last *Sodome et Gomorrhe*, namely Saint-Loup's inversion, the wartime scenes and the hero's last encounter with an elderly Charlus chaperoned by Jupien. Between 1929 and 1932 the 'definitive' edition of *À la recherche* appeared. The existing eight volumes were reduced to seven by grouping the two *Côté de Guermantes* and the two *Sodome et Gomorrhe* (which *de facto* erased all vestige of its once-intended series): the editorial canon was born. In the meantime, Gallimard's request that *Albertine disparue* were republished from its 'original manuscript' fell on deaf ears;[15] Robert Proust nevertheless preserved the typescript which was rediscovered in 1986.[16] Today, *À la recherche* still awaits a complete edition that will not camouflage its unfinished composition, and allow us to better understand the history of its extraordinary genesis, propelled, from the start to the end, by the power of fiction.

Notes

1 A. Pugh, *The Growth of 'À la recherche du temps perdu': A Chronological Examination of Proust's Manuscripts from 1909 to 1914*, 2 vols. (University of Toronto Press, 2004). No comparable study exists for the years 1914 to 1922.

2 *Cahiers 1 à 75 de la BnF* (Turnhout: Brepols–BnF, 2008–).

3 For easy access: www.item.ens.fr/index.php?id=578147.

4 *Proust 45* (NAF 16636); *Carnet* 1; seventy-five folio sheets (lost; see *Carnet* 1, fol. 7v); *Cahiers* 3, 2, 5, 1, 4, 31, 36, 7, 6, 51; to which several 1908–9 letters must be added.

5 B. de Fallois (ed.), Gallimard, 1952; P. Clarac (ed.), Gallimard, 1971; M. B. Bertini, L. Keller (eds.), H. Scheltel (trans.), Suhrkamp, 1997.

6 *Cahier* 3, fol. 6r.

7 *Carnet* 1, fol. 7v: 'Le côté de Villebon et le côté de Méséglise'.

8 They have been partially published by Fallois, 1952.

9 *CSB*, 1952, 'Préface'.

10 See *Matinée chez la princesse de Guermantes. Cahiers du 'Temps retrouvé'*, ed. H. Bonnet and B. Brun (Paris: Gallimard, 1982).

11 See *'Bricquebec': Prototype d''À l'ombre des jeunes filles en fleurs'*, ed. Richard Bales (Oxford: Clarendon Press, 1989).

12 See III, 34, var. b, pp. 1300–53.

13 Nathalie Mauriac Dyer, *Proust inachevé* (Paris: Champion, 2005), p. 179 ff.

14 See Mauriac Dyer, *Proust inachevé*.

15 See N. Mauriac Dyer, A. Rivière and P.-E. Robert (eds.), *Les Années perdues de la Recherche. Correspondance pour l'édition des volumes posthumes d''À la recherche du temps perdu'* (Paris: Gallimard, 1999), pp. 137–44.

16 Mauriac Dyer, *Proust inachevé*.

PART II

Historical and cultural contexts

i. The arts

CHAPTER 6

Proust's reading

Caroline Szylowicz

In a chapter titled 'First Steps Toward a History of Reading', cultural historian Robert Darnton wrote:

> [M]ost of us would agree that a catalogue of a private library can serve as a profile of a reader, even though we don't read all the books we own and we do read many books that we never purchase. To scan the catalogue of the library in Monticello is to inspect the furnishings of Jefferson's mind. And the study of private libraries has the advantage of linking the 'what' with the 'who' of reading.[1]

These words echo those of Georges Andrieux, the Parisian bookseller who, in 1930, had overseen the auction of the library of Paul Souday (1869–1929), the famed literary critic and contemporary of Proust. In the foreword to the auction catalogue, Andrieux remarked:

> Thanks to [the catalogue], those who desire to find, for some study, personal notes or documents written by Paul Souday, will be able to take steps to find out in which library an item has been preserved. Thus, even if scattered, these books will always be accessible, and the product of so much work, of so many meditations and controversies will not be lost.[2]

Following these recommendations, W. Silverman noted, in her examination of the auction catalogue of the library of another contemporary of Proust, Count Robert de Montesquiou-Fezensac (1855–1921): 'A study of his bibliophilia, an area of his esthetic pursuits that has received surprisingly scant attention from critics, lends further support to the recent reappraisal of his role as a foremost esthetic guide and educator of his contemporaries.'[3]

How, then, is one supposed to 'inspect the furnishings of Marcel Proust's mind', when no auction of his books was organized after his death, and no catalogue ever compiled?

After the novelist's death on 18 November 1922, his brother, Dr Robert Proust, inherited all his belongings and transferred most of them from rue

Hamelin to his home on avenue Hoche. He spent the next few years supervising the publication of the remaining volumes of *À la recherche*, while pursuing his career as a professor of medicine and as a surgeon. Following Dr Proust's death in May 1935, his widow decided to move out of the home on avenue Hoche. L. Foschini, in her account of collector Jacques Guérin's lifelong quest for Proustian memorabilia, pieced together the fate of the estate.[4] Suzy Mante-Proust, the only child of Dr and Mme Robert Proust, kept her uncle's manuscripts and associated literary documents, as well as some of his furniture. In preparation for the move, Mme Robert Proust asked a dealer named Werner and the bookseller Henri Lefebvre to help her dispose of her late brother-in-law's remaining belongings, furniture, books, papers, many of which were reportedly burned or discarded. Werner brought some corrected proofs and other papers to Lefebvre and was planning to auction off any remaining items. It was at that time that the young Guérin happened to visit Lefebvre's bookshop. Lefebvre put Guérin in contact with Werner, who took him back to the apartment, empty but for a bookcase, a desk, and 'in the entryway, stacks of books . . . piled up to the ceiling'.[5] These books had belonged to Marcel Proust but Mme Robert Proust had systematically removed whatever dedications she could find to erase her late brother-in-law's name.[6] On a mantelpiece, copies of Robert de Montesquiou's *Les Hortensias Bleus* and *Les Chauves-Souris*, inscribed to Proust, had escaped the purge.

'Home furnishings'

A small number of books survived the treatment described by Foschini and remained within the Proust family, or passed to private collectors, and to a much smaller extent, libraries. An examination of four major exhibition catalogues uncovers about three dozen books known to have belonged to Marcel Proust.[7] They include works by Léon Daudet, Charles Maurras, Paul Bourget, Ernest Renan, Anatole France, Maurice Barrès, André Gide, François Mauriac, Jean Cocteau, Colette, André Breton, Pierre Mac Orlan, Blaise Cendrars, John Ruskin of course, and Robert de Montesquiou.

The Musée Marcel Proust in Illiers-Combray owns a small collection of books, although the absence of provenance information for most of the pieces suggests that these books were added to enhance the Combray decor when the museum was established. Nineteenth-century sets of *Lettres de Madame de Sévigné*, *Mémoires du duc de Saint-Simon* and a copy of an 1870 edition of George Sand's *François le Champi* donated by Suzy Mante-Proust are likely intended to conjure up the familiar maternal presence.

Other titles, such as Mallarmé's translation of poems of Edgar Poe, a study of Whistler by Théodore Duret, or a volume on penal colonies dated 1843 could plausibly have belonged to Proust or his relatives. Two items have clear provenance: a bound score of Gounod's *Roméo et Juliette* bearing the initials of Proust's mother, 'J. W.', donated by Jacques Guérin, and *Histoire de la littérature hindoue*, inscribed to the young Marcel Proust by its author, Dr Cazalis, writing under the pen name Jean Lahor.

The Bibliothèque nationale de France also owns at least three of Proust's books. The Département des estampes received in 1969 the copy of Ruskin's *The Bible of Amiens* which Proust used and annotated to prepare his translation.[8] The other two titles, Montesquieu's *Lettres persanes* and *La Sainte Bible ou l'Ancien et le Nouveau Testament*, were part of a donation from Dr Robert Le Masle, which also included several medical and scientific texts that had belonged to Drs Robert and Adrien Proust.[9]

In addition, two photographs provide a glimpse into the Proust family home decor and its book furnishings. The first shows Jeanne Proust, in profile, sitting in a distinctive Empire-style chair, caught in the act of reading, seemingly oblivious to the camera. In the background, a bookcase with four glass doors, filled with rows of books in matching bindings, is clearly visible. Although out of focus, a pile of books or magazines can be made out in the foreground.[10] The second photograph, taken at Proust's last residence in rue Hamelin, shows Proust's desk and a chair, possibly the same as that used by Jeanne Proust in the previous image, or at the very least from the same set. To the left of the desk a four-sided revolving bookcase is filled with books of various formats, and topped with more large volumes.[11]

'Mind furnishings'

While no catalogue of Proust's books was compiled in 1922, or even in 1935, Proust's correspondence, unsurprisingly, reveals much about the readings and the reading habits of its creator. Proust's letters, augmented by Philip Kolb's meticulous annotations, which were later compiled in a general index,[12] inspired a young researcher, J. Lambilliotte, to suggest a model database to reconstitute Marcel Proust's library.[13] While this model remains unfinished, it prefigures the sort of 'data-mining' that would be made possible with a new digital edition of the letters. Because this database would include every single piece of evidence that Proust had come into contact with a book, or had some knowledge of it, or sought to find more about it, it would offer a much more precise and dynamic view, across time, of the writer's mental furnishings than an auction catalogue ever could. Indeed such a catalogue could only record books which were found to be present at the time of the sale. In the case of bibliophiles such as Montesquiou and Souday, that date might correspond to a point of 'maximum accumulation'.

'We read many books that we never purchase'

This is certainly the case with Proust, who was never a collector. Instead, the systematic parsing of Proust's letters makes it evident that, while Proust read or came in contact with large numbers of books (Lambilliotte reports gathering more than 650 entries for the period 1883–1904),[14] he did so without necessarily owning them.

As a boy, he received books as gifts from family and friends, as rewards for earning top place in school rankings, but his parents and grandparents made much use of neighbouring 'cabinets de lecture', commercial circulating libraries where they maintained subscriptions. Books were passed around the family circle, mailed back and forth among friends, forgotten in cabs. From a relatively young age, Proust began to receive books directly from their authors, a trend which grew along with his reputation as literary critic and published author in later years. When doing research, whether for his work on John Ruskin, or during the writing of À la recherche, Proust often called on a network of friends and acquaintances to answer his queries, or to suggest suitable books, and often to lend books to him. Borrowed books were generally given back: 'Every day I hope to be well enough to bring you back the *Carpaccio* in person the day after. But since this "day after" is taking a long time to come I've resigned myself to sending it back by post' (*Corr*, xv, 62). Sometimes not: 'But what worries me most is not knowing to whom I must send back the tattered book on emblems. It was infinitely useful, but this is no reason not to return it to the bookseller' (*Corr*, xxi, 121). Robert de Billy has described how, in 1901, he lent Proust his copy of Émile Mâle's *L'Art religieux du XIII siècle* and received it back, four years later, missing its cover and 'bear[ing] the marks of all the misfortunes that can befall a book, read in bed, in close proximity to medicines'.[15]

Proust did not avail himself of libraries for his research. Most references to Parisian libraries in the geographic section of the general index refer either to bibliographic annotations in the correspondence, or to young Proust's unenthusiastic 'career' as an unpaid assistant at the Bibliothèque Mazarine, between 1895 and 1900. Although, on his first day there, on 6 June 1895, he writes to Robert de Montesquiou to offer to do some research on his behalf while at the Mazarine, there is only one documented instance of Proust as library patron, about the time when he became interested in the writings of John Ruskin. In October 1899, having recently returned from Évian, Proust wrote to his friend Pierre de Chevilly that 'I led him [François d'Oncieu] only to such exalted places as the Louvre and the Bibliothèque nationale (where I have at last found, read, and loved Ruskin's *Seven Lamps of Architecture* in *La Revue générale*...)' (*Corr*, II, 367).

Proust also lent or gave away his own books. In January 1917, in a letter to the young Jacques Hébertot, a theatre critic for the daily newspaper *Gil Blas*, who was serving at the time as an officer in a heavy artillery unit, Proust announced the shipment of 'a translation of *St Mark's Rest*, another of *Stones of Venice*, and *Swann*'. He added: 'The copies I am sending you (except for *Swann*) have been used by me and are quite damaged, so please have no qualms about keeping them if they please you or throwing them away if they are an encumbrance. In any case they are now yours' (*Corr*, XVI, 37).

Comparisons between the correspondence, its index, and the indices of critical editions of *À la recherche* and other collected writings of Proust, such as his four pocket notebooks or *carnets*, yield many interesting findings and clues for researchers. Authors mentioned in the letters also appear in the *Recherche*, or their name may be omitted, although their words remain, absorbed and woven in Proust's own writing. Scholars have unearthed many such intertextual exchanges. Because the correspondence itself is a corpus that continues to evolve and grow as unpublished letters emerge, and because scholars continue to uncover intertextual elements in Proust's manuscripts, our understanding of the furnishings of Proust's mind requires periodic rearranging.

'We don't read all the books we own'

While most extant books belonging to Proust remain in private collections and can usually be seen only during major exhibitions, at which point they are locked in display cases, they contain many clues to the way Proust read and handled them. N. Mauriac Dyer and D. Ferrer examined Proust's copy of *La Chartreuse de Parme* when it was exhibited in advance of an auction in 2003.[16] They show that Proust heavily annotated his copy, commented on issues of style, plot or vocabulary, and that he planned to use these elements in future writings.

N. Mauriac Dyer, describing the inscribed copy of *Gustave Flaubert, 1821–1880: sa vie – ses romans – son style*, which Proust received from the critic Albert Thibaudet in June 1922, notes that it is possible to distinguish the pages that were cut by Proust, in a very rough manner, from those that were neatly sliced opened, probably by the binder, after Proust's death.[17] The pages cut by Proust are gathered around only three specific chapters.

A third book in private hands, *Le Repos de Saint-Marc* translated into French by K. Johnson, shows the same pattern of selective reading.[18] Only the first pages of the translator's preface and a few scattered pages throughout the volume have been carelessly opened, torn more than cut. Proust leafed through three or four separate passages but read the three-page translator's preface very attentively, judging by his written reactions in the margins. He mocked the nonsensical use of English idioms in a French translation, underlined redundant words, and berated the translator for the lack of precision in his or her praise of Ruskin. The front cover of the book, made of a vellum-like paper, which bears a wrinkled, circular indentation probably made by a wet glass or bottle, and multiple grey and brown stains, evidence of splatters or burns, is reminiscent of the misfortunes described by R. de Billy. Philip Kolb received this volume as a gift from Suzy Mante-Proust, during his first research trip in France in 1935–6. The existence of this copy raises some interesting questions of provenance. If this is the copy that Proust sent to Hébertot in 1917, how did it return into Suzy Mante-Proust's possession? Did Hébertot carefully hold on to it until the end of the war, without reading it, and returned it later to Proust or his heirs? Or did Proust own a second copy?

These three examples and the Bibliothèque nationale's annotated copy of *The Bible of Amiens* retain the physical traces of Proust's acts of reading, which N. Mauriac Dyer vividly describes:

> We thus witness Proust in his most daily activity as reader, thinker, writer, but also as man of letters involved in the literary debate of his time: he receives a book, reads its table of contents, roughly cuts with his finger, an envelope or a stray piece of paper the few pages that interest him. He glances through them, and he reacts.[19]

It is likely that Proust engaged in this lively dialogue with more than just four books. It can only be hoped, then, that some of the books 'orphaned' by Mme Robert Proust in 1935 still exist on bookshelves, and that it is just a matter of time until they find their way into the hands of Proust enthusiasts capable of recognizing the novelist's distinctive handwriting.

Notes

1 Robert Darnton, *The Kiss of Lamourette: Reflections in Cultural History* (New York: Norton, 1990), pp. 154–87.

2 'Bibliothèque de Paul Souday: éditions originales dédicacées et correspondances autographes d'auteurs contemporains. Vente les 12, 13, 14 et 15 mars 1930.' Georges Andrieux, expert [auction catalogue].

3 W. S. Silverman, 'Unpacking His Library: Robert de Montesquiou and the Esthetics of the Book in Fin-de-siècle France', *Nineteenth-Century French Studies*, 32 (2004), 316–31.

4 Lorenza Foschini, *Proust's Overcoat*, trans. by Eric Karpeles (New York: Ecco, 2010).

5 Foschini, *Proust's Overcoat*, p. 45.

6 Foschini, *Proust's Overcoat*, p. 46.

7 *Marcel Proust and His Time 1871–1922* (London: Wildenstein Gallery, 1955), items 339, 345, 349, 352, 356, 362; *Marcel Proust* (Paris: Bibliothèque nationale, 1965), items 51, 69, 83, 119, 160, 195, 245, 302, 339, 394, 473, 479, 485; *Marcel Proust en son temps* (Paris: Musée Jacquemart-André, 1971), items 34, 61, 120, 129, 217, 224, 233, 264, 281; *Marcel Proust: l'écriture et les arts* (Paris: Bibliothèque nationale de France, 1999), items 65, 75, 237, 244, 248, 250, 252, 254, 256, 258, 260–3, 265–7, 270.

8 Anne Borrel, 'Proust et Ruskin: l'exemplaire de *La Bible d'Amiens* à la Bibliothèque nationale de France', *48/14 La Revue du musée d'Orsay*, 2 (1996), 74–79.

9 *Lettres persanes de Montesquieu. Éloge par d'Alembert* (Paris: P. Pourrat frères, 1834), call number Z LE MASLE- 255. *La Sainte Bible ou l'Ancien et le Nouveau Testament, version de J. F. Ostervald* (Paris, Brussels: Société biblique britannique et étrangère, 1898), call number RES- Z LE MASLE- 43. The donation is noted as 'Legs Le Masle' in the corresponding catalogue records of the Bibliothèque nationale de France.

10 Photograph reproduced in Jérôme Picon, *Passion Proust, l'album d'une vie* (Paris: Textuel, 1999), p. 96; Évelyne Bloch-Dano, *Madame Proust, a Biography*, trans. by Alice Kaplan (University of Chicago Press, 2007), facing p. 155. A closer view of the empty bookcase is published in Foschini, *Proust's Overcoat*, p. 87.

11 Photograph reproduced in André Maurois, *The World of Marcel Proust*, trans. by Moura Budberg (New York, London: Harper & Row, 1974), p. 262. The desk and bookcase were acquired in 1935 by Jacques Guérin, who turned them over to the Musée Carnavalet, together with other objects, in later years.

12 *Index général de la correspondance de Marcel Proust d'après l'édition de Philip Kolb*, ed. by Kazuyoshi Yoshikawa (Presses de l'Université de Kyoto, 1998).

13 Julie Lambilliotte, 'La bibliothèque de Marcel Proust: de la lecture à l'écriture', *Bulletin d'informations proustiennes*, 30 (1999), 81–9.

14 Lambilliotte, 'Bibliothèque', 83.

15 Robert de Billy, *Marcel Proust: lettres et conversations* (Paris: Éditions des Portiques, 1930), p. III.

16 Nathalie Mauriac Dyer and Daniel Ferrer, 'L'exemplaire annoté de *La Chartreuse de Parme*', *Bulletin d'informations proustiennes*, 35 (2005), 9–17.
17 Nathalie Mauriac Dyer, 'Défense de Flaubert 1919–1922', *Bulletin d'informations proustiennes*, 30 (1999), 29–48.
18 John Ruskin, *Le Repos de Saint-Marc. Histoire de Venise pour les rares voyageurs qui se soucient encore de ses monuments. Traduit de l'anglais par K. Johnston* (Paris: Librairie Hachette et Cie, 1908).
19 Mauriac Dyer, 'Défense', 40.

CHAPTER 7

Decadence and the fin de siècle

Marion Schmid

In French literary history, Proust occupies the position of an interstitial, 'entre-deux' writer poised between the literary experiments of the second half of the nineteenth century (spearheaded by, amongst others, Flaubert, Baudelaire and Mallarmé) and the high modernism that was to challenge traditional genre conventions in the period between the two world wars. The young Proust made his first steps in literary criticism and fiction during the last decades of the nineteenth century and this transitional period with its effervescent intellectual atmosphere, rugged literary landscapes and diverse cultural preoccupations was to have a lasting influence on the future author of the *Recherche*. Like his fellow early modernists Joyce, Thomas Mann and Gide, Proust found in the cultural and literary imaginary of the fin de siècle a vast repertoire of themes and motifs which he appropriated for his own writing in a complex process of absorption, distancing and, ultimately, overcoming. The Zeitgeist of the fin de siècle, and more specifically the figures and aesthetics of one of its most prominent artistic movements – Decadence – offered him ample raw material for a novel that is both a reflection and a catalyst of the influences that have shaped it.

Before examining the negotiation of fin-de-siècle cultural discourses and representations in his writing, it is necessary to circumscribe the rather diffuse and not altogether synonymous (though they are often used as such) terms 'fin de siècle' and 'Decadence'. Beyond its temporal reference to a specific period in the history of Western civilizations, that is, the last two decades of the nineteenth century, the notion 'fin de siècle' describes above all a cultural phenomenon characterized by philosophical pessimism, the belief that contemporary civilization was undergoing an inevitable phase of decadence and decline and an acute sense of political and social crisis. Paul Verlaine's poem 'Langueur' (1884) with its vision of a Decadent civilization soon to be swept away by 'white barbarians' sums up the collective feeling of degeneracy, ennui and

51

exhaustion in the aftermath of the Franco-Prussian war and the 1871 Paris Commune. Rapid social and technological change, threatening demographic decline – especially in view of the sharp increase in birth rates and the aggressive politics of Wilhelminian Germany –, looming class conflict and endemic political corruption not only caused widespread feelings of insecurity, but brought about a profound questioning of the values and intellectual foundations of the young Third Republic, notably the positivist creed of faith in progress as a vehicle of collective well-being and advancement. Far from promising unlimited knowledge and universal happiness, for the fin-de-siècle generation the twilight of the nineteenth century became symbolic of an end time, echoed in the scientific alarmism and secular millennialism of the era.

In literature, this spiritual malaise found its most prominent expression in the movement called 'Decadence' which crystallized in France in the last decades of the nineteenth century around authors such as Huysmans, Rachilde, Octave Mirbeau and Jean Lorrain (plus a host of minor poets and prose writers largely forgotten today). A worldview and a symptom rather than a coherent theory of literature – and here lies perhaps its main difference from its successor and, some would argue, second incarnation, symbolism –, Decadence feeds on and perpetuates fin-de-siècle fears and preoccupations, yet, contrary to most cultural commentators of the period who lament the debasement and degradation of contemporary society, its proponents tend to embrace and even celebrate degeneracy. Artistically disparate, uneven in its achievements, and temporally fluid, Decadent writing nonetheless shares a number of common artistic and intellectual concerns, characteristic of a radicalized subjectivity and a disregard for social and aesthetic tradition: the primacy of art over nature, the subversion of normative gender and sexual roles, a penchant for the morbid, the perverse and the grotesque, the quest to escape banal, everyday life through the cultivation of heightened sensations and immersion into artificial paradises and exotic fantasies.[1]

We do not know with any certainty whether Proust had read major Decadent authors such as Huysmans, but his contacts with the wider – and more international – artistic movement were numerous: first and foremost through one of his mentors in the 1890s, the poet, art collector and dandy Robert de Montesquiou (the model for Huysmans' Decadent anti-hero Des Esseintes and a major influence for Charlus in the *Recherche*); but also via his translations of Ruskin, selective readings of Walter Pater and interest in Pre-Raphaelite painting, which familiarized him with British aestheticism (a major influence on the formation of a

Decadent sensibility in France); and, not least, thanks to his passion for Richard Wagner and Gustave Moreau, two artists at the confluence of Decadence and symbolism. Having felt some 'vague Decadent impulses'[2] himself, Proust at first defends Decadent writing in the literary journals to which he contributes in the 1880s, but quickly distances himself from the stylistic flourishes, morbid sensibility and religion of beautiful forms of language he discerns as some of its pitfalls. His ambivalence towards the movement, which seems to have held a considerable fascination for him, but from which he was anxious to demarcate himself, crystallizes in a series of articles on Montesquiou – most importantly, 'De la simplicité de Robert de Montesquiou' (1893) and 'Un professeur de beauté' (1905) – in which he endeavours to free the poet from the epithet 'Prince of Decadence' that his eccentric lifestyle and over-ornate poetry have earned him. Like Baudelaire before him, Proust argues, Montesquiou is the victim of a false Decadent appropriation, yet his minute style and vast erudition do in fact designate him as a proud successor of the French classical tradition. Paradoxical as it may seem, especially in light of the fervent attack against the obscurantist rhetoric and mannered style of the young generation of Decadent and symbolist poets he formulated in the polemical 'Contre l'obscurité' (1896), his rehabilitation of the Decadent poet is part of a wider break with the contemporary avant-gardes: by aligning Montesquiou with the classical tradition, Proust deals a blow to the Decadent generation, whom he deprives of one of its leaders and main models.[3] Later, in a response to a survey on 'Classicism and Romanticism', he would effect a similar re-evaluation with regard to Baudelaire, whom Théophile Gautier had co-opted to Decadence in his 1868 preface for *Les Fleurs du mal*, but here he reorients the debate by postulating the classicism of the avant-gardes: they are classical 'great artists who, for as long as they were misunderstood, were called romantics, realists, decadents, etc.'[4] Classicism, for Proust, then, does not mean timelessness, but rather discordance with respect to contemporary artistic fashions.[5] Contrary to the numerous epigones of Decadence, who engage in derivative, inauthentic writing, Baudelaire is classical precisely because of his originality.

Proust's critical evaluation of Decadence thus revolves above all around questions of authenticity and inauthenticity, originality and borrowing – a dialectics that will be played out in his fiction. His first published book, *Les Plaisirs et les jours* (1896), a work at the intersection between Decadence and symbolism, shows a strong affinity with the Decadent sensibility. Its luxurious presentation and intermedial gesturing (it includes piano scores by Reynaldo Hahn and original drawings by the salon hostess Madeleine

Lemaire) situate the volume in the tradition of the Wagnerian *Gesamt-kunstwerk* in which different forms of art reunite in a harmonious whole. The heteroclite nature of the volume, composed of novellas, prose and verse poems, pastiches and philosophical essays, however, recalls the fragmentation and dispersal that Désiré Nisard, Paul Bourget and Nietzsche had identified as main characteristics of Decadent aesthetics. More explicitly, intertextual references to Baudelaire, Montesquiou, Maeterlinck and Wagner, the melancholy pessimism of its upper-class protagonists, languid atmosphere of death and decline and portrayal of morbid love and guilty sexualities firmly inscribe the book within a fin-de-siècle Zeitgeist. In this polyphonic volume, where a wealth of styles from 'écriture artiste' to Russian realism after the manner of Tolstoy dialogue with one another, Proust for the first time extensively experiments with the practice of literary pastiche, which, in avowed or tacit form, will play a major role in his artistic development. A privileged means of what he calls 'literary criticism in action', the pastiche enables him to imitate and evaluate other authors' styles with a view to forging his own authentic voice. For, as he states in 'À propos du style de Flaubert' (1920) ['On Flaubert's Style']: 'we need to . . . produce a voluntary pastiche so that afterwards we can become original once more and not produce involuntary pastiche all our lives' (*ASB*, 269; *CSB*, 594).

In 1908–11, when Proust wrote the first drafts for what was to become the *Recherche*, Decadence as an artistic and literary fashion was passé. Paris, once again at the pinnacle of artistic experimentation, was shaken by the advent of a new avant-garde, notably cubism and futurism. Yet whilst the artistic revolution of the early twentieth century undoubtedly, as critics have shown, impacted upon Proust's vision and style, he nonetheless continues to draw on a fin-de-siècle imaginary in his writing. Many of the novel's great themes – the struggles for social hegemony and the end of an era, the critique of aestheticism and idolatry, the subversion of gender and sexual roles, hereditary degeneracy and the collapse of the old social order – are indebted to Decadence. Take for example the panoply of female temptresses in early drafts for the novel: the promiscuous chambermaid of Mme de Picpus – a 'marvellous Giorgione' disfigured in a steamer accident (IV, 710–35) –, the upper-class prostitute Mlle de Courgeville (IV, 664–5), or the audacious young woman who presses her breasts against the Narrator at a ball (III, 960–1) are all spectres of one of the favourite (stereo)types of Decadent femininity – the femme fatale. Salome and Medusa, Galatea and Helena, perverted adolescent and vile courtesan, these Decadent figures, as

Antoine Compagnon has shown, disappear from the drafts in 1913 with the creation of a new couple: Albertine and Morel, that is, Sodom and Gomorrah.[6] If Proust was eager to erase all too explicit Decadent references from his novel, he shows an affinity with the 'sexual anarchy' critics such as Elaine Showalter have detected in fin-de-siècle fiction in his profound questioning of normative gender roles and sexualities. In the wake of sexologist discourses, most importantly, Magnus Hirschfeld's theory of the 'third sex', the *Recherche* not only accords a central role to homosexuality – no mean feat given the repressive social climate of the time – it probes the lesser charted waters of polyvalent sexual identities and practices. Albertine's sodomist fantasies (5: 384; III, 840) and Morel's intermittent lesbian identity (5: 237–8; III, 720–1) – which perturbs Charlus's more traditional sexual taxonomy of 'en être' or 'ne pas en être' [being, or not being, 'one of them'] – destabilize any binary classifications into hetero-, homo- or bisexuality. In tune with Decadent writers such as Rachilde, sexuality and gender are conceived of as unstable and in flux, to be performed and re-enacted in elaborate *mises en scène*. In the lineage of Sade and Sacher-Masoch – two beacons of Decadence – and echoing the blasphemous sexualities of Baudelaire, Barbey d'Aurevilly and Villiers de l'Isle-Adam, Proust stages a series of theatres of cruelty (most importantly the Montjouvain episode in *Du côté de chez Swann* and its counterpart, Charlus's flagellation in the bordello for homosexual men in *Le Temps retrouvé*) where evil, ritual and excess form a subversive alliance. Yet, fitting for the belatedness of his own writing with regard to the literary models he pastiches and for the growing critical distance that separates him from the universe of Decadence, favourite tropes of the period – the black mass, blasphemy and debauchery, profanation and defilement – are conjugated with irony. Shocking as they will have been to contemporary readers and daring as they remain in our much more liberal century, Proust's sadomasochistic rites do not lack humour. Their agents are fully conscious of the limitations and repetitive nature of the spectacles of evil they perform. As remarks the Narrator, echoing Charlus's disappointment at the feigned cruelty of his torturers: 'Nothing is more limited than pleasure and vice. In that sense one may say truly, altering slightly the meaning of the phrase, that we revolve always in the same vicious circle' (6: 169; IV, 406).

In his mature work, then, Proust increasingly parodies and pastiches the forms and figures of Decadence, particularly in his critical engagement with aestheticism and the Decadent aesthetic. The author shares with British aestheticism and the French 'l'art pour l'art' the cult of art and the concept of the autonomy of the artwork, but he rejected the primacy of art over life and the 'banal aestheticism' promoted by one of his contemporaries, Oscar Wilde (*Corr*, XVIII, 268). In the *Recherche* the dangers of an aestheticism lacking in philosophical meaning and the pitfalls of artistic idolatry are dramatized through a host of aesthetes and dilettantes who forsake creation for artistic contemplation or content themselves with amateurish artistic practice. As counter-models for his own vocation, Bloch, Legrandin, the young Marquise de Cambremer and the sculptor Ski alert the Narrator to the threats that dilettantism and *mondanité* pose for the aspiring writer, for as he will discover in *Le Temps retrouvé*: 'real books should be the offspring . . . of darkness and silence' (6: 257; IV, 476). The quasi-religious cultivation of art practised by the Verdurin clan, in particular Mme Verdurin's hysterical aestheticism and grotesque transformation into a living artwork, are the source of much comedy and caricature. More seriously, through the aesthete Swann, who seeks to elevate banal life by assimilating it into the artistic sphere – as reflected in the accrued prestige bestowed upon Odette thanks to her resemblance with Botticelli's Zephora – Proust stigmatizes the attitude of the idolater who confuses art and reality (he had made a similar reproach to Ruskin in his preface to *La Bible d'Amiens* and to Montesquiou in 'Un professeur de beauté'). The Narrator, who is similarly guilty of valorizing people, objects and even cities through artistic mediation, runs the risk of becoming a 'celibate of Art', were it not for the series of epiphanies in the final Guermantes matinee that teach him that true art must penetrate beneath the world of appearances to extract some general essence.

As a modern Bildungs- and Künstlerroman, the *Recherche* traces the journey that leads the Narrator from inauthenticity to authenticity and from idolatrous contemplation to creation. In a narrative strongly indebted to fin-de-siècle topoi of decadence and renewal (the last chapters are replete with metaphors of apocalyptic destruction and messianic rebirth, especially in the great spectacle of war), his symbolic death and resurrection through art in the last volume allegorize the overcoming of sterile Decadence and the advent of a new form of writing. Already in 'Contre l'obscurité', the young Proust had advised symbolist and Decadent poets to take inspiration in nature. The poetics he devises in the programmatic parts of *Le Temps retrouvé* re-invests nature with the power to enchant the artist and lead him towards aesthetic revelation. Art no longer, as in the Decadent aesthetic, seeks to replace nature, but, as the only possible form of redemption, helps unveil a deeper reality.

On a stylistic level, this overcoming of the Decadent aesthetic is put into practice in the famous Goncourt pastiche in *Le Temps retrouvé*, which continues the 'literary criticism in action' Proust effected in *Les Plaisirs et les jours* and the series of pastiches around the Lemoine Affair he wrote in 1908–9 (especially the satirical 'Dans le "*Journal* des Goncourt"'). This bravura stylistic exercise in the form of a miniature portrait of the Verdurin clan again revolves around aestheticism's elevation of art over nature. Lexically and syntactically, the pastiche emulates the 'spectacle of style'[7] characteristic of *style décadent*: rare or technical vocabulary, predilection for foreign words or words with a Latin or Greek root, neologisms formed from already existing common words, emphatic expression, syntactic expansion, ante-position of adjectives, and so forth. Proust insisted in a 1922 interview that the critique he effects in the Goncourt pastiche was 'ultimately laudatory' (*CSB*, 642). In 1917, when he composed this implicit pastiche, Annick Bouillaguet explains, the Goncourts are no longer 'a counter-model to reject, but a model to surpass'.[8] It is no coincidence, then, that this second Goncourt pastiche is situated shortly before the cataclysmic events of the war chapter and the 'Bal de têtes': the overcoming of Decadent style is part of a wider liberation from Decadent sensibilities in the last volume. If the Narrator initially doubts his own literary talent upon reading the Goncourts' flamboyant prose, he quickly discovers the limitations of their heightened pictorial style, an aesthetic lesson which will allow him to formulate his own definition of style, no longer as a matter of technique, but of vision.

Long neglected by literary criticism, Decadence has come to be recognized as an aesthetic category in its own right as well as an important cultural transition between the Romantic crisis of subjectivity in which it has its roots and the nascent experiments of twentieth-century modernism.[9] Indeed, for many critics today, it is an integral part of the consciousness of crisis and rejection of aesthetic tradition that propelled modernism. Proust, as we have seen, quickly distanced himself from minor, derivative forms of Decadent writing, but the Decadent imaginary with its rich tropes and themes – artificiality and aestheticism, sickness and sensibility, sexual anarchy and cultural decline – was to have a prolonged influence on his writing from his juvenilia to the *Recherche*. Assimilated and renegotiated, parodied and pastiched, emulated and eventually overcome, on a thematic as well as a stylistic level, Decadence was a sensibility and an aesthetics against which he could position himself in the quest for his own voice and vision. As both influence and counter-model, it was a vital step in Proust's modernist journey.

Notes

1 For an excellent overview of the movement see Hannah Thompson, 'Decadence', in William Burgwinkle, Nicholas Hammond and Emma Wilson, eds., *The Cambridge History of French Literature* (Cambridge University Press, 2011), pp. 541–8. For a detailed study of the influence of the Decadent movement on Proust see Marion Schmid, *Proust dans la décadence* (Paris: Champion, 2008).

2 See Marcel Proust, *Écrits de jeunesse, 1887–1895* (Illiers-Combray: Institut Marcel Proust International, 1991), p. 64.

3 See Jean-Yves Tadié, *Marcel Proust: biographie* (Paris: Gallimard, 1996), p. 216.

4 See 'Classicisme et romantisme', *CSB*, 617–18 (618).

5 See Antoine Compagnon, *Proust entre deux siècles* (Paris: Seuil, 1989), p. 29.

6 Compagnon, *Proust entre deux siècles*, pp. 125–6.

7 The term is borrowed from David Weir, *Decadence and the Making of Modernism* (Amherst: University of Massachusetts Press, 1995), p. 42.

8 'Proust lecteur des Goncourt: du pastiche satirique à l'imitation sérieuse', in J.-L. Cabanès, ed., *Les Frères Goncourt: art et écriture* (Presses universitaires de Bordeaux, 1997), p. 348.

9 See Weir, *Decadence and the Making of Modernism*.

CHAPTER 8

Paris and the avant-garde

Hugues Azérad

It does not require much imagination to picture Marcel Proust, absorbed by the creation of the *Recherche*, sipping his café au lait, and glancing at an article on the front page of the *Figaro* dated 20 February 1909, enigmatically entitled 'Le Futurisme'. Its introit is preceded by a cautionary caption stipulating that the author, Marinetti, was the representative of the most advanced and mettlesome of all past and present 'schools'. Proust reads on and becomes immersed in a swirl of garish images extolling the beauty of planes, locomotives and cars, before the young futurists start proclaiming the eleven commandments of their manifesto. Once past his initial surprise, he may have been laughing up his sleeve when hitting the fourth point: 'We say that the world's magnificence has been enriched by a new beauty; the beauty of speed. A racing car whose hood is adorned with great pipes, like serpents of explosive breath ... is more beautiful than the *Victory of Samothrace*.' Proust was yet to write the apocalyptic passages of *Le Temps retrouvé*, whose images are suffused with futurist overtones (no longer induced by imagination, but by the shock of the aerial bombings of the First World War). However, fifteen months earlier (19 November 1907), he had himself published an article 'Impressions de route en automobile' on the front page of the *Figaro*, in which he rendered the lived experience of speed and movement during motoring trips in Normandy. This hymn to the motorcar was unequivocal: a new world of perceptions and sensations was offered to the budding artist, revealing aspects of reality which had been previously hidden from view. Not only are nature and its processes metamorphosed by the speed of the motorcar, but time and space are intertwined in order to reverse the pre-modern perception of the world. Nature, architecture and spatial hierarchies are 'metaphorized' (metaphor being the trope for 'transport'): 'Now, between the propagating steeples below which one saw the light which at this distance seemed to smile, the town, following their momentum from below without being able to reach their heights, developed steadily by

59

vertical increments the complicated but candid fugue of its rooftops' (*CSB*, 64). The technological revolution of the motorcar – combined with that of the train, the aeroplane, chronophotography, cinema and the telephone – creates a revolution in perception and in the way the 'artistic eye' interprets the world and is shaped by it. This *Ur*-text of Proustian modernism will be transplanted into the *Recherche* in the episode of the steeples of Martinville (even though the car reverts to being a carriage to chime with the temporal framework of the 1880s), creating a series of self-referential moments, as it is the only piece of writing penned by the hero which will eventually be published (in *Le Figaro* in *Albertine disparue*). As Sara Danius puts it, the 'Impressions de route' betoken 'the emergence of writing' and how it is 'intimately linked to technologies of velocity and the new spaces of representation they burst open'.[1]

Many other episodes featuring instruments of modernity will pepper the *Recherche* (Proust is alleged to have introduced the word 'looping' for the first time in a novel, when describing Giotto's airborne angels in *Albertine disparue*) where they are more than tokens of modernity, playing instead a crucial role in the development of the narrative and the aesthetic which underpins the novel. Seemingly impervious to the revolutions occurring in the arts between 1908 (the birth of cubism with Braque and Picasso) and 1922 (the end of the Dada movement in Paris and incipient signs of surrealism) – particularly cubism, futurism and cinematography – Proust's novel follows a parallel trajectory in the way art and the artist incorporate technological mediation in their aesthetics of perception. By 1910, as Virginia Woolf intimated in an essay written in 1924,[2] 'human character changed' and there was no turning back.[3] This is explicitly stated during another motoring expedition in *Sodome et Gomorrhe*: 'Distances are only the reflection of time and space and vary with it ... Art is modified by it also, since a village which seemed to be in a different world from some other village becomes its neighbour in a landscape whose dimensions are altered' (4: 457; III, 385).

In the eyes of early criticism and of many of Proust's contemporaries, the world of the *Recherche* appeared distant from modernity and resolutely steeped in the salons of the Belle Époque. Proust was often (mis)construed as an anti-modernist and compared with Baudelaire, whose ambiguous stance towards modernity and opposition to progress was a mainstay of romanticism and symbolism. Furthermore, Proust never missed an occasion to assert his predilection for classicism, except that he defined it as what is 'out of step with its own times' and not simply as classical.[4] These categorizations notwithstanding, a corrosive modernist narrative is to be found beneath the more superficially traditional one. Far from being an epiphenomenon of modern machine culture, the *Recherche* enacts and triggers an epistemic change which is tightly bound up with renewed aesthetics: 'classical modernism represents a shift from idealist theories of aesthetic experience to materialistic ones . . . the emergence of modernist aesthetics signifies the increasing internalization of technological matrices of perception'.[5]

Visions induced by technology may thus provide a link between Proustian and futurist and cubist aesthetics. The exhibition of futurist paintings at the Galerie Bernheim-Jeune held in February 1912 was very well covered by the press, and in the catalogue Boccioni explains how he introduced dynamism, simultaneity and lines of force, in painting: 'We interpret nature on canvas by rendering objects as the beginning or continuation of the rhythms that those same objects imprint on our senses.'[6] This material transcendentalism finds echoes in Proust's conception of inner reality, as the 'impression' which corresponds to the sole reality deemed worthy of existence in a work of art: 'When an idea – an idea of any kind – is left in us by life, its material pattern, the outline of the impression that it made upon us, remains behind as the token of its necessary truth' (6: 234; IV, 458–9). The differences between literature and painting do not preclude interesting parallels between Proust and the futurist, particularly regarding the role of intelligence and memory: 'It's not simply about making a painting abstract or intellectual, as everyone believes. It's also about reifying and – by way of a refinement of taste – making malleable and concrete that which until now we considered intangible, impossible to shape, invisible.'[7]

Only one contemporary critic, Jacques Rivière, was able to perceive Proust's forays into avant-garde techniques. In a letter of July 1922, Rivière addresses Proust's cubism, even though his notion of cubism – perspectivism, analytical cubism (decomposition) and synthetic cubism (recomposition) – overlaps with futurist elements (dynamism, simultaneity, movement):

> A thing that's struck me for the first time is your relationship to the cubist movement – and more profoundly, your profound immersion in contemporary aesthetic reality . . . never have the same statements been presented from so many different angles; to the point, no doubt, that they seem to lose all meaning, and would lose all meaning, if the movement and ceaseless continuation of your narration didn't ensure their restoration. (*Corr*, XXI, 376)

In two other essays, Rivière had evinced the rich ambivalence of Proust's aesthetic: its anti-symbolist and anti-realist stance within a profoundly understood classicism, its radical psychology and its 'pure experience' based on 'no preconceived ideas'. This attempt at reaching for the lived experience, the pure sensation of the object, past the *a priori* nets of mimetic representation, is a mainstay of Proustian, cubist and futurist aesthetics, however different each is in practice.[8]

It is tempting but perhaps misleading to label various episodes of the *Recherche* as particularly cubist or futurist, for Proust effects his own transformative aesthetic: the hero and the Narrator strive to define objects, reality and individuals as they 'see' them and not as they 'know' them.[9] Nowhere is this more visible than in a series of portraits in *Le Côté de Guermantes*. At first glance, the 'close-up' portrait of the Narrator's attempt to kiss an ungraspable Albertine seems cubist-like ('during this brief journey of my lips towards her cheek, it was ten Albertines that I saw', 3: 421; II, 660), whilst Saint-Loup's fist fight with a 'shadow', whose referent is as intractable as Albertine, is more explicitly futurist.[10] In the latter, 'lines of force', 'simultaneity', 'plasticity', and 'dynamic sensation' are foregrounded:

> Suddenly, as an astral phenomenon flashes through the sky, I saw a number of ovoid bodies assume with a giddy swiftness all the positions necessary for them to compose a flickering constellation in front of Saint-Loup. Flung out like stones from a catapult, they seemed to me to be at the very least seven in number. They were merely, however, Saint-Loup's two fists, multiplied by the speed with which they were changing place in this – to all appearance ideal and decorative – arrangement. (3: 205; II, 480)

Yet this rather direct reference to boxers painted by futurists (Carra, Boccioni) is also a clear indicator of a possible pastiche or parodic fragment: the Narrator gives us a clue a few lines later when he debunks the entire scene and the 'style' he adopted in its depiction, by reducing his vision to mere 'ornament', a trivial aesthetic flight of fancy belied by the real blood spilled on the pavement. Reality trumps aesthetics, as Proust's narrative trumps its own rendering of futurist painting – self-parody and pastiches being recurring, structuring features of the *Recherche*. If parody always implies a twist in meaning or genre, and if pastiche implies distancing via imitation of style,[11] Proust is taking a stand against the excessive aesthetic prowess of the contemporary avant-garde, intimating that behind such gestures lurks a possible drift towards violence, heralding the unleashing of technological warfare. Perhaps Proust never forgot the futurist glorification of war that formed the apex of Marinetti's 1909 manifesto.

In June 1919, Proust replied to Jean Cocteau after reading his *Le Coq et l'arlequin* and commented upon a few of his aphorisms: 'Whenever a work seems ahead of its time, it's simply because the times haven't kept up with the work' and 'an original artist is unable to copy. So all he has to do to be original is copy.' Proust's comments reveal his profound engagement with the arts of his time and expert navigation of the Parisian literary field. Each line in the letter gives us clues about his positioning with regard to tradition, the avant-garde, music and critical reception. Proust corroborates Cocteau's quip about works of art being ahead of their times even though they seem 'arrière-garde': 'Swann, if you've truly read it, and what you've read of *À l'ombre des jeunes filles en fleurs*, proves what we always thought about the art of the period' (*Corr*, XVIII, 267–8). Proust is here referring to his disquisition on artistic innovation in *À l'ombre des jeunes filles*:

> No doubt it is easy to imagine ... that all the revolutions which have hitherto occurred in painting or in music did at least respect certain rules, whereas that which immediately confronts, be it Impressionism, the pursuit of dissonance ... Cubism, Futurism ... differs outrageously from all that has occurred before. (2: 121; 1, 522–3)

The letter bristles with references to other artists and the question of originality (a tricky issue to be raised with Cocteau who was often accused of ransacking other artists' findings); it also indicates Proust's refusal to pander to a jarring use of words and avant-garde images, which he rejected as a resurgence of romantic excess.

The whole of Proust's correspondence is testament to his tactical positioning in the swirling world of Parisian art. Proust's positioning differs only in form, not in spirit or tactics, from the constant rivalries, denunciations, alliances, betrayals and requests for favours which occurred between the various groupings of the avant-garde, as was exemplified by the fraught relationship between the short-lived little magazines (*SIC, Nord-Sud, Littérature, Le Mot, Action, 391*), between Reverdy and Max Jacob, between the Left Bank artists (around Adrienne Monnier, who never liked Proust) and the Right Bank coteries, and eventually between Breton, Picabia and Tzara. Proust took his place in the literary field by buttressing his own conception of what constitutes true art, taking flak from the most boisterous avant-gardists (he was rated 'o' by *Littérature* in 1921), and staying on good terms with the moderate modernists and the rear guard (Gide, Paulhan, Rivière, Gallimard, the worldly élite) that still reigned in Paris. He made sure to emphasize the modernist credentials of *Swann* via interviews for various journals shortly before its publication: 'You know there is plane geometry and solid geometry. Well, for me, the novel is not only plane psychology, but psychology in time' (*ASB*, 234; *CSB*, 557).[12] This preoccupation with geometry and time as a 'fourth dimension' was in fact the talk of the town thanks to Apollinaire's texts in *Les Peintres cubistes* (1913). Proust's anxiety of reception never subsided, as shown by his letters which continued to reinforce his aesthetic dogmatism and his sense that by 1920 he was ahead of his peers (*Le Côté de Guermantes* and *Sodome et Gomorrhe* being published just before his death).

By 1919, it is true, most avant-garde movements were in the doldrums, either through the effect of the *retour à l'ordre* [call to order][13] or because of internecine conflicts of interest among the avant-garde (the death of Apollinaire in 1918 and the first issue of *Littérature* in 1919 were turning points). However, in 1920, an unassuming Romanian – Tristan Tzara – knocked on Picabia's door and was introduced to Breton and Soupault. Tzara was a founding father of Dada, the subversive aura of which had been felt in Paris since its inception in Zurich in 1916. Now Tzara arrived in Paris to reignite the Dada spirit. Nine months later, the Dadaists (Picabia, Breton, Soupault, Eluard, Tzara) had launched their first event and inundated the Right Bank (where Proust lived) with leaflets, tags and issues of *Bulletin Dada*.[14] Proust and Breton had a strange encounter. Breton ('Dada en chef' according to Rivière) was correcting the proofs of *Le Côté de Guermantes*, and through a fascinating slip of the pen (or rather repressed admiration, given the brilliance of the hallucinatory, pre-surrealistic sequences of Doncières), he had left a slew of typos ('the novels of Bergson' for 'the novels of Bergotte' being highly symptomatic). Naturally Proust was horrified when he received a copy of the book. Ever merciful (having read Breton's and Soupault's *Champs magnétiques* whilst Breton was botching the proofs), Proust wrote to Gallimard of 'Monsieur (the charming dada who oversaw the proofs and whose name escapes me thanks to momentary amnesia)' (*Corr*, XIX, 438). Proust's playful forgetting of the name of his new rival did not last long. Four days later he wrote to Soupault in admiration: 'I'd have loved so much to congratulate you and Monsieur Breton for your *Magnetic Fields*', but not without subtly sending up its alleged revolutionary style (qualifying it as 'chant [song]' and 'verset'), and picking a particularly 'romantic' and therefore passé line: 'this river that overflows with our despair' (*Corr*, XIX, 445).

These numerous points of contact between Proust and the avant-garde are more than anecdotal. They show that Proust was not isolated from the epistemic and artistic changes taking place around him in what was then the capital of the arts. Until 1913, and whilst writing the *Recherche*, Proust catalysed these various movements and technological revolutions, not passively but actively, always aware of the transience attached to art, and the shackles of history, class and personal obsession. Proust was not only geographically close to the most radical of twentieth-century avant-gardes (the Dadaists were based at the Café Certà, passage de l'Opéra), but aesthetically, too. One only needs to think of Proust's creative use of collage and montage as part of the fabric of the *Recherche* (the famous *paperoles*),[15] or of the subversive use of pastiche applied to writers: the various Lemoine pastiches anticipate Dada hoaxes, troubling the assumed relationship between signifier and signified. As in Hofmannsthal's *Letter to Lord Chandos* or in the Dada manifestos, Proust questions the authority of language, near-dismantling it by pushing syntax to the limits ('The only people who defend the French language ... are those who "attack" it', *Corr*, VIII, 276).

Proust advertised the idea of his own isolation: 'real books should be the offspring of darkness and silence' (6: 302; IV, 476). But the two brightest interpreters of the arts – Cocteau and Rivière – were among his closest friends. The latter was the first critic to understand that Proust was ushering in a revolution in writing under a veneer of classical forms; he was also the first to understand that Dada's true preoccupation was with language (seen as transformative political *praxis*): 'Scepticism in matters of syntax is coupled with a sort of mysticism ... the dadas continue to lean towards this surrealism which was Apollinaire's ambition.'[16] There was a third critic then intermittently living in Paris – Carl Einstein – who theorized the revolution enacted by cubism first, then by Dada. He did so by debunking the 'romanticism' of the avant-gardes and by remaining faithful to the 'revolution of the eye' that cubism – by now an 'old' movement – had triggered in the first decade of the century. In a letter of 1923, Einstein wrote:

> writers think they're very modern when they replace violets with automobiles or aeroplanes ... one expresses oneself through the dimensions of memory or of the future, not in a Futurist way – instead the individual person rises or falls in volume, in their sensations of self or of things, approaching as closely as possible to lived experience, the symptoms of which are ... that which we agree to call things.[17]

Einstein, the most cutting-edge theoretician of the avant-garde and still acknowledged as cubism's best critic, was dreaming of a novel to come that would become an 'inner spiritual realism'. The *Recherche* would realize this dream.

Notes

1 Sara Danius, *The Senses of Modernism: Technology, Perception, and Aesthetics* (Ithaca, NY: Cornell University Press, 2002), p. 133.
2 Quoted in David Bradshaw and Kevin J. H. Dettmar, eds., *A Companion to Modernist Literature and Culture* (Oxford: Wiley-Blackwell, 2008), p. 216.
3 On Proust and his supposedly fractious or fertile relationship with the avant-gardes, in 'Further Reading', see the essays by Fraisse, Keller and Savy.
4 See 'Classicisme et romantisme' (*CSB*, 617–18).
5 Danius, *Senses of Modernism*, pp. 1–2.
6 Umberto Boccioni, *Dynamique plastique* (Lausanne: L'Âge d'Homme, 1975), p. 77.
7 Boccioni, *Dynamique plastique*, p. 78.
8 Jacques Rivière, *Études: 1909–1924* (Paris: Gallimard, 1999), pp. 591, 612, 613, 617.
9 For a full list of paintings Proust could have seen, see Keller and Savy in 'Further Reading'. Proust's knowledge of cubism was much sketchier, and came mainly from Cocteau and Jacques-Émile Blanche (he saw a few Picasso paintings and drawings and was entranced by the ballet *Parade* in 1917).
10 See also Saint-Loup walking down the brothel stairs (6: 148; IV, 389), a possible reference to Duchamp's *Nu descendant un escalier* (1912).
11 See 'Parodie' and 'Pastiche' entries in Annick Bouillaguet and Brian G. Rogers, eds., *Dictionnaire Marcel Proust* (Paris: Champion, 2004).
12 See Luzius Keller, 'Proust au-delà de l'impressionnisme', in Sophie Bertho, ed., *Proust et ses peintres* (Amsterdam: Rodopi, 2000), pp. 57–70.
13 See Kenneth Silver, *Esprit de corps* (London: Thames and Hudson, 1989).
14 Michel Sanouillet, *Dada in Paris*, trans. by Sharmila Ganguly (Cambridge, MA: MIT Press, 2008), pp. 110–11.
15 N. Savy, 'Jeune roman, jeune peinture', in Jean-Yves Tadié, ed., *Marcel Proust: l'écriture et les arts* (Réunion des musées nationaux, 1999), pp. 55–65 (60).
16 'Reconnaissance à Dada', in Sanouillet, *Dada in Paris*, p. 145.
17 In *Bébuquin* (Dijon: Les Presses du réel, 2000), pp. 94–5. All my thanks to Anthony Cummins for translating quotations into English.

CHAPTER 9

The novelistic tradition

Hugues Azérad and Marion Schmid

The publication of *À la recherche du temps perdu* between 1913 and 1927 constitutes both a *summa* of and a new departure for western literature. With its guiding theme of an artistic vocation, its sensitive portrayal of a sentimental education from childhood to maturity and its quest for deeper metaphysical truths beyond the confines of the material world, the novel aligns itself with a tradition of foundational texts that have shaped European literature for almost a thousand years. Dante Alighieri's *Divina Commedia* with its allegory of a spiritual peregrination; the analytical novel in the tradition of Madame de Lafayette; the Bildungsroman in the style of Goethe's *Wilhelm Meister* – not to forget the great Russian novel with its complex narrative construction and epic portraits of society – are but some of the models that resonate in Proust's novel. The author's use of a first-person narrative, sharp characterization and satirical descriptions of upper-class society recall the *Mémoires* of Saint-Simon – a major influence on the *Recherche* – while his probing analysis of human nature and relationships evokes the nineteenth-century French personal novel of authors such as Benjamin Constant, Nerval and Chateaubriand. The novel's doubling up as a philosophical treatise and an aesthetic manifesto, finally, puts it in the lineage of essayistic works such as Montaigne's *Essais* and Pascal's *Pensées* while heralding the heightened self-reflexivity that characterizes modernist and postmodern fiction. Just how indebted the *Recherche* is to its literary predecessors and how readily its author engages in intertextual games and pastiches can be gleaned from the extensive literary references in the text, ranging from Homer, Saint-Simon and Racine to George Eliot, Balzac and Dostoyevsky. Proust's quasi-encyclopaedic knowledge of western literature across the ages and his subtlety and flair as a literary critic have enriched and nourished his novel, endowing it with an intertextual and generic complexity matched perhaps only by his fellow modernist James Joyce. As Jean-Yves Tadié comments, '*À la recherche* recapitulates the entire literary tradition, from the Bible to Flaubert and Tolstoy, and all literary genres.'[1]

67

And yet, perhaps paradoxically, the novel as the genre in which Proust was to excel and which he would propel into uncharted territory did not come readily to him. With hindsight, one may be surprised that his first creative attempts were in verse and prose poetry as well as in shorter literary forms such as novellas, pastiches and philosophical essays. His first published book, the heteroclite *Les Plaisirs et les jours* (1896), gives an idea of the fragmentation that characterizes – and to a certain extent compromised – Proust's juvenilia. A 'bouquet of many different flowers', the volume, though evincing a certain thematic coherence, appears unbalanced and dispersed.[2] The same holds true for his novel *Jean Santeuil*, begun in 1895, but abandoned some four years later for want of a structure. The manuscript contains many scenes recycled in the *Recherche*, yet the novel's third-person narrative, combined with the linear plot of a nineteenth-century Bildungsroman, ultimately proved too restrictive with regard to the structurally and philosophically more ambitious work Proust had in mind.[3] In *Jean Santeuil*, as in the *Recherche*, involuntary memory triggers literary creation, but its rich potential remained unexploited without the technique of double internal focalization – that is, the splitting-up of the first person into a narrated and a narrating self – eventually adopted in the *Recherche*. Moreover, aesthetic reflection was not yet subordinated to the wider theme of a vocation, and, most importantly for Proust himself, the fragments were lacking in stylistic originality and vision.[4]

After the failure of *Jean Santeuil*, Proust relinquished any further novelistic project until 1908, devoting himself instead to his translations of Ruskin as well as to articles and reviews. A fresh start came early in the year when he was once again firmly embarked on a new novel that announced the *Recherche*, but of which little more than an outline is preserved. However, this project also faltered quickly, being superseded by an essay against Sainte-Beuve in the autumn. Proust at first hesitated between a traditional essay and a dialogue between a first-person Narrator and his mother that would embed literary criticism in a fictional narrative. He developed both the narrative and the theoretical parts simultaneously, in his habitual manner of composing textual units to be assembled at a later stage – anticipating the *montage* technique of modern cinema popularized by Sergei Eisenstein and fellow Soviet filmmakers some twenty years later. Eventually the fictional parts outgrew the theoretical ones and eclipsed the Sainte-Beuve project, after a solution for linking hitherto disparate fragments presented itself in the form of a retrospective narrative, which helped reconcile different time frames.[5]

The genesis of the *Recherche*, then, is shaped by a productive tension between fragment and whole as well as between essay and fiction, which reverberates in the published text and informs Proust's thinking about novelistic form. Even at a time when the new aesthetics of collage was changing traditional forms of composition, Proust remained preoccupied by the conflict between romantic (open) and classical (closed) form – or, in fin-de-siècle terms, between Decadence (fragmentation) and vitalism (organicity) – that had informed nineteenth-century aesthetic discourses.[6] Revealingly, in the *Recherche*, the Narrator aligns himself with two nineteenth-century artists, Balzac and Wagner, who both, by dint of an 'illumination', intuited a unifying principle for their works *après coup*. Their creations are all the more authentic, he argues, since their unity was unplanned: 'Not factitious, perhaps indeed all the more real for being ulterior, for being born of a moment of enthusiasm ... a unity that was unaware of itself, hence vital and not logical, that did not prohibit variety, dampen invention' (5: 177; III, 667). Proust's own novel, like-wise, seeks to accommodate plurality within an overarching unity, to unravel general laws behind the manifold experiences of the human condition. Nothing, the author reiterates in his correspondence, is more alien to him than gratuitous detail, pure ornament and documentary realism. If there is one thing that is new in his novel, he asserts in a letter to Robert Dreyfus, it is its absence of denotative signifiers: 'Not once does one of my characters close a window, wash his hands, put on an overcoat or introduce people to one another' (*Corr*, XII, 394). For, according to his compositional principles of harmonious integration and fusion, 'one must above all subordinate, not be carried away by an amusing anecdote and give one line more to a detail than it should have in the balance of the overall text' (*Corr*, XIX, 118).

The tension between fragment and whole that informs Proust's think-ing about novelistic form also needs to be placed in the flurry of aesthetic debates launched by new novelists who were vying with one another to claim the first place, vacated by Zola only a few years before. Proust was one of the contenders in this race to pre-eminence, whereby authors were venturing beyond the quicksand of symbolism, naturalism and psycholo-gism, but in fact, apart from a few exceptions, ended up recycling old principles. Most of these turn-of-the-century writers (Anatole France, Henri Bordeaux, Paul Bourget, Octave Mirbeau, Rémy de Gourmont, Maurice Barrès, Jules Renard) have now fallen by the wayside of literary history; Proust, after the unfinished *Jean Santeuil*, was aware of these false starts, able to discern that untrodden paths were open before him, particularly after his own 'illumination' of 1908/9. The dead end in which the French novel found itself around 1910 (which, incidentally, Proust, Jacques Rivière and André Gide were the only ones to recognize), goaded Proust into outlining the aesthetic principles that would liberate his forthcoming novel from the positivist edicts that reigned in the narrow, mostly Parisian literary circles of the early twentieth century. Nowhere is this more apparent than in Proust's letter (6 February 1914) to Rivière, where he sets out his theory of the novel and vents his fear of being misunderstood:

> At last I find a reader who can tell that my book is a principled work, a structure ... As an artist I found there was more integrity and subtlety in not letting on that I was engaged only in the search for truth ... I do so detest those ideological works in which the narrative amounts to nothing more than the failed intentions of the author, which I'd rather not mention ... No, if I had no intellectual convictions, if I sought only to recollect, and to make with these recollections a redundant souvenir of days gone by ... I wouldn't take ... the trouble to write. (*Corr*, XIII, 99)

Proust was intent on describing his novel as 'dogmatique' and a 'construction' in order to distance himself from the image bestowed upon him by Gide and the editors of the *Nouvelle Revue française*, who had rejected his manuscript, having mistaken him for an outmoded stalwart of Decadent writing and a mere darling of aristocratic salons. He was also keen to demarcate himself from his most pressing rivals. His dismissal of Romain Rolland – the author of the acclaimed *Jean-Christophe* (1904–12) and inventor of the term 'roman fleuve' – is a case in point. According to Luc Fraisse,[7] Proust had read *Jean-Christophe* with great attention and even used some of Rolland's writings to nourish the Narrator's reflections on German music in the *Recherche*, but he nonetheless wrote some scathing remarks in an article later published in *Contre Sainte-Beuve*: 'Unfortunately, when Jean-Christophe ... leaves off speaking, M. Romain Rolland continues to pile banality on banality, and when he searches for a more precise image, the effort is one of search not of discovery' (*ASB*, 97; *CSB*, 208).

Proust's critical eye pinpointed *Jean-Christophe*'s aesthetic flaw: Rolland's groundbreaking approach to music was overlaid with a didactic style which spoiled the novel as a whole, turning it into a 'roman à thèse'. Suffice it to say that Proust was right, and *Jean-Christophe*, in spite of gem-like passages, ultimately disappoints due to the narration's nineteenth-century style, which is superimposed on a traditional Bildungsroman. *Jean-Christophe* perfectly illustrates the kind of novel that *Jean Santeuil* could have been and that Proust rejects in *Le Temps retrouvé*. Its contemporaneity with the genesis of the *Recherche*, and, thus, its inevitable threat of artistic rivalry (Proust was writing the novel whilst reading Rolland's volumes in succession) probably reinforced the author in his decision to cut off all links with the French novelistic tradition and to strengthen the aesthetic principles of his work. It is perhaps not a coincidence that the aesthetic 'manifesto' of *Le Temps retrouvé* was written in draft form as early as 1911, and one wonders whether Proust was not bent on sketching out ideas which he knew were revolutionary in scope and content, with a view to undergirding the theoretical foundations of a work still pregnant with its futurity.

Even after he had successfully embarked on writing the *Recherche* and fended off immediate rivals, Proust became aware of how difficult it would be to navigate the Parisian literary fields of the 1910s, and to inflect the way his work would be received, not only during his lifetime, but more importantly, after his death. A less visible side of creation is what Hans Robert Jauss calls the 'horizon of reception', that is, the integral part the book's reception plays in its existence as a novel, given that its meaning stems from a dialogue between its aesthetic effect and the way contemporary and future readerships will decode it.[8] The introduction of radical novelty ripples through literary fields in unpredictable ways, and Proust was acutely aware of the uncertainty surrounding the reception of his novel, an uncertainty that even the award of the Goncourt Prize in 1919 could not dispel. This anxiety is evidenced in the 'new writer' episode of *Le Côté de Guermantes*, where Proust dramatizes how tradition is ruptured by illusory novelty and how genuine innovation is often mistaken for superficial shifts in public taste. The author foreshadows the *Recherche*'s own reception and retrospectively stages the pressure exerted by literary fashion on himself through an ironic *mise en abyme*, whereby the Narrator falls prey to a new form of idolatry, that of the 'new', abandoning his previous worshipping of Bergotte, who finds himself superseded by the 'new writer':

> I no longer had the same admiration for him as of old ... But a new writer had recently begun to publish work in which the relations between things were so different from those that connected them for me that I could understand hardly anything of what he wrote ... only I felt that it was not the sentence that was badly constructed but I myself that lacked the strength and agility necessary to reach the end. I would start afresh ... and each time ... I would fall back again ... I felt nonetheless for the new writer an admiration which an awkward boy who gets nought for gymnastics feels when he watched another more nimble. (3: 374–5; 11, 622–4)

The episode is imbued with a profound ambiguity. On the one hand, the Narrator comes to the conclusion that true innovation in art is never properly understood at first, as the revolutionary artist's stylistic vision is perceived as too distorting and at too great a variance with the expectations and habits of the public. Proust has recourse to his recurring analogy of the optician to expand on this idea: '"Now look". And, lo and behold, the world around us (which was not created once and for all but is created afresh as often as an original artist is born) appears to us entirely different from the old world, but perfectly clear' (3: 376; II, 623). But this optical correction induced by the artist-as-optician needs time to allow for the process of accommodation to occur in the public. Until another 'optician' will turn up a few years later and provide yet another way of looking at the world, once again 'correcting' the public sight after an inevitable period of neglect: 'Such is the new and perishable universe which has just been created. It will last until the next geological catastrophe is precipitated by a new painter or writer of original talent' (3: 377; II, 623). On the other hand, the multiple ironic asides, the humorous analogy between gymnastics and artistic prowess, and the tautological emphasis on originality ('new original writer') debunk the Narrator's thesis as to how artists shape public taste. Given the non-synchronous synchronicity between the author, the Narrator and the protagonist, which is one of Proust's most daring innovations, one cannot but notice how much positivist language (the intellect is foregrounded as the sole instrument of interpretation and aesthetic evaluation) the Narrator-protagonist uses throughout this passage about artistic innovation, ending on a comparison between art and science and a reflection on the concept of progress in literature ('each new original writer seemed to me to have advanced beyond the stage of his immediate predecessor' (3: 377; II, 623)). Through this ironic *mise en abyme* of the Narrator as a 'new writer' to come, and of the author of the *Recherche* as a 'new writer' in actuality, Proust raises the spectre of the ephemerality and contingency of artistic innovation, however genuine, for it not only has to contend with public reception (and attendant misinterpretation), but with inevitable supersession. Proust knows that this spectre may well turn into an 'artistic law' and that he, also, will be swept aside by new artists. At the same time, he hopes that in writing the *Recherche*, he is hatching a more fundamental innovation which will endure not only the test of public reception, but also that of time.

In 1919, T. S. Eliot published 'Tradition and the Individual Talent',[9] in which he subsumed the issue of originality and innovation into a deeper problematic, that of the retrospective 'reception' of new works of art; not how they upturn public taste or arrogate a leading role to themselves for a short while, but the ways in which they reshape tradition as a whole:

> the historical sense compels a man to write not merely with his own generation in his bones, but with a feeling that the whole of literature of Europe from Homer ... has a simultaneous existence ... No poet, no artist of any art, has his complete meaning alone ... His significance, his appreciation is the appreciation of his relation to the dead poets and artists ... what happens when a new work of art is created is something that happens simultaneously to all the works of art which preceded it. The existing monuments form an ideal order among themselves, which is modified by the introduction of the new (the really new) work of art among them.[10]

Proust was reaching similar conclusions in *Le Temps retrouvé* in his dismissal of avant-garde and literary journals that focus on what is superficial and ephemeral ('multiplication of reviews and literary journals ... and with them of factitious vocations as writer or artist' (6: 250; IV, 199)), instead of, as Eliot put it, setting their work in the temporal and the timeless simultaneously. The anxiety of reception which plays an integral part in Proust's correspondence and the early volumes of the *Recherche* gradually gives way to reflection on how his own work engages with the literature that preceded it: the truly innovative work casts a look backwards at a tradition it not only inflects but 'corrects', like the optician of Combray, and, therefore, salvages (as the *Recherche* did with many past writers, from Racine to Nerval and Baudelaire). By concretizing and actualizing the reception of his work among past and present French literary traditions – in his novel, but also via his letters – Proust did away with his potential critics and with his own anxiety. As the Narrator realizes in *Le Temps retrouvé*, true innovation is a universal – and therefore timeless – principle, whereas the public and the critics are only interested in its short-lived particularity: 'whereas the reality of talent is something universal, whether it be a gift or an acquirement, and the first thing that a reader has to do is to find out whether this reality is present beneath a writer's superficial mannerisms of thought and style, it is upon just these superficial mannerisms that criticism seizes when it sets out to classify authors. Because he has a peremptory tone, because he parades his contempt for the school that preceded him, criticism hails as a prophet a writer who in fact has no message that is new' (6: 251; IV, 200). Proust, like his fellow modernist Eliot, knew that the only reception and judgment that count are those bestowed by tradition itself, 'the timeless as well as the temporal',[11] and that the place and 'prizes' accorded to their works will be proportionate to the alteration they create in its harmonious whole.

Notes

1 Jean-Yves Tadié, 'Introduction', in Marcel Proust, *À la recherche du temps perdu*, 4 vols. (Paris: Gallimard, 1987–9), vol. 1, x.

2 Pierre Daum, '*Les Plaisirs et les jours' de Marcel Proust: étude d'un recueil* (Paris: Nizet, 1993), p. 184.

3 See Jean-Yves Tadié, *Proust* (Paris: Belfond, 1983), p. 147.

4 Tadié, *Proust*, p. 147.

5 For a detailed discussion of the *Recherche*'s genesis see Chapter 5 above and Marion Schmid, 'The Birth and Development of *À la recherche du temps perdu*', in Richard Bales, ed., *The Cambridge Companion to Proust* (Cambridge University Press, 2001), pp. 58–73.

6 See Antoine Compagnon, *Proust entre deux siècles* (Paris: Seuil, 1989), p. 42.

7 Fraisse, *La Petite Musique du style: Proust et ses sources littéraires* (Paris: Garnier, 2011), p. 334.

8 See Fraisse, *La Petite Musique*, p. 643.

9 T. S. Eliot, 'Tradition and the Individual Talent', in *Selected Prose*, ed. John Hayward (Harmondsworth: Penguin, 1963), pp. 21–9.

10 Eliot, 'Tradition', p. 23.

11 Eliot, 'Tradition', p. 23.

CHAPTER 10

Philosophy

Thomas Baldwin

Like many students, Marcel Proust enjoyed a night out. By early 1895, at the age of twenty-three, and in stark contrast to the popular image of Proust the sickly, bed-ridden recluse, he had become a 'well-known personality' in Parisian society, 'a sort of dandy figure out of Balzac'.[1] According to Jean-Yves Tadié, between January and April 1895, Proust was seen at some eighteen soirées and performances (musical, theatrical). Meanwhile, in spite of the frenetic rhythm of his social and night life, Proust also completed a bachelor's degree in literature and philosophy at the Sorbonne. Between October 1894 and March 1895, he attended lectures in the Latin Quarter delivered by the psychologist and epistemologist Victor Egger (receiving an unremarkable 11/20 for an essay on 'Socrates' philosophy'), by the idealist philosopher of science and religion Émile Boutroux (whose lectures in 1894–5, judging by the topics set for the written examinations, focused on Descartes and his relation to classical philosophy), and by the aesthetician Gabriel Séailles, under whose instruction Proust became familiar with the work of the German idealists F. W. J. Schelling and Arthur Schopenhauer. He also took private lessons with Alphonse Darlu, his former philosophy master at the Lycée Condorcet (where Proust was a pupil between 1882 and 1889), on whom M. Beulier, the teacher in *Jean Santeuil*, is often said to be based.

While little is known about the precise content of the philosophical curriculum Proust followed either between 1894 and 1895 or in earlier years, it was, according to Tadié, Boutroux and Darlu who made the most profound impression on the young student. Through their teaching, he was introduced to 'the notions of faith in the human spirit, Kantian idealism, . . . in a reality hidden behind appearances, and the rigours of analysis, which flew in the face of the misty imprecision dear to the Symbolists and sometimes to Bergson' (we shall return to the influence of Bergson in due course).[2] For Tadié, 'this year of studying for his philosophy degree was just as vital for Proust's development as his

75

emotional or social life'.[3] Indeed, in a questionnaire completed around 1895, Proust names Boutroux and Darlu as his 'heroes from real life' (*ASB*, 114; *CSB*, 337).

At a time when the influence of positivism remained quite strong, Darlu and Boutroux embraced an idealist metaphysics. Whereas the positivists maintained that the source of all authentic knowledge lay in the data of sensory experience accompanied by certain logical operations,[4] Darlu and Boutroux proposed that reality – or reality as we can know it – is in essence mentally constructed, or otherwise immaterial:

> in an age when the positivism and scientism that were inherited from Taine were still highly influential, here was a French philosophy that was derived from Aristotle and, in particular, from Kant, along with Ravaisson, Renouvier, Fouillée and Boutroux . . ., which defended the cause of metaphysics, idealism and spiritualism.[5]

In a short article entitled 'L'irréligion d'état' ['State Irreligion'], first published on 3 May 1892 in *Le Banquet*, a literary magazine founded by Proust with a number of his friends (including Robert Dreyfus, Fernand Gregh and Daniel Halévy),[6] Proust (who signs the article 'Laurence') derides the 'materialist philosophy' of 'the radicalism of those in power', positioning himself on the side of the 'great idealist philosophers' (*CSB*, 348). In his short biography of Proust, Edmund White suggests that 'once Proust's idealism is noticed it appears in nearly every line of his great novel'.[7] By way of example, White cites a passage from the end of *Du côté de chez Swann* in which the Narrator goes in search of Gilberte at the Champs-Élysées. Marcel observes that

> like the idealist philosopher whose body takes account of the external world in the reality of which his intellect declines to believe, the same self which had made me greet her before I had identified her now urged me to seize the ball that she handed to me (as though she were a companion with whom I had come to play, and not a sister-soul with whom I had come to be united). (1: 483; 1, 394)[8]

For Tadié, the influence on Proust of French neo-Kantian (idealist) thought is so profound – and so much in evidence in *À la recherche* and elsewhere – that the attempts of other critics to situate him within the orbit of German philosophical idealism, and of Schelling and Schopenhauer in particular, are futile:

> This [Darlu's teaching] is what prevents us from making Proust into an inheritor of German Romanticism and the philosophy of Schelling and Schopenhauer. For him, as with Kant's French disciples, such as Darlu,

Lachelier ... or Boutroux, concepts were always lucid and defined, examples were precise, reasoning was flawless, the writing unostentatious since it was necessary to reject effects of style, obscure illusions and the alibi of imagery.[9]

Tadié's unequivocal claims are, at least in part, a response to Anne Henry. In her remarkable *Marcel Proust: théories pour une esthétique*, Henry contends that, from *Jean Santeuil* onwards, Proust provides a literary transposition of Schelling's philosophy of nature, art and identity.[10] Elsewhere, Henry asserts that just as 'Vinteuil's score is written by Schopenhauer', so *À la recherche* is 'the most literal translation' of Schopenhauer's *The World as Will and Representation* (1818).[11]

Such emphatic statements, as Joshua Landy has observed, 'should come as a bit of a surprise'.[12] While it may be true, as Henry claims, that Proust is an ingenious exploiter of Schopenhauer's or Schelling's ideas, Proust's writings do not accord on 'every single point and down to the finest detail with a given philosophical system', be it Schopenhauer's, Schelling's, or anyone else's, nor, as is Henry's and Tadié's belief, are they '*generated* from that system, each character or event representing one of its aspects, in a vast and slavishly accurate allegory'.[13] Indeed, so far as the influence of the philosophy of Schopenhauer is concerned, Proust may in fact end up in a position very similar to Nietzsche's 'simply by reacting in the same way [as Nietzsche] against Schopenhauer, while knowing almost nothing of Nietzsche's work'.[14] There are, of course, echoes throughout Proust's immense œuvre of an impressive number of philosophers, including, as Duncan Large points out, 'the pre-Socratics, Plato, and the neo-Platonics through Descartes, Leibniz, and Spinoza, Locke, Kant, and Hegel, to Kierkegaard and Emerson' – a number of whom he may never have read.[15]

The dangers of presenting Proust as no more than a philosophical copycat are just as apparent if we consider him in relation to the work of John Ruskin and Henri Bergson. Beginning in 1895, Proust spent several years reading Ruskin and Ralph Waldo Emerson. Through his reading and subsequent translation of Ruskin's work, Proust began to refine his own theories of art and the role of the artist in society. Famously, in *Le Temps retrouvé*, Marcel recalls having translated Ruskin's *Sesame and Lilies* (see 6: 175; IV, 411–12). While, like Ruskin, Proust's Narrators are frequently delighted by common natural glories (buttercups, hawthorn, lilacs and so on), they do not simply assimilate Ruskin's ontology or his aesthetics without modification or displacement. In fact, on several occasions, what looks like a modernistic inversion of Ruskin turns out to be a very close fit with the words of Emerson. Consider, for example, Marcel's description in

À l'ombre des jeunes filles of the break of dawn which he studies through the train window during his journey to Balbec (2: 267–8; 11, 15–16). While this passage is overwhelmingly Ruskinian – in so far as it gives priority to the imagination and to the 'seen' rather than to confining intellectual notions and the 'known' – it is also, as Sara Danius suggests, deeply un-Ruskinian in one important respect.[16] The Narrator admires a series of richly evocative scenes through a window, but it is the window of a train, whose rapid movement through the country affords him the sight of not one scene but many. This would not have appealed to Ruskin at all, for he loudly reviled most modern technology and architecture, especially trains and railway stations, despite Turner's rare efforts to render steam and speed sublime. In *The Seven Lamps of Architecture*, he remarks sourly that the 'whole system of railroad travelling is addressed to people who, being in a hurry, are therefore, for the time being, miserable'.[17] At first sight, then, it appears that Proust pays tribute to Ruskin's aesthetic values and at the same time turns his thoroughly anti-modern stance on its head. But we should be careful in suggesting, as Danius does, that this inversion implies an entirely or unambiguously modern, 'avant-garde' approach to an old-fashioned nineteenth-century aesthetic programme. Emerson's comments suggest that Proust's treatment of the scenes observed through the train window is perhaps not (wholly) post-Ruskinian, and therefore not as paradoxical or modern as it might at first seem. For example, in 'Nature' (1836), he exclaims: 'What new thoughts are suggested by seeing a face of country quite familiar, in the rapid movement of the railroad car! Nay, the most wonted objects (make a very slight change in the point of vision), please us most.'[18] It is very surprising (though not at all inexplicable, perhaps) that Proust mentions Emerson on only one occasion in *À la recherche* (3: 318; 11, 574), for he seems to be clearly reflected not only in Proust's description of the landscape seen through the train window, but also in descriptions of objects seen from trains, carriages – the Martinville steeples being the most obvious example – and cars which occur in *À la recherche*.

It is often said, casually, that Proust's thinking was deeply affected by his encounter with Bergson, who married Proust's cousin Louise Neuberger in 1892. He heard Bergson speak at the Collège de France in 1900 and had read and annotated *Matière et mémoire* (1896) by 1911. Nevertheless, the novelist and the philosopher shared the wish that the connection not be overstated, and critics do not agree on the extent and significance of Bergson's influence. For Tadié, 'Bergson without Proust is no more surprising than Proust without Bergson'; indeed, for Bergson, Tadié claims, the author of *À la recherche* was merely the person who had supplied him with earplugs to help him sleep.[19] Roger Shattuck observes that the line near the beginning of *Du côté de chez Swann*, 'when a man is asleep, he has in a circle round him the chain of the hours, the sequence of the years, the order of the heavenly bodies' (1: 3; 1, 5), is reminiscent of Bergson's claim in *Matière et mémoire* that 'a human being who *dreamed* his life ... would probably thus keep constantly in sight the infinite multitude of details of his past history'.[20] In contrast, Anthony Pilkington argues that 'while it is true that both [Bergson and Proust] draw a distinction between two radically different modes of memory, they do not draw the same distinction': Bergson's 'habit memory' is not found in Proust, he suggests, and the 'pure memory' of *Matière et mémoire*, which may be 'congruent with the account of memory found in *À la recherche*, ... is not identical with the Proustian "mémoire involontaire"'.[21] Proust's own exasperated observations support Pilkington's analysis: in the newspaper *Le Temps* on 12 November 1913, he denies that *Du côté de chez Swann* is a 'Bergsonian novel', insisting that his work is 'dominated by the distinction between involuntary and voluntary memory, a distinction which not only does not figure in the philosophy of M. Bergson, but is even contradicted by it' (*ASB*, 235; *CSB*, 558). Similarly, in a letter of 1914 to Henri Ghéon, he expresses frustration at the Bergson comparison: 'I already have enough to do without trying to turn the philosophy of M. Bergson into a novel!' (*Corr*, XIII, 39). Thus, while there are certainly affinities between their works (both writers explore questions of memory, time, habit, laughter, sleep, dreams, morality, religion and psychology, for example), Proust cannot be viewed as a mere Bergsonian.[22]

À la recherche is a novel. It is not a philosophical treatise. As Vincent Descombes has observed, Proust's 'task is not to illustrate philosophical themes, but to compose a narrative'.[23] How, though, did Proust's contemporaries understand the term 'philosophical', and in what sense might Proust's narrative now be described as a philosophical one? In an 1896 article entitled 'Contre l'obscurité', Proust argues that a philosopher's concern for logic confers the right to be obscure: 'Because he is not appealing to our logical faculties, the poet cannot benefit from the right which any profound philosopher has of seeming at first obscure' (*ASB*, 137; *CSB*, 392). This comment provides an insight into the philosophical context in which Proust worked; it points to a distinction that obtained, for a number of Proust's contemporaries, between philosophy and literature. According to Descombes, 'the philosophers whose lessons Proust may have learned [including Boutroux and Darlu] did ... teach that man possesses, in addition to his "sensitive" (and therefore "poetic") faculties, a group of logical faculties'.[24] For these thinkers, philosophy 'was generally accepted as meaning the construction of a *world-system* more satisfying than one constructed by *common sense*'.[25] This system is more satisfying because it is 'free of the contradictions ... in the views of the ordinary man'.[26] Indeed, it is precisely because the philosopher's system is by definition superior to the common view of things that it must inevitably appear obscure. While the philosopher embraces an uncommon logical clarity, the writer and the artist are 'the partisans of the anti-philosophical, of that element of the world that has not found its proper place in the rational system of the world'.[27] Descombes's observation may support Tadié's view that, for philosophers such as Darlu and Boutroux, philosophical 'concepts were always lucid and defined, examples were precise, reasoning was flawless'.[28] Nevertheless, while the influence of these thinkers on Proust is undeniable, *À la recherche* cannot be enlisted in support of their view of the novel as 'anti-philosophy', even if its concepts and reasoning are not entirely watertight. Indeed, for Descombes, Marcel's philosophical pronouncements and digressions are logically incoherent, prescribing 'constructions that prove to be impossible'.[29] It is not in them that we should look for the philosophical import of Proust's novel: 'the philosophy of the novel is not to be sought in this or that thought content, but rather in the fact that the novel requires of the reader a *reformation of the understanding*'.[30] In other words, there is a philosophy of the novel that resides not in its many passages of a speculative character, but rather in the effects of style derided by Proust's philosophical contemporaries and teachers as 'anti-philosophical' – in Marcel's efforts 'to elucidate what was obscure' and 'to exact *intellectual and moral work*'[31] through the rich linguistic workings that the narrative and descriptive passages of *À la recherche* provide.

Notes

1 Jean-Yves Tadié, *Marcel Proust: A Life*, trans. by Euan Cameron (Harmondsworth: Penguin, 2000), p. 211.
2 Tadié, trans. Cameron, *Marcel Proust*, p. 204.
3 Tadié, trans. Cameron, *Marcel Proust*, p. 205.
4 As a philosophy of science, positivism was developed in the early nineteenth century by the philosopher and sociologist Auguste Comte and in later years by the critic and historian Hippolyte Taine. Outside France, Bertrand Russell's *The Problems of Philosophy* was published in 1912, one year before *Du côté de chez Swann*. Russell prioritizes empirical knowledge over metaphysics: if we can observe sense data, he argues, there is no reason to doubt the existence of

objects. Later on, as a *logical* positivist influenced by the Vienna Circle, Russell espoused a theory of meaning which held that only statements about empirical observations and formal logical propositions are meaningful.

5 Tadié, trans. Cameron, *Marcel Proust*, p. 79.

6 For the second edition of *Le Banquet*, published in April 1892, Proust produced four 'studies'. These appeared after an article by Halévy and Gregh on Nietzsche and extracts from Nietzsche's *Beyond Good and Evil* (this was the first time Nietzsche's text, or passages from it, had been made available in French).

7 Edmund White, *Proust* (London: Weidenfeld & Nicolson, 1999), p. 29.

8 As instructive as White's example may be – it demonstrates, among other things, that Marcel compares himself explicitly to an idealist philosopher – he also elides Marcel's philosophy with Proust's. The distinction between Proust and Marcel is, as a number of critics have observed, one that matters. See, for example, Joshua Landy, *Philosophy as Fiction: Self, Deception and Knowledge in Proust* (Oxford University Press, 2004), pp. 14–49.

9 Tadié, trans. Cameron, *Marcel Proust*, p. 204; translation modified.

10 See Anne Henry, 'La révélation d'une philosophie de l'art', in *Marcel Proust, théories pour une esthétique* (Paris: Klincksieck, 1981), pp. 45–97.

11 Anne Henry, 'Proust du côté de Schopenhauer', in *Schopenhauer et la création littéraire en Europe*, ed. Anne Henry (Paris: Klincksieck, 1989), pp. 149–64 (p. 24). We hear distinct echoes here of Samuel Beckett's 1931 monograph on Proust, in which he surmises that 'the influence of Schopenhauer on this aspect [music] of the Proustian demonstration is unquestionable'. Samuel Beckett, *Proust and Three Dialogues with Georges Duthuit* (London: John Calder, 1965), p. 91.

12 Landy, *Philosophy as Fiction*, p. 6.

13 Landy, *Philosophy as Fiction*, p. 7; emphasis in original.

14 Landy, *Philosophy as Fiction*, p. 6.

15 Duncan Large, *Nietzsche and Proust: A Comparative Study* (Oxford University Press, 2001), p. 18.

16 See Sara Danius, 'The Aesthetics of the Windshield: Proust and the Modernist Rhetoric of Speed', *Modernism/Modernity*, 8 (2001), 100–26 (106).

17 John Ruskin, *Selected Writings*, ed. Kenneth Clark (Harmondsworth: Penguin, 1991), p. 246.

18 Ralph Waldo Emerson, *Selected Essays*, ed. Larzer Ziff (Harmondsworth: Penguin, 1982), p. 64.

19 Tadié, trans. Cameron, *Marcel Proust*, p. 128.

20 Henri Bergson, *Matière et mémoire*, cited in Roger Shattuck, *Marcel Proust* (Princeton University Press, 1982), p. 144.

21 Anthony E. Pilkington, *Bergson and His Influence: A Reassessment* (Cambridge University Press, 1976), p. 173.

22 See White, *Proust*, p. 44.

23 Vincent Descombes, *Proust: Philosophy of the Novel*, trans. by Catherine Chance Macksey (Stanford University Press, 1992), p. 35.

24 Descombes, *Proust*, p. 74.
25 Descombes, *Proust*, p. 74; emphasis in original.
26 Descombes, *Proust*, p. 74.
27 Descombes, *Proust*, p. 76.
28 Tadié, trans. Cameron, *Marcel Proust*, p. 204.
29 Descombes, *Proust*, p. 52.
30 Descombes, *Proust*, p. 35; emphasis in original.
31 Descombes, *Proust*, p. 35; emphasis in original.

CHAPTER 11

Painting

Gabrielle Townsend

Of the three art forms that Proust chooses to feature in *À la recherche du temps perdu* – painting, music and literature – painting is undoubtedly given the greatest prominence: first, through the sheer number of references to works of art and their creators that abound throughout the novel and, second, through the relative levels of detail devoted to the descriptions of the work of the three fictional artists portrayed: Vinteuil, the composer, Bergotte, the writer, and Elstir, the painter. It is also significant that Proust's imagery has been shown to be predominantly visual.[1]

The music of the composer Vinteuil is an important motif in *Un amour de Swann*: the 'little phrase' from his violin sonata is the 'national anthem' of Swann and Odette's affair, and his septet makes a profound impression on the Narrator later in the novel. But Vinteuil himself is a relatively minor character whose genius is not recognized until after his death. Conversely, although we receive a somewhat more detailed impression of the writer Bergotte, we learn little about his work in terms of its subject matter. The most significant insight into his writing is Bergotte's own analysis of a painting, the *View of Delft*, which compares prose with paint, the textual with the visual. But his perception of a lack of richness in his own writing leads to a sense, at the moment of death, of having failed as an artist. Style thus takes precedence over content as a criterion for judging the worth of a work of art – a conviction Proust never fails to underline, as we shall see. And the description of Bergotte's books in the window of a bookshop: 'his books, arranged three by three, kept vigil like angels with outspread wings' (5: 209; III, 693), as guardians of Bergotte's resurrection, presupposes the survival of the artist's work beyond death, as also in the case of Vinteuil. In contrast to this immortality is the relative insignificance of individual artists' lives.

But Elstir is a more fully developed character, and his work and working methods are described in considerably more detail. Why this should be is a question I shall return to; I shall first look at the range of artistic reference

83

that Proust employs in his novel. Over 100 artists and over 200 individual works of art are mentioned in *À la recherche*.[2] The range of reference is temporally and stylistically vast: from the Renaissance to cubism, from the great masters to formerly fashionable minor painters of the nineteenth century, now forgotten. Proust's purpose in inserting these references varies greatly: sometimes the reference merely serves as a visual analogy to enrich the texture of his prose; sometimes his descriptions will illuminate a philosophical concept; sometimes a citation will be used sociologically, to illustrate a character's taste, or, in a mildly satirical way, to ridicule mistaken artistic judgment.

Proust's knowledge of art

Proust acquired his impressive knowledge of art in various ways. He saw many pictures at first hand: as a schoolboy and young man he spent hours in the Louvre studying the old masters. His knowledge is reflected in his poems 'Portraits de peintres', devoted to Cuyp, Paulus Potter, Watteau and Van Dyck, included in *Les Plaisirs et les jours*. Then, on becoming an habitué of the salons of the Faubourg Saint-Germain, he had access to the jewels of aristocratic collections, just as the Narrator, invited to dinner, asks the Duc de Guermantes to let him view his collection of Elstirs. Seeing art was the main purpose of the rare but vividly memorable trips he made abroad. The first was to Holland in 1898 to see a Rembrandt exhibition in Amsterdam. In 1902 he went with his friend Bertrand de Fénelon to Belgium and again to Holland – to Haarlem, to see the work of Frans Hals (which the Narrator confesses to having missed, to the Duchesse de Guermantes' somewhat pretentious indignation) and to the Hague, where Vermeer's *View of Delft* made a lasting impression on him. He wrote to his friend the critic Jean-Louis Vaudoyer that 'Ever since I saw the *View of Delft* in the museum in The Hague, I have known that I had seen the most beautiful painting in the world' (*Corr*, xx, 226). He also said that Vermeer had been his favourite painter since he was twenty and that he had chosen him to be the object of Swann's studies. Proust saw the picture again when it was shown in Paris in 1921, the year before his death, his struggle to get to the exhibition reflected in the description of the dying Bergotte's visit. His trip to Venice in 1900 acquainted him with Carpaccio, the Bellini family, Titian and Veronese, all of whom are frequently cited in the novel. Most importantly, he went to Padua, where seeing the Giotto frescoes in the Scrovegni chapel was one of the most important artistic experiences of his life; the Vices and Virtues portrayed there play a major role in the novel. He never visited Rome or Florence, so never saw the work of Botticelli, whose Zipporah, from the Sistine Chapel frescoes, Swann identifies with Odette.

Sources of reference

Ill health increasingly restricted Proust's ability to travel and to visit galleries, with the result that when writing he was extremely reliant on secondary sources for references that he needed either to recall a painting he had seen perhaps years earlier, or to describe a work he had never seen at first hand.[3] We should also recall that the Narrator's first acquaintance with works of art is via the reproductions that his grandmother and Swann gave him – engravings when possible, as she regarded these as more artistic than photographs. Among the most important of these reference works was *Les Villes d'art célèbres*, a collection of illustrated books published by Éditions Laurens that included volumes on Milan, Amsterdam and Haarlem, Padua and Verona, Venice and Florence. Laurens also published a collection called *Les Grands Artistes*. Proust used both sets of volumes extensively, and a substantial proportion of the works of art mentioned in *À la recherche* are to be found in these books.[4] He also frequently consulted the *Gazette des Beaux-Arts*, an illustrated journal owned by another friend, Charles Ephrussi, one of the first patrons of painters such as Monet, Manet and Renoir, and one of the models for Swann. Proust contributed to the journal from 1900 onwards and also wrote for its weekly, non-illustrated sister publication *La Chronique des arts et de la curiosité*.[5] He regularly visited the offices of the *Gazette* to consult the journal, collect review copies of books submitted to it and to read other publications, such as the *Burlington Magazine*. He often consulted the *Gazette*'s secretary, the art historian and critic Auguste Marguillier, for specialist advice. Thus Proust must be seen as more than a dilettante – rather as someone who made a serious study of all kinds of art.

An important source of his artistic knowledge and interest came from his lengthy and intense involvement with the writings of Ruskin, whose work he translated: another set of illustrated books that Proust referred to constantly was the Library Edition of Ruskin's complete works, the first set of which he received in January 1905.[6] He wrote to Marie Nordlinger, his friend and collaborator in translating Ruskin, 'I have been given the splendid new edition of Ruskin as a New Year's present . . . You will see what fine new illustrations there are' (*Corr*, v, 42). It was Ruskin's watercolour copy of Botticelli's *Zipporah* (the frontispiece to volume XXIII of the Library

Edition, which contained *Mornings in Florence* and *Val d'Arno*) that Proust drew on for his description of Zipporah in *Un amour de Swann*.

It is worth noting that Proust, although wealthy enough to buy some original paintings, never had much interest in becoming a collector, although he wrote that he would perhaps have bought old masters, specifically Italian primitives, if he could have afforded them; but such valuable works were beyond even his means – or so he claimed. More important to him than possession is the capacity of paintings to stimulate memory by their power of association, like the madeleine: 'If I were rich, I wouldn't buy masterpieces ... but pictures that preserve the smell of a town or a damp church, like curios that evoke dreams as much by the association of ideas as in themselves' (*Corr*, VI, 337). Elsewhere he mentions his interest in buying copies of famous paintings 'which would fulfil my desire for paintings at a lower cost than originals and without the fatigue of going to Dresden or even visiting the Louvre' (*Corr*, X, 88). Not merely was Proust indifferent to the status of originals, and happy to use reproductions: he can be said in many respects to *prefer* a secondary source. For example, when researching the details of a garment created by Fortuny, the (real) Venetian designer, that he will describe Albertine wearing in the novel, he specifically declines an offer from a friend to lend him an actual gown, and requests rather a book with, if possible, 'the *flattest* description of her coat, as it would be in a catalogue, listing fabric, colours, design' (*Corr*, XV, 63). It is as if the presence of an original object would, in its insistent specificity, inhibit the creative process by limiting it to simple description, rather than permitting it to be transformed by the writer's imagination.

Proust's use of paintings in *À la recherche*

Just as the Narrator's grandmother prefers to give him reproductions of works of art depicting famous landmarks rather than photographs, in the belief that they represented 'a stage higher in the scale of art' encompassing 'several "thicknesses" of art' (I: 46; I, 40), Proust introduces references to paintings to give an allusive richness to his text. Characters' appearance is often likened to that of figures in paintings, as for example when the Narrator's father appears with his head wrapped in a scarf, resembling Abraham in a picture by the fifteenth-century Florentine artist Benozzo Gozzoli, an engraving of which had been given to the Narrator by Swann. Similarly, Swann has the habit of comparing features of people of his acquaintance with elements of portraits: 'in the colouring of a Ghirlandaio, the nose of M. de Palancy; in a portrait by Tintoretto ... the penetrating stare, the swollen eyelids of Dr du Boulbon' (1: 267–8; 1, 219). And Swann's identification of Odette with Botticelli's Zipporah allows him the legitimization of an infatuation that would otherwise seem demeaning. It is Swann who points out to the Narrator's family the resemblance of their pregnant kitchen maid to Giotto's Charity, a figure from the frescoes Proust had seen in Padua. But whereas Swann's comparisons are frivolous, Proust draws moral conclusions from this association, in particular from the discrepancy between appearance and character, in contrast to the convention that links one to the other. The maid's face, swollen in pregnancy, does recall the features of Giotto's Virtues: 'her face and squarish elongated cheeks, did distinctly suggest those virgins, so sturdy and mannish as to seem matrons rather, in whom the virtues are personified in the Arena Chapel' (1: 95; 1, 80). But Charity's face – 'vulgar and energetic' (1: 95; 1, 80) – does not seem to express any quality of charity, just as Envy looks more like an illustration in a medical textbook. Initially the Narrator does not see any merit in the Vices and Virtues. But later he comes to appreciate the significance of the way abstract qualities are represented:

> I came to understand that the arresting strangeness, the special beauty of these frescoes derived from the great part played in them by symbolism, and the fact that this was represented not as a symbol (for the thought symbolised was nowhere expressed) but as a reality, actually felt added something more precise and more literal to the meaning of the work. (1: 96; 1, 81)

The true face of goodness is 'impassive, unsympathetic, sublime' (1: 96; 1, 81). Thus Proust is claiming that art must reject sentimentality and convention, and rather use specific physical elements to convey its intention. That a banal detail – such as Vermeer's famous 'little patch of yellow wall' (5: 245; III, 692) – or a humble subject can be transformed by art is for Proust an important aesthetic concept, expressed most forcefully in the article 'Chardin et Rembrandt' (*ASB*, 122–31; *CSB*, 372–82), in which he claims that a great artist such as Chardin, master of the still life, can reveal to the viewer the beauty of everyday objects. The way a subject is treated, not the subject itself, is the essential criterion for valuing a work of art, and this principle is the foundation stone of Proust's aesthetic philosophy.

Elstir and *Le Port de Carquethuit*

No single artist was the inspiration for Elstir, although his name is an obvious partial anagram of Whistler. Critics have suggested artists as various as Degas, Hokusaï, Renoir, Helleu, Vuillard, and the American marine painter T. Alexander Harrison, as models.[7] Certainly the salient features of his painting *Le Port de Carquethuit*, to which Proust devoted extensive description and analysis, owe much to Monet's Impressionist paintings of the coast of Normandy, but also to Turner's marine paintings, which Proust knew well from illustrated editions of Ruskin's works *Modern Painters* and *The Harbours of England*. Both these artists blur the distinction between land and sea, earth and water, and Proust invests Elstir's painting with the same intentional dissolving of boundaries to harness the power of metaphor: 'the charm of each of them [the marine paintings] lay in a sort of metamorphosis of the objects represented, analogous to what we in poetry call metaphor, and that, if God the Father had created things by naming them, it was by taking away their names or giving them other names that Elstir created them anew' (2: 479; II, 191). Elstir creates metaphor by linking elements to form a new vision, greater than the sum of its parts, 'by employing, for the little town, only marine terms, and urban terms for the sea' (2: 480; II, 192). His metaphors reveal an inner reality – the essence of the world: 'metaphors that express the essence of the impression made for us by an object but that we cannot penetrate until genius has unveiled it for us'.[8] The Narrator had previously accounted for his disappointment on seeing a statue in the porch of Balbec church he had long wished to view by his 'incapacity for looking at things properly' (2: 274–5; II, 21). Elstir's role in the narrative is thus to be the agent who will teach the Narrator how to look at his subject before he can create a work of art. This means seeing and recording with a fresh and unprejudiced eye. As the critic Pierre-Henry Frangne suggests, 'for Proust and Elstir, to paint an impression is to paint sensations before the reasoning and calculating mind gets involved and produces delimited and hence predetermined representations'.[9] This unique personal vision transcends everyday reality to create a work of art of universal relevance and enduring value, achieving immortality through the continual *recre-ation* it undergoes as it speaks directly to each individual recipient.

Proust returns to the subject of metaphor in *Le Temps retrouvé* as he reflects on his conception of what art must be, and, ultimately, on his own vocation:

> [the writer] can describe a scene by describing one after another the innumer-able objects which at a given moment were present at a particular place, but truth will be attained by him only when he takes two different objects, states the connexion between them – a connexion analogous in the world of art to the unique connexion which in the world of science is provided by the law of causality – and encloses them in the necessary links of a well-wrought style;

truth – and life too – can be attained by us only when, by comparing a quality common to two sensations, we succeed in extracting their common essence and in reuniting them to each other, liberated from the contingencies of time, within a metaphor. (6: 246; IV, 468)

Thus the greatest truth the Narrator must grasp is one he has learnt from a painter, underlining the centrality of the visual in Proust's artistic universe.

Notes

1 Victor E. Graham has calculated that 62 per cent of Proust's images are visual, particularly those to do with memory. Victor E. Graham, *The Imagery of Proust* (Oxford: Blackwell, 1966), p. 8.
2 An invaluable comprehensive guide to the works of art alluded to in the novel is Eric Karpeles, *Paintings in Proust: A Visual Companion to 'In Search of Lost Time'* (London: Thames & Hudson, 2008).
3 I discuss Proust's reliance on reproduced images in Gabrielle Townsend, *Proust's Imaginary Museum: Reproduction and Reproductions in 'À la recherche du temps perdu'* (Oxford and Bern: Peter Lang, 2008).
4 See Jérôme Picon, '"Un degré d'art de plus"', and Valérie Sueur, '"Impressions et réimpressions": Proust et l'image multiple', in *Marcel Proust: l'écriture et les arts* (Paris: Gallimard/Bibliothèque nationale de France/Réunion des musées nationaux, 1999), pp. 81–7; pp. 89–101.
5 See Philip Kolb and Jean Adhémar, 'Charles Ephrussi (1849–1905); ses secrétaires: Laforgue, A. Renan, Proust; "sa" Gazette des Beaux-Arts', *Gazette des Beaux-Arts*, January 1984, pp. 29–41.
6 *The Works of John Ruskin*, ed. E. T. Cook and Alexander Wedderburn, 39 vols. (London: George Allen, 1903–12).
7 See (among others) D. F. Wakefield, 'Proust and the Visual Arts', *The Burlington Magazine*, vol. CXII, 806 (1970), 291–6 (294); and Michel Butor, *Les Œuvres d'art imaginaires chez Proust* (London: Athlone Press, 1984), p. 19.
8 From *Cahier* 28, quoted in Claudie Chelet-Hester, 'La galerie des Guermantes ou la leçon de vérité d'Elstir', *Bulletin d'informations proustiennes*, 22 (1991), 37–49 (39).
9 Pierre-Henry Frangne, 'La peinture selon Proust et Mallarmé', in *Proust et les images: peinture, photographie, cinéma, vidéo*, ed. Jean Cléder and Jean-Pierre Montier (Presses Universitaires de Rennes, 2003), pp. 51–67 (63).

CHAPTER 12

Music

Julian Johnson

Music has been one of the great passions of my life . . . It has brought me indescribable joy and knowledge, and the certitude that something exists beyond the 'void' with which I have struggled for so long. It runs like a guiding thread throughout all of my work. (Marcel Proust, 1922)[1]

Had Proust never made this declaration, in an interview six months before he died, one might surely have surmised it from his work;[2] his fascination with music is clear enough throughout his novels and his correspondence. A decade later, Samuel Beckett concluded his 1931 study of Proust with a brief reflection on the importance of music, characterizing it with a similarly dynamic and energetic metaphor – music, he said, was 'the catalytic element' in Proust's work.[3] A whole book could be written on the subject, Beckett ventured and, in the eighty years since, many have been.[4] Approached by scholars working in both literature and musicology, the topic recurs with 'pendulum-like regularity'.[5] But what was clear then, and remains so today, is that a few themes and approaches have remained constant. These include investigations of Proust's musical world (in terms of his own musical experiences and the wider cultural milieu), studies of the presence of music in his novels (as cultural markers for different characters and in terms of literary style) and explorations of the structural and philosophical significance of music to Proust's larger project. Though it would be foolish to say that any of these have been exhausted, there is probably little more of interest left to say on the undoubted importance of Wagner or on the somewhat pointless question of exactly which Sonata for Violin and Piano provided the model for the fictional Vinteuil *Sonate* that plays such an important role within *À la recherche*. There is still a great deal to learn, however, about what Proust's *Recherche* tells us about the nature of music, and what, according to Proust's account, music might tell us about time, memory and particularity.

Proust's own musical world was exceptionally rich; never was Paris a more important and vibrant centre of musical culture than during his lifetime and it is clear that he was fully immersed in the new developments that were then changing the landscape of modern music. The importance of Wagner and *wagnerisme* to his work cannot be overstated and he absorbed the quasi-religious respect for Beethoven (particularly the late works) then current. But it was his association with contemporary composers that drew him to reflect most on the parallels between his own literary project and the nature of music. He had access to the leading musical salons of his time and knew not only Saint-Saëns, Fauré and Franck, but also Debussy, Ravel and Reynaldo Hahn.[6] In later life, as he became increasingly withdrawn from society, Proust still found ways to hear musical performances. There are famous tales of the Capet Quartet being woken in the middle of the night to play the Debussy String Quartet for him in his flat, and on another occasion the Poulet Quartet being asked for a private performance of the Franck Quartet.[7] But he also made use, from 1911 onwards, of the *théâtrophone* ('a telephone service that allowed the subscriber to listen to whatever happened to be on at the Opéra, Opéra-Comique or any of half a dozen other Parisian theatres').[8]

However closely modelled on real-life characters and situations, the insights offered by Proust's work into the musical life of the Belle Époque are always given through the filter of subjective experience. He writes about music in a manner almost antithetical to the attempts at objective analysis that were, just at this time, beginning to define the discipline of musicology and for that reason his rhapsodic literary flights have often been neglected. Leo Bersani, for example, not only suggests that the discussions of art in general in *À la recherche* are of 'rather uneven quality' but that the descriptions of music in particular are given 'with what is often an irritating literary virtuosity'.[9] For others, it is precisely the musical quality of Proust's language at such moments that becomes the object of study, as for Jean Milly in *La Phrase de Proust* with its detailed textural analysis of the sonorous and musical qualities of the language used to discuss the music of Vinteuil.[10]

That said, there is no lack of fascinating analysis of the social role of music. Using the index of the first Pléiade edition of *À la recherche*, Georges Matoré and Irène Mecz identified some forty musicians who appear in its constituent volumes, of whom the most frequently recurring are Wagner (35 times), Beethoven (25) and Debussy (13).[11] Music is often used as a cipher for the sensibility and taste of a character, often ironically, to suggest that someone's outward social pretensions and snobbery are betrayed by an inward lack of sensibility. Mme Verdurin, for example, is described as 'a goddess of Wagnerism and migraine' (5: 281, trans. mod.; III, 753) whose 'salon was understood to be a Temple of Music' (4: 309; III, 263) and famously suffers from a host of physical symptoms, so sensitive is she to the power of music. A wonderful example occurs in *Du côté de chez Swann*, at a soirée held by the Marquise de Sainte-Euverte. Mme de Franquetot watches a pianist plays Liszt as anxiously as she might follow a trapeze artist at a circus. Meanwhile, Mme de Cambremer ('as a woman who had received a sound musical education') is 'beating time with her head, transformed into the arm of a metronome, the sweep and rapidity of whose oscillations from one shoulder to the other ... so increased that at every moment her diamond earrings caught in the trimming of her bodice, and she was obliged to straighten the bunch of black grapes which she had in her hair, though without any interruption to her ever accelerating motion' (1: 395, trans. mod.; 1, 323).

The most important musical figure in *À la recherche* is, however, neither Wagner nor Beethoven but the fictional composer Vinteuil, and the most important musical works are his equally fictional Sonata for Violin and Piano and Septet. There are plenty of works by real composers that have received less attention than these and much ink has been spilled on their possible sources. In particular, the origin of the recurrent motif from the Sonata, known as 'la petite phrase', which plays such an important role across the broad span of *À la recherche*, has occupied several generations of commentators. In fact, the question was largely exhausted before the exhaustive search began, because Proust himself was entirely clear about the insignificance of its one small point of direct contact with a real piece. In a now famous inscription to Jacques Lacretelle in 1918, he made clear the multiple and conflated sources of the phrase, but with a disclaimer that should have put an end to the matter. 'Insofar as reality has been of use to me (which is not very much, to be honest)', he began, before identifying the source of 'la petite phrase' as a 'charming but ultimately mediocre phrase of a sonata for violin and piano by Saint-Saëns, a musician I do not care for.'[12] He went on to mention a disparate set of further musical resonances including the 'Good Friday Spell' from Wagner's *Parsifal*, Franck's Violin Sonata and String Quartet, the Prelude to Wagner's *Lohengrin*, and a phrase of Schubert. Plenty of other works have been added to the mix since.[13] Like the Sonata, the Septet also has multiple sources, as Kazuyoshi Yoshikawa's study of the 'extremely composite' origins of the work has shown.[14]

Far more important, however, than the disparate sources of Vinteuil's Sonata and Septet is the role that these two works play within the novel.

The sense that they 'form one of the pillars of the complex design of the *Recherche*',[15] with the Sonata in the first volume and the Septet preparing the ground for the last, suggests a structural importance for music which Proust seems to have realized only in the process of developing the work as a whole. Pierre Costil's essay, 'La construction musicale de la *Recherche du temps perdu*', published in two parts in 1958 and 1959,[16] was, in the words of Nattiez, 'the first to establish beyond doubt the essential role played by the Sonata and Septet in the work's structure: it is the Narrator's meditation on the nature of music that leads him to see in it the ideal model for literature and to decide to devote his life to literary work'.[17] Since then, the key role played by music in the novel has been generally acknowledged, running through the novel largely unseen, yet generating some of its key moments, like the 'guiding thread' of music in Proust's own life. It may break the surface relatively seldom and occupy a small proportion of the thousands of pages, but the musicalization of time and experience shapes the novel's central theme. As Roger Shattuck puts it, music contains 'in miniature' the affective memory that normally operates over a far broader time scale. Hence, on hearing the Septet, 'Marcel finally hears and understands that the shape of music is the shape of fiction, and the shape of life itself properly lived.' Key to this is music's presentation of material events that are then left behind, only to be recovered again, 'the same and yet different' but within a matter of minutes rather than years. For Proust, Shattuck insists, 'Nothing has fully happened if it happens only once. Life – and music insofar as it recapitulates life – is a twice-told tale.'[18]

This is underlined the first time we encounter the Vinteuil Sonata, as Swann hears it played by a pianist chez Verdurin (1: 247–50; 1, 203–5). But for Swann himself, hearing the piece on this occasion provokes the memory of having it heard it once before, about a year earlier. His recollection is revelatory because whereas his initial experience literally had no name (he was unable to find out what the piece was) the rehearing in the Verdurin salon is associated with being able to identify the piece and thus to take possession of it. On the one hand, Proust underlines Swann's 'mishearing' of the music in merely material ways ('At first, he had appreciated only the material quality of the sounds'; 1: 250; 1, 205); on the other, he underlines Swann's openness to the charm of the music that overcomes him like a scent. 'Perhaps it was owing to his ignorance of music', the Narrator concludes, 'that he had received so confused an impression, one of those that are none the less the only purely musical impressions, immaterial, entirely original, and irreducible to any other kind. An impression of this order, for an instant, is, so to speak, *sine materia*' (1: 250, trans. mod.; 1, 206).

While Swann may have begun in the purely material realm of musical sounds, his recollection of the Sonata nevertheless delivers far more than a merely sensuous experience. Not only does it produce in him a happiness at once 'unintelligible, and yet precise', but occasions in him a change of life, 'a sort of rejuvenation', as he turns away from everyday pleasures and seeks out something more ideal (hence his project on Vermeer) (1: 251–2; 1, 207). Much later a similar feeling will be provoked in the Narrator. Picking out the themes of the Sonata at the piano as he waits for Albertine in *La Prisonnière*, he is momentarily transported back to Combray and his earlier desire to be an artist. 'Could life console me for the loss of art? Was there in art a more profound reality, in which our true personality finds an expression that is not afforded it by the actions of life?' (5: 174; III, 664). Most commentators, however, see Swann as failing to fully grasp Vinteuil's music because he too readily equates it with his love for Odette. Just as music opens up a world beyond the materiality of phenomena (the influence of Schopenhauer is most audible here) Swann rushes in and fills the space with the name of Odette (1: 261–3; 1, 215–16). Thus Odette becomes the worldly object for the longing provoked by the music, the inadequate figure of desire for its evocation of the *Ewig-Weibliche*. Central to the later development represented by the Narrator is that he will not make the same mistake: 'Music, unlike Albertine's company, helped me to descend into myself, to discover new things there: the variety that I had sought in vain in life, in travel, but a longing for which was none the less renewed in me by this sonorous tide whose sunlit waves, came to break at my feet' (5: 175, trans. mod.; III, 665).

Nattiez suggests that the various appearances of Vinteuil's music throughout the novel 'act as milestones in the Narrator's discovery of his vocation as a writer, of the nature of the "true life" and of the recovery of Time through the literary work'.[19] It is thus on hearing the Septet, chez Verdurin, that the Narrator reverses his earlier conclusion that art is meaningless and gives himself up to the 'hypothesis that art might be real', considering that what it conveys must 'correspond to some definite spiritual reality, or life would be meaningless' (5: 427–8; III, 876). The key epiphanic moments of the novel – the madeleine, the spires at Martinville, the trees on the road to Balbec – are explicitly related to the effect of the music at this point. Music thus provides a vehicle for those moments of self-possession found in recollecting experience through the particularity of its sensuous details, rather than in abstract or logical ideas. But whereas the memory of people and places always results in disappointment, such that the Narrator concludes the goal to which they point is 'unrealizable', he nevertheless recalls that 'the septet of Vinteuil had seemed to point to the contrary conclusion' (6: 230; IV, 455). In providing 'a fragment of time in the pure state', music anticipates the Narrator's revelation that 'a minute freed from the order of time has re-created in us, to feel it, the man freed from the order of time' (6: 224–5; IV, 451).

Music thus provides the model for what the novel aspires to achieve. On the one hand it presents time in a linear form as a kind of quest or journey in which motifs change and become non-identical with themselves, like people as material life moves on; on the other hand, it constantly revisits and recoups the past, remaking it in the present. Memory in music is also involuntary; its associative logic also deranges the self in productive and poetic ways, exploring in the plural times of the self a complex mediation of the external materiality of social existence and the interiority of memory and imagination. As Mauro Carbone points out, Proust figures 'a different description of the relationship between the sensible and the intelligible'.[20] That he does so in a way that places music at its centre is not only of literary interest, but raises a question about music, as a kind of thinking through sensible particularity, whose consequences have hardly begun to be explored.

Notes

1 Jacques Benoist-Méchin, *Retour à Marcel Proust* (Paris: Pierre Amiot, 1957), p. 192.

2 Benoist-Méchin interviewed Proust in June 1922, publishing the result as *La Musique et l'immortalité dans l'œuvre de Marcel Proust* in 1926, later reprinted as *Retour à Marcel Proust*.

3 Samuel Beckett, *Proust* (New York: Grove Press, 1931), p. 71.

4 André Coueroy's article, 'La musique dans l'œuvre de Marcel Proust', printed in English as 'Music in the Work of Marcel Proust', appeared in *The Musical Quarterly*, 12 (1926), 132–51. This was followed by Florence Hier's *La Musique dans l'œuvre de Marcel Proust* (New York: Columbia University Press, 1933) and Louis Abatangel's *Marcel Proust et la musique* (Paris: Recherches, 1937). A steady stream of studies devoted to the topic has followed; the principal ones are cited in the course of this chapter.

5 Jean-Jacques Nattiez, *Proust as Musician*, trans. Derrick Puffett (Cambridge University Press, 1989); originally published as *Proust musicien* (Paris: Christian Bourgois, 1984).

6 For an overview of Proust's musical world see Georges Piroué, *Proust et la musique du devenir* (Paris: Denoël, 1960), Part I.

7 Piroué, *La Musique du devenir*, pp. 32 and 34.

8 Cormac Newark, 'Proust and the soirée à l'Opéra chez soi', in *Opera in the Novel from Balzac to Proust* (Cambridge University Press, 2011), n. 1, p. 247.

9 Leo Bersani, *Marcel Proust: The Fictions of Life and Art* (Oxford University Press, 1965), pp. 200–1.

10 Jean Milly, *La Phrase de Proust – des phrases de Bergotte aux phrases de Vinteuil* (Paris: Larousse, 1975). Ève-Norah Pauset also comments on musical structures in the literary text in *Marcel Proust et Gustav Mahler: créateurs parallèles* (Paris: L'Harmattan, 2007), p. 31.

11 Georges Matoré and Irène Mecz, *Musique et structure romanesque dans la 'Recherche du temps perdu'* (Paris: Klincksieck, 1972), p. 30.

12 See *Corr*, XVII, 193; translation taken from *Letters of Marcel Proust*, trans. and ed. Mina Curtis (New York: Helen Marx Books, 2006), pp. 434–5.

13 The 'petite phrase' is consistently identified as a phrase in F major that first appears in bars 76–83 of the first movement of Saint-Saëns's Sonata for Violin and Piano in D minor. Luigi Magnani analyses the different sections to show how Swann's account of it matches Saint-Saëns's score in *La Musica in Proust* (Turin: Giulio Einaudi, 1978), pp. 29–32.

14 Kazuyoshi Yoshikawa, 'Vinteuil ou la genèse du Septuor', *Cahiers Marcel Proust 9. Études proustiennes III* (Paris: Gallimard, 1979), 289–347 (305).

15 Mauro Carbone, 'Composing Vinteuil: Proust's Unheard Music', *RES: Anthropology and Aesthetics*, 48 (2005), 163–65 (163).

16 *Bulletin des Amis de Marcel Proust et des Amis de Combray*, 8 (1958), 469–89; and 9 (1959), 83–110.

17 Nattiez, *Proust as Musician*, p. 8.

18 Roger Shattuck, 'Making Time: A Study of Stravinsky, Proust and Sartre', *The Kenyon Review*, 25 (1963), 248–63 (252).

19 Nattiez, *Proust as Musician*, p. 8.

20 Carbone explores how this 'new theory of ideas' is exactly what preoccupied Merleau-Ponty before his untimely death. See Carbone, *An Unprecedented Deformation: Marcel Proust and the Sensible Ideas* (State University of New York Press, 2010), p. 9.

CHAPTER 13

Theatre and dance

Áine Larkin

Theatre looms large among the many art forms discussed and enjoyed in *À la recherche du temps perdu*, where the protagonist Marcel as a stage-struck boy runs to the Morris column near his home each day to view new playbills (1: 86; 1, 72), and buys a photograph of the actress La Berma to dream over (2: 68; 1, 478). The frequency and diversity of references to the stage in Proust's work reflect its contemporary cultural significance; while dance, though rarely evoked in comparison with other arts, is an important source of entertainment, as well as a required accomplishment in Marcel's milieu.[1] References to plays, playwrights, theatres, performers and especially actresses litter the narrative or play significant roles in it, and dance is an unsettling spectacle, from the waltzing *jeunes filles* at the Casino at Incarville to the male ballet dancer who sparks a vicious argument between Saint-Loup and his mistress (the actress) Rachel in a Paris theatre. To speak of Proust, theatre and dance, one must attend to three areas: theatre and dance as they appeared in Proust's own time, as they intersected with his personal life, and as they inform his fiction.

'The fascination for a visual and live spectacle, on stage, was part of Parisian life in the *Belle Epoque*',[2] and throughout the nineteenth century in France, together with the expanding capital, the theatre business grew consistently (though by the end of the nineteenth century it had become 'more an exceptional indulgence than a weekly habit'):[3] it was the principal form of entertainment because financially accessible to all, and because the variety of theatres catered to every taste, whether for tragedy, comedy, melodrama, slapstick, vaudeville, or mime. Proust's correspondence confirms his fascination with theatre from his youth onwards, and his education, though privileging knowledge of the classics, also encouraged interest in contemporary literature. Theatre is present as both high culture and popular entertainment in *À la recherche*, with Comédie-Française actors, Montmartre *chansonniers*, contemporary dramatists, directors and choreographers all acknowledged. Dance in Parisian theatres was popular

97

in Proust's lifetime, the Opéra de Paris being the home of classical ballet; however, ballet as an élite art was gradually displaced in the late nineteenth century to boulevard and variety theatres and music halls, until the development of Russian ballet reinvigorated the art in the early twentieth century, most particularly thanks to Diaghilev's Ballets Russes which visited Paris annually 1909–15, in 1917, and 1919–29.[4] Other dance forms besides ballet, such as the waltz, mazurka, polka, Boston and tango, were ubiquitous both on stage and off: 'dance is the sport of women and the cult of Parisian society', observes Louis Énault in 1856, 'in Paris one learns to dance quickly and well; all the world's *steps* meet there',[5] and this preoccupation with dance as a social skill is discernible in the many dance classes mentioned in the early volumes of *À la recherche*, for Marcel, Gilberte and young girls at Balbec.[6]

Playwrights and stage performers were household names in Proust's Paris, and fiction meets reality in his representation of the theatre, where real-life stars rub shoulders with his invented artists: among the many names dropped are Sarah Bernhardt, Maubant, Réjane, Sir Henry Irving and Febvre. Proust's evocation of the theatre is thus rooted in his own experience as spectator and informed by contemporary perceptions of the theatre and its luminaries. Particular to theatre as opposed to other arts is its re-creation of an original written text – when he watches La Berma in Racine's *Phèdre* for a second time, Marcel realizes that the actress is 'a window opening upon a great work of art' (3: 46; II, 347). This understanding of the actor's inherently fugitive art may explain the privileged position of theatre in Proust's novel, itself so concerned with making readers aware of the worth of their own lives as fleeting time lived and remembered. The choice of Racine's classical play is also pertinent, since its exploration of a troubled city state, undone by a volatile queen beset by incestuous desires which lead to her death and her stepson's, echoes the changing values and social structures of twentieth-century French society so minutely explored throughout the novel.[7]

As regards Proust's interest in dance, Diaghilev's Ballets Russes is the most relevant phenomenon in the early twentieth-century dance world; Proust attended the opening night of the company's second tour in Paris in 1910, was struck by Nijinsky's fame and talent, and was particularly taken with Léon Bakst's modern, richly coloured stage designs (*Corr*, x, 141). He also saw Nijinsky's scandalously erotic death throes in Debussy's *L'Après-midi d'un faune*, a ballet based on Stéphane Mallarmé's poem of the same title.[8] The Ballets Russes astounded audiences around the world with their innovative performances, costumes, music and stage designs.

As with theatre, mentioning real companies and dancers such as the Ballets Russes, Nijinsky and Mistinguett anchors Proust's representation of the dance world firmly in early twentieth-century Paris, providing a coherent framework for his fictional dancers, whose performances display and so underline the elusive nature of any object of desire: sexual, social or professional. In the late nineteenth century, the Opéra de Paris ballet world was notable as the source of 'a complex cultural mythology that intertwined ideals of femininity and bourgeois masculine desire', where the fantasy of the woman dancer was available to all, and the institutionally promoted mingling of privileged Jockey Club members with dancers backstage meant that the dancer came to embody 'a variety of contradictions around issues of class, sexuality, and politics'; as a result, popular fiction and non-fiction about dancers proliferated in the mid to late nineteenth century, exploiting the figure of the dancer in terms of a well-worn binary opposition of ethereal, ideal feminine beauty and available prostitute.[9] Dance scenes in Proust's novel are no doubt informed by this mythology, particularly with regard to the *jeunes filles*, whose ambiguous social and moral status Marcel notes the first time he sees them at Balbec, where even while walking, their bodies retain 'that immobility which is so noticeable in good waltzers' (2: 427; II, 147). The practice of 'keeping' a dancer is also mentioned three times, underlining the banality of this habit for upper-class men during the Belle Époque. At Balbec, Marcel wonders if the *jeunes filles* are the mistresses of champion cyclists staying there. However, Proust subverts the traditional relation of available female dancer to desiring male spectator by introducing the possibility of female homosexuality. In so doing, he radically reworks the established literary and artistic trope of the dancer in ways that Marcel and other male spectators find disturbing, and demonstrates the significant influence of the early twentieth-century dance world as a space for the projection of a homosexual identity and desire.

The term 'dance' necessarily covers a vast array of forms, and for Proust it largely implies rhythmic movements of the body in time to music, typically in the form of established steps and sequences of steps, to be danced in a wide variety of potential venues: so, at Balbec, the stylish young Octave 'took prizes in all the dancing competitions, for the boston, the tango, and what-not' (2: 530; II, 233), and Swann is described as having 'the same regard ... for the little families with small incomes who asked him to dances in their flats ... as for the Princesse de Parme who gave the most splendid parties in Paris' (1: 324; I, 265). The year 1912 saw the first tango craze in Paris, its origins in working-class port areas of Buenos Aires and the seduction inherent in the tango ensuring its popularity. Such stylized dance steps and movements may be regarded as a kind of non-verbal language, signifying unambiguously;[10] but in Proust's work, both amateur and professional dancers' movements are perceived to signify quite different things from one observer to another. Marcel can be seen as serving an apprenticeship to signs, as Gilles Deleuze affirms, and dance is one of the many sign systems he must attempt to decipher.[11] Guillemette Bolens remarks that

> kinesic interpretation of a real situation is a priori an exchange in which the perception of signals emitted by others is simultaneous with the emission of signals by the person who is observing. The perception of a face is always subject to the influence of the face, itself perceptible, of the person perceiving.[12]

Scenes of dance in Proust involve exchanges between more than one pair of individuals, causing an ungovernable multiplicity of points of view on the dancers. Dance resists verbal expression, a fact of which it seems Proust was acutely aware; and dance performances in his work point up the disparities in perception that alternately fascinate and alienate human beings from each other, producing the effects of displacement and disloca-tion which dance theorist Dee Reynolds affirms are possible for both performer and spectator.[13]

It is Dr Cottard, at Incarville, who first suggests openly that Albertine is a lesbian (4: 224–5; III, 190–1). Lacking male partners, Albertine and Andrée waltz pressed against one another, as another of the *petite bande* plays the piano in an otherwise deserted Casino: at first glance, they function as mirror images reflecting the same sex back to one another instead of the traditional complementariness of the man/woman couple, in conventional waltzing as in mainstream heterosexual relations. The theatre-like Casino has of course served hitherto as a space for their dance lessons (and the scandal surrounding Bloch's cousin and Mlle Léa (2: 559; II, 257)); here the performance the men witness takes on worrying conno-tations. Thinking perhaps along the same lines as George Bernard Shaw, to whom is attributed the maxim that dancing is the vertical expression of a horizontal desire legitimized by music, Dr Cottard expresses professional disapproval. His comical assertion – he cannot actually see the girls clearly without his spectacles – that the pair must be sexually aroused since "'women derive most excitement through their breasts'" (4: 225; III, 191) shows the misinformation which ignites Marcel's jealous suspicion. His remarks have an insidiously destructive effect. Not having previously read anything sinister into the girls' dancing, Marcel's suspicions about Albertine's sexual life both past and present now grow. Once nascent doubts about her sexual orientation have been aroused, Marcel reconsiders previously dismissed comments, and retrospectively reassesses aspects of her behaviour as proof of carefully concealed homosexual vice. So much head- and heartache thanks to a myopic doctor's prurient indiscretions by the dancefloor!

The waltz shocked polite society, which initially considered it 'too sexually dangerous for "respectable" women', because of its closed form, the couple's consequent independence, and their physical proximity.[14] Derived from German country dancing, it developed into several new styles in France in the late nineteenth and early twentieth century. In waltzing to their friend's piano-playing, in an empty space typically used for the purpose of public display, Albertine and Andrée release themselves from bourgeois behavioural norms of gender performance and create a self-sufficient totality, through the medium of a modern dance form with a somewhat scandalous history. They perform both the male and female roles of the dance, reducing their spectators to the role of passive desiring observers of their movement; and in blurring the conventional gender distinctions of the waltz, their actions throw up the anxiety-inducing suggestion of a more intimate kind of exclusive, transgressive female activity.[15]

Theatre and dance coalesce around the character Rachel, a sometime actress and Saint-Loup's lover. Rachel was the name of an actress revered in mid-nineteenth-century France for her revival of classical French theatre; Jewish, independent and successful, as is Proust's Rachel, she died in 1858. Once again, despite the anachronism, there is a blurring of boundaries between the real and fictional theatrical worlds, suggesting a homage to the great actress of the past, as well as another link with Racine. At a theatre where she is performing, Marcel and Saint-Loup go on stage to mingle with hangers-on and performers during the interval. As with the Incarville Casino, we witness a performance space outside the norms usually governing our spectatorship; here this is due to Saint-Loup's aristocratic privilege and wealth, like Jockey Club members at the Opéra. Into this space comes a rehearsing male dancer, for whom Thierry Laget believes Nijinsky to have served as model, and whose emancipation from any and all norms of gender performance captures Marcel's imagination as he witnesses him 'describing graceful patterns with the palms of his hands' (3: 199; II, 475), free as a butterfly.[16] These delicate hand movements, which he repeats and pastiches for Rachel, make him an attractively ambiguous man/woman in her eyes. Her initial, faintly sexually suggestive admiration becomes explicit, and it is his feminine grace that Rachel singles out; she thus confounds the seemingly ultra-masculine, financially powerful and controlling Saint-Loup (who, we later discover, is actually homosexual). The dancer's effeminate hand movements, scarlet skirt and vivid make-up underline his gender ambiguity, and obscure the distinct gender roles inherent in the classical ballet tradition, the blurring of which Théophile Gautier so deplored for its emasculation of the male dancer in anything other than action/pantomime parts.[17] Malcolm Bowie observes 'the exploitation of art for other than artistic ends' in *À la recherche*, and this graceful, knowing dancer with his self-mocking gestures and mysterious smile is touting his talents in both the artistic and the sexual domains.[18] What we find here is the subversion not only of gender roles, but of the hegemonic patriarchal gaze towards which the female classical ballerina directs her performance. It is to Rachel that the dancer presents and flaunts himself, and when her ocular consumption of his gestures becomes verbal suggestions of less symbolic uses of those same movements, the gender and sexual ambiguity of the scene is further complicated by her appeal to his very femininity. He is male; his movements are decidedly not, for Rachel; he is more womanly than she is, which is precisely why she likes him. Dance is the means by which traditional constructs of masculinity are challenged through the body of this Nijinsky-inspired dancer; the androgynous Nijinsky was himself homosexual and the iconography surrounding the hugely successful Ballets Russes is firmly rooted in the history of an emerging gay culture in the early twentieth century.

The popular theatre so beloved of Belle Époque audiences is the principal analogy found and evoked at the 'Bal de têtes' in *Le Temps retrouvé* where Marcel is unsettled by his aged upper-class friends. This experience of the effects of time threatens his newly minted creative ambitions: the alterations in his friends' appearance and their difficulty moving suggest by turns a fancy-dress ball or theatrical entertainment; a puppet show, more dispiritingly; and a theatrical pageant (6: 287–93; IV, 500–4). The variety of theatrical styles underlines the grotesquerie of the dreadful change he witnesses, and in the midst of it, an old dancer friend, remembered as a 'marvellous waltzer', a 'feather-light fair girl', now a 'ventripotent old campaigner' (6: 311; IV, 519), figures the truly sobering significance of Time's power. She who once circled blithely through space and time now lumbers across the floor. Her forces are all but spent – a chilling portent for Marcel himself.

Theatre and dance as exploited in *À la recherche* reflect the dynamism, diversity and exhilarating modernity of these creative forms in Belle Époque

Paris. Proust links them securely to his over-arching themes of homosexuality and the ephemeral individual experience of time, whilst honouring the genius of the hard-working individual dramatic artists and artists in movement who so inspired him in his efforts to fix words on the page.

Notes

1 Michèle M. Magill notes that in all 25,000 lines of Proust's novel, 'scarcely a dozen relate to dance', in 'Pas de pas de deux pour Proust: l'absence de la danse dans *À la recherche du temps perdu*', *Dalhousie French Studies*, 53 (2000), 49–55 (49). This and all subsequent translations from the French are the editor's.

2 Cynthia Gamble, 'From *Belle Epoque* to First World War: The Social Panorama', in Richard Bales, ed., *The Cambridge Companion to Proust* (Cambridge University Press, 2001), pp. 7–24 (13).

3 F. W. J. Hemmings, *The Theatre Industry in Nineteenth-Century France* (Cambridge University Press, 2006), p. 4.

4 Jane Pritchard, ed., *Diaghilev and the Golden Age of the Ballets Russes 1909–1929* (London: V&A Publishing, 2010), pp. 222–9.

5 Louis Énault, 'Les Jardins', in Alexandre Dumas, Théophile Gautier, Arsène Houssaye, Paul de Musset, Louis Énault and Du Faye, eds., *Paris et les Parisiens au XIXe siècle: mœurs, arts et monuments* (Paris: Morizot, 1856), pp. 284–309 (303).

6 Dance classes are mentioned during Marcel's infatuation with Gilberte Swann (2: 114 and 181; 1, 516 and 572) and at Balbec where the *jeunes filles* and the Jewish girls attend classes at the Casino (2: 368, 425, 535, 547; 11, 98, 145, 237, 247).

7 See Peggy Schaller, 'Theatre in Proust – the Fourth Art', in *Proust et le théâtre, Marcel Proust aujourd'hui*, 4 (2006), 51–70 (57).

8 Jean-Yves Tadié, *Marcel Proust: A Life*, trans. by Euan Cameron (London: Penguin Books, 2001), pp. 542–3.

9 Julie Townsend, *The Choreography of Modernism in France: La Danseuse, 1830–1930* (Oxford: Legenda, 2008), pp. 10–20. Townsend focuses exclusively on the female dancer, but the latter point seems relevant to the male dancer also.

10 Judith Lynn Hanna, *Dance, Sex and Gender: Signs of Identity, Dominance, Defiance, and Desire* (Chicago and London: University of Chicago Press, 1988), pp. 13–16.

11 Gilles Deleuze, *Proust et les signes* (Paris: Presses universitaires de France, 1964).

12 Guillemette Bolens, *Le Style des gestes: corporéité et kinésie dans le récit littéraire* (Lausanne: Éditions BHMS, 2008), p. 29.

13 Dee Reynolds, *Rhythmic Subjects: Uses of Energy in the Dances of Mary Wigman, Martha Graham and Merce Cunningham* (Plymouth: Dance Books, 2007), pp. 2–3.

14 Jane C. Desmond, 'Embodying Difference: Issues in Dance and Cultural Studies', in *Meaning in Motion: New Cultural Studies of Dance* (Durham, NC, and London: Duke University Press, 1997), p. 32.
15 Judith Butler, *Gender Trouble* (London and New York: Routledge Classics, 2006), pp. 185–8.
16 See Laget's editorial note to the Pléiade edition (11, 1609).
17 Ann Daly, 'Classical Ballet: A Discourse of Difference', in Desmond, ed., *Meaning in Motion*, pp. 111–20 (113).
18 Malcolm Bowie, *Proust among the Stars* (London: HarperCollins, 1998), p. 73.

PART II

Historical and cultural contexts

ii. Self and society

CHAPTER 14

Freud and psychoanalysis

Céline Surprenant

The question as to whether Marcel Proust (1871–1922) read or at least knew about Sigmund Freud (1856–1939) is invariably raised whenever it is a matter of situating Proust in relation to psychoanalysis. This is so even though Proust himself had provided a categorical answer that could have sufficed to put an end to any further enquiry. Responding to Roger Allard's review of *Sodom and Gomorrah* in 1921, in which the critic had made a rapprochement between aspects of the novel and Freud's theory of the dream held by what Allard called the 'Freudian' school of thought, which saw the dream as 'an effort on the part of the physical being for fulfilling an unavowable desire', Proust had hastened to state that if he had not understood 'the sentence on Freud', it was because 'he had not read his books' (*Corr*, xx, 447).

The question, then, as to what unites Freud and Proust with respect to their modernity is not new.[1] Allard's review, or René Rousseau's 1922 article entitled 'Marcel Proust et l'esthétique de l'inconscient' ['Marcel Proust and the Aesthetics of the Unconscious'] are some of the earliest rapprochements, before Jacques Rivière delivered a series of lectures in 1924 under the heading of 'Marcel Proust. L'Inconscient dans son œuvre', later published in the *Nouvelle Revue française*, which were important for disseminating both Proust's work and Freud's ideas during the 1920s.[2] These articles follow soon after the first translations of Freud's work into French, and it is useful to recall a few dates. It was only in 1907 that the Swiss psychiatrist Alphonse Maeder published didactic articles on Freud's theories.[3] It was also in 1907 that Proust published his most 'psychoanalytical' article, 'Sentiments filiaux d'un parricide' ['Filial Sentiments of a Parricide'], based on Henri Van Blarenberghe's killing of his mother, which ends, 'like one of Freud's essays'.[4] In 1913, Emmanuel Régis and Angelo Hesnard published a landmark article on 'La doctrine de Freud et de son école' in *L'Encéphale*, the same year that *Swann's Way* appeared. For these authors, 'Freud's system' was said apparently to consist in 'one of the

107

most important scientific movements of the current psychological epoch'. The authors had reservations towards it, because it was after all a 'medico-philosophical system'.[5] They nevertheless conceded that it provided an interesting 'affective psychology, a sort of mechanics of the mind', which anticipates how we now characterize Proust's endeavour in *À la recherche*.[6] It was also in 1913 that the first one of Freud's articles, entitled 'L'intérêt de la psychanalyse' ['The Claims of Psycho-Analysis to Scientific Interest' (1913)], was first translated into French and printed in the Italian journal *Scientia* (*The Interpretation of Dreams* was first translated into French only in 1926).[7]

Between these early articles and Jean-Yves Tadié's recent study, only a few monographs have dealt specifically with the two authors.[8] The pairing of any literary author and psychoanalysis calls to mind 'applied psycho-analysis', which has been deemed to be a reductive methodology, whether the analytic framework should be applied to the author, characters or plots. It is, however, particularly awkward to speak of 'applied psychoanalysis' in relation to *À la recherche*. Since the publication of *Contre Sainte-Beuve* in 1954, we know that the novel grew out of what began as an essay seeking to critique 'the Method of Sainte-Beuve', which consists in

> not separating the man from the work … to surround oneself with all the possible facts about a writer, to collate his correspondence, to question the people who knew him, talking with them if they are still alive, reading what they may have written about him if they are dead. (*ASB*, 12; *CSB*, 221)

Before understanding his error, the young hero in *À la recherche* entertains that kind of curiosity towards the writer that he admires, just as Odette asks Swann the wrong kind of questions about Vermeer, because life and writing are not easily separable (1: 96; 1, 237). However, the method is wrong because, as Proust has it in the Sainte-Beuve essay, 'a book is the product of a self other than that which we display in our habits, in company, in our vices' (*ASB*, 12; *CSB*, 221). In *Contre Sainte-Beuve*, then, Proust seemed to have invited a psychoanalytic reading of sorts, by designating 'un autre moi' ['another self'], perhaps even an unconscious self, as the source of creative works, while situating access to that other self elsewhere than in the author's biography.

The novel, moreover, does not offer a unified theory of memory, or the unconscious, sexuality, love and hate, perversion, mourning and so on, themes that have been deemed 'Freudian' in the novel, and which Freud dealt with throughout his writings. For both Proust's Narrator and Freud, I am moved by unconscious motivations that undermine, in puzzling, and sometimes painful, ways my sense of being a unified self. Proust proposed fictional explanations of them, which did not have to have a therapeutic value, while Freud found truths about the unconscious in fiction. *À la recherche* tells the story of someone who delights in making theories about unconscious motivations, from a stock of literary, cultural and scientific sources, that are not, however, external to the narrative as though they could explain it. The Narrator's theories on the mechanisms of involuntary memory, habits and dreams, are not any more helpful for interpreting the Narrator's or characters' motivations than are the theories of art contained in the novel for interpreting *À la recherche*.[9]

Proust could well have read if not Freud's writings, at least articles about psychoanalysis. He could also have heard about 'Freud's system' during evening receptions.[10] Given that *À la recherche* draws its scientific, cultural and literary references from the end of the nineteenth century, and re-stages them anachronistically in a twentieth-century novel, as Antoine Compagnon has convincingly argued, Proust's psychological discourse is closer to Freud's pre- and early psychoanalytic writings than to his later work.[11] The genesis of Proust's novel is co-extensive not only with the elaboration, but also with the dissemination and contestation of psychoanalytic ideas in the early decades of the twentieth century. Freud's theories emerge out of late nineteenth-century Romantic and positivist science, and for both Proust and Freud, it is those joint sources that have been most obscured.[12]

We find nineteenth-century medical and psychiatric themes in *À la recherche*: the Narrator-hero suffers from a 'maladie de la volonté' ['ailment of the will'], or even from neurasthenia. One of the novel's medical doctors, Cottard, a member of the Verdurin 'clan', is said to bear some of Adrien Proust's characteristics. These themes have raised exegetical questions. Proust's readers have been puzzled by the apparently genuine psychological contents of the novel, and its genesis during the period of emergence of nineteenth-century experimental psychology, and, we could add, that of psychoanalysis.[13]

Adrien Proust (1834–1903), the author of a *Traité d'hygiène* [*Treatise on Hygiene*, 1877], and, in collaboration with Gilbert Ballet, of *L'Hygiène du neurasthénique* [*Hygiene of the Neurasthenic*, 1897], among other works, shared psychiatric knowledge with Freud, who, from October 1885 until March 1886, studied neuropathology in Jean-Martin Charcot's laboratory at La Salpêtrière in Paris. In 1866, Adrien Proust had successfully passed the *concours d'agrégation* in medical studies, partly under Charcot's supervision. Reading his father's works, we could imagine Marcel Proust enquiring about the strangeness of the unconscious mental life revealed by hypnosis.

It was to a large extent from Charcot's separation of neuroanatomy and psychology that Freud refined the idea that mental pathology can be explained in relation to unconscious mechanisms, and that what is true for neurotics (including hysteria), is true for the human psyche in general. It was in this context that he developed his paper 'Some Points for a Comparative Study of Organic and Hysterical Motor Paralysis', one of four articles on hysteria and obsessional neuroses published in French during the 1890s.[14]

Freud was indebted to German-inspired theories of association and the physiological orientation of nineteenth-century experimental psychology. An association takes place between ideas and their 'quota of affect' or 'affective value', and 'the arm will be paralysed in proportion to the persistence of this quota of affect or to its diminution by appropriate psychical means' (*SE* 1: 171). The affective value of the repressed idea increases as time passes, and what is at stake is soon the *memory* of an impression or of an idea, manifesting itself through the body (*SE* 1: 172). Such blocked-off childhood memories most often touched on sexuality, whose development, Freud argued, began in infancy and was then forgotten, after a period of latency. Certain ideas could thus be repressed, and continue to produce effects and disturbingly return in various forms (dreams, slips of the tongue, errors and neurotic symptoms), which means that repression is an essentially dynamic process.[15]

Proust's Narrator seems to have experienced the affective process that Freud was describing. The opening passage on the bodily memory anticipates that displayed in 'The Intermittencies of the Heart' in *Sodom and Gomorrah*, where the Narrator leaning to untie his boots, realizes belatedly his grandmother's absence at the level of his body (4: 179–81; III, 153–4). The emphasis is placed upon the Narrator's affective relation with the space whose image and size return in half-sleeping states, thanks to the body's capacity to store past impressions, the ribs', the knees', the shoulders' memory acting as markers of past inhabited spaces and circumstances (1: 4–5; 1, 6). The return of the *impression* is contingent. In all other instances but during the second stay in Balbec, the return of the past brings about a 'félicité'; in *Le Temps retrouvé* the puzzlement about the experience of memory involved in the unequal paving stone or the noise of the spoon brings about an 'énigme du bonheur' (6: 217; IV, 445–46).

By contrast, Freud aimed to provoke the return of the repressed so as to undo the repression of affectively charged ideas and situations. The cure at first involved hypnosis, then the use of pressure of the hands on the forehead to incite patients to remember. It soon became a 'talking cure', in which patients said everything that came into their head, to let unconscious material emerge, and lift resistances against its return. As in Proust's novel, psychical work has something physical about it: 'the bringing back of ... lost memories is opposed by a certain resistance which has to be counterbalanced by work proportionate to its magnitude' (*SE* 3: 296). Eventually, the cure rested on transference, that is, on the affective relation between the patient and the analyst thanks to which it was possible to understand earlier relations by remembering them. The return of the past in both authors partly converges around contingency, except that in Freud, there is conflict. Something opposes the return of the past, but a chance association may lead me to it.

For René Rousseau, Proust could be compared to a clock-maker who would prefer to worry about the 'cogs, the weights and the pendulum' rather than about the conventional meaning of time that the clock registers.[16] Proust, moreover, had adopted 'a genre that presented the character of the unconscious', by weaving together writing, sleeping and dreaming.[17] However, the material on dreams in *À la recherche* is not mostly Freudian. The dream is there not quite a disguise of repressed desires, even though it consists in a 'particular *form* of thinking, made possible by the conditions of the state of sleep', whose characteristics seem to be based on Freud's treatise.[18] Proust and Freud shared a body of knowledge and practices on dreams with the nineteenth-century *savants rêveurs*, such as, for example, Alfred Maury (1817–92), the author of *Le Sommeil et les rêves* (1861).[19] The debate touched on the measure of mental acts, in which Proustian introspection also consists;[20] among other topics, these authors wondered whether thought could accelerate excessively in dreams, as Maury claimed to have experienced in his 'guillotine dream', which condensed a whole epoch – the Terror – within a span of a few seconds. Swann's dream in *Swann's Way* reproduces features of that landmark dream (1: 456–9; 1, 373–4), which also serves as a point of reference for illustrating narrative speed: a novelist can make a character grow old in one page, and indeed across the duration of a novel (cf. the Narrator's comments about the 'prodigious speed' of dreams (6: 274, trans. mod.; IV, 490–1)).

Nevertheless, Swann's dream calls upon displacement, one of the dream's four mechanisms according to Freud, thanks to which charged ideas are placed on unimportant supports, and through which repressed desires make themselves known.[21] That process is at work not solely in the novel's fictional dreams. In *Swann's Way*, for example, our attention is drawn to the detail of a flower, while what is going on is the disturbing nature of sexuality, a procedure that is taken up again through Darwin's mediation in *Sodome et Gomorrah* (4: 1–9; III, 3–9).[22]

Freud and Proust were united in their passion for explaining. That passion is most at play in Freud around the idea of memory-traces, that is, the system of imprints of which the psyche is made, and which he touched on, among other places, in 'The Project for a Scientific Psychology' (1895), and took up again in *Moses and Monotheism: Three Essays* (1939), when imagining the transmission of psychical traces in the Jewish people's immemorial past.[23] In one discussion on forgetting and sleep, Proust's Narrator points to an immemorial and forgotten past from which he deduces the possibility of life in another body or on another planet (4: 443–4; III, 374). Freud and Proust here followed parallel paths; however, it is perhaps in this instance that the convergence is the most compelling.

We asked at the beginning whether Proust had read Freud, but had Freud read Proust? In 1926, Freud confessed to Marie Bonaparte that he had not enjoyed *Swann's Way* very much because of the 'style': 'Proust doesn't finish his sentences, and would seem to cultivate a taste for depths.'[24] Did Freud not enjoy the so-called 'Freudian' themes in the volume? Oddly, Freud reproached Proust for having a 'taste for depths', whereas both authors undeniably shared a suspicion towards depth. The unconscious was not a matter of inaccessible depths, but of consciousness. Successful repression leaves nothing to be seen, said and analysed. From that angle, the theory of the unconscious may illuminate the founding paradox of *À la recherche*, concerning 'les vérités de l'intelligence' ['the truths of the intelligence'] which are 'inferior' to that of the 'instinct', but which are alone able to establish that inferiority (*ASB*, 8; *CSB*, 216). This is not because we can propose a psychoanalytic reading of the novel. Rather, by bringing Freud and Proust together, we might experience that the intellect's other, whether it be the unconscious or involuntary memory, and whatever theoretical, fictional or theoretico-fictional route it may make us take, still has something very intellectual about it.

Notes

1 See for example, N. Deschamps, 'Critique psychanalytique', in A. Bouillaguet and B. G. Rogers, eds., *Dictionnaire Marcel Proust* (Paris: Champion, 2004), pp. 268–71 (268).
2 Concerning Freud, see A. de Mijolla, 'Freud connu en France 1920–1925', in *Freud et la France 1885–1945* (Paris: Presses universitaires de France, 2010), pp. 191–331. See also Jacques Robertfrance, 'Freud ou l'opportuniste' (1924) in L. Hodson, ed., *Marcel Proust: The Critical Heritage* (London: Routledge, 1989), pp. 284–5.

3 See Mijolla, 'Freud connu en France', pp. 90–1.
4 Antoine Compagnon, *Proust entre deux siècles* (Paris: Éditions du Seuil, 1989), pp. 163–4. See also Jean-Yves Tadié, *Le Lac inconnu: entre Proust et Freud* (Paris: Gallimard, 2012), p. 76.
5 Mijolla, 'Freud connu en France', p. 143.
6 See K. Haustein, 'Proust's Emotional Cavities: Vision and Affect in *À la recherche du temps perdu*', *French Studies*, 63 (2009), 161–73, for a reading that emphasizes affectivity in Proust, albeit in relation to the romantic idea of emotion rather than the Freudian theory of affect, to which the psychoanalyst André Green had called attention in *Le Discours vivant* (Paris: Presses universitaires de France, 1973).
7 Mijolla, 'Freud connu en France', p. 146.
8 See Deschamps, 'Critique psychanalytique', for a survey of publications on the topic, including Malcolm Bowie's groundbreaking study, *Freud, Proust and Lacan: Theory as Fiction* (Cambridge University Press, 1987).
9 For the status of theories in *À la recherche*, see, among others, V. Descombes, *Proust: philosophie du roman* (Paris: Éditions de minuit, 1987).
10 *Journal de l'abbé Mugnier* quoted in Mijolla, 'Freud connu en France', p. 172.
11 Compagnon, *Proust entre deux siècles*, p. 26.
12 J.-M. Quaranta, 'Génétique et intertextualité', in *Marcel Proust* 4 (2004), 53–74 (56), on the occultation of the positivist dimension of Proustian aesthetics.
13 See, for example, Joshua Landy, 'Proust among the Psychologists', on Edward Bizub's *Proust et le moi divisé: 'La Recherche', creuset de la psychologie expérimentale (1874–1914)* (Geneva: Droz, 2006), in *Philosophy and Literature*, 35 (2011), 375–87.
14 *The Standard Edition of the Complete Psychological Works of Sigmund Freud*, vols. I–XXIV, ed. James Strachey, Anna Freud, Alix Strachey and Alan Tyson (London: Hogarth Press and the Institute of Psychoanalysis, 1953–1974), vol. III. Henceforth abbreviated as *SE*, followed by the volume and page number in the text. The term 'psycho-analyse' is used for the first time in French in 'Heredity and the Aetiology of Neurosis' (1896), *SE* 3: 141–56.
15 See Jean-Louis Baudry, *Freud, Proust et l'autre* (Paris: Éditions de minuit, 1984), for an analysis of the Freud and Wilhelm Fließ correspondence, which began when Freud started his 'auto-analysis' around 1897. See also in this regard J. M. Masson, ed. and trans., *The Complete Letters to Wilhelm Fließ (1887–1904)* (Cambridge, MA: Harvard University Press, 1985).
16 'Marcel Proust et l'esthétique de l'inconscient', in *Le Mercure de France*, 15 January 1922, 361–85 (365).
17 Rousseau, 'Marcel Proust', p. 369.
18 'The Interpretation of Dreams', *SE* 5: 506.
19 See J. Carroy, *Nuits savantes: une histoire des rêves (1800–1945)* (Paris: Éditions EHESS, 2012), pp. 79–112.
20 For Bowie, introspection in *À la recherche* consists in: 'comprendre, calculer, mesurer, constater, induire' (*Freud, Proust and Lacan*, p. 56).

21 'The Interpretation of Dreams', *SE* 4: pp. 305–9.
22 Dominique Fernandez broaches this topic in *L'Arbre jusqu'aux racines: psychanalyse et création* (Paris: Grasset, 1992), pp. 328–9.
23 *SE* 1: 283–397; *SE* 23.
24 É. Roudinesco, 'Freud et Proust: un parallèle impressionniste', www.cifpr.fr/+Freud-et-Proust-parallele+, 12 juin 2012.

CHAPTER 15

Sexuality

Elisabeth Ladenson

Proust would doubtless have been somewhat horrified by his current status as an icon of gay modernism. *À la recherche du temps perdu* was the first major literary work in France to take on the issue of same-sex sexual relations directly and in an apparently objective manner. Its semi-autobiographical Narrator is heterosexual, just as he is non-Jewish, and his intense interest in both homosexuality and Jewishness (which he often treats as related and analogous phenomena) is presented as the product of an anthropological curiosity strictly devoid of any personal stake in these subjects. The representation of sexuality in the novel was, accordingly, greeted by critics as a courageously unflinching and objective treatment of a problematic subject, while in the later volumes, in which homosexuality takes on increasingly greater importance, the emphasis on alternative sexualities was often viewed as compromising the work's appeal to 'universal' experience. Proust was at once intensely interested in depicting same-sex relations and, given the opprobrium attached to the subject at the time, unwilling to identify himself – or his ambiguously autobiographical Narrator – as homosexual.

Sexuality is present from the opening pages of *Swann's Way*, in the form of a wet dream, with the mention of a woman born 'from an awkward position of my thigh' while the protagonist is asleep (1: 3, trans. mod.; 1, 5). Later on in 'Combray' masturbation is mentioned in passing, as one of the activities in which the hero indulges in the privacy of an orris-scented water-closet lockable from the inside. The protagonist's sexuality – and Proustian sexuality in general – is largely masturbatory, and the importance of masturbation for the novel's conception may be gauged by an early version of the opening section, in which the phrase 'à la recherche de' makes its inaugural appearance in the form of a reference to 'cette exploration que je fis alors en moi-même, à la recherche d'un plaisir inconnu' ['that exploration into myself that I undertook at that time, in search of an unknown pleasure']. The suppression of this overt emphasis on solitary pleasure may have been the result not only of an effort to make the opening pages of the novel more generally acceptable, but also of the fact that masturbation was during the early years of the twentieth century still to some extent viewed as a highly pernicious activity, potentially leading to neurasthenia as well as host of other nervous ailments.[1] Proust's correspondence includes a letter he wrote as an adolescent to his grandfather asking for money to visit a brothel, as his father is trying to cure him of his penchant for masturbation and a first visit failed to yield the desired results (*Corr*, XXI, 550–1). Sexuality in the *Recherche* is nonetheless strongly marked by both masturbatory solipsism and a related pessimistic anxiety over the inability to 'know', carnally or otherwise, another person. The protagonist's sexual relations with women are depicted as non-penetrative and tend to follow the model of the wet dream in the novel's opening pages; notable examples of this are his orgasm while play-wrestling with the apparently complicit Gilberte on the Champs-Élysées in *Swann's Way*, and, much later, his frottage-style lovemaking with (or rather on) Albertine while she is asleep in *The Captive*.

Although there is no indication that Swann's sexual practices tend similarly to the non-penetrative, his first sexual encounter with Odette inaugurates a key theme in the novel's depiction of sexual relations, as he looks forward to 'the act of physical possession (in which, paradoxically, one possesses nothing)' (1: 281; I, 230). 'Possession' had long served as the standard acceptable term for penetrative heterosexual intercourse. Swann's insight that the notion of physical 'possession' is in the end nothing more than an inaccurate euphemism resonates throughout the novel, as first he and then the protagonist, as well as various secondary characters, are repeatedly confronted with the basic Proustian truth that it is impossible fully to 'possess' or know another person, and least of all the object of one's most ardent desire. This idea is explored through the hero's vain attempts to 'possess' Gilberte and then Albertine, and also with reference to the theme of prostitution. Both Swann and Saint-Loup fall in love with women who are essentially whores, which is to say women who are in theory available to be 'possessed' in exchange for money. Odette was 'sold' by her mother at an early age; when Swann first encounters her she has managed to reach the upper echelons of a prostitutional gamut ranging from common streetwalker to prosperous courtesan. She is a *demimondaine*, a 'kept woman' whose livelihood depends on the financial support of a series of wealthy men who may or may not be married (generally to women of their own class). Saint-Loup's girlfriend, Rachel, is an actress, a profession often linked to and concomitant with a career as a prostitute during this period. We first encounter her in the novel when the hero is offered her services in a brothel, long before he meets her again with Saint-Loup. In both these cases, what is evident is that prostitution is in the eye of the beholder; women who would seem to be available to all comers with enough money become literally priceless when they are the object of a desire to 'possess' them fully, rather than merely in the conventional sense. Price rises according to demand, and ultimate demand – the desire to possess in some 'real' sense – depends on the idea that price is no object, that is, on the illusion that the desired object is not in fact in it for the money. Desire, in Proust's world, both arises from and creates inaccessibility. Swann falls in love with Odette when she is not available to him, and once Odette realizes that Swann loves her, she knows that his desire will only increase the more she withholds herself. Charlie Morel offers a homosexual variant of this same theme in the later volumes when the baron de Charlus becomes obsessed with him. Swann, of course, marries Odette, but this form of 'possession' only occurs once he no longer desires her for herself (but rather for their daughter, Gilberte).

Proust's depiction of prostitution in its various guises owes much to nineteenth-century French literature as well as to the prominence of courtesans during the period in question. Writers such as Balzac, Flaubert, Zola and Maupassant had emphasized the full range of prostitutional activities throughout the nineteenth century. In Balzac's *La Vieille Fille* (1836), a laundress named Suzanne leaves Alençon for Paris, where she eventually reappears (in this and later volumes of *La Comédie humaine*) as the courtesan Suzanne de Val-Noble. Rachel owes much to the mythology of the beautiful Jewish prostitute as seen in works such as Balzac's *Illusions perdues* (1837–43). Odette de Crécy's story is not much different, at least in its beginnings, from that of a variety of these characters, many of whom (e.g. Balzac's Coralie, Flaubert's Rosanette in *L'Éducation sentimentale*, and Zola's Nana) recount similar narratives of having been sold off by their mothers at an early age to an older man in the provinces and then making their enterprising way to Paris. While Odette appears to have been based largely on Laure Hayman, a courtesan whom Proust knew in his youth (she seems to have been the mistress of both his great-uncle and father), her trajectory also recalls those of late nineteenth-century and Belle Époque courtesans such as Émilienne d'Alençon, Valtesse de la Bigne (whose bed inspired that of Nana in Zola's novel), and Liane de Pougy. Unlike those of all the above, however, Odette de Crécy's aristocratic name, which appears to be assumed, turns out, ironically enough, to be genuine, the product of an early brief marriage.

In terms of sexuality, though, Proust's work is best known for its groundbreaking representation of same-sex relations. In a letter to Louis d'Albuféra in 1908, Proust wrote about his projects – most of which ended up being included in his magnum opus – among which he lists 'an essay on pederasty (not easy to place)' (*Corr*, VIII, 113). What we call homosexuality was an object of much fascination at the time and, as Proust knew, a difficult subject to write about. The vocabulary of same-sex relations was in great flux during this era. In a notebook entry, Proust can be seen grappling with the question of how to name men whose sexual preference was other men. He observes that the word which best suited his purposes, the slang term *tante* ('auntie'), was unavailable to him, because he was not Balzac and could therefore not allow himself the use of this evocative 'word that wears a skirt' (Esquisse IV; III, 955). The word he settled on, *inverti*, 'invert', was borrowed from the vocabulary of late nineteenth-century sexology, as was *homosexuel* and other terms used during this period (e.g. *unisexuel*). Proust preferred 'invert' to 'homosexual' both because of the latter word's hybrid Greek-Latin provenance and, notably, because his conception of the phenomenon in question is predicated not on the idea of same-sex attraction per se but rather on the *anima muliebris in corpore virili inclusa* (the soul of a woman trapped in the body of a man) model first theorized in *Memnon*, the 1868 manifesto of the German sexologist Karl Heinrich Ulrichs.[2] According to Ulrichs and similar subsequent accounts, the *Urning* (in German) or *Uranien* (in French) – thus termed in homage to Pausanias's speech in Plato's *Symposium* positing love between men as the highest form of love, inspired not by Aphrodite Pandemos ('vulgar') but by Aphrodite Ourania ('celestial') – is attracted to other men because he himself is in some innate way feminine. (Here the borrowing from Plato stops, as the men animated by Aphrodite Ourania in the *Symposium* are in no way depicted as feminine.) Proust prefers the term *inversion* because the same-sex attraction displayed by the male characters in the *Recherche* is in fact essentially heterosexual, since they only desire men to the extent to which they are themselves in some inherent way feminine (the Narrator at one point refers to 'what is sometimes, most ineptly, termed homosexuality' (4: 8; III, 9)).

The novel's 'Gomorrheans', the female counterparts to his Sodomites, alone escape the inversion model, displaying something like a true 'homosexuality' in the sense that they seem to desire their like rather than their opposite. This would seem to be the product of narrative expedience more than any attempt to theorize sexual asymmetry. Since almost all the lesbian characters are also objects of male desire and (therefore) jealousy, they could not be truly masculine; at most they are attractively boyish (Mlle Vinteuil is something of an exception, a holdover from Proust's early stories, in which lesbianism did duty for male homosexuality).[3] It was not, in any case, Proust's portrayal of lesbianism (another word he eschewed) that garnered the most attention when the volumes were first published, but his account of Sodom. French literature was replete with depictions of female homosexuality, from the lesbian mother superior who tries to seduce the heroine of Diderot's *La Religieuse* (first published in 1796, although written some decades earlier), through Balzac's *La Fille aux yeux d'or*, Gautier's *Mademoiselle de Maupin* (both 1835), Baudelaire's *Fleurs du mal* (1857, originally to be entitled *Les Lesbiennes*), Zola's *Nana* (1880), and Colette's *Claudine* series (notably *Claudine à l'école* (1900) and *Claudine en ménage* (1904)), to name but a few. Male homosexuality, however, had been treated overtly only by Balzac, in his Vautrin cycle, especially *Illusions perdues* (1836–43) and *Splendeurs et misères des courtisanes* (1838–47). When Proust writes that he would like to use the word *tante* to depict his Sodomites, but, 'not being Balzac', he will have to make do with *inverti*, he is referring to Balzac's discussion of homosexual prison slang in *Splendeurs et misères*. He does not explain what he means by this exactly, and at first glance it might seem to indicate simply that he has neither the fame nor the reputation for heterosexuality of his illustrious predecessor, and therefore cannot afford to write about such matters in an overly familiar way with impunity. Beyond this, though, it is also relevant that in the 1830s, before same-sex relations had been theorized, Balzac was free to portray Lucien's ardent friendship with David in the opening passages of *Illusions perdues* as explicitly analogous to heterosexual love, without any suggestion of a sexual relationship between the two, even though the beautiful Lucien will fall under the spell of the diabolical Vautrin at the end of that novel, and become his *mignon* in its sequel (*Splendeurs*). The development of sexological theories of same-sex relations in the late nineteenth and early twentieth centuries, along with the burgeoning discourse of psychoanalysis, had rendered the depiction of intimate male friendship problematic, which doubtless goes a long way towards explaining the Narrator's austere denunciations of friendship in *À l'ombre des jeunes filles*, when the protagonist is befriended by the beautiful aristocrat Robert de Saint-Loup (who also, much later, turns out to be an invert).

Homosexuality was a fraught subject when Proust was beginning to write his magnum opus, making this aspect of his project both more urgent and more problematic. Not only had sexologists been delineating new scientifically framed conceptions of what had previously been depicted as, alternatively, a crime or a sin, a number of scandals had brought the topic to the fore. The trials of Oscar Wilde in England in the mid 1890s had made homosexuality a much-discussed subject; convicted of 'gross indecency', Wilde had died in 1900 in Paris after serving two years' hard labour. More recently still, the Eulenburg Affair in Germany, in which members of Kaiser Wilhelm's entourage were accused of homosexual activities in a series of well-publicized trials, again brought same-sex relations to the forefront of current events in Europe in 1907–9. As a result, when Proust was beginning his vast novel, homosexuality was at once highly visible and highly controversial. While the subject had been featured in various ways in fiction ranging from Georges Eekhoud's *Escal-Vigor* (1899, the object of an obscenity trial in Belgium) to Binet-Valmer's *Lucien* (1910) and Francis Carco's *Jésus-la-caille* (1914), Proust's novel was regarded as the first objective treatment of same-sex relations in a serious literary work. The Wilde affair is referred to in the *Recherche*, via Charlus, who speaks of Wilde's remark that the death of Lucien de Rubempré in Balzac's *Splendeurs* was one of the great traumas of his life, adding that the man in question (whom he does not name) was to learn that life reserved greater sorrows for him.

Proust's depiction of 'inversion' was generally greeted as a courageous and even-handed treatment of a difficult subject. Not everyone, however, was happy with it, André Gide being a particularly virulent critic. Gide, who was open about his own 'pederasty', preferring the Greek term for relations between men and adolescent boys or young men, objected to Proust's portrayal of 'inversion', on the grounds that his depiction emphasized what Gide felt to be the worst aspects of same-sex love, notably the idea that homosexual men are necessarily feminine. Gide's own ideas, drawing on 'Greek love', rigorously eschewed femininity, and indeed seem to have been based in a profound misogyny. He delineated his approach in *Corydon*, a Platonic dialogue between a pederast and a heterosexual, which includes an explicit refutation of Proust's account of inversion. Although Gide had written earlier versions which he circulated among his circle of friends, he did not publish it until 1924, two years after *Sodome et Gomorrhe* appeared, and after Proust's death.

Proust's often-quoted assertion about the depiction of homosexuality that 'you can tell anything, but on condition that you never say: "I"' comes from an entry in Gide's *Journal* from 1922.[4] Having recorded this observation from a conversation between the two, Gide adds: 'ce qui ne fait pas mon affaire' ['but that won't suit me']. This reported moment is remarkable for several reasons: first, that one of Proust's most famous pronouncements on the subject comes not from anything he himself wrote but rather from the diary of someone with whom he entertained lengthily charged and problematic relations (Gide had initially rejected *Swann* for the Nouvelle Revue française, before realizing the error and convincing Proust to allow the *NRF* to bring out the entire work; he was also, while appalled by Proust's account of homosexuality, reluctant to publish his own treatments of the subject until after publication of *Sodome et Gomorrhe*, following which he expressed great frustration at not having been first). Perhaps most notably, though, the observation that Gide records emphasizes an important aspect of Proust's depiction of homosexuality that has been relatively little remarked upon. The idea that one may say anything on condition of not saying 'I' is in fact explored in the pages of the novel itself, in the form of Charlus's manifestly erroneous conviction that he can talk about inversion with impunity as long as he does so in the third person. He thus becomes the laughing-stock of the Verdurin clan, who encourage him to deliver expansive lectures on the subject without his ever realizing that his personal investment in it has not gone unperceived by his interlocutors. (This phenomenon is deftly analysed by Eve Kosofsky Sedgwick as 'the glass closet' in the chapter on Proust in *Epistemology of the Closet* (1990).) Proust's apparently naïve stance as reported by Gide has thus been pre-deconstructed, as it were, by the author himself in his work. Charlus is there to let us know Proust is aware that even the most rigorously 'objective' account of homosexuality cannot guarantee impunity.

Ironically enough, it was not *Sodome et Gomorrhe*, with its lengthy taxonomy of same-sex practices, that led the general audience to understand that Proust himself was implicated in his examination of homosexuality. This did not occur until after his death, when *La Prisonnière* was published, depicting the protagonist's sequestration of Albertine in his parents' apartment while they are away. Readers were bothered by the lack of verisimilitude in the story of a young bourgeois boy whose parents would have allowed him to keep a girl in their apartment. It was this violation of bourgeois mores, rather than the Narrator's ethnography of homosexuality in the earlier volume, that finally 'outed' Proust among the general public.

Notes

1 Onanophobia, or fear of masturbation as a highly dangerous and even deadly activity that could lead to a panoply of ills including syphilis, madness and death, was an idea that gained currency during the eighteenth century, continued throughout the nineteenth, and only began to wane in the twentieth

with the popularization of sexology and psychoanalysis. See Thomas Laqueur's *Solitary Sex: A Cultural History of Masturbation* (New York: Zone Books, 2003).

2 *'Memnon': Die Geschlechtsnatur des mannliebenden Urnings. Eine naturwissenschaftliche Darstellung.* Vol. 11 (Schleiz, 1868).

3 See Elisabeth Ladenson, *Proust's Lesbianism* (Ithaca, NY, and London: Cornell University Press, 1999) for a full discussion of this topic.

4 *The Journals of André Gide*, trans. and ed. by Justin O'Brien (New York: Knopf, 1947), vol. 1, p. 304; André Gide, *Journal 1889–1939* (Paris: Gallimard, 1951), vol. 1, p. 692. For an extensive discussion of this see Michael Lucey, *Never Say I: Sexuality and the First Person in Colette, Gide, and Proust* (Durham, NC: Duke University Press, 2006).

CHAPTER 16

Health and medicine

Michael R. Finn

Marcel Proust comes to literary maturity at a watershed moment in the evolution of late nineteenth- to early twentieth-century thinking about illness. On the one hand, he is the uneasy inheritor of nineteenth-century obsessions about hysteria and maladies of the nervous system. Many of his characters suffer from problems of the nerves, his asthmatic Narrator in the first instance, not to speak of Proust's friends such as the writers Daniel Halévy and Anna de Noailles. At another level, the fin de siècle is preoccupied with the idea of degeneration, both of the tainted individual and of society itself, and traces of this sense of downwardness persist in the final volumes of *À la recherche du temps perdu*. A more specific, personal problem posed itself for Proust as the century turned: in 1898, a prominent French psychiatrist was still writing that most doctors considered 'sexual inversion, the spontaneous sensual, sentimental or intellectual attraction to a person of the same sex, as a sign of degeneracy'.[1]

Increasingly, as Freud and Breuer published their first essays on hysteria, medicine was turning away from the physical and beginning to discover psychosomatic maladies. Proust reached his twenties in the heyday of a new psycho-medical condition called neurasthenia – a kind of latter-day chronic fatigue syndrome – the symptoms of which (episodic nervous exhaustion and a lack of willpower and decisiveness) began to be widely identified, particularly in men. During the same period, there was much discussion of willpower deficits, especially after the psychologist Théodule Ribot published *Les Maladies de la volonté* [*Ailments of the Will*] in 1883. In the wake of that essay, a rising star, the novelist and critic Paul Bourget, became a kind of prophet of the weak-will syndrome in literary personalities. According to Bourget, willpower deficit was not only a seminal idea in the novels of the Goncourt brothers, it was the underlying theme of Zola's *Rougon-Macquart* and at the heart of Alphonse Daudet's characters. The same malady, he wrote in a text that Proust would have read avidly, almost prevented Maxime Du Camp from electing the proper form for

123

his writing. Du Camp dabbled in every possible writing genre before realizing that the correct vehicle for his thought was history, the history of Paris.[2]

Charcot himself prefaced Fernand Villain's study on neurasthenia in 1891. Proust's father Adrien published *L'Hygiène du neurasthénique* in 1897, and the typical patient he describes – a cultured but unfocused member of the idle, privileged classes caught up in a physically debilitating, soul-destroying social whirl – seems to be personified in his social gadfly son, that slow-to-produce man of letters Marcel. A question ever present in Marcel Proust's mind from the mid 1890s until *À la recherche* was actually underway, was: how will my nervous condition affect or inhibit my writing?

Proust was conceived in 1870 during the siege of Paris by the Prussian armies and the pregnancy, in a time of high anxiety and privation, produced what was called at the time 'un enfant de siège', a delicate child whose Jewish mother Jeanne always had an especially close and protective relationship with her first-born.[3] Proust was an asthmatic, suffering his first serious attack in his tenth year. As a mature writer, he was known for the constant anti-dust fumigations of his bedroom, the cork sound-proofing of that bedroom and, as he worked increasingly at night and slept during the day, his use of a mixed regime of stimulants alternating with sleep-inducing narcotics. It is said he would drink strong coffee at any time of the day or night, and in 1902 he suffered his first bouts of heart palpitations and tachycardia.[4] The cause of his premature death at age fifty-one seems to have been pneumonia followed by a pulmonary abscess or embolism.

An absence of will

Portraits of Proust's early hero Jean Santeuil present an individual suffering from emotional crises that he is unable to control. A visiting doctor opines that the young fellow is 'a nervous child', and Jean's mother therefore attributes his weakness to an involuntary nervous state 'absolving him of all responsibility' (*JS*, 33; 210). At this, Jean feels immediate relief, but the long-term result is guilt at his own debility. Proust's fiction and non-fiction show him closely following the medical theme of willpower deficit right up to the time *Contre Sainte-Beuve* begins to become *À la recherche du temps perdu*. In his introduction to the translation of Ruskin's *Sesame and Lilies*, Proust discusses Coleridge's grand projects that came to naught because of a lack of decisiveness and, in making a glowing reference to the study of Théodule Ribot, *Les Maladies de la volonté*, which it is clear he has read, Proust seems to sketch the portrait of reluctant, indecisive individuals much like himself. Such persons resemble, by their laziness and attraction to frivolity, patients who are truly spiritually inert: 'They live on the surface in a perpetual forgetfulness of themselves, in a sort of passivity which makes them the plaything of every pleasure' (*ASB*, 212; *CSB*, 179).

One of the most revealing remarks made by Proust about willpower deficits shows his concern that such debility can in fact represent a medical deficiency of the creative psyche. He feels he can detect the problem in two of his favourite writers, Baudelaire and Nerval. That is, their practice of attempting to express the same idea in their poetry and their prose – similar lines in Baudelaire's *Fleurs du mal* and his *Petits poèmes en prose*, a phrase from Nerval's 'Sylvie' that almost replicates verse from his poem 'El Desdichado' – is a weakness that may well be part of an actual psychological condition: 'In such geniuses the inner vision is very sure, very strong. But, be it *a malady of the will* or the lack of a determinate instinct . . . they try in verse and then, so as not to waste the original idea, in prose, etc.' (my emphasis; *ASB*, 26; *CSB*, 234–5).

It is difficult to resist the conclusion that it is Proust's own wavering instinct and indecisiveness that lie behind these lines, for concurrently with his reflections on the works of Nerval and Baudelaire, one of his notebooks shows how anxious and undecided Proust is about the written form his ideas ought to take: 'La paresse ou le doute ou l'impuissance se réfugiant dans l'incertitude sur la forme d'art. Faut-il en faire un roman, une étude philosophique, suis-je romancier?'[5] ['Laziness or doubt or impotence taking refuge in uncertainty over artistic form. Should it be a novel, a philosophical study, am I a novelist?'] And indeed, the work that initially proceeded from this uncertainty, *Contre Sainte-Beuve*, was a bastard composition, largely a philosophico-literary essay, but also partly a novel.[6]

Doctors real and fictional

Proust grew up in a medical family and a medical milieu. The Proust apartment and dining table often hosted physicians or the diplomats who accompanied Dr Adrien Proust to the international conferences where he led the fight against infectious diseases, particularly cholera. He devoted the last twenty years of his life to the idea of creating 'cordons sanitaires' to hold back foreign contagions. The high point of his career in medicine was his nomination to a Chair of Hygiene at the Faculty of Medicine in Paris. Marcel's younger brother, Robert, following in his father's footsteps, became a well-known Parisian gynaecologist and surgeon.

The emerging medical specialization of hygiene also had a more down-to-earth meaning for Adrien Proust, not only principles of careful cleanliness and anti-infection, but also a set of fresh-air lifestyle guidelines: a healthy day was not complete without a shower, a bit of fencing or gymnastics, a bicycle outing. Adrien drove these principles home in his preface to the work of Dr Édouard Brissaud on asthma, *L'Hygiène des asthmatiques*, and in *L'Hygiène du neurasthénique*, which he co-authored with Dr Gilbert Ballet. Of course, Dr Proust had both a serious asthmatic and, as we have seen, a model for neurasthenia at home. But Marcel, the consummate self-protecting invalid, had no interest whatsoever in the bland recipes of medical hygiene.

The turn of the century and his reaching the age of thirty in 1901 did not bring the satisfactions of maturity for Marcel. Part of the problem was, no doubt, his frustration at feeling inextricably involved in derivative writing, translations of works by John Ruskin, critical articles and society columns, rather than something creative of his own. In 1904 he writes to Maurice Barrès, 'I still have two Ruskins to translate and after that I will try to give expression to my poor soul, if it hasn't expired in the interim' (*Corr*, IV, 93).

Moreover, during the period from 1900 to 1905, Marcel's health was ever more troubling: his asthma did not relent and he suffered from coughing fits, sensations of smothering, general pulmonary congestion, ultra-delicate digestion and extreme sensitivity to cold. These years also correspond to those when both of his parents died, and for both health and psychological reasons, Proust consulted an increasing number of doctors including Paul Dubois, author of a study (1904) on the psychological treatment of nervous disorders. In complete despair after his mother died, Marcel sought advice from the asthma specialist and family friend Édouard Brissaud on treatment for his insomnia and nervous exhaustion. He considered treatment from either Dubois or Jules-Joseph Déjerine of the Salpêtrière Hospital but in the end checked himself into the clinic of the hysteria specialist Dr Paul Sollier in December 1905. Proust's poet friend Anna de Noailles, also on the advice of Brissaud, had twice sojourned there. For the six weeks he stayed, the inveterate correspondent Marcel had difficulty following the house regimen of isolation from family and friends, but the relative calm and quiet did him good.

The reasons that medicine and doctors are treated with scepticism if not cruelty in *À la recherche* are not difficult to imagine. Proust clearly felt a sense of rebellion against medical experts, especially those who were self-important or peremptory in their judgments, for all were ineffective in curing his lifelong afflictions. However, another reason was surely the dogmatic, sometimes crude attitudes of Marcel's father, for example when he encouraged Marcel to counter his 'bad habits' by frequenting bordellos.[7] Nor were his admonitions to his son to live a healthier lifestyle and choose a 'real' profession – the law, the magistrature, diplomacy – met with sympathy. Among the many portraits of doctors in *À la recherche* is one of a provincial physician (Adrien was from the small town of Illiers) who devotes long years in Paris to 'purely material studies'. The result is that he never develops into a genuinely cultivated person (4: 508; III, 428). Certain of Proust's texts are gentler, highlighting the good heart of paternal figures, but the same texts almost always stress their naïveté and lack of cultural savoir-vivre.

Doctors, like diplomats, have a prominent role to play in Proust's novel. The diplomat-in-chief of the story, Norpois, seems to have a little of the doctor in himself, sharing as he does both Adrien Proust's preference for literature that has to do with 'reality', and the style of Adrien's own publications, highly coloured language full of clichés, learned terms and authoritarian aphorisms.[8] There are perhaps two main types of doctors in *À la recherche*, Cottard (who shares his name with Adrien Proust's colleague Jules Cotard), and Du Boulbon. Cottard is no bright light, but in spite of his bad jokes and periodic dimwittedness, he has a practical flair for diagnostics and identifies the precise treatment needed for the youthful Narrator's pulmonary congestion and spasms. He is 'a great clinician' (2: 82, trans. mod.; I, 490). In contrast, Du Boulbon, a noted specialist in nervous diseases, is imaginative and cultured. Charcot has said of him that he will reign over the fields of neurology and psychiatry. However, when he is called to the bedside of the Narrator's grandmother, he suggests without examining her that she be more active and attempt some outings to the Champs-Élysées. Told that the problem is albumin in the woman's urine, Du Boulbon retorts that he has researched the question of 'mental albumin'. This dangerous deposit, a sign of the kidney malfunction from which she will shortly die, is thus classified as 'imaginary' by the prestigious visitor (3: 342–52; II, 596–602). There is no doubt that Proust encountered doctors with similar views; for them, since his symptoms were nervous in origin, his suffering was also 'imaginary'.

Proust and nineteenth-century medicine

As observed at the beginning of this essay, Proust's thinking about malady was much influenced by the research on hysteria and nervous conditions of the final twenty years of the nineteenth-century. Asthma, insomnia and hypochondria, he writes of Jean Santeuil, are part of Jean's talent and, in fact, these afflictions are effects of the young man's genius. Is this meant facetiously, as a reprise of the nineteenth-century cliché, 'genius is a neurosis'? Probably not, for years later Proust writes, 'I believe that physical illness (in our degenerate age) is almost a precondition for any intellectual force that has a touch of genius, even if this is due solely to the creative value of suffering.'[9]

From the 1850s on, the other great question about human deficiencies, besides hysteria, was that of degeneracy, the idea that most if not all nerve-weakened individuals possessed hereditary markers that guaranteed they were destined for physical and mental deterioration, paralysis, madness, death. Some of Proust's stories from the 1890s where sexual themes are important such as 'La confession d'une jeune fille' and 'La fin de la jalousie', plus the lesbian tale, 'Avant la nuit', end with a death, and thus share the type of ending of pathographies of the period like *Sodome* (1888) by Henri d'Argis where the gay hero ends up paralysed and insane, or the novel *Méphistophéla* (1890) by Catulle Mendès whose lesbian heroine declines into insanity and death. It is as though the morbid dénouements of Proust's stories are partly 'atmospheric', that is, inherited from the ambient literature of degeneracy.

The vocabulary of nervous ailments is constantly in evidence in Proust's fiction, characterizing men and women from the earliest stories to his Narrator in *À la recherche* and major characters like Swann and Charlus. Again and again, we read of the nervous flaws of characters, the 'nervous weaknesses' of Charlus (4: 408; III, 344), the 'neurotic venom' (5: 180; III, 669) of the neurasthenic Charlie Morel which has him committing cruel acts, then regretting them. A doctor notes that Mme Verdurin also suffers from 'certain neurasthenic symptoms' (1: 247; I, 203). The diplomat Vaugoubert possesses an 'hysterical ardour' (4: 51; III, 44), Mme de Cambremer discovers a volume of Scarlatti with 'an hysterical shriek' (4: 409; III, 345), and a number of homosexuals whose inner imbalance causes them to reveal themselves appear 'convulsed ... by an hysterical spasm' (4: 23; III, 21). These constant references underline the fin-de-siècle nature of Proust's novel in that they reposition many characters in the rhetoric and diagnoses of nervous morbidity characteristic of the 1880s and 1890s. At another level, they reinforce what many a reader of Proust senses in the final volumes of the novel, that is, that society is in decline.

But as other characters decline, the star of the Narrator/writer rises, and the concerns about willpower and perseverance fade. It is curious, though not entirely illogical, to reflect that Proust's early anxieties and guilt about a clinical lack of willpower transitioned into a belief that involuntary phenomena were infinitely more authentic and productive for a creative writer than the products of the rational intelligence. The Narrator discovers that the beauty of art, of emotional reality and indeed of existence is not available through willed, dogged, intellectual efforts, but comes to us involuntarily through the revelation of long-hidden sensations and memories. Hampered for years by his lack of decisiveness, the Narrator realizes that his weakness is his strength. When he wrote the famous line, 'Chaque jour j'attache moins de prix à l'intelligence' (*CSB*, 211) ['Daily, I attach less value to the intellect' (*ASB*, 3)] and began to spin out his theory of involuntary memory, Proust was in fact announcing a victory of the 'un-willed' over the recipes of positivist science and medicine.

Notes

1 C. Féré, *Étude de la descendance des invertis* (Paris: Progrès Médical, 1898), p. 3.
2 Proust knew Bourget personally and was certainly familiar with his essays. See P. Bourget, *Essais de psychologie contemporaine* [1883] (Paris: Gallimard, 1993), pp. 330, 333. Besides brief references to willpower problems in the major novelists, Bourget wrote substantial texts on willpower maladies in Amiel and Du Camp (pp. 405–31).
3 According to the research of the distinguished psychiatrist Legrand du Saulle, of ninety-one children conceived during the siege of Paris, sixty-four were found to have physical, intellectual or affective anomalies. The other eighteen [sic] were in general small in size and sickly. See George Barral's preface to Dubut de Laforest's novel, *Le Faiseur d'hommes* (Paris: Marpon and Flammarion, 1884), p. xxi.
4 See Dr R. Soupault, *Marcel Proust du côté de la médecine* (Paris: Plon, 1967), p. 220. As we know, an early title for Proust's great work was to be *Les Intermittences du cœur*, a phrase which in Proust's mind had medical overtones.
5 *Le Carnet de 1908*, ed. Philip Kolb (Paris: Gallimard, 1976), p. 61.
6 Are Lois Bragg and William Sayers correct when they write that the Narrator Marcel is more heavily burdened with willpower problems than was Proust the neurasthenic? See their article, 'Proust's Prescription: Sickness as the Precondition for Writing', *Literature and Medicine*, 19 (2000), 165–81 (165).
7 See Jean-Yves Tadié, *Marcel Proust: Biographie* (Paris: Gallimard, 1996), pp. 69–71 for Adrien Proust's attempts to correct Marcel's 'bad [sexual] habits', and pp. 51–2 for a discussion of Adrien and Robert Proust's extra-marital adventures.
8 Marie Miguet-Ollagnier discusses these patterns in her comparison of Norpois and Adrien Proust in 'Le Père Norpois et le roman familial', *Revue d'Histoire Littéraire de la France*, 90 (1990), 191–207.
9 Quoted by J. Yoshida, 'Proust et la maladie nerveuse', *Revue des Lettres Modernes: Histoire des Idées et des Littératures*, 1067–72 (1992), 101–119 (118).

CHAPTER 17

Technology and science

Sarah Tribout-Joseph

> Few authors foreground the arts quite so comprehensively as Proust; certainly, none made them so central to their own literary production. Proust's whole life was saturated with love of the arts, and so too was to be his great novel: probably no other work of literature celebrates the arts as totally as his, or is so convincing in this pursuit.[1]

Thus Richard Bales hails Proust as champion of the arts. Yet it is no doubt for this very reason that the scientific bent of the author has tended to be overlooked. Nevertheless in recent years there has been a reassessment of the 'supposed Proustian preference [for] art to science'.[2] Contemporary writers were indeed aware of Proust's 'double vision' as this assessment by Virginia Woolf makes clear:

> The mind of Proust lies open with the sympathy of a poet and the detachment of a scientist ... It is as though there were two faces to every situation; one full in the light so that it can be described as accurately and examined as minutely as possible; the other half in shadow so that it can be described only in a moment of faith and vision by the use of metaphor.[3]

Science and the arts belong to different paradigms. Is there both a scientific and a poetic Proust as Woolf suggests? What evidence of crossover emerges between the arts and the sciences in Proust? The modernist period in which Proust was writing is characterized by rapid technological advance, including notably the introduction of electricity, telephony, radiography, photography and the motor car. 'To be sure', remarks Sara Danius, 'most scholars and critics agree that avant-garde movements such as cubism, futurism, surrealism, and vorticism must be understood in relation to technology.' Nevertheless she sees that traditional accounts of modernism have been marked 'by an antitechnological bias'.[4] Such misreadings of modernism are accounted for by the alleged separation of high and low culture and the championing of artistic autonomy over what Adorno and the Frankfurt School see as degraded mass culture:

> For the antitechnological bias operates in conjunction with the clichéd notion that high-cultural art is inherently better and more deserving of scholarly attention because, among other reasons, it is less or not at all informed by technologized production, and likewise, that its low-cultural counterpart, mass culture, is inauthentic or mediocre because, among other reasons, it is far removed from the activity of the creative mind of the artist. (D, p. 7)

Danius goes on to describe *À la recherche* as 'an unsurpassed chronicle of the advent of modern technology' (D, p. 11). In her reading of Proust: 'the smell of petrol is as epiphanic as the taste of a madeleine dipped in tea; the airplane above the treetops in Balbec as sublime as a sea storm' (D, p. 94). How does modern mass-technologized consumer society fit with Proustian aesthetics? In line with current critical thinking, I shall argue here that, beyond thematic representation, science and technology are an integral part of Proustian aesthetics. I shall explore first how Proust charts the impact of technological and scientific advance at the end of the nineteenth century and the beginning of the twentieth. I shall then question Proust's sources and understanding to determine whether the use he makes of science goes further, beyond even the imaginative engagement and creative stimulation which science affords, to engage with science's epistemological premises.

The *Recherche* certainly charts the impact of technological advance. Some of the more memorable examples are no doubt the photograph of the grandmother and her voice on the telephone. In both cases the Narrator experiences a sense of incomprehension before the new technology: human sensory perception is baffled before the machine. The disembodied voice and the ghostly presence in the photo make for a dehumanizing experience. The abstract notion of 'progress' is notably countered in the literary text by the portrayal of the destabilizing effect of estrangement before the novelty of the new technology, as evidenced in the case of the telephone here:

> My grandmother could no longer hear me; she was no longer in communication with me; we had ceased to be close to each other, to be audible to each other; I continued to call her, groping in the empty darkness, feeling that calls from her must also be going astray. I quivered with the same anguish which I had felt once before in the distant past, when, as a little child, I had lost her in a crowd, an anguish due less to my not finding her than to the thought that she must be searching for me, must be saying to herself that I was searching for her, an anguish not unlike that which I was later to feel, on the day when we speak to those who can no longer reply and when we long for them at least to hear all the things we never said to them, and our assurance that we are not unhappy. It seemed to me as though it

> was already a beloved ghost that I had allowed to lose herself in the ghostly world, and, standing alone before the instrument, I went on vainly repeating: 'Granny! Granny!' as Orpheus, left alone, repeats the name of his dead wife. (3: 150–1; II, 432)

Technology is thus seen to impact on an individual's life and the way he/she apprehends the world. The new is also perceived as an encroachment into the lives of individuals. Mme Cottard expresses a dubious reaction to the telephone and to its invasion of domestic space:

> Just fancy, the sister-in-law of a friend of mine has had the telephone installed in her house! She can order things from her tradesmen without having to go out of doors! I confess that I've made the most bare-faced stratagems to get permission to go there one day, just to speak into the instrument. It's very tempting, but more in a friend's house than at home. I don't think I should like to have the telephone in my establishment. Once the first excitement is over, it must be a perfect racket going on all the time. (2: 211; I, 596)

Certain utilities which are now taken for granted are described as a 'charming luxury' and as such they function as a measure of social status: there is stupefaction at the idea that 'the new house Mme Verdurin has just bought is to be lighted by electricity' (2: 211; I, 596). Mme Verdurin thus betrays herself as a social climber: access to technology allows social status to be bought and technologization leads to massification and announces modern consumer society.

That Proust buys into the new technology is evident from his palpable enthusiasm for such inventions as the motorcar and the *théâtrophone*, which enabled him in his ill health to listen to whole operas without going outside. The changed perception of distance occasioned by the introduction of the motorcar is likened to 'two and two mak[ing] five' (4: 457; III, 385). If part of the pleasure of jaunting in the countryside can be attributed to a liking for his chauffeur, Alfred Agostinelli, Proust nevertheless poeticizes a revolutionary breakup of the visual plane afforded by speed and played out before him thanks to the windshield.

Technological advances are of course only permitted by advances in science. The period in which Proust wrote the *Recherche* was one of intense activity which saw many discoveries of fundamental importance. It gave rise to the birth of many new fields of science and significant breakthroughs in others, including non-Euclidean geometry, quantum mechanics, atomic theory, evolutionary biology, thermodynamics, field theory, genetics, relativity, geology and optics, and such advances are represented in Proust's novel. If *À la recherche* can thus be read as a document on the dissemination and impact of scientific ideas and technological progress, the interaction of science and the arts also mutually enhances both disciplines with science affording imaginative engagement and creative stimulation, as well as a model of enquiry for curious minds.

As such, scientific metaphors in the text are drawn from every branch of science. Particularly abundant are metaphors taken from botany, optics and medicine.[5] The most notable botanical metaphor in the text is used to represent the attraction of the homosexual couple, Charlus and Jupien, and is calqued on the image of the bee fertilizing the orchid.[6] But Proust, on this occasion as on others, goes beyond the poetry of the metaphor to address broader epistemological concerns. The ethical issues at stake here relate to the limits of science and challenge the masquerade of spurious scientific discourse in the form of 'biological' theories of homosexuality prevalent at the time.

Whilst older studies such as those of Reino Virtanen and Charles Scribner Junior are useful in cataloguing scientific metaphors in the text,[7] Danius, Thiher and Luckhurst's recent works are more ambitious in attempting to show how the arts can borrow from the sciences to provide a theoretical framework which shapes the epistemological premises of the novel. Thiher and Luckhurst indeed argue that Modernist writers are motivated by the same questions that drive scientific enquiry. Luckhurst undoubtedly offers one of the best appraisals of the function of science in the *Recherche*. She argues that 'the authority of science and scientific law is a key epistemological question of the "modernist" period, and as such, it opens out onto related issues: How do hypotheses become theories? How do models, or metaphors, and theories interact?'[8] Luckhurst's study brings together two strands in Proustian criticism: the metaphor of the 'poet' and the maxim of the 'scientist', alerting us to the fact that although

> the interplay of maxim and metaphor ... is one of the fundamental paradoxes of [the *Recherche*] the common reader's experience ... is pre-empted by a tradition which promotes a certain type of sentence, one which is abundant, lyrical, and often metaphor-laden, and bars entry to the more austere, analytical, and indeed moralistic Proust.[9]

Yet the case must not be overstated. Earlier versions of the text feature the character Vington, a natural historian. He, however, is later transformed into Vinteuil, the composer. For Luckhurst such a substitution is 'emblematic of the progressive fragmentation and refiguration of science in the novel', whereby 'in the earlier drafts scientific metaphors are extended, more discursive, and linked to stronger statements of purpose than those which survive in the final text'.[10] Indeed the shift away from scientific certainty is voiced during the Narrator's series of revelations on life and the nature of art at the end of the book, when he declares that: 'A work in which there are theories is like an object which still has a price-tag on it' (6: 236; IV, 461).

One obvious question which arises concerns the extent to which Proust was actually familiar with the scientific developments of his times. His own interest in botany would account for its prevalence in the text. As a boy he even won the natural history prize at the lycée Condorcet. Natural history is also one of the more easily accessible branches of science. *Du côté de chez Swann* was published in 1913, at a time when Einstein's theory of relativity was becoming widely known. Proust was flattered by Camille Vettard's comparison of his work to that of Einstein's whilst at the same time he denied any understanding of the latter's work.[11] In a letter to his friend the Duc de Guiche, Proust writes: 'It is all very well to say I am indebted to [Einstein], I do not understand a single word of his theories, not knowing algebra. And I would very much doubt whether he has read my novels. It seems we have analogous ways of deforming Time' (*Corr*, xx, 578). Nevertheless Proust was to ask his friend Vettard for regular updates and it seems that such a consultation of friends was one of the ways in which Proust kept himself informed of scientific developments.[12]

Proust's own father and brother were of course doctors and the medical aspect of Proust's work has been well documented.[13] Proust's father notably wrote *The Hygiene of the Neurasthenic* with his assessment that: 'Nothing is more likely to cause depression and hypochondria in patients than continued attention, constant questions concerning their health and advice from those around them.'[14] In describing the nervous, emotionally charged state of the 'Neurasthenic', the father seems to be performing a case study of his own son and the work reads like an avant-texte of the *Recherche*. The influence of the father is similarly apparent in Bizub's recent book in which the author even questions whether Proust is not plagiarizing his father. In the final version of the *Recherche*, the highly sensitive Narrator will deplore his lack of willpower when it comes to writing, before finally overcoming his weakness. Michael Finn, reading Proust through the medium of the father's medical writings, examines the idea that the first, 1910–11, version of *Recherche*, is the 'autobiography of a Neurasthenic'.[15] He proposes that 'writing the *Recherche* could be con-sidered as a therapeutic exercise for a Neurasthenic', and goes on to analyse 'to what extent the aesthetics and framework of the book revise the various diagnoses of patients suffering from a lack of willpower in order to reverse values concerning certain medical ideas of the times'.[16] If Proust's father published widely in esteemed medical journals, such a critical conjuncture in the *Recherche* is missing and is replaced by the sceptical reception of the general public. If Proust's father was one of the first to advocate the 'cordon sanitaire' to combat cholera, Proust's text indicates that the general public erects a similar sort of barrier between themselves and medical and scientific practices with, for example, the Narrator's grandmother respectfully listening to the doctor but having no actual intention of carrying out his orders (2: 327; II, 64;).

Proust was certainly familiar with popularizers of science, such as Guiche, though it is difficult to determine the extent to which this was so. Critics have focused on the one mention of Poincaré in the text (3: 126; II, 414). The latter was both a mathematician and a philosopher of science. His work is notable in the field of relativity for his conclusion on the problem of three bodies moving in space, which was to give rise to chaos theory. Whilst Thiher's argument that Proust's 'Three Steeples' scene is an application of Poincaré's three-body theory is difficult to maintain given Proust's limited knowledge of the debate,[17] there seems to be more of a case for the influence of Poincaré's method of epistemological enquiry. As Luckhurst remarks:

> Proust's science seen through Poincaré's science is no longer simply a body of laws but an imaginative and speculative process – the desire to cast experiments, to hypothesize and model, the need to formulate and to justify the formulation of laws – which underlies creativity in both art and science.[18]

It can be concluded that the Narrator sees himself, like the scientist, as an experimenter trying to arrive at a perspective on the world that will allow him to understand not the particular but the laws governing the general (6: 442; IV, 618). Proust shares the scientist's aim of reaching the truth. His search, his research, and his most notable literary findings such as his theory of metaphor or involuntary memory are all indicative of a spirit of scientific enquiry. Nevertheless, approaching Proust from a scientific background, François Vannucci flags up the novelist's departure from scientific rigour.[19] Ultimately science is only an analogy in Proust and it is artistic style which makes the text:

> la vérité ne commencera qu'au moment où l'écrivain prendra deux objets différents, posera leur rapport, analogue dans le monde de l'art à celui qu'est le rapport unique de la loi causale dans le monde de la science, et les enfermera dans les anneaux nécessaires d'un beau style. (IV, 468)

> but the truth will be attained by him only when he takes two different objects, states the connexion between them – a connection analogous in the

world of art to the unique connexion which in the world of science is provided by the law of causality – and encloses them in the necessary links of a well-wrought style. (6: 246)

Notes

1 Richard Bales, 'Proust and the Fine Arts', in Richard Bales, ed., *The Cambridge Companion to Proust* (Cambridge University Press, 2001), p. 183.

2 Malcolm Bowie, *Proust, Jealousy, Knowledge* (London: Queen Mary College, 1979), p. 2.

3 Virginia Woolf, 'Phases of Fiction', in *Granite and Rainbow* (New York: Harcourt Brace, 1958), p. 125.

4 Sara Danius, *The Senses of Modernism: Technology, Perception, and Aesthetics* (Ithaca, NY: Cornell University Press, 2002), p. 2. Hereafter 'D'.

5 For an analysis of optics see Roger Shattuck's *Proust's Binoculars* (London: Chatto & Windus, 1964).

6 See Diane de Marjerie's *Le Jardin secret de Marcel Proust* (Paris: Albin Michel, 1994).

7 Reino Virtanen, 'Proust's Metaphors from the Natural and the Exact Sciences', *PMLA*, 69 (1954), 1038–59; Charles Scribner, Jr, 'Scientific Imagery in Proust', *Proceedings of the American Philosophical Society*, 134 (1990), 243–308.

8 Nicola Luckhurst, *Science and Structure in Proust's 'À la recherche du temps perdu'* (Oxford University Press, 2000), pp. 3–4.

9 Luckhurst, *Science and Structure*, p. 12.

10 Luckhurst, *Science and Structure*, p. 68.

11 Camille Vettard, 'Proust et Einstein', *Nouvelle Revue française*, August 1922; see *Corr*, XXI, 247.

12 For an account of the interconnected developments of art and science in Proust's time, see Stephen Kern, *The Culture of Time and Space: 1880–1918* (Cambridge, MA and London: Harvard University Press, 2003 [1983]).

13 See Chapter 16 above; also, L. A. Bisson, 'Proust and Medicine', in *Literature and Science* (Oxford: Blackwell, 1955), pp. 292–8; François-Bernard Michel, *Proust et les écrivains devant la mort* (Paris: Grasset, 1995); Robert Soupault, *Marcel Proust du côté de la médecine* (Geneva: Plon, 1967); Edward Bizub, *Proust et le moi divisé: 'La Recherche' creuset de la psychologie expérimentale (1874–1914)* (Geneva: Droz, 2006); Michael R. Finn, *Proust, the Body and Literary Form* (Cambridge University Press, 1999).

14 Adrien Proust and Gilbert Ballet, *L'Hygiène du neurasthénique* (Paris: Masson, 1897), p. 80 [my translation].

15 Michael R. Finn, 'Proust et le roman du neurasthénique', *Revue d'histoire littéraire de la France*, 96/2 (1996), 266–89 (267).

16 Finn, 'Proust et le roman', p. 268 [my translation].

17 Allen Thiher, *Fiction Rivals Science: The French Novel from Balzac to Proust* (Columbia: University of Missouri Press, 2001), p. 207.

18 Luckhurst, *Science and Structure*, p. 47.

19 François Vannucci, *Marcel Proust à la recherche des sciences* (Monaco: Rocher, 2005).

CHAPTER 18

Religion

Margaret Topping

A novel of crossings, frictions and fusions, the *Recherche* is also a site of productive aesthetic and moral tensions in its engagement with religion.[1] Proust's own Catholic/Jewish heritage situates him at the intersection of different rituals, practices and beliefs, just as his historical context provided the stage for a turbulent clash between the two traditions. The Dreyfus Affair became the trigger for widespread anti-Semitic feeling, while also entrenching and intensifying a strand of right-wing Catholic thinking prevalent since the late nineteenth century.[2] This was also a period of increased interest in Eastern religions and in alternative belief systems such as spiritualism, all of which leave their traces on the novel.[3] Occupying a privileged, 'in-between' space afforded Proust some of the detachment of the quasi-ethnographic observer who considers religion as a means of cementing group identities, attributing value or establishing and maintaining principles of conduct. In addition, this ethnographer uses the lens of religious ritual in order to make sense of the secular. Yet the ethnographer's mask of objectivity also slips, most obviously in his portrayal of characters who are the self-professed embodiments of religious belief and/or those who are rejected by it.

Proust *croyant*?

Proust's personal correspondence offers a rich mine of references to religious belief that tempt us into pinning down his own faith (or lack thereof). Yet Proust's desire to comfort or connect with his addressee inflects his letters, such that evidence of belief here remains a tantalizing source of 'frictions'. In a letter to Georges de Lauris in 1906, for instance, Proust asks 'whether your mother was religious, found consolation in prayer. Life is so dreadful that all of us must turn to it' (*Corr*, VI, 220); while a letter of 1908 urges Mme Straus: 'In Heaven's name, not a word about any of this to Mme Ganderax. In Heaven's name . . . in which, alas,

137

neither of us believes' (*Corr*, VIII, 278). A more nuanced attitude progressively prevails, as in the following contemplative excerpt from a 1915 letter to Lionel Hauser:

> even though I do not have Faith ... religious concerns are never absent a single day from my life ... I deny nothing, I believe in the possibility of everything; objections [to belief] based on the existence of Evil etc are absurd, since Suffering alone seems to me to have raised and to continue to raise man above the status of a savage, but from that position to certainty, even to Hope, there is a long journey. I have not yet completed that journey. Will I ever? (*Corr*, XIV, 218).

Arguably, these meditations on religion position Proust most closely to agnosticism, but of greater significance than any attempt at a resolution of this 'biographical' friction is how these fluctuating perspectives are echoed in the fictionalized construct of the novel. For Albert Thibaudet, 'the presence of God, the consent to God are as evident, as necessary and as absolute in the work of Balzac ... as the absence, the inexistence of God in the work of Proust';[4] and this vision of a godless fictional landscape persisted from the publication of the *Recherche* for at least three decades. Yet, as René Girard pointed out in the 1960s, 'the vocabulary of transcendence is astonishingly rich in the work of this novelist who never – or almost never – speaks of metaphysics or religion'.[5] More recently, too, such influential figures as Malcolm Bowie have argued compellingly for the profound morality of the *Recherche*,[6] a concept not restricted to organized religions but certainly enshrined within them. As Claude Vallée subtly attests, these critical 'frictions' may, in fact, fuse: 'Doubtless here, there is no longer any God, but everything has become God – objects, ideas, passions, and those ideas of themselves that are men ... A sacred book, a pious work, but written by a sacrilegious hand.'[7]

Christianity and Judaism

Vallée's observation encapsulates the complexities of Proust's handling of religion as, variously, a tool for social satire or celebration, a vector for the rituals and beliefs that define the secular world, or a multi-tonal comedy of self-glorification. In all cases, Proust playfully negotiates a fine balance between reverence and irreverence. The novel's portrayal of religious characters or of characters via religious motifs ranges from indulgent mockery to sharp indictment, with something akin to ethnographic curiosity between the two. It is, though, representatives of Christianity – and, in particular, Catholicism – who are most commonly present at the extremes. The Narrator's affectionate satire of Léonie's dual devotion to health and Church, for example, is comically underscored by Proust's description of the crown of thorns that is her wig (1: 61; 1, 51–2) or of her multi-purpose bedside table:

> At one side of her bed stood . . . a table which served at once as dispensary and high altar, on which, beneath a statue of the Virgin and a bottle of Vichy-Célestins, might be found her prayer-books and her medical prescriptions, everything that she needed for the performance, in bed, of her duties to soul and body, to keep the proper times for pepsin and for vespers. (1: 60; 1, 51)

At the other extreme, we witness a biting satire on the brother-in-law of the Narrator's grandmother, a monk who peeps through slightly spread fingers to assess the impact of his piety on those around him and to measure that of the Narrator, while ostensibly lost in prayer at the grandmother's deathbed (3: 390–1; 11, 635). Judaism, in contrast, is harnessed to quite different purposes.

Proust's evocations of Judaism are based on the distinction Juliette Hassine has noted between 'Judaism as a religion, Jewishness [judéité] as a cultural identity, and Jewdom [judaïcité] as a human community'.[8] The first of these features only as a metaphorical undercurrent in the novel, as in the sanctity accorded to Saturdays in the young Narrator's family which recalls the Jewish Sabbath. Jewish characters in the novel, notably Bloch, his family, and Swann, are present primarily as embodiments of the second – 'Jewishness as a cultural identity' – and notwithstanding the process of 're-judaicization' that Swann undergoes as a result of the Dreyfus Affair, it is primarily 'Jewdom as a human community' that he comes to embody rather than an active religious observance. Suspicions surrounding Jewish 'nationhood', a central tenet of anti-Semitic feeling, are portrayed in the *Recherche* even before the Dreyfus Affair, and critics such as Wolitz have argued that all of Proust's characters are/have been anti-Semitic to some extent.[9] The Narrator's family, for instance, disapprove of his Jewish friends, while his grandfather's humming of melodies from the operetta *La Juive* in the presence of these friends exemplifies the acceptability, indeed the seeming innocence, of such religious and/or cultural classifications. Charlus likewise expresses extravagant anti-Semitic sentiments, yet his fascination with Bloch as the alluring embodiment of an oriental exoticism/eroticism provides a subtle pivot to the intertwining of Judaism and homosexuality later in the novel. Proust's Narrator remains ostensibly neutral when the Dreyfus Affair erupts in *Le Côté de*

Guermantes, with this crisis offering, above all, a mechanism for the exploration of group psychologies. However, the landscape shifts by *Sodome et Gomorrhe*, for as the idea of Jewish nationhood and the associated concept of Diaspora are transposed onto the stateless, ostracized 'race' of homosexuals, Proust's observational tone falters, and the 'moral theorist' emerges in the face of the intolerance suffered by these two persecuted groups.

Proust as moral theorist

Malcolm Bowie introduces the term 'moral theorist' to encompass the fluctuating voices of the Narrator: at times moral philosopher, at others *moraliste*, and occasionally, *moralisateur*.[10] Yet, the three appear to coalesce in his approach to these marginalized groups:

> like the Jews again . . ., shunning one another, seeking out those who are most directly their opposite, who do not want their company, forgiving their rebuffs, enraptured by their condescensions; but also brought into the company of their own kind by the ostracism to which they are subjected, the opprobrium into which they have fallen, having finally been invested, by a persecution similar to that of Israel, with the physical and moral characteristics of a race, . . . and seeking out (as a doctor seeks out cases of appendicitis) cases of inversion in history, taking pleasure in recalling that Socrates was one of themselves, as the Jews claim Jesus was one of them, without reflecting that there were no abnormal people when homosexuality was the norm, no anti-Christians before Christ, that the opprobrium alone makes the crime. (4: 18–19; III, 18)

Cracking the surface of quasi-ethnographic study are hints here of compassionate outrage, or at the very least a call for recognition of injustice and moral relativism. Subsequently, it is through Proust's new dramaturgy of Racine's Biblical tragedies, *Esther* and *Athalie*, that he extends and plays out this analogy between the position of the Jews and that of the homosexual 'race'.[11] Not only does his conception of the homosexual man's enforced role-playing chime with this theatrical intertext, but through a multifaceted overlaying of 'noble' and 'vulgar' styles and situations, Proust effectively re-evaluates the meaning of tragedy in a twentieth-century context. Racism and bigotry, whether endured by homosexuals or Jews, are the true twentieth-century tragedies, Proust seems to be saying, albeit that the frequently humorous tone which creeps into Proust's depiction of the former group – in particular Charlus – precludes their treatment in high classical mode, yielding instead something more akin to tragicomedy. Conscious innuendo, gender inversion, and sexual and spiritual devotion fuse, for instance, in the wake of Charlus's revelations about the ambassador Vaugoubert's attempts to surround himself only with homosexual employees, thus creating a 'diplomatic Sodom' (4: 86; III, 74):

> But, being accustomed from my childhood to apply, even to what is voiceless, the language of the classics, I read into M. de Vaugoubert's eyes the lines in which Esther explains to Elise that Mordecai, in his zeal for his religion, has made it a rule that only those maidens who profess it shall be employed about the Queen's person. 'And now his love for our nation has peopled this palace with daughters of Zion, young and tender flowers wafted by fate, transplanted like myself beneath a foreign sky. In a place set apart from profane eyes, he' (the worthy ambassador) 'devotes his skill and labour to shaping them.' (4: 75–6; III, 65)

Proust thus subverts religious devotion, while also rewriting Biblical narrative. This latter is perhaps best epitomized by his mythology of homosexual desire which travesties the doctrine of an omniscient God by attributing the homosexual Diaspora to the fortuitous error of a God who naïvely placed heterosexual angels on the guard at the gates of Sodom and Gomorrah. These angels therefore believed the tales of enthusiastic heterosexuality told them by the inhabitants in a bid to escape the cities' destruction and permitted them to pass (4: 36–7; III, 32–3). Within a single extended metaphor, not only is the ultimate outcome of the Biblical narrative inverted, in the Diaspora rather than the destruction of the inhabitants of Sodom and Gomorrah, but individual fragments of this larger metaphorical mosaic are also reconfigured: the inhabitant of Sodom changes gender through an analogy with Lot's wife, and this figure is looking back out of sexual interest in a passing young man, not what we assume in the Biblical evocation of Lot's wife to be regret at the destruction of her home. More broadly, the displacement of an all-knowing God destabilizes not only monolithic doctrinal certainties but also, by extension, heteronormative sexual certainties and, as discussed below, fixed social crystallizations.

Proust ethnographer or satirist?

As the preceding examples suggest, the voice of the moral theorist may fuse with that of the satirist, and it is primarily through Proust's metaphorical appropriation of Christianity that a satirical perspective is made possible on the secular ethnography of rituals and codified practices to which as much importance is ascribed by 'devotees' as by believers to organized religion. The Verdurin 'petit clan' is the extreme model of the rituals which, through the figure of Mme Verdurin herself, dictate social life with an inquisitorial zeal.[12] However, in ways that hint at, or call for, an acknowledgment of the democratic nature of *belief* despite the hierarchical structure of religious *institutions* (and thus a social 'levelling'), the Narrator also perceives the extent to which the servants' lunchtime at Combray has sacred status in the eyes of Françoise. She is transformed into a priest celebrating mass, at the culmination of which a bell would signal not the miracle of transubstantiation, but the sacrilegious usurpation of the moment by the Narrator's family summoning a servant (3: 10–11; II, 317). The differing tones that rub against one another in these examples alone dramatize the shifting textures of Proust's reinvention of religion: an attempt to deflate the Verdurins' dictatorial hegemony through satire, for example, goes hand in hand with a recognition of the importance of secular rituals such as mealtimes; and the elevation of cooking to a sacred art-form elsewhere in the novel nuances this gentle mockery of Françoise's fearful rule of the kitchen by transforming this culinary artist – one of many artists in the novel – into a demiurgic creator. Choosing the ingredients for the dinner for Norpois, she is likened to Michelangelo, who 'spent eight months in the mountains of Carrara, choosing the most perfect blocks of marble for the monument of Julius II' (2: 18; I, 437). The Narrator's young, intradiegetical self does not come away unscathed in Proust's religious analogies either, this metaphorical field offering a means to communicate the enormity of certain traumas – such as the 'drame du coucher' – to him,[13] and at the same time the disproportion of his reactions in the mind of the more mature, knowing, writing self.

Conclusion: Proust's religion of art

The overarching narrative within which these 'frictions' between the naïve young Narrator/protagonist and the mature Narrator/writer are played out maps the evolution from the former's misplaced worship of artists such as Bergotte and La Berma, to a genuine valorization of the creative process whether textual, visual, sonic, culinary or driven by the demands of fashion. Critics from Bucknall to Chaudier have argued that the ultimate epiphany for the Narrator is the creation of a religion of art as a means to transcendence and atemporality, not in the conventional sense of immortality through the legacy of the works of art the artist leaves behind, but in the sense that the work of art 'alleviates' contingency and the isolation of individual moments, creates connections, fusions, overarching meanings. At the end of the *Recherche*, Proust searches for a metaphor to express the novel the Narrator/protagonist is to write. Combining both small and great things, lofty and trivial, sacred and secular, he toys with a range of images: a church, a druidic monument, a cathedral, but ultimately, he settles on a simple dress (6: 431–2; IV, 610).

As is well known, Proust had originally planned to structure his novel in relation to the physical layout of a cathedral, with individual sections entitled nave, transept, apse, etc.: a seemingly fitting metaphor, one might argue, for this singularly monumental and illuminating text. Yet, the metaphor is rejected by Proust. For him, the reader's engagement with the novel cannot be a passive one. His or her role does not end at the final pages of the novel. To cast his novel as a cathedral may thus have been too suggestive of monolithic conclusions, of fixed wisdom, an authoritative vision. In many respects, Proust's novel comes full circle with cycles of apprenticeship completed, but the *Recherche* is also grounded in a calculated refusal of closure, an openness, a space for self-discovery. In contrast to the fixed certainties implied by the image of the cathedral, the dress implies the knitting together of fragments, the capacity to transform and to be transformed, a mobile, changing, democratic space in which to challenge accepted beliefs, ethics and values.

Notes

1 I first analysed Proust's handling of religion in Margaret Topping, *Proust's Gods: Christian and Mythological Figures of Speech in the Works of Marcel Proust* (Oxford University Press, 2000). The ideas explored here owe something to this earlier discussion, especially Part II, 'Christian and Biblical Figures of Speech', pp. 97–157.

2 See Theodore Zeldin, *A History of French Passions 1848–1945*, vol. II, *Intellect, Taste and Anxiety* (Oxford University Press, 1993): 'Religion and Anticlericalism', pp. 983–1039.

3 See Barbara J. Bucknall, *The Religion of Art in Proust* (Urbana: University of Illinois Press, 1969), Stéphane Chaudier, *Proust et le langage religieux* (Paris: Champion, 2004), and Margaret Topping, *Supernatural Proust: Myth and Metaphor in 'À la recherche du temps perdu'* (Cardiff: University of Wales Press, 2007).

4 Preface to H. de Balzac, *Le Père Goriot* (Paris: Flammarion, 1966). As recorded by Juliette Hassine in her article, François Mauriac also criticized Proust's novel on account of 'the total absence from it of God'; see Hassine, 'The Creation of Eve in the Writings of Marcel Proust', in David H. Hirsch and Nehama Aschkenasy, eds., *Biblical Patterns in Modern Literature* (Chico, CA: Scholars Press, 1984), pp. 95–104 (96).

5 René Girard, *Mensonge romantique et vérité romanesque* (Paris: Grasset, 1961), p. 83.

6 Malcolm Bowie, *Proust among the Stars* (London: HarperCollins, 1998), pp. 175–208.
7 Claude Vallée, 'La Religion dévoyée', in G. Cattaui and P. Kolb, eds., *Entretiens sur Marcel Proust* (Paris: Mouton, 1966), pp. 168–93 (170).
8 Juliette Hassine, 'Le personage juif proustien face à la critique des années 1970–1980', *Yod* (1982), 7–23 (14).
9 Seth L. Wolitz, *The Proustian Community* (New York University Press, 1971), pp. 158–68.
10 Bowie, *Proust among the Stars*, p. 176.
11 Proust's conception of homosexuality is certainly a product of his time. See J. E. Rivers, *Proust and the Art of Love: The Aesthetics of Sexuality in the Life, Times and Art of Marcel Proust* (New York: Columbia University Press, 1980). However, the 'gaps' in his understanding highlighted by more recent approaches to the study of sexuality and desire do not devalue the challenge his work represents to contemporary prejudices.
12 See the opening pages of 'Un Amour de Swann' (1: 225–6; 1, 185–6).
13 The Narrator's mother's much-longed-for kiss is, for instance, likened to 'a host for an act of peace-giving communion' (1: 13; 1, 13).

CHAPTER 19

Travel

Margaret Topping

The only real journey ... would be to travel not towards new landscapes, but with new eyes, to see the universe through the eyes of another, of a hundred others. (5: 237; III, 762)

Banality is never in the world. It is always in the gaze.[1]

The interconnectedness of space, place, modernity and desire in Proust has preoccupied critics from Georges Poulet to Sara Danius,[2] but little attention has been granted to Proust's relationship to contemporary cultures of travel and to the theories of travel that evolved in the course of the twentieth century. Yet the striking overlap between his observation above and that of contemporary travel theorist, Jean-Didier Urbain, also establishes Proust as a time-traveller. In the period between Proust's and Urbain's aphoristic comments, writers as diverse as Georges Perec, Henri Michaux and cultural anthropologist Claude Lévi-Strauss were, with differing inflections, pronouncing or implying 'la fin des voyages'.[3] With a sense of exhaustion of the possibilities of geographical exploration, each was calling for, or enacting, a form of virtual travel based on a freshness of perception, a willingness to see the world differently. As Urbain continues:

> What is important is not whether (or not) the world is 'washed of its exoticism' ['rincé de son exotisme'], but whether it might one day be perceived as such. Whether it is 'washed' or not, what is essential is surely to rid oneself of this disagreeable impression and to reinvent the exoticism of the world.[4]

Opening up the world

Urbain's urgent call for a renewal of travel and a rethinking of exoticism is evidenced in the works of post-Second World War travel writers but, in the early twentieth century, Proust was already signalling a new approach to travel and doing so, paradoxically, at a moment when geographical

145

travel was becoming increasingly democratized. Thomas Cook's first foray into group travel dates from 1841.[5] At this time, he organized an eleven-mile, publicly advertised train journey conveying 540 people to a temperance meeting in Loughborough at the price of a shilling per head. Prior to, but particularly during, Proust's lifetime, Cook's enterprise expanded its geographical reach and moved beyond its initial ideological impetus. By the 1860s, Cook's guided tours were established throughout Europe and America, and by the 1870s, further afield: his first round-the-world trip, lasting 222 days, dates from 1872, and his celebrated Nile Tours enjoyed particular popularity from the 1880s onwards. Closer to home – and prominent in the *Recherche* – technological developments facilitating physical travel are a source of both wonder and anxiety. This oscillation is captured in Anne Green's compelling discussion of the railway, which, she explains, was viewed variously as 'a positive symbol of progress, a disturbing emblem of change, or a bleak reflection of a frustrated and alienated society'.[6] Recent advances in air travel similarly prompt reactions fluctuating between thrill and caution;[7] whilst car travel provides the opportunity for a new form of digression, or 'zigzagging' as it has been referred to by contemporary travel writers seeking to eschew pre-ordained itineraries and modes of travel.[8] Like the stylistic meanderings of Proust's prose, car travel offers freedom from a fixed endpoint or teleology: 'Then we got back into the car. And it started back, down little, twisting paths where the winter trees, hung in ivy and brambles, looked as if they should lead to a magician's lair' (5: 158; III, 680).[9] Digression may, in fact, be the necessary condition of the novel's conclusion; the zigzagging enabled by car travel may be essential to the completion of the Narrator's journey, for chance and peripeteia are key factors in this voyage of discovery, this process of looking at the world with new eyes. Likewise conceived in mythologized form is the new possibility of virtual travel offered by the telephone, but, here as elsewhere, anxiety and excitement coalesce:

> For this miracle to happen, all we need do is to approach our lips to the magic panel and address our call ... to the Vigilant Virgins whose voices we hear every day but whose faces we never get to know; ... the forever fractious servants of the Mysteries, the shadowy priestesses of the Invisible ... the Young Ladies of the Telephone! (3: 130; II, 432)

All of these technological advances are mythologized by Proust in ways that convey both genuine wonderment and a gentle self-satire.

Proust: an agoraphile or claustrophile traveller?

The sense of enormity that the young Narrator/protagonist projects on to the prospect of geographical travel echoes that of the figure Jean-Didier Urbain terms the 'agoraphile' traveller.[10] The rhetoric of the agoraphile, for Urbain, is that of a grand adventurer ploughing a path through uncharted territory. This is the persona of the traveller associated above all with the period of empire whose writing is inflected by a discourse of 'mastery, conquest and colonization'.[11] Such travellers dissociate themselves categorically from the 'touriste', an attitude hinted at in Proust's subtly satirical reference to an activity he perceives more as a symbol of social status to be vaunted retrospectively than as an experience appreciated in the moment: 'think of the [tourists] who are uplifted by the general beauty of a journey they have just completed, although during it their main impression, day after day, was that it was a chore' (2: 56; 1, 472). Yet, despite this agoraphile posture, what the reader intuits is that the intradiegetical Narrator is closer to the identity of the 'claustrophile', the traveller who undertakes journeys of proximity (geographically, the furthest he travels is to Venice), thus disentangling the notion of travel from that of physical mobility: 'Mobility is a movement in space whereas travel [le voyage] is an idea.'[12] Initially, this *décalage* between the agoraphile and claustrophile offers a means for the Narrator to satirize his young fearful self who – overwhelmed by the enormity of even the shortest of journeys beyond the habitual – imbues the trip to the train station from which he will travel to Balbec with all the disproportionate trepidation of an ascent to Golgotha (2: 224; 11, 6).

The adventurer rhetoric which was prevalent in travel writing of Proust's time, with its emphasis on distant, untrodden territories and on discovery, is thus ironically applied to a rather more domestic journey. The Narrator's 'claustrophile' identity need not, though, be understood as limiting, for it is precisely Urbain's claustrophile – like Perec in *Espèces d'espaces* – who prompts us to see the familiar with fresh eyes. This is the ultimate revelation of the Narrator of the *Recherche*, quoted at the beginning of this chapter, who, in a microcosm of the *apprentissage* he undergoes more generally, realizes that 'truth', revelation, discovery lie not outside himself – in other works of art, in other people, in a trip to see La Berma in Racine's *Phèdre*, or in a much-longed-for journey to Venice – but in a subjective apprehension that transcends the commonplace wisdom or path. Patterns of travel and return (whether physical or metaphorical) structure the novel: the Narrator moves back and forth between a limited number of geographical locations (Paris, Balbec, Combray), but reflecting the mythical structures of the novel, return is not to be equated with a failure to progress. The journey away from, and back to, one's starting point brings challenge, growth and thus a renewal of perception for the traveller/writer and also for the reader. The Narrator's return to origins is thus inseparable from eschatology myths which embody both the perfection and the certainty of new beginnings at the end of each natural cycle.

The *Recherche* as travel literature?

The *Recherche* is thus a metaphorical journey of (self-)discovery in which multiple physical journeys are portrayed. Can one therefore consider Proust's novel to be a form of travel literature? Francophone Swiss traveller-writer Nicolas Bouvier (1929–98) describes his own philosophy of travel and the representation of travel in the following terms in *Routes et déroutes*: 'I bring together little fragments of knowledge, as one would gather the scattered pieces of a shattered mosaic, wherever I can, with no attempt to impose a system';[13] whilst at the other end of the spectrum, critic Jean-Marc Moura has identified the 'musealization of the world' as a dominant strategy in the contemporary touristic imaginary. This strategy, he argues, is based on an 'exhibiting of the world [mise en spectacle du monde]' born of a 'heritage syndrome' in which all human artefacts are to be 'labelled, preserved and secured'.[14] In bringing his gaze to rest on his own culture (if we accept that the true voyages, are not to unfamiliar lands, but based on seeing the familiar differently), how does Proust's Narrator reflect these paradigms?

Proust's *monde-mosaïque*

Bouvier's evocation of a mosaic implies a refusal of any attempt at a systematic appropriation of the world. In the context of physical travel, such a philosophy is rooted in a post-colonialist, post-Orientalist set of values which eschews monolithic, homogenizing narratives of the culture represented. It also aims to set aside limiting or preconceived points of reference and thus to break down the boundaries between self and other, albeit without negating the existence of difference.

In a multiplicity of ways, Proust's novel is grounded in self–other encounters: these are not typically encounters with a cultural other to the Narrator, but are conceived rather in terms of sexual, gender, social or artistic otherness. Yet, in representing these encounters, Proust has recourse to images of intercultural contact, travel and exoticism.[15] Proust brings the exotic home; he defamiliarizes the familiar, and it is precisely in this way that he encourages a freshness of perception. In wartime Paris, for instance, the city at night is as if transported to Baghdad with all of the 'exotic' sexual piquancy associated with the *Mille et Une Nuits*.[16] What Proust introduces us to is 'the pleasure of experiencing Diversity [le plaisir de sentir le Divers]', to quote Victor Segalen, be that understood culturally or, more broadly, in terms of psychological, gender, sexual or artistic difference. The phrase quoted is from Segalen's *Essai sur l'exotisme* which he wrote contemporaneously to Proust (between 1904 and his premature death in 1918). Segalen's essay was never completed, and published only in fragmented form in 1978; but on account of this, and the works published during his lifetime, Segalen is now celebrated as redefining exoticism in the twentieth century.[17] Yet one might argue that Proust's work too embodied an aesthetics of diversity: the Narrator relishes and savours otherness, as evidenced in his delight in Elstir's Turneresque paintings where the distinction between sea and land is reconfigured; he is fascinated likewise by the intricate diversity of human desire, and on a metatextual level, an aesthetics of diversity is keenly felt by first-time readers of Proust. The novel is initially disconcerting and elusive, just as Segalen's also were.[18] This ideal pleasure in Diversity reaches its limits, however, when the Narrator himself is emotionally implicated. While Albertine's profound otherness may be a means for Proust to comment on the fundamental unknowability of any human being and also arguably on the differences between homosexual and lesbian desire, her resistance to knowledge and capture is, for the intradiegetical Narrator, a source of frustration.

Proust's *monde-musée*

Proust's socio-historical context was a threshold one: he was witness to a new century, to the First World War and the dramatic upheaval and social mobility that this conflict prompted. The *Recherche* willingly engages with these upheavals, and there is almost a greedy fascination and delight in the processes by which, in the supreme example of social 'travel', Mme Verdurin becomes the Princesse de Guermantes in the wake of the First World War. Proust is not nostalgic for the old hierarchies, but he does appreciate the value of the long view, the realities of historical contingency, the inevitabilities of repetition and return. As such, the *Recherche* arguably embodies an impulse to salvage that recalls Proust's contemporary Albert Kahn whose *Archives de la planète* charted, in photographic form (between 1909 and 1931), what Kahn saw as the diversity of a world being lost.[19]

The photographers Kahn commissioned travelled the globe, but Western Europe, including France – and indeed Paris – was also a locus of attention as a world where traditions, rituals, customs were disappearing.

Proust's fascination with etymologies of place-names, genealogies, rituals and traditions may be, in part, a means of representing the naïve young Narrator's illusions surrounding the aristocracy, but for the mature Narrator/writer, these arguably betray a desire to preserve – like contemporaries such as Segalen or Kahn – what is being lost through social, historical, political, artistic mobilities. In this sense, one might argue for a musealization of the world of the Belle Époque being evident in the *Recherche*. Crucially, though, this is not to be equated in Proust's perception with stasis or mummification, or a decontextualized form of museology, an idea subtly dramatized in Raoul Ruiz's cinematic version of *Le Temps retrouvé* when, at the 'bal de têtes', seemingly sculpted figures, the embodiments of both the ageing process and the co-presence of past and present social worlds and destabilized hierarchies, glide around within a moveable set.[20]

Conclusion

The mosaic of self–other encounter is thus constantly reconfigured in a movement which paradoxically allows for the coalescence of the *monde-mosaïque* and *monde-musée*. The mosaic marks the appreciation and, at times, the shock of diversity; it represents the valorization of mobilities, both social and perceptual – indeed the majority of references in Proust's novel to the nomadic or the 'vagabond' relate to memories, the gaze, the workings of the mind. The mosaic embodies the desire to transcend broad brushstroke preconceptions; it is also Proust's complex textual mosaic. Yet this is, at the same time, a mosaic which preserves, conserves and, in some sense, exhibits a world poised on the threshold of modernity.

Notes

1 Jean-Didier Urbain, *Secrets de voyage: menteurs, imposteurs et autres voyageurs impossibles* (Paris: Payot, 1998), pp. 438–9; all translations are my own.

2 Georges Poulet, *L'Espace proustien* (Paris: Gallimard, 1963); Sara Danius, 'The Aesthetics of the Windshield: Proust and the Modernist Rhetoric of Speed', *Modernism/Modernity*, 8.1 (2001), 99–126.

3 In *Espèces d'espace* (Paris: Galilée, 2000), Perec advocates travelling to a different floor of one's apartment building. Although a journey to distant cultures, Michaux's *Un barbare en Asie* (Paris: Gallimard, 1986) prompts a rethinking

of physical travel by renegotiating cultural difference, while Lévi-Strauss famously proclaimed in the section of *Tristes Tropiques* entitled 'The End of Travel' ['la fin des voyages'] that 'Humanity is settling into monoculture' (Paris: Plon, 1955), p. 26.

4 Urbain, *Secrets de voyage*, p. 439.

5 For an analysis of the growth of Cook's Tours, see F. Robert Hunter, 'Tourism and Empire: The Thomas Cook & Son Enterprise on the Nile, 1868–1914', *Middle Eastern Studies*, 40.5 (2004), 28–54. See 'Further Reading' for material on the history of Cook's success.

6 Anne Green, *Changing France: Literature and Material Culture in the Second Empire* (London: Anthem Press, 2011), p. 64 (see Green's Chapter 3, 'Transport', pp. 35–64). See also Jean-Christophe Gay, 'L'espace discontinu de Marcel Proust', *Géographie et cultures*, 6 (1993), 35–50.

7 See 4: 495; III, 417 for the Narrator's emotion on first seeing an aeroplane, and 6: 66–7; IV, 337–8 for his conversation with Saint-Loup in which German bombers are likened to Valkyries.

8 The use of the term in relation to travel dates from Rodolphe Töpffer's *Voyages en zigzag* (Paris: Hoëbeke, 1999 [1836]). For the ways in which the term has been adopted by twentieth-century travel writers, see Charles Forsdick, 'L'Orient quoi! Bouvier and the Post-Orientalist Journey', in M. Topping, ed., *Eastern Voyages, Western Visions: French Writing and Painting of the Orient* (Oxford, Bern: Peter Lang, 2004), pp. 325–45 (344–5).

9 See Pierre Bayard, *Le Hors-sujet: Proust et la digression* (Paris: Éditions de Minuit, 1996); and my 'Errant Eyes: Metaphor, Digression and Desire in Proust's *In Search of Lost Time*', in A. Grohmann and C. Wells, eds., *Digressions in European Literature: From Cervantes to Sebald* (London: Palgrave Macmillan, 2011), pp. 106–77.

10 See Jean-Didier Urbain, *Ethnologue, mais pas trop* (Paris: Payot, 2003), for a discussion of the 'tyrannie agoraphile' dominating travel writing in this period (p. 187); and 'Further Reading' for additional sources that develop these categorizations.

11 Charles Forsdick, Feroza Basu and Siobhán Shilton, *New Approaches to Twentieth-Century Travel Literature in French: Genre, History, Theory* (Oxford, Bern: Peter Lang, 2006), p. 45.

12 Jean-Didier Urbain, 'Les catanautes des cryptocombes: des iconoclastes de l'Ailleurs', *Nottingham French Studies*, 'Errances urbaines' special issue, ed. Jean-Xavier Ridon, 39.1 (2000), 7–16 (14).

13 Nicolas Bouvier, *Œuvres* (Paris: Gallimard, 2004), p. 1280.

14 From a paper entitled 'Littérature et imaginaire touristique du temps: portraits du Caraïbe en paradis atemporel' delivered at the 'Borders and Crossings' conference (Melbourne, 2008); my translations.

15 See Margaret Topping, 'Les Mille et Une Nuits proustiennes', *Essays in French Literature*, 35–6 (1999), 113–30.

16 This metaphorical field is also used in relation to cross-cultural encounter. Venice, for instance, is conceived as the gateway to the East.

17 Victor Segalen, *Essai sur l'exotisme: une esthétique du divers* (Paris: Livres de Poche, 1999). Segalen writes, for instance, that 'Exoticism is not therefore that kaleidoscopic state associated with the tourist or the mediocre viewer, but the acute, curious reaction to the clash [choc] of a strong individuality against an objectivity whose difference from itself it perceives and savours' (p. 43; my translation).

18 His *René Leys* [1922], for example, not only plunges the reader into a moment of unstable knowledge, as does Proust's own, but it dramatizes too the impossibility of knowing the cultural Other (here China's Imperial City at a moment of transition from the dynastic tradition to social revolution, but also the impenetrability of all that is other to us in the broadest terms (Paris: Gallimard, 2000).

19 See David Okuefuna, *The Wonderful World of Albert Kahn: Colour Photographs from a Lost Age* (London: Random House, 2008). The Musée Albert-Kahn website is also a useful resource: http://albert-kahn.hauts-de-seine.net.

20 Raoul Ruiz, *Le Temps retrouvé*, available on DVD from Artificial Eye (2000).

CHAPTER 20

Journalism

Christine M. Cano

Proust between two dailies: *Le Figaro* and *Le Temps*

Just a few years after Émile Zola published his earth-shaking series of pro-Dreyfus articles in *Le Figaro* (November–December 1897), Marcel Proust became a regular contributor to the paper with a series of society columns and pastiches.[1] Zola, at the height of his literary glory, was able to secure in the pages of *Le Figaro* a conspicuous venue for his fiery defence of Dreyfus. Proust, at the threshold of a career in letters, signed his society columns with a pseudonym and carefully guarded his incognito. He was to maintain an uneasy distance between journalism and literature throughout his writing life.

The contrast between these two instances of journalism – between Zola's public indictment of the French justice system and Proust's discreet chronicles of his visits to literary and aristocratic salons – tells us as much about the life of the French press as it does about Zola and Proust as journalists. How had *Le Figaro* evolved in those six years between Zola's *dreyfusard* articles and Proust's first society column ('Le salon de S.A.I. la princesse Mathilde', 25 February 1903)? The numbers tell it all: *Le Figaro*'s circulation, from a robust 80,000 copies at the end of the nineteenth century, dropped to 20,000 in the heat of the Dreyfus Affair.[2] Conservative and moderately republican, with an aristocratic and high-bourgeois readership, *Le Figaro* assumed a surprisingly pro-Dreyfus stance from the start of the Affair and lost subscribers by the thousands. Zola himself notes that he barely got his third article on the Affair, 'Procès-Verbal' (5 December 1897), into the newspaper's troubled pages as its readers abandoned it.[3] By the time Proust's series of 'Salons' began appearing in *Le Figaro*, the paper's fortunes were on the rise again. Under the leadership of Gaston Calmette, it had recovered its traditionally conservative profile and minimized its coverage of politics. Readers were returning to an elegant *Figaro* which gave ample press to arts and letters, *fêtes mondaines*, and the growing world of sports.

153

Proust's 'Salons' and 'Pastiches,' light, witty, ironic and incisive, embody the spirit of *Le Figaro* in the first decade of the twentieth century. These pieces represent only a fraction of his journalistic output (he was active as a journalist from 1892 to 1922), but they gave him his early reputation as a superficial writer who published only in the society pages – his concealed identity having quickly come to light. As Léon Pierre-Quint put it in his 1925 biography, even in Proust's immediate circle of friends it was commonly held that Marcel would never be anything other than 'Horatio' from the *Figaro*.[4] What was required of a successful *chroniqueur* at the turn of the century? According to Yves Sandre, the *chroniqueur* of 1900 was expected to demonstrate, rather than depth and rigour, 'spontaneity, sparkle and irony; a talent for vulgarization and for accessible expository prose'.[5] Proust, now widely known for attributes other than spontaneity and accessibility, had mastered the art of the *chronique* with its striking portraits of contemporary figures and brief, memorable formulae.

Proust was writing for newspapers during what is often called the golden age of the French press: the Belle Époque.[6] Historian Pierre Albert describes the transformation of newspapers into popular consumer products at the end of the nineteenth century. After 1871, industrial and social developments made possible the growth of an inexpensive, large-circulation press. Technical improvements sped up the printing process; the spread of literacy created new readerships in the working and artisanal classes; newspapers increased their pagination and diversified their content. The Parisian press, in particular, boomed. The number of dailies appearing in the capital rose dramatically, as specialized titles devoted to sports, finances, literature and fashion multiplied. Non-specialized dailies such as *Le Figaro* expanded their rubrics to cover these and other topics. *Le Figaro* increased the number of pages in each issue from four to six (it would eventually rise to eight), and other French titles followed suit.

In an age when newspapers had ceased to be an expensive product reserved for a social minority, Proust wrote for a social and cultural élite. The publications in which his *chroniques* appeared belonged to the political centre (*Le Figaro*, after its Dreyfus Affair debacle), the right-wing press (*Le Gaulois*; *La Presse*; *L'Intransigeant*, after the Boulangist crisis), or the 'literary' press. In this last category were *Le Gil Blas*, which bore the subtitle 'the most literary – the most Parisian of newspapers'; Alfred Vallette's avant-garde literary review *Le Mercure de France*; and periodicals such as *La Revue d'art dramatique*, *La Revue hebdomadaire*, *La Renaissance latine* and *La Nouvelle Revue française*. If we include his articles on Ruskin and on the English painter Dante Gabriel Rossetti, the list extends to art journals: *La Chronique des arts et de la curiosité* and *La Gazette des Beaux-Arts.*[7]

Contained within this list of titles is a deeper dimension of Proust's relationship with the press of his time: his social ties to leading figures in journalism. The most notable of these was Gaston Calmette, chief editor of *Le Figaro* from 1894–1914, to whom Proust dedicated *Du côté de chez Swann.*[8] Robert Proust, in a preface to *Chroniques* (1927), his posthumous collection of Marcel's writings for the press, praised the 'most affectionate kindness' which Calmette had shown his brother in offering him the 'hospitality' of *Le Figaro*. As for Robert de Flers, who succeeded Calmette as literary editor, he and Marcel were linked by 'ties of deep friendship' that went back to middle school.[9] Indeed, it was Flers who became Proust's primary connection to *Le Figaro* after Calmette's tragic death. But as Proust wrote in a June 1914 letter to André Gide, Flers was less influential than his predecessor and could not always make things happen at *Le Figaro* (*Corr*, XIII, 253–4). Alfred Vallette, the founder and managing editor of *Le Mercure de France*, though not a social acquaintance like Calmette and Flers, remained an important contact for Proust after publishing one of his essays on Ruskin in 1900. Since *Le Mercure de France* doubled as a publishing house, Proust offered Vallette his two Ruskinian translations, *La Bible d'Amiens* (1904) and *Sésame et les lys* (1906). Vallette rejected his next offering – an early version of *À la recherche* – out of hand. But he graciously obliged when, a few years later, Proust asked him to reprint excerpts of Jacques-Émile Blanche's favourable review of *Du côté de chez Swann* from *L'Écho de Paris* (*Corr*, XIII, 151–2).

Proust's correspondence traces the day-to-day exchange of social currency that helped to keep him active in the world of journalism. In a May 1914 letter to Flers, he asked his former classmate to try to get him a rubric – *any* rubric – at *Le Figaro*: 'If ever any rubric is without an author, such as the weather, dogs run over in traffic, music, theatre, the stock exchange, society, I would be thrilled to take it over.' He assured Flers he was capable of being 'brief and practical' rather than literary (*Corr*, XIII, 195–6). But if Proust insisted on his 'journalistic' qualities when addressing a longtime friend like Flers, who had always known him as a *littéraire*, he faced the opposite image problem when seeking a publisher for *À la recherche*. For an independent literary publisher like the Nouvelle Revue française (the publishing wing of the periodical *La Nouvelle Revue française*), Proust was typecast in an instant as a dilettante who wrote for *Le Figaro* – and his manuscript summarily cast aside. In the words of Pierre Assouline, 'They rejected Marcel Proust *a priori*. In the eyes of the NRF, he embodied everything they hated: frivolity and dilettantism, high society and idleness, duchesses and *Figaro*.'[10]

Proust's talents and interests as a journalist coincided with an era at *Le Figaro*: the years in which it rediscovered its identity as a *journal mondain* under Calmette. His close collaboration with *Le Figaro* and its literary supplement all but ended with Calmette's disappearance, but his writings for the press in general were already becoming rarer as *À la recherche* came to life. Paradoxically, as Proust took his distance from journalism to devote himself to his novel, he became even more immersed in the world of the press – as a new literary figure whose reputation was being made.

Just as *Le Figaro* had played the dominant role in his dealings with the press in the decade preceding the publication of *Du côté de chez Swann*, the sober French daily *Le Temps* (1861–1942) took centre stage after 1913. These two rival publications of the centre cultivated markedly different images: *Le Figaro* had its chateaux and salons, *Le Temps* its embassies and foreign policy columns. 'Serious to the point of tedium', according to Pierre Albert, *Le Temps* distinguished itself by its large European readership and its authority in international affairs.'[11] Its literary rubric, *Les Lettres*, was signed during Proust's time by a series of illustrious literary critics: Anatole France, Gaston Deschamps and Paul Souday. Souday took up his post as literary critic at *Le Temps* in 1912 and kept it until his death in 1929, his influence spanning the most important years of Proust's career.

In an October 1913 letter to Proust, as *Du côté de chez Swann* was about to be launched, publisher Bernard Grasset gave an expert glimpse into the process of seeking publicity from the press. 'There are three journalistic ways of writing about a book; in chronological order, they are: *indiscretions*, excerpts, and articles. By "indiscretions", I mean those little notes in which a book is announced before its publication . . . Most newspapers have a rubric dedicated to these literary indiscretions' (*Corr*, XIII, 408). Grasset considered *Le Gil Blas*, *L'Intransigeant*, *Le Temps* and *Le Figaro* to be the most desirable publications in which to place a 'literary indiscretion' or *écho* (as they were called at *Le Figaro*). Excerpts were a more selective matter, since 'an important newspaper will rarely publish excerpts if another one already has'; he advised focusing their efforts on *Le Temps*. (In the end, *Le Gil Blas*, *Le Temps* and *Les Annales* published different excerpts within the space of a week.) Articles, finally, were the most important part of the publicity process. A front-page article, or *premier Paris*, in *Le Figaro* would be 'extremely advantageous', Grasset explained, especially if written by André Beaunier. They would also need one from Souday of *Le Temps*, Henri Chantavoine of *Le Journal des Débats* and Gustave Lanson of *Le Matin*.

Beginning with journalist Élie-Joseph Bois's interview of Proust, which appeared under the title '*À la recherche du temps perdu*' on 12 November 1913, *Le Temps* was enlisted in the vanguard of the launching of *Du côté de chez Swann*. This high-profile interview gave Proust a chance to explain how his forthcoming novel fitted into a larger ensemble, to unveil his conception of the art of the novel (a 'psychology in time'), and to introduce his concept of 'involuntary memory'. Much to his chagrin, *Le Temps* edited out his expressions of admiration for the book's dedicatee, Calmette. Was the article too long, or did *Le Temps* want to avoid casting a spotlight on *Le Figaro*'s influential chief editor? Whatever the case, Proust expressed his disappointment and regret in a letter to Calmette just before the interview was published. He went on to note that *Le Figaro* was 'the *only* newspaper dealing with literature' that had not announced his book. 'Perhaps you could publish an *écho* announcing the interview in *Le Temps*,' he added (*Corr*, XII, 308). A few days later, *Le Figaro* placed a prominent *écho* announcing *Du côté de chez Swann* – but made no allusion to the interview. It followed up its announcement eleven days later with a front-page review penned by Proust's friend Lucien Daudet (and not Beaunier, as Grasset had suggested).[12] Laudatory, personal and eloquent, Daudet's *Figaro* article was for Proust 'a sort of offering made to the past of an ancient friendship' (*Corr*, XII, 345).

Although *Le Figaro* was not without its unpleasant surprises, it was friendly territory. *Le Temps* was on another plane. Proust was blindsided by Souday's five-column review of *Du côté de chez Swann* in the 10 December issue of *Le Temps*. Souday offered no shortage of serious critiques: *Swann* had no structure; its subject was insignificant; it was written in a convoluted style. But above all, he imputed the book's many typographical and printing errors to its author – an affront to Proust's honour. Proust considered responding to the critic in the pages of *Le Temps*, but decided against it. The day after the review appeared, he began a private letter to Souday by alluding to the French *droit de réponse*:

> Monsieur, I do not wish to make use of a procedure that you might find offensive by responding to you in print, as I have the legal right to do ... My book may demonstrate no talent. But it at least presupposes and implies enough culture that it is not morally plausible that I would make errors as glaring as those you point out. (*Corr*, XII, 380–1)[13]

Whatever the tenor of Proust's first exchanges with Souday, *Du côté de chez Swann* benefited from the considerable prestige of being featured in *Le Temps* three times in the month following its publication.

As *À la recherche* expanded, Proust followed the press ever more closely. The reception of each volume, especially after the award of the Goncourt Prize (1919), was increasingly complex. Proust continued to engage each journalist-critic in a discussion of his or her article, as he had done with Souday – often in an effort to 'win them over to his cause', as Philip Kolb put it (*Corr*, XIX, iv). The landscape of the post-war press saw Jacques Boulenger at the head of *L'Opinion*, Jean de Pierrefeu (whom Proust considered the enemy) attached to *Le Journal des Débats*, and the eternal Souday at *Le Temps*. A November 1920 letter to Souday marks the evolution of Proust's relations with the critic and with published criticism. 'Three or four days ago, I had a "bad Souday"', Proust wrote, referring to Souday's review of *Le Côté de Guermantes* (4 November 1920). 'I would have thought so in the past. But now that I know you, now that I have shared in your grief [for the loss of Madame Souday] ... my disappointment at not being able to see you is all that counts and getting a "bad Souday" is nothing in comparison' (*Corr*, XIX, 574). Proust had developed with Souday a relationship that transcended the vicissitudes of literary judgment.

The dominance of *Le Temps* in the latter part of Proust's career is strangely reflected in its fictional representation in *À la recherche*. Among the twenty-five real-life titles mentioned in the novel, *Le Temps* alone is associated with the ritual mocking of a journalist (Brichot, pilloried by the Verdurin clan for his pedantic articles in *Le Temps*). Brichot's bombastic style can be traced back, in many of its characteristics, to a wartime column Proust detested: Joseph Reinach's 'commentaires de Polybe' in *Le Figaro*.[14] This leaves us with an interesting question. Given Brichot's strong genetic link to a *Figaro* journalist, why did Proust cast him as a writer for *Le Temps*? Perhaps to protect *Le Figaro*'s well-known function in the novel as the gateway to the hero's literary vocation – and his own image of *Le Figaro* as his one-time journalistic 'home'.

Notes

1 Zola's pro-Dreyfus *Figaro* articles of 1897, 'Monsieur Scheurer-Kestner' (25 November), 'Le Syndicat' (1 December), and 'Procès-Verbal' (5 December), launched his campaign to transform public opinion in the Affair. Proust's series of 'Salons' appeared in *Le Figaro* from February 1903 to May 1905, his 'Pastiches' from January 1904 to March 1909.

2 Claire Blandin, *Le Figaro: deux siècles d'histoire* (Paris: Armand Colin, 2007), pp. 61–2.

3 *L'Affaire Dreyfus: la vérité en marche* (Paris: Fasquelle, 1901), p. 26.

4 *Marcel Proust: sa vie, son œuvre* (Paris: Éditions du Sagittaire, 1925), p. 66. 'Horatio' and 'Dominique' were favourite Proustian pseudonyms.

5 'Proust chroniqueur', *Revue d'histoire littéraire de la France*, special issue: 'Marcel Proust', 71 (1971), 771–90 (772).

6 Pierre Albert, *Histoire de la presse* (Paris: Presses universitaires de France, 1970), p. 64. My summary here is based on Chapter 5, 'Le développement de la presse populaire à grand tirage (1871–1914)', pp. 55–75; and on Albert's chapter 'L'apogée de la presse française (1880–1914)', in Claude Bellanger, Jacques Godechot, Pierre Guiral and Fernand Terron, eds., *Histoire générale de la presse française*, 5 vols. (Paris: Presses universitaires de France, 1972), III, pp. 239–405.

7 Proust republished two of his essays on Ruskin, in modified form, in *Pastiches et mélanges* (1919). Others appear in *CSB*.

8 Calmette was assassinated in the offices of *Le Figaro* on 16 March 1914, by the wife of former prime minister Joseph Caillaux, after mounting a campaign against the politician in the pages of his newspaper. He was replaced by Robert de Flers (literary editor) and Alfred Capus (political editor).

9 Marcel Proust, *Chroniques* (Paris: Gallimard, 1927), p. 7.

10 Preface, *Autour de 'La Recherche': lettres* (Paris: Éditions Complexe, 1988), p. xv. I discuss the NRF's rejection of Proust's manuscript in Christine M. Cano, 'Mea Culpa: Gide, Proust, and the Nouvelle Revue française', *Romance Quarterly*, 50 (2003), 33–42.

11 Albert, 'L'apogée de la presse française', p. 352.

12 Daudet's article appeared on 27 November 1913. Beaunier, an important critic whose friendship Proust had cultivated for years, refused to write a review until the entire *Recherche* had appeared. In a series of letters to the critic in December 1913, Proust deftly encouraged him not to wait for such an uncertain completion. Beaunier died in 1925, without having published a line about Proust's novel.

13 Philip Kolb suggests in a note that Proust's original sentence expresses the opposite of what he means to say. The original gives the equivalent of: '. . . it is not morally *im*plausible that I would make errors as glaring as those you point out'. My translation follows Kolb.

14 See Christine M. Cano, 'Proust and the Wartime Press', in A. Watt, ed., *'Le Temps retrouvé' Eighty Years After/80 ans après: Critical Essays / Essais critiques* (Oxford: Peter Lang, 2009), pp. 133–40.

CHAPTER 21

Politics and class

Edward J. Hughes

Proust's public involvement in political campaigning preceded the years he spent working on *À la recherche*. His eager defence of Dreyfus is conveyed in *Jean Santeuil* where he delivers a forthrightly moral condemnation of judicial and military power, which is depicted as acting squarely in defence of *la raison d'État*. The other major issue on which he campaigned was Church–State relations. As an outspoken critic of the Combes government's policy of laicity, he opposed the separation of Church and State which was brought about in 1905. His 'La mort des cathédrales' ['Death of the Cathedrals'] (*Le Figaro*, 16 August 1904) provides a cultural defence of France's religious heritage, seen in his lofty yet implicitly political view as the legacy of a medieval, Christian faithful who form 'a great silent democracy' (*CSB*, 149). Writing to Georges de Lauris on 29 July 1903 (in a letter which Proust refers to as stupid and embarrassing, and one to be destroyed by its addressee), he provides a revealing snapshot of his political thinking at this time. Reflecting both on 'the dangerous mindset that gave rise to the [Dreyfus] Affair etc' prevalent in the late 1890s and on the growth in anticlericalism, Proust argues that in both cases, 'on travaille à faire deux France' (*Corr*, III, 382) ['the thrust of political life is to divide the country in two']. Concerned by 'the fermenting of hatred among the French' (*Corr*, III, 383), Proust notes how the press reinforces prejudice in the laicity debate and stifles independent thinking. He was to restate this view in *Le Temps retrouvé* where Charlus points to newspaper readers' deluded belief in their autonomous actions: '"ce public qui ne juge ainsi des hommes et des choses de la guerre que par les journaux est persuadé qu'il juge par lui-même". En cela M. de Charlus avait raison' (IV, 367) ['"this public which judges the men and events of the war solely from the newspapers, is persuaded that it forms its own opinions". In this M. de Charlus was right' (6: 122)]. Suspicious of virulent forms of nationalism during the First World War, Proust shows press influence to be a key agent of ideological formation.

160

Proust was born into a middle-class, Parisian family with liberal conservative political leanings, one that prospered within the structures of the Third French Republic, with his father, Dr Adrien Proust, rising to high rank in the field of public health. In his writing, Proust was both to share, and to take ironic distance from, the values, beliefs and prejudices of his class. In the first volume of *À la recherche*, social class barriers appear deeply embedded. Combray has a caste-like system within which domestic servants play their ancillary roles, an aloof aristocracy (the local Guermantes family) enjoys the deference paid to it from below, and the bourgeoisie represented by Marcel's family are solid defenders of the social order as evidenced by the moral disquiet they voice in relation to Swann's marriage to Odette. In *Un amour de Swann*, the situation of the middle-class Verdurins, whose salon is modestly positioned in social terms, appears to be no less rigidly set. Yet the overdetermined way in which social class fixity is conveyed in *Du côté de chez Swann* heightens the effect created later when the class configuration comes to mutate. By the end of the novel, Mme Verdurin, twice widowed and in her third marriage, has become the Princesse de Guermantes, while her earlier protégée, Odette de Crécy, has likewise joined the ranks of the aristocracy as Mme de Forcheville. By contrast, the standing of the Duchesse de Guermantes has fallen. 'Le pur du pur' ['the purest of the pure'] (6: 396; IV, 582) in terms of her genealogy – she was born a Guermantes and married a Guermantes –, she pursues her love of literature and the theatre while erroneously believing that this bohemian turn in no way threatens her situation. These individual life narratives point to a wider social revolution (hastened by the First World War) which, in very broad terms, sees the political and social triumph of the bourgeoisie and the decline of the aristocracy.[1]

Staying at Balbec's Grand Hôtel exposes the young Marcel to the mindset of France's provincial bourgeoisie, as does his relationship with Albertine. If the 'jeunes filles en fleurs' dazzle the Parisian adolescent with their seemingly exotic, bird-like provenance, their parents, who are suspicious of the Third Republic and the rhetoric of laicity, espouse an all too familiar, conservative, anti-Jewish politics. The provincial families boycott a concert in the town hall, from where, consistent with the secular culture promoted by the State, an image of Christ has been removed to the great shock of Andrée's mother. The animus directed at the nation's republican government extends to parents writing to the *Le Gaulois* newspaper to protest about the morally unsuitable questions featuring in their daughters' examination papers (2: 542; II, 243).

The exposure given to subaltern lives in *À la recherche* comes principally through evocation of the world of domestic service, within which rivalries to do with position and hierarchy are as present as in other social classes. Françoise seeks to eliminate any threat to the favour she enjoys within Marcel's family, her long-term service contrasting with the short stay of the kitchen-maid (Giotto's 'Charity') she has driven out (1: 147; 1, 122). But in her conversations with male domestic employees, her vulnerability emerges, as when she fearfully recalls the events of 1870 and discusses patriotism and military desertion with the gardener (1: 104; 1, 87). In a much later conversation with the maître d'hôtel as war breaks out in 1914, a politics of gender sees the male domestic sadistically heightening the fears of the woman-servant by perversely exaggerating the likely outcomes of the conflict (6: 71; IV, 327–8). At Balbec's Grand Hôtel, the management and ancillary staff emerge, in the Narrator's exuberant fresco, as though from a Pandora's box (2: 281; II, 26). And in the brothel scene in *Le Temps retrouvé*, Saint-Germain and Belleville meet as the working-class male prostitutes mix with their clients in a cross-class cohabitation that sees many aristocrats happy to stay away from high society in an atmosphere redolent of a wider social decadence (6: 180; IV, 414).

A range of political and ideological positions is represented and tested in *À la recherche*. While the tensions aroused by the Dreyfus Affair feature prominently in the account of the salon of Mme de Villeparisis in *Le Côté de Guermantes I*, the often ironic, significantly detached treatment of the affair in *À la recherche* contrasts markedly with the tone of moral protest which it attracts in *Jean Santeuil*. Broader political debate is also present in the mature novel. In *À l'ombre des jeunes filles en fleurs*, the Baron de Charlus and his socialist nephew Saint-Loup adopt conservative and progressive stances respectively on a range of issues. If pacifism, democratization, disarmament and leniency towards wrongdoers are all advocated by Saint-Loup, the Narrator undermines the liberal outlook by arguing that such steps may trigger more criminality, more war and a loss of international prestige (2: 389; II, 116). Yet putting a brake on Saint-Loup's progressivism does not equate to political reaction on the part of the Narrator, and in the same debate, he also rejects Charlus's social imaginary with its quirky conflation of art, upper-class prestige and social paternalism. In the aftermath of the First World War, we see Proust rejecting both aggressive nationalism and internationalism. In a letter to Daniel Halévy (*Corr*, XVIII, 334), he derides the cultural narrowness of 'Le Parti de l'Intelligence', whose nationalist manifesto appeared in *Le Figaro* on 19 July 1919, while also being mistrustful of internationalism of the kind promoted by Roman Rolland in a rival manifesto, 'Un appel: fière déclaration d'intellectuels', which appeared in *L'Humanité* (26 June 1919).

At Balbec, the new culture of leisure in early twentieth-century France sees rival social classes drawn into contiguity and the Narrator evokes with ludic pleasure the steps taken by the Marquise de Villeparisis to stem the flow of cross-class contact (2: 296–7; II, 38–40). Likewise, the train journey made by guests of Mme Verdurin heading to La Raspelière brings them into contact with local peasants, an encounter described by the Narrator in subversively comic terms (4: 305–7; III, 259–60). This irreverential handling of snobbery by the Narrator and the faltering steps taken by the young Marcel in his apprenticeship in the politics of social class demonstrate that the often ludic depiction of class rivalries is fundamental to Proust's narrative.

In *À la recherche*, the Marquis de Norpois provides the main conduit to the world of professional politics. Marcel's father, who is keenly interested in foreign affairs, enjoys close working relations with the career diplomat, who had the ear of Napoleon III in the run-up to the Franco-Prussian War, continued to exercise power after the Republican victory over President Mac-Mahon and the consolidation of the Third Republic in 1877, and, on the occasion of the state visit of King Theodosius, is reported by the press as conversing at length with the monarch at the Paris Opéra (2: 5–8; 1, 426–8). While far from being awestruck by Norpois's ability to maintain political influence over decades, Proust's Narrator nevertheless reflects analytically on how power sustains itself. He sees in Norpois's 'negative, methodical, conservative spirit' (2: 6; 1, 427) a mindset suited to the pursuit of state interests, as is Norpois's disdain for 'the methods of procedure, more or less revolutionary and at the very least improper, which are those of an Opposition' (2: 6; 1, 427). If the use of free indirect style sees the Narrator work seamlessly into the discourse of 'la Carrière' (1, 427), a theatrical effect is generated by the Narrator allowing the reader access to the copious expositions of the careerist Norpois. As Bowie observes, Norpois's class and profession 'licence him to speak voluminously, and to tyrannise his social inferiors with opinions and reminiscences'.[2]

The world of national and international politics is also accessed obliquely in Proust's work. For Vincent Descombes, Proust reduces much of *À la recherche* to an evocation of 'la vie mondaine' or worldliness, with 'the rest of life – business, scandals, crises, war, work – ... seen only as refracted in this world'.[3] This process of refraction is visible in the cognitive link made by the Narrator between the conduct of political and social life as he attempts to understand the unpredictable workings of power in the faubourg Saint-Germain. Thus, to comprehend the Duchesse de Guermantes' arbitrary manner and the 'epigrammatic malice' (3: 545; II, 763) which displays itself in the capricious verdicts she passes on social acquaintances, the Narrator looks to press coverage of parliamentary proceedings. For the theatricality and bombast in evidence in the Chamber of Deputies and the perverse unpredictability with which common-sense views are there ridiculed parallel the 'artificial and dramatic decisions' (3: 549; II, 766) which Oriane is given to making. With Proust able to 'represent politics as a cruel dreamlike charade', power works as seductively in the Chamber as it does in Saint-Germain.[4] Thus while political moves to expose wrongdoing, to make the rich pay more than the poor, and to secure peace and not war may seem routine in the Narrator's view, thunderous applause in the Chamber can be used – shockingly, he reflects – to make such moves appear scandalous. If Proust's urge is to fathom the volatilities present in opinion-formation, the herding instinct which he sees as underpinning the creation of majorities can turn common sense on its head. To draw again on Bowie, in Proust, 'politics itself is the science of contradiction in the social sphere'.[5] In *Jean Santeuil*, a fictional transposition of Jean Jaurès's intervention sees Couzon speak out in the Chamber against the Armenian massacres of 1894–6 only for his protest to be drowned out by right-wing deputies, the force of whose stupidity and sneering contempt for 'Truth' is seen as morally repugnant by the Narrator (*JS*, 602).

In *À la recherche*, the twinning of politics and salon life thus allows for exploration of the herding instinct. The Verdurin salon provides an instructive example: Saniette plays the role of scapegoat or 'souffre-douleur' and, like Charlus later in the novel, undergoes an 'exécution' (I, 272) ['[is] finished … off' (I: 333)] there; Swann is expelled from the clan; and Brichot is ridiculed when he rises to become a high-profile, patriotic journalist of the First World War. The string of exclusions illustrates paradigmatically Proust's method of 'analy[sing] social life in terms of *election* and *exclusion*'.[6]

A logic of political mutation forms part of the long view inscribed by Proust in *À la recherche*. The same Verdurin salon, once a forum for anti-Semitism, undergoes evolution in a manner which, for the Narrator, is as hard to imagine as, in another era, a salon that might declare itself loyal to the cause of the Paris Commune: 'The little clan was in fact the active centre of a long political crisis which had reached its maximum of intensity: Dreyfusism' (4: 166; III, 141). Culture wars run their course, a point illustrated anecdotally by the case of the Duc de Guermantes. Swayed by three intelligent, aristocratic women whom he meets at a spa town, he becomes a Dreyfusard, the Narrator observing that countries, like individuals, undergo periodic change: 'many countries which we have left full of hatred for another race . . . six months later, have changed their minds and reversed their alliances' (4: 162; III, 138).

With political causes thus changing, so too does the designation of those who are publicly demonized. Opponents of 'la loi de trois ans' – the law which extended military service to three years and was introduced in 1913 as part of the growing militarization that preceded the war – take the place of once-denigrated Dreyfusards, one of whom, M. Bontemps, is closely involved in framing the new legislation and can thus bathe in nationalist approval (5: 44; IV, 305). Likewise Joseph Reinach, earlier vilified on account of his very public support for Dreyfus, enjoys rehabilitation as an enthusiastic advocate of 'l'Union Sacrée' (6: 276; IV, 492).

The Narrator's telescopic social survey prompts the conclusion that individual changes of social fortune are 'quasi-historical' (4: 164; III, 140):

> Dans une certaine mesure les manifestations mondaines (fort inférieures aux mouvements artistiques, aux crises politiques, à l'évolution qui porte le goût public vers le théâtre d'idées, puis vers la peinture impressionniste, puis vers la musique allemande et complexe, puis vers la musique russe et simple, ou vers les idées sociales, les idées de justice, la réaction religieuse, le sursaut patriotique) en sont cependant le reflet lointain, brisé, incertain, troublé, changeant. (III, 139–40)

> To a certain extent social manifestations (vastly less important than artistic movements, political crises, the trend that leads public taste towards the theatre of ideas, then towards Impressionist painting, then towards music that is German and complicated, then music that is Russian and simple, or towards ideas of social service, ideas of justice, religious reaction, outbursts of patriotism) are nevertheless an echo of them, distant, disjointed, uncertain, changeable, blurred. (4: 164)

If politics, culture and 'la vie mondaine' all share the propensity to mutate, Proust's choice of five epithets aimed at establishing the homology points to its elusive character. The sense of ideological connections working across high society and politics extends to the linkage between the emotional life of individuals and affairs of state. Thus the successive fraught love affairs of Marcel's life come to be understood via an analogy with the sequence of hatreds governing national and international affairs. In both private and public domains, passion blights perspective. Saint-Loup and Marcel hold distorted views of Rachel and Albertine respectively, just as the Narrator confesses to Germanophobia (6: 275; IV, 491). Signalling the ideological hold of prejudice, Proust constructs a genealogy of collective antagonisms (anticlericalism, anti-Semitism, anti-German feeling, 6: 276; IV, 492). In this compacting together of hatreds, Proust's Narrator demonstrates the free availability of prejudice surfacing afresh in new socio-political configurations (2: 103; 1, 508).

Notes

1 René Girard comments on the radical way in which Proust demystifies the lure of the faubourg Saint-Germain: see René Girard, *Mensonge romantique et vérité romanesque* (Paris: Grasset, 1961), p. 221. For an exploration of how culture played a central role in the bourgeois erosion of aristocratic hegemony, see Catherine Bidou-Zachariasen, *Proust sociologue: de la maison aristocratique au salon bourgeois* (Paris: Descartes & Cie, 1997).
2 Malcolm Bowie, *Proust among the Stars* (London: HarperCollins, 1998), p. 160.
3 Vincent Descombes, *Proust: Philosophy of the Novel*, trans. by Catherine Chance Macksey (Stanford University Press, 1992), p. 178.
4 Bowie, *Proust among the Stars*, p. 132.
5 Bowie, *Proust among the Stars*, p. 157.
6 Descombes, *Philosophy of the Novel*, p. 186; emphasis in the original.

CHAPTER 22

The Dreyfus Affair

Edward J. Hughes

In *Le Temps retrouvé*, Proust's Narrator complains about politics invading the space of literature. Thus writers who put before the demands of literature the search for justice, as in the Dreyfus Affair, or the advocacy of national unity in the context of the First World War, are rebuked by the Narrator: 'How many ... turn aside from writing!' (6: 233; IV, 458). While this could be read biographically as the view of an author long embarked on a career of literary production, the forthright defence of the claims of literature belies the fact that the younger Proust responded with some urgency to major political events of his day. Thus in a letter of December 1919, a quarter of century after Dreyfus's initial conviction, Proust could still boast of his early role as an active defender of Dreyfus, who had been found guilty of spying for Germany in December 1894: 'My signature was on the very first of the pro-Dreyfus lists and I was an ardent Dreyfusard, sending a copy of my first book to Picquart in the Cherche-Midi prison' (*Corr*, XVIII, 545).

The representations of the Dreyfus Affair in Proust's work are to be found principally in *Jean Santeuil* and *À la recherche du temps perdu* and they demonstrate a significant evolution in response, from the campaigning eagerness of the early novel to the retrospective consideration in the *Recherche* of a crisis, the intensity of which had been substantially diminished by the time of composition of the novel. Proust was an early believer in the innocence of the Jewish captain from Alsace who was humiliatingly stripped of his military rank at a degradation parade in January 1895 and imprisoned on L'Île du Diable. He worked to secure the support of Anatole France for the Dreyfus cause and in a letter of January 1899 congratulated the high-profile novelist on his intervention (*Corr*, II, 272).

In *Jean Santeuil*, Proust reflects this period of intense national crisis principally through the trial of Émile Zola. This followed on a month after the latter's defiant 'J'accuse' (published in *L'Aurore* on 13 January 1898) in which he protested Dreyfus's innocence. Proust highlights the opposition

167

between two principal figures in the court proceedings: General de Boisdeffre and Colonel Picquart. If the former exudes an overweening military power, Picquart is idealized as a figure unambiguously wedded to truth. Proust draws a parallel with the portrait of Socrates in Plato's *Phædo* (*JS*, 342; 641), the comparison highlighting the sacrificial pursuit of truth, which the young Proust was keen to champion. The Narrator in *Jean Santeuil* explains:

> C'est ce sentiment qu'on pouvait éprouver en entendant le colonel Picquart et qui nous émeut tant dans le *Phédon*, quand en suivant le raisonnement de Socrate nous avons tout d'un coup le sentiment extraordinaire d'entendre un raisonnement dont aucune espèce de désir personnel n'est venue altérer la pureté, comme si la vérité était supérieure à tout. (*JS*, 641)

> That was the feeling one had in listening to Colonel Picquart, the same feeling of which we are chiefly conscious, which moves us so deeply, in reading the *Phædo*, when following Socrates' arguments we are suddenly overwhelmed by the realization that we are listening to a process of logical reasoning wholly undebased by any selfish motive, as though nothing ... could have any meaning except truth in all its purity. (*JS*, 342)

If Picquart embodies witness to the Truth ('Vérité' and 'Justice' are capitalized by Proust, *JS*, 602), the young novelist similarly welcomes the intervention of Auguste Scheurer-Kestner, vice-president of the Senate who publicly asserted Dreyfus's innocence in the summer of 1897 (*JS*, 351, 651). Science provides another counter to the workings of corrupt power in *Jean Santeuil*, the objective testimony of graphologists in the Zola trial being heralded as an edifying expression of commitment to analytical rigour. Indeed in 'La Vérité et les opinions', the Narrator commends, in cases of litigation, the scrupulous establishment of legal and medical truth based on scientific detachment, a fearless scrutiny of evidence and indifference to the workings of public opinion (*JS*, 350–1, 649–51).

Beyond the intensely public sphere of the court room, the early novel also focuses significantly on the private world inhabited by Mme Santeuil, a passionate, if closet, defender of Dreyfus. 'Madame Santeuil et l'Affaire' (*JS*, 657–9), a biographical transposition of how Proust's Jewish mother, Jeanne Weil, responded to the events, constructs an emotional portrait of the maternal figure who, notwithstanding the conventional bourgeois marriage within which she plays a subservient role, rebels privately against state injustice and empathizes intensely with Picquart, who is facing imprisonment for having maintained that the incriminating memorandum allegedly penned by Dreyfus was the work of Major Esterhazy. While far from being a public radical, Mme Santeuil, 'en proie à la torture d'un mal'

(*JS*, 657) ['burdened by deep suffering'] thus lives the Affair with an intensity that amounts to a form of martyrdom. This private inflection signals a more general movement in Proust whereby public drama is often captured prismatically through interior worlds.

While Dreyfus was to be rehabilitated, being decorated with the Légion d'honneur in 1906, and Zola, the once vilified advocate of Dreyfus's innocence, was to be posthumously honoured in 1908 with the depositing of his ashes in the Panthéon, Proust was less drawn to these later twists in the public narrative of the Affair. Yuji Murakami explains this turning away from intense identification with the Affair in biographical terms, identifying a number of critical factors: the serious illness of Proust's mother in 1899 (she was to die in 1905, two years after the demise of Professor Adrien Proust), Proust's decision to embark on the work of translating Ruskin, and his unease about the cultural politics surrounding the separation of Church and State brought about by the Combes government in 1905. In *Pastiches et mélanges* (1919), Proust was to reflect on the ephemeral nature of political passion: 'combien, à quelques années de distance, les mots changent de sens et combien sur le chemin tournant du temps, nous ne pouvons pas apercevoir l'avenir d'une nation plus que d'une personne' (*CSB*, 142) ['how words change their meaning in the space of a few years, and how it is that, on the twisting road of time, we are no more able to see the future of a nation than that of a person'], Proust observed.

The reminder about the fallibility that undermines our attempts to grasp the course of events signals not only a dispersal of political intensity but also the question of the retrospective depiction of that intensity. In the case of the Dreyfus Affair, it has an afterlife in Proust's work. As Murakami reminds us, Proust retains from the earlier drama the crucial image of the scapegoat, which he was to weave into his later writing, most notably in *Sodome et Gomorrhe* where the homology of the Jew and the homosexual, who are paired as victims of social oppression forced to pursue furtively their cause and desire, forms a central plank in Proust's platform for the defence of homosexuality.[1]

Alongside the sympathetic evocation of those on the side of justice in the Dreyfus case, the *Recherche* harnesses the energies of anti-Semitism released across the nation by the Affair. Already in *Jean Santeuil*, the accommodation of the voices of racial and religious bigotry is signalled: 'juif, nous comprenons l'antisémitisme, et, partisan de Dreyfus, nous comprenons le jury d'avoir condamné Zola' (*JS*, 651) ['If we happen to be Jews, we make a point of trying to understand the anti-Semite point of view: if believers in Dreyfus, we try to see precisely why it was the jury found against Zola' (*JS*, 353)]. The suggestion of a protean narrative acting as resonance chamber for the circulation of prejudice sees Proust's Narrator working promiscuously both inside and outside the mindset of the anti-Semite. This siding with the enemy entails an internalization of the adversary's viewpoint that will later manifest itself in the insertion of venom of the kind heard, for example, at the salon of Mme de Villeparisis in *Le Côté de Guermantes I*. There, an atmosphere of generalized anti-Semitism prevails, the view of the Prince de Guermantes 'qu'il fallait renvoyer tous les juifs à Jérusalem' (II, 532) ['that all the Jews ought to be sent back to Jerusalem' (3: 267)] epitomizing the mood of hostility. Catherine Bidou-Zachariasen identifies 'the logic that had constructed Dreyfus's guilt and that had been set in motion by a social elite in decline and reduced to a tense nationalism and anti-Semitism'.[2]

The Dreyfus Affair also serves paradigmatically as an indicator of how the workings of power entail a will to monopolize truth. Thus in *Le Temps retrouvé*, the Narrator argues that with the Dreyfus Affair, as with the war and the world of medicine, those in power – 'les gens du pouvoir' – make authoritarian claims about the rightness of their judgment: 'j'avais vu ... croire que la vérité est un certain fait, que les ministres, le médecin, possèdent un oui ou un non qui n'a pas besoin d'interprétation, qui fait qu'un cliché radiographique indique sans interprétation ce qu'a le malade, que les gens du pouvoir savaient si Dreyfus était coupable' (IV, 493) ['I had seen everybody believe ... that truth is a particular piece of knowledge which cabinet ministers and doctors possess, a Yes or No which requires no interpretation, thanks to the possession of which the men in power *knew* whether Dreyfus was guilty or not' in the same way that an x-ray photograph is supposed to indicate without any need for interpretation the exact nature of a patient's disease (6: 278)].

In contrast with *Jean Santeuil*, *À la recherche*, far from idealizing the role of individual protagonists in the Affair, points not only to the intense animosities the events aroused but also to the unpredictable developments that came in their wake. Chronologically removed from the immediacy of the earlier conflict, Proust thus has his Narrator note in *Le Temps retrouvé* that the sons of noblemen who had vilified Dreyfus (the aristocracy having formed part of the bedrock of anti-Dreyfus opinion) embrace the Affair as an exotic, fashionable cause. More generally, the Narrator reflects on how strongly held judgments are both powerful and ephemeral. This aura of transience is reinforced when the Narrator describes how prominent Dreyfusards who had been demonized now come to be embraced, a decade later, by ultra-nationalists in wartime France:

j'avais déjà vu dans mon pays des haines successives qui avaient fait apparaître, par exemple, comme des traîtres – mille fois pires que les Allemands auxquels ils livraient la France – des dreyfusards comme Reinach avec lequel collaboraient aujourd'hui les patriotes contre un pays dont chaque membre était forcément un menteur, une bête féroce, un imbécile, exception faite des Allemands qui avaient embrassé la cause française. (IV, 491–2)

I had already seen in my country successive hates which had, for example, at one time condemned as traitors – a thousand times worse than the Germans into whose hands they were delivering France – those very Dreyfusards such as Reinach with whom today patriotic Frenchmen were collaborating against a race whose every member was of necessity a liar, a savage beast, a madman, excepting only those Germans who ... had embraced the French cause. (6: 276)

If the rehabilitation of the deputy Joseph Reinach epitomizes the new order, the realignment is consistent with the politics of 'L'Union Sacrée' which actively sought the suppression of memory of the Dreyfus Affair in the pursuit of national unity. As part of the same new consensus, Brichot can refer to the Dreyfus Affair as forming part of prehistory (6: 45; IV, 306). In reflecting on what he presents as a sequence of successive hatreds, Proust's Narrator thus establishes a diachronic perspective on the channels of social exclusion and demonization. Likewise, he sees the social advantage accruing from an opportunistic political alignment. Hence the inexorable rise of Mme Verdurin, whose once anti-Semitic salon rapidly acquires prestige by becoming Dreyfusard in orientation and counting Zola and Picquart among its guests. The strategic embrace of progressivism which this signals throws into relief the selfless pursuit of truth evoked in relation to the Zola trial in *Jean Santeuil*.

More generally in *À la recherche*, Proust's Narrator relishes the fluctuations that mark individual responses to the Dreyfusard cause long after the earlier, intense phase of the crisis. Thus Robert de Saint-Loup, who had been conspicuous in aristocratic circles as someone sympathetic to the cause, comes to align himself with the military. For Charles Swann, who embraces the Dreyfus cause years later with the same naïveté that he had shown when he married Odette, his Dreyfusism nevertheless ensures greater personal authenticity in the Narrator's eyes by estranging him from the aristocratic circles to which he had become used. This restores him, honourably as the Narrator insists, to the social class of his ancestors: 'ce nouveau déclassement eût été mieux appelé "reclassement" et n'était qu'honorable pour lui' (II, 870) ['this new "declassing" would have been better described as a "reclassing" and was entirely to his credit' (3: 673)]. Meanwhile Mme Swann covers up the background of her husband by joining with aristocratic women in the aggressive pursuit of anti-Semitism (3: 288; II, 549).

There is abundant evidence of the Narrator's ludic evocation of prejudice in the *Recherche*. Thus the Duchesse de Guermantes, who sees as natural her absence of dealings with Jews, complains of the disturbance in social hierarchy whereby opponents of Dreyfus see this as a passport to contact with like-minded anti-Semites regardless of their social class:

> je trouve insupportable que, sous prétexte qu'elles sont bien pensantes, qu'elles n'achètent rien aux marchands juifs ou qu'elles ont 'Mort aux Juifs' écrit sur leurs ombrelles, une quantité de dames Durand ou Dubois, que nous n'aurions jamais connues, nous soient imposées par Marie-Aynard ou par Victurnienne. Je suis allée chez Marie-Aynard avant-hier. C'était charmant autrefois. Maintenant on y trouve toutes les personnes qu'on a passé sa vie à éviter, sous prétexte qu'elles sont contre Dreyfus. (II, 535)

> I do think it perfectly intolerable that just because they're supposed to be right-thinking and don't deal with Jewish tradesmen, or have "Down with the Jews" written on their sunshades, we should have a swarm of Durands and Dubois and so forth, women we should never have known but for this business, forced down our throats by Marie-Aynard or Victurnienne I went to see Marie-Aynard a couple of days ago. It used to be so nice there. Nowadays one finds all the people one has spent one's life trying to avoid, on the pretext that they're against Dreyfus. (3: 271)

As Proust accurately reflects, anti-Semitism was to be found in all social classes in the Third Republic. Aimé demonstrates its populist expression by protesting that the captain is guilty a thousand times over (2: 446; II, 164); in *À l'ombre des jeunes filles en fleurs*, Albertine reveals how within the provincial Catholic bourgeoisie, anti-Semitic bigotry was rife as when she comments on Marcel's friend Bloch: 'Je l'aurais parié que c'était un youpin. C'est bien leur genre de faire les punaises' (II, 235) ['I would have betted anything he was a Yid. Typical of their creepy ways!' (2: 533)]; in *Combray*, Marcel's grandfather, aware that his young grandson has invited a Jewish friend home, hums lines from various operatic sources in a veiled, anti-Semitic jibe (1: 107–8; 1, 90–1); and the Baron de Charlus draws perverse pleasure from his vilification of Jews who reside at addresses that recall a would-be pure, medieval Christian heritage (4: 586; III, 491). But alongside the ubiquitous prejudice that transcends social class, Proust also signals Jewish anti-Semitism, as when those culturally assimilated Jews refer condescendingly to central European immigrants, whose recent arrival in France accounts for their conspicuously Jewish form of dress. Thus Bloch, standing on the beach at Balbec, utters 'des imprécations contre le fourmillement d'Israélites qui infestait Balbec' (II, 97) ['a torrent of imprecation against the swarm of Jews that infested Balbec' (2: 367)].

Working with, but also seeking to detach from, the intensities of the political moment, Proust's Narrator uses the metaphor of the social kaleidoscope to capture the volatility in intense ideological alignments: 'L'affaire Dreyfus … amena un nouveau [changement] … Tout ce qui était juif passa en bas … et des salons nationalistes obscurs montèrent prendre sa place' (I, 508) ['The Dreyfus case brought about another [change] … Everything Jewish … went down, and various obscure nationalists rose to take its place' (2: 103)]. Indeed the Narrator, arguing that any sense that social affairs might follow a settled pattern is illusory, prefers to see the social – which is only ever 'momentanément immobile' (I, 508) ['momentarily stationary' (2: 104)] – in a perpetual state of transmutation.

Notes

1 Yuji Murakami, 'L'Affaire Dreyfus dans l'œuvre de Proust' (doctoral thesis, Université de Paris-Sorbonne, 2012), p. 512.
2 C. Bidou-Zachariasen, *Proust sociologue: de la maison aristocratique au salon bourgeois* (Paris: Descartes & Cie, 1997), p. 92.

CHAPTER 23

The First World War

Brigitte Mahuzier

À la recherche du temps perdu as we know it is a product of the war. When the First World War broke out, in August 1914, Proust, who was forty-three, asthmatic, and in poor health (he would live only another eight years), had just published the first volume, *Du côté de chez Swann* (1913). At this point, the *Recherche* was in its author's mind only a trilogy, a Hegelian structure with a redemptive *Aufhebung.* To the notion of 'lost time' (in the first volume) would correspond that of 'time regained' (in the third volume). In between, *Le Côté de Guermantes* would be a sort of 'crossing of the desert,' time wasted rather than lost ('perdu' has both meanings), which in the end would be redeemed through Art, an episode called 'Adoration perpétuelle'.

The overall structure, time lost/time regained, of the cathedral-like novel endured. But the volume in between, *Le Côté de Guermantes*, which was ready for the press, did not. A moratorium on publication prevented Grasset, then Gallimard from publishing it, and as the surprisingly long war extended the moratorium, it gave Proust time to dismantle this first *Guermantes* and reconstruct, expand and modify the middle section in ways he had not anticipated.

The war affected not only the sheer length of the novel – it grew from three to seven volumes – but the movement of writing itself as well as its content. On the model of the 'intermittences du cœur', a 1908 overall title which Proust had abandoned in 1913 only to incorporate it as a subtitle in *Sodome et Gomorrhe II*, he imparts his novel with large 'mouvements de balancier' (pendulum movements, a metaphor often found in the *Recherche* to evoke the beatings of the heart). He moved backwards by adding *À l'ombre des jeunes filles en fleurs* before his new *Côté de Guermantes*, and frontwards, with a series of volumes in which his recent personal loss (the abrupt departure and death of Alfred Agostinelli who 'disappeared' in an aeroplane accident off the Mediterranean coast just before the outbreak of the war) would take on a larger, national dimension, inaugurating the

174

'disappearance', in similarly obscure conditions, of so many young men during the war. The two unpredictable events that took place in 1914 a few months apart, Agostinelli's death and the start of the war, would profoundly alter the novel. But as Proust introjected the character of Albertine and developed his *Sodome et Gomorrhe* series (*La Prisonnière* and *Albertine disparue* were, until 1922, titled *Sodome et Gomorrhe III* and *IV*), he was also pursuing his early plan of writing a very serious yet 'indecent' novel where the sodomite and gomorrhean themes would be intertwined.

From the outbreak of the war until the day he died (in November 1922), Proust would never cease adding to the inner sections of the novel, expanding it to dimensions which, had he lived longer, would have been yet larger. Working from within his overall structure, and from within his cork-lined room, his bed littered with daily papers, military reports and combat analyses, Proust, like Aunt Léonie in her bedroom in Combray, was immersed in the world outside, the chronicle of which he followed day by day, studying and commenting on military strategies and deployments of troops with unflagging interest. In *Le Temps retrouvé*, Robert de Saint-Loup, a career officer and close friend of the Narrator, his inside source of information on the life in the frontline and on military strategy, compares a good writer to a general on a battlefield, who, realizing that his original plans have deviated as the battle itself evolved, must re-adjust them according to the well-known diversion strategy:

> A general is like a writer who sets out to write a certain play, a certain book, and then the book itself, with the unexpected potentialities which it reveals here, the impassable obstacles which it presents there, makes him deviate to an enormous degree from his preconceived plan. You know, for instance, that a diversion should only be made against a position which is itself of considerable importance; well, suppose the diversion succeeds beyond all expectation, while the principal operation results in a deadlock: the diversion may then become the principal operation. (6: 86; IV, 341)

What is stressed here is that a good diversion strategy, aiming to surprise the enemy (here the reader), must be deployed on a point which, from the beginning, has been considered important enough to become the main operation. In other words, the interference of the Great War, which was to deviate the novel from its original project, gave Proust the opportunity to make of inversion, a theme already important before the war, a perfect diversion.

It is not surprising, given that the queer spectacle of war was viewed from an invalid's bed, that relatively little attention has been accorded to the treatment of the war in the novel. The war episode itself was relegated to the end of the novel, in *Le Temps retrouvé*, and for a long time the *Recherche* appeared as the antithesis of a war novel, its world peopled with 'partouzards indécis attendant leur Watteau, toujours' ['irresolute smut-fingering seekers always awaiting their Watteau'] to quote Louis-Ferdinand Céline's inimitable style in his *Voyage au bout de la nuit*.[1] In this gritty semi-autobiographical novel, a modern epic which takes the reader from the mud of the trenches to the mud of the Paris suburb, and revolutionized the literary landscape when it was published in 1932, Céline's caricature of Proust and the Parisian idle rich of the rear, was in keeping with his denunciation of the war and with a certain image of Proust as a 'ghost' belonging to a world both past and feminine.

In 1919, when the Académie Goncourt, a group of belles-lettristes in charge of awarding a prize for the best novel of the year, chose Proust's second volume, *À l'ombre des jeunes filles en fleurs*, over Roland Dorgelès's immensely successful war novel, *Les Croix de bois*, they enshrined an image of Proust and his world as feminine, pre-war and peaceful.[2] Proust's 'jeunes filles' were seen as the absolute opposite of the virile 'poilus', the heroes of the trenches. In short, Proust was the anti-Céline. According to a contemporary critic, Philippe Dufour, who has studied the impact of the war on modernist realism, Proust, unlike Céline to whom he is compared, had missed the boat: the Great War, he writes, 'vient buter contre la *Recherche*' ['stumbles on/bangs against the *Recherche*'], it just did not affect its Belle Époque world.[3]

Proust indeed seemed the very opposite of a 'poilu' author, and his 'trenches' were entirely situated in the Parisian world of the rear. Unlike his younger brother, Robert, who reported for duty and insisted on being sent as medical officer to the frontline, near Verdun, on the first day of the war, the author used his connections to be discharged and was declared unfit for service. Aside from his usual trip to Cabourg (3 September–14 October 1914), made once he had ascertained that his brother's family had safely reached Pau, he stayed in Paris when it was dangerous to do so and when he could have easily fled to a safer place (like Gilberte who takes cover in Combray), in particular during the January 1916 zeppelin raids and the late 1918 poundings of the German canons, misnamed by the Parisians the 'Grosse Bertha'.

From the first day of the war, Proust feared for the safety of his brother, his friends, Reynaldo Hahn, Bertrand de Fénelon, Robert d'Humières, for the 'millions of men [who] are going to be massacred in a war of the worlds comparable to that of Wells because it is advantageous for the Emperor of Austria to have access to the Black Sea' (as he puts it in a letter sent to his financial advisor, Lionel Hauser, the night he accompanied his brother to the Gare de l'Est, *Corr*, XIII, 283). Yet, despite his denunciation, made in his correspondence, of the immoral nature of the so-called Great War and his lack of concern for his own safety, Proust is often catalogued as a suspiciously disengaged and apolitical writer, belonging to the world of *planqués* (ones who hide from danger), the Brichot or Norpois type he mocks so sarcastically in *Le Temps retrouvé*.

The war episode, as a separate piece which Proust included in *Le Temps retrouvé* in 1916 and 1917, reinforces this image of the author as a somewhat distant observer. The critic Maurice Rieuneau, commenting on this episode in the 1970s, argues that the war, as it loses its specifically historical aspect, becomes one more element (like love, inversion, social life and political passions) incorporated into the novel's 'quête intérieure psychologique' ['interior psychological quest'].[4] Rieuneau's approach reinforces the image of Proust as primarily a philosopher and an artist, who, although obsessed with the war, considers it 'from a great distance'. Proust himself served to attenuate the impact of the war as a historical event by the image we have of him as a writer who elevated his art 'above the mêlée', inciting his reader to replace the daily paper with a selection from Pascal's *Pensées*, as Swann had ironically (which for him meant seriously) suggested that one should do.

In recent years, socio-historically minded critics, such as Michael Sprinker, Edward Hughes and Jacques Dubois, have taken a close and bracing look at the war episode, stressing Proust's immense talents as a socio-historical moralist as he depicted the effects of the war on people's behaviour and mentalities.[5] Proust, in this light, is a sort of 'moraliste du grand siècle', his characters – Mme Verdurin, Charlus, Bloch, Morel, Brichot, the gardener-turned-manservant, even Françoise – becoming during the war caricatures of their pre-war selves. Offering no moral rules of conduct, imbued with the irony and detachment of the seventeenth-century *moraliste*, as well as the scientific distance and dispassionate detachment of the entomologist Jean-Henri Fabre for his insects, Proust would seem to have included the war episode to prepare the reader for the final Goyesque tableau, the 'Bal de têtes', before the artistic redemption of 'L'adoration perpétuelle'.

In the theoretical and overall framing part of *Le Temps retrouvé*, there is a clear indictment of two related forms of art, descriptive and prescriptive literature, both of which could encompass war literature: 'littérature de notation' (IV, 473), another term for descriptive literature (6: 253), and literature with an agenda, in this case 'patriotic art' (6: 237; IV, 466). His rejection of patriotic art, which was directed at such novels as Barrès's 'romans de l'énergie nationale', was in direct line with Flaubert's art-for-art's-sake stance, his suspicion of 'littérature de notation', applied to war literature, as well as from Stendhal's 'soupçon' about language's inability to translate a battlefield experience. As Saint-Loup demonstrates in his letters from the front, where he reclaims worn-out expressions such as 'passeront pas' [they shall not pass] or 'on les aura' ['we'll get them'], ready to write with them a national epic, participation in war offers no certificate of authenticity, and proves insufficient to turn war witnesses into adequate translators of their own experience. The only time Saint-Loup is true to himself and adequately representing his experience on the front is when he describes his impression of the war as if he were on a duck hunt. Language being inadequate to the task, the war could not be written by those who were fighting it on the front. If war could be translated into language, it would be written directly on the bodies of those who lived it, like the mark on Saint-Loup's forehead (*front* in French) as he came back to Paris for a last period of leave.

The front was a mystical place, a place of hell, of death, of the Real, whatever is beyond representation, and Proust, through his Narrator who remains throughout the *Recherche* very sensitive about language, its use and misuse, collaborated with that perception. Effectively casting himself out of the war, in the world of *planqués* or *embusqués* who play at war, exploit it in new creative ways, and disgrace its heroes and potential epic, nation-building narratives, Proust seemed to resemble his own caricatures: Mme Verdurin and her *petite église* transformed into an intelligence and espionage centre, and Charlus with his hotel exploiting young soldiers for his own personal pleasure and fantasy, when not chasing men in uniforms through the dark streets of Paris.

This *planqué* image that we have of him is also due to his own anti-Beuvian stance on the separation between life and work. 'Le monsieur qui dit "je"' whose opinions on the war appear to be tepidly patriotic and mostly non-committal, does not speak for the author, whose voice on the war is disseminated and more often heard coming from the Germanophile and defeatist Baron de Charlus. Proust's critique of the war, through Charlus in particular, is very close in content to his own. This is clear in Charlus's long diatribe against war journalism as 'warspeak'.[6] It is also surprisingly close to Romain Rollands's opinions, which he expressed in a series of anti-war letters published from Geneva between 1914 and 1915 in *Le Journal de Genève*. But whereas Rolland proclaimed them loud and clear, and was branded defeatist and anti-patriotic, Proust's comments were reserved for his friends in the privacy of his correspondence.[7] As Marion Schmid demonstrates, in her socio-genetic analysis of an early draft of 'Monsieur de Charlus pendant la guerre', in the writing and rewriting of the war episode, Proust censored his own private opinions on the war while using 'oblique strategical ways' to express them.[8] One such approach is via the Baron de Charlus.

Proust not only disseminated his personal critique of the war through one of his 'tantes', a crazy, anti-Semite SM queen turned pederast at the end of his life, who is viewed with a mixture of suspicion and disgust by the Narrator; he also projected a number of his more intimate convictions and feelings on Charlus's nephew, Robert de Saint-Loup. Saint-Loup's love for the Army (which recalls the embellished memory of Proust's own military service in 1889–90 as 'paradis militaire'), his fascination with war strategy (which Proust ingurgitated each day as a remedy against his nevralgic obsession with the war), his patriotic love, rooted in his attachment to places and place-names, a necessary mute form of love which he compares to the one between mother and son, all this made Saint-Loup the necessary double of Charlus. As Rieuneau puts it, Proust's 'heart was with Saint-Loup but he remained lucid enough to judge his compatriots along with Charlus'.[9] In other words, it took at least two characters, the uncle and the nephew, to disseminate the author's own controversial and highly contradictory position at the time: his patriotism coupled with a love for the Army and an attraction to the Army's values and lifestyle on the one hand which was and still is confused with right-wing nationalism and militarism, and his left-wing severe criticism of war which brings him close to Jaurès, and anticipates, as Marion Schmid points out in the above-mentioned article, Althusser's critique of ideology in *Ideology and Ideological State Apparatus*.

Post-First World War literature is replete with real and metaphorical voyages, through darkness, despair and derision: whether written by war veterans (such as Céline's *Voyage au bout de la nuit*, or Bernanos's *Sous le Soleil de Satan* (1926)), or by home-front writers such as Colette's *La Fin de Chéri* (1926) or Mauriac's *La Fin de la nuit* (1935). These novels mark the disappearance of a world that had vanished with the war. The *Recherche* is no different. As the protagonist learns from a second letter written by Gilberte (who witnessed the battle of Méséglise, which she describes with the same technical details as Verdun), there is nothing left of his beloved church of Combray, all sites of memory which he shared with Gilberte have been desecrated by the war; there is no returning to Combray. What matters now is that long walk taken by the Narrator in the company of

Charlus, through the night in wartime Paris, during which is finally accomplished the *nunc erudimini* (now learn for your profit) that the Baron had unsuccessfully offered the Narrator during his visit at the end of *Guermantes* (3: 647; II, 847). It is at this point that the novel turns Balzacian, that Charlus, and with him the 'race des tantes', becomes a model for a writer or a poet, his unspeakable desire forcing him to continue his search, 'l'empêche de s'arrêter, de s'immobiliser dans une vue ironique et extérieure des choses' ['he cannot get stuck in an ironical and superficial view of things', 6: 173, translation modified; IV, 410].

Notes

1 Louis-Ferdinand Céline, *Voyage au bout de la nuit* (Paris: Gallimard, 1952), p. 74.

2 See Antoine Compagnon's 'La *Recherche du temps perdu* de Marcel Proust', in Pierre Nora, ed., *Les Lieux de mémoire* [1984–92], 'Quarto' edition, 3 vols., III 'Les France' (Paris: Gallimard, 1997), pp. 3835–69.

3 Philippe Dufour, *Le Réalisme: de Balzac à Proust* (Paris: Presses universitaires de France, 1998), p. 22.

4 Maurice Rieuneau, in 'La guerre dans *Le Temps retrouvé*', in *Guerre et révolutions dans le roman français de 1919 à 1939* (Paris: Klincksieck, 1974), pp. 112–33 (131).

5 Michael Sprinker, *History and Ideology in Proust* (Cambridge University Press, 1994); Jacques Dubois, 'Proust et le temps des embusqués', in Pierre Schoentjes, ed., *La Grande Guerre: un siècle de fiction romanesque* (Geneva: Droz, 2008), pp. 205–25; Edward J. Hughes, 'Cataclysm at One Remove', in Elyane Dezon-Jones, ed., *Approaches to Teaching Proust's Fiction and Criticism* (New York: MLA, 2003), pp. 38–43; and *Proust, Class, and Nation* (Oxford University Press, 2011).

6 See Christine Cano's 'Proust and the Wartime Press', in Adam Watt, ed., *Le Temps retrouvé Eighty Years After/80 ans après: Critical Essays/Essais critiques* (Oxford and Bern: Peter Lang, 2009), pp. 133–40.

7 See Pascal Ifri's 'La première guerre mondiale dans la *Recherche* et la correspondance: un parallèle', *BAMP*, 62 (2012), 19–30.

8 Marion Schmid, 'Ideology and Discourse in Proust: The Making of "Monsieur de Charlus pendant la guerre"', *Modern Language Review*, 94 (1999), 961–77.

9 Rieuneau, 'La guerre', p. 130.

PART III

Critical reception

CHAPTER 24

Critical reception during Proust's lifetime

Anna Magdalena Elsner

In *Le Temps retrouvé*, the Proustian Narrator describes the discouraging experience of one's work being misunderstood: 'Before very long I was able to show them a few sketches. No one understood anything of them ... Those passages in which I was trying to arrive at general laws were described as so much pedantic detail' (6: 442; IV, 618). This experience haunts not only the fictional Narrator, but also his creator up until his death, which is why Proust took such an interest in his public and, as his correspondence shows, often responded to his reviewers. These letters constitute an active participation in critical debates and this is, as has recently been remarked, one of the reasons for separating the history of the reception of Proust's *œuvre* before and after his death.[1] While Proust was always supported by a number of influential friends, a cursory overview of the early reception of his work shows that long before he was an author of established fame, Proust had to cope with being read as an unserious and superficial writer. His readership increased with the publication of each volume of the *Recherche* and led critics increasingly to focus on the literary value of his work. But Proust's reception during his lifetime is always set against the backdrop of often-hostile criticism, frequently based on the myth of the sickly, reclusive snob writing from the safety of his cork-lined room.

1895–1906

Even if Proust had already published short stories and poems in *Le Gaulois*, *Le Banquet* and *La Revue blanche* in 1895, his literary debut only came a year later with *Les Plaisirs et les jours*. This luxury edition, illustrated by Madeleine Lemaire, was reviewed by the major French newspapers and literary publications (*Le Figaro*, *Le Gaulois*, *Le Temps*, *La Revue Blanche* and *La Revue de Paris*), but hardly changed Proust's social reputation as a *mondain* dandy. While the publication of *Du côté de chez Swann* in 1913

183

and *À l'ombre des jeunes filles en fleurs* in 1919 are major turning points in Proust's reception, he remained a marginal, if not entirely unnoticed figure on the Parisian literary scene up until 1913. Particularly unfavourable criticism for *Les Plaisirs* came from his Lycée Condorcet friends Léon Blum and Fernand Gregh who accused him of dilettantism and criticized his association with his elegant society sponsors.[2] Not all critics were as hostile, and while clearly underlining that *Les Plaisirs* is a work of youth, Anatole France compared Proust to Bernardin de Saint-Pierre and Petronius in his laudatory preface. Paul Perret claimed that Proust was 'truly a "modern"',[3] while Charles Maurras takes Proust to be a classicist.[4] What further contributed to the view that Proust's position was a traditionalist one was his 1896 essay 'Contre l'obscurité', published in *La Revue blanche*, in which he critiques the intellectualism of symbolism and thereby offended Mallarmé. This tension between a modern and a classical Proust, already apparent in the critical debates surrounding the early work of the author, is one that critics will return to throughout his lifetime.

After these early literary experiments, which hardly led to a breakthrough, Proust published two translations of works by John Ruskin: *The Bible of Amiens* in 1904 and *Sesame and Lilies* in 1906. Both were reviewed and praised by a number of important newspapers, but did not transform Proust's reputation into that of a serious writer.[5] Nevertheless, Henri Bergson noticed that *La Bible* was more than a translation,[6] and another, substantial, article by Albert Sorel in *Le Temps* remarks upon Proust's magisterial use of the French language.[7] Due to its preface 'Sur la lecture', which anticipates many of the themes of the *Recherche*, the translation of *Sesame and Lilies* was more important in establishing Proust as a writer, but it received less attention from the press, despite André Beaunier's enthusiastic reviews on the front page of *Le Figaro*. Beaunier compared the way Proust read Ruskin to the way Montaigne read Plutarch, remarking that within this translation there is an independent literary voice being born – but before this voice is acknowledged as such, Proust had to overcome the obstacle of finding a publisher for his magnum opus.[8]

1913–1914

Proust's difficulty in getting the first volume of the *Recherche* published is notorious.[9] Refused by journals and newspapers (even if *Le Figaro* published selected extracts in 1912) and also by three major publishing houses, Fasquelle, the Nouvelle Revue française (NRF) and Ollendorf, Proust published *Du côté de chez Swann* at his own expense with Grasset. This further heightened Proust's anxiety about being misunderstood and, forced to act as his own publicity manager, he pulled all possible strings in order to place extracts and announcements of his book in newspapers prior to its publication. As part of this campaign, Proust arranged an interview with Élie-Joseph Bois, published by *Le Temps*, in which he spells out what separates him from the philosophy of Bergson and highlights the importance of involuntary memory for his work.[10] As Douglas Alden rightly remarks, while the terms in which Proust defines his book are significant today, they 'must have appeared enigmatic to the readers of 1913', as only very few critics picked up the 'philosophical' or 'psychoanalytical' content of the novel.[11] But after the publication of *Swann* in late November, the attention critics paid to the book is nonetheless unanimous, if not unanimously favourable, and we should not overlook how the reactions solicited from friends differed from those of professional critics in that respect. This is certainly true for the praise *Du côté de chez Swann* received from Jean Cocteau, Lucien Daudet or Maurice Rostand: Rostand assigned Proust a place alongside Shakespeare and Dante, Cocteau described *Swann* as 'a *giant miniature* full of mirages, silhouettes and gardens, with playful games of space and time and big fresh touches of colour à la Manet superimposed on them',[12] and Daudet closed his review on the front page of *Le Figaro* with the visionary statement: 'in the years to come, when M. Marcel Proust's book is mentioned, it will appear as an extraordinary manifestation of human intelligence in the twentieth century'.[13] In the same article, Daudet also already mentions the moral quality of Proust's work, which, as the topic of homosexuality begins to emerge within the *Recherche*, becomes an ever more central aspect of its early reception.

Professional critics might have been less enthusiastic, but they certainly did not ignore the publication of the first volume of the *Recherche*: the most important – and most devastating – review came from Paul Souday at *Le Temps*. Souday mentioned Proust's talent, but criticized the style and grammar of his French, and furthermore noted that the book was 'chaotic' with too much attention devoted to detail, that nothing extraordinary happened in these autobiographical 'memories of childhood', and that what did happen was 'rather banal'.[14] Many of the early critics, like Souday, seem to act on the assumption that Proust's work is autobiographical, but the relationship between the author and his Narrator does not immediately become a major point of interest for criticism.[15] As Alden notes, 'strangely enough, the critics of 1913–1914 were not especially perplexed by the novelty of Proust', and it is mainly discussions revolving around elements of style, absence of plot and the seemingly whimsical structure which dominate the reviews.[16]

With the publication of *Swann*, Proust also began to build a reputation outside France – Mary Duclaux enthusiastically reviewed it for the *Times Literary Supplement* and Rainer Maria Rilke wrote to his publisher in Germany enquiring about a possible translation.[17] However, the most important reactions with regard to the future of the *Recherche* were certainly those emerging from members of the NRF. André Gide turned down Proust's manuscript for the NRF, but he later wrote to Proust that he considered this the major shortfall in the publishing history of the NRF and apologized for having dismissed Proust as a 'snob, mondain amateur' (*Corr*, XIII, 50). Starting with this apology and ending with their taking over the publication of Proust's novel after the First World War, the NRF's reaction epitomizes a major change in Proust's reception. Henri Ghéon reviewed *Swann* for the January 1914 issue of the NRF and claimed that the novel had no structure and logic and was the result of Proust's *mondain* indolence,[18] but the final paragraph of his otherwise severe review already suggests a more positive and even admiring take on the novel. Only days after Ghéon's review was published, Gide and Jacques Rivière wrote to Proust stating their admiration, and in March 1914 Gide made the formal offer to publish the rest of the *Recherche* – a project that had to be postponed following the outbreak of the First World War.

1919–1922

Not only did the war shape the internal growth of the *Recherche*, but it also changed the fate of Proust's public reception. This, as Jean Giraudoux explains in 1919, is because after four years of bloodshed and despair, all people want is to read peaceful, poetic stories like Proust's.[19] While the general reaction to Proust was more favourable after the war, Giraudoux's opinion was not unanimously shared by the French public, and when *À l'ombre des jeunes filles en fleurs* appeared in 1919, it got only a few short, reservedly positive reviews in the *Revue de Paris, Le Figaro, Comœdia* and *Le Crapouillot*. Proust nevertheless continued to be supported by his friends, amongst them Robert Dreyfus who, under the name 'Bartholo', described the book as 'a monument of psychology, both subtle and mysterious' on the front page of *Le Figaro*.[20]

The general attitude towards Proust changed with the award of the prestigious Goncourt Prize on 10 December 1919, which triggered the first serious debate about the value and novelty of Proust's writing, even if this debate was initially still dominated by a questioning of Proust's entitlement to the award. He was criticized for his friendship with a jury member, Léon Daudet, and for being too old to be awarded a prize intended for young, up-and-coming authors. More criticism unrelated to the literary value of the book was also voiced on politico-historical grounds, namely that one year after the First World War, a work like Roland Dorgelès's *Les Croix de bois* would have been more suitable for the award, as it not only deals directly with the war, but also openly manifests political engagement.

The simultaneous publication of a collection of articles under the title *Pastiches et mélanges* in 1919, even if these articles had previously been published in newspapers during the pre-war years, further sparked the critics' interest in questions of style, which remained a key thread in the critical reaction to Proust in the post-Goncourt years. While some critics were outspokenly hostile to Proust's style,[21] others praised it, as did Gide, who also defended the structure of Proust's novel, claiming that there was a 'hidden plan' to it.[22] Further arguments in Proust's defence after he won the Goncourt Prize were proposed by Léon Daudet and Rivière, who already fervently defended him before the war. Daudet assigns Proust a place amongst the great French 'moralists and chroniclers of the human heart' and is the first critic to mention the comical quality of Proust's writing.[23] In the same vein, Rivière claimed that Proust's 'study of the human heart' does nothing less than re-invent the 'psychological novel'.[24] The vocabulary used by Daudet and Rivière points to the two major themes in Proust criticism after the war: Proust's 'classicism', which culminated in another of Rivière's articles published in February 1919, where he argued that Proust had renewed the classical tradition à la Racine and led French literature back into its own, namely 'the study of feelings' and a 'discourse on human passions';[25] and Proust's status as a *moraliste*. In the debates relating to *À l'ombre des jeunes filles* the term is still to be understood in the classical sense, namely as an observer of human behaviour, but this debate gradually distanced itself from the term's classical meaning and moved towards the more ambiguous territory of human morality.[26]

A major change of attitude in the period between the Goncourt and Proust's death is, as Hodson observes, that critics in France and elsewhere, whether favourable or unfavourable, knew they were dealing with an established author.[27] While the publication of *Le Côté de Guermantes I* in 1920 does not lead criticism in new directions, the publication of *Le Côté de Guermantes II* with *Sodome et Gomorrhe I* attached to it, divided critics. Proust's depiction of homosexuality becomes a major point of contention: Gide noted his disappointment in his diary,[28] and others, such as André Germain openly displayed their discontent with the turn Proust's work was taking.[29] Others, in particular the authors of the *NRF*, amongst them Roger Allard, continued to defend Proust as an observer of morals in the classical sense.[30] François Mauriac also pleads that the *Recherche* is a 'classical work' that has 'renewed the novel'; however, his mentioning 'immorality', even if he still argues against it, already anticipates the religious foundation of his criticism after Proust's death.[31] When *Sodome et Gomorrhe II* was published in 1922, it was clear that what might have been mistaken for a temporary turn in Proust's work had become a central subject of the novel. Some critics urged Proust to return to his pre-*Sodome* days, while others, such as Allard, again, appealed to Proust's 'moral relativity'.[32] An important defence announcing the posthumous age of Proust's reception came from René Rousseau, who defined Proust as a 'psychologist' and outlined important links between the *Recherche* and Freudian psychoanalysis.[33]

In 1920, Rivière noted that 'only masterpieces have the privilege to instantly conciliate such a consonant chorus of enemies'.[34] When Proust died in November 1922, the moral debate was still in full swing, but Proust was considered an established author with literary fame that stretched well beyond French borders. Proust's works were reviewed in a number of foreign presses,[35] and an English translation by Charles Scott Moncrieff was underway with the first volume published as *Swann's Way* in September 1922. The tributes paid to Proust shortly after his death show that despite the latest turn in criticism during his life – and despite the fact that it proved that he was, to some extent, still misunderstood – there was consensus that Proust had revolutionized French literature.

Notes

1 Pascale Fravalo-Tane, '*À la recherche du temps perdu' en France et en Allemagne (1913–1958): 'Dans une sorte de langue étrangère ...*' (Paris: Honoré Champion, 2008), p. 43.

2 Léon Blum, 'Les Livres', *La Revue Blanche*, 1 July 1896, 44–8; Fernand Gregh, *La Revue de Paris*, 15 July 1896, reprinted in F. Gregh, *Mon amitié avec Marcel Proust* (Paris: Grasset, 1958), pp. 11–12.

3 Paul Perret, *La Liberté*, 26 June 1896, p. 2 (English translations are taken from Leighton Hodson, ed., *Marcel Proust: The Critical Heritage* (London: Routledge, 1989), p. 61).

4 Charles Maurras, 'La vie littéraire', *La Revue encyclopédique*, 22 August 1896, p. 584.

5 *La Bible d'Amiens* is reviewed in *Le Temps, Les Arts de la Vie, La Chronique des Arts et de la Curiosité* and *La Revue de Paris*; *Sésame et les lys* in *Le Figaro* and *Le Mercure de France*. For a full press review see Jean-Yves Tadié, *Lectures de Proust* (Paris: Armand Colin, 1971), p. 9.

6 Henri Bergson, '*La Bible d'Amiens*, de Ruskin', *Séances et Travaux de l'Académie des Sciences morales et politiques*, 162 (1904), 491–2 (492).

7 Albert Sorel, 'Pèlerinages de beauté', *Le Temps*, 11 July 1904, p. 3.

8 André Beaunier, *Le Figaro*, 5 June 1906 and 14 June 1906, p. 1.

9 See Christine M. Cano, *Proust's Deadline* (Urbana/Chicago: University of Illinois Press, 2006) and Henri Bonnet, *Marcel Proust de 1907 à 1914* (Paris: Nizet, 1971).

10 Élie-Joseph Bois, *Le Temps*, 13 November 1913, p. 4.

11 Douglas Alden, *Marcel Proust and His French Critics* (New York: Russell & Russell, 1940), p. 9.

12 Jean Cocteau, *Excelsior*, 23 November 1913 (Hodson, *Critical Heritage*, p. 14).

13 Lucien Daudet, *Le Figaro*, 27 November 1913 (Hodson, *Critical Heritage*, p. 88).

14 Paul Souday, *Le Temps*, 10 December 1913 (Hodson, *Critical Heritage*, pp. 94–7).

15 Some critics are more prudent: Francis Chevassu writes that 'at first glance [*Swann*] does not fit into any genre' and Lucien Daudet speaks of an 'apparently autobiographical account' (Hodson, *Critical Heritage*, pp. 92, 85).

16 Alden, *French Critics*, p. 22.

17 Mary Duclaux, 'Art or Life? "A Small Boy and Others"', *Times Literary Supplement*, 4 December 1913, p. 585. For *Swann*'s reception in Germany, see Fravalo-Tane, *Une sorte de langue étrangère*, pp. 51–64.

18 Henri Ghéon, *NRF*, 1 January 1914, 139–43.

19 Jean Giraudoux, 'Du côté de Marcel Proust', *Feuillets d'art*, 1 (1919), 1–4.

20 'Une rentrée littéraire', *Le Figaro*, 7 July 1919, p. 1 (Hodson, *Critical Heritage*, p. 20).

21 See for example Pierre Lasserre, *La Revue universelle*, 2 (1920), 19–32.

22 André Gide, 'Billet à Angèle', *NRF*, 1 May 1921, pp. 586–91 (Hodson, *Critical Heritage*, p. 155).

23 Léon Daudet, 'Un nouveau et puissant romancier', *L'Action française*, 12 December 1919, p. 1 (Hodson, *Critical Heritage*, p. 127).

24 Jacques Rivière, 'Le Prix Goncourt', *NRF*, 1 January 1920, 152–4 (Hodson, *Critical Heritage*, p. 131).

25 Rivière, 'Marcel Proust et la tradition classique', *NRF*, 1 February 1920, pp. 192–200 (Hodson, *Critical Heritage*, p. 138).

26 For an important account of the early reception regarding the novel's moral dimension, see Eva Ahlstedt, *La Pudeur en crise: un aspect de l'accueil d' 'À la recherche du temps perdu' de Marcel Proust (1913–1930)* (Paris: Touzot, 1985).

27 Hodson, *Critical Heritage*, p. 21.

28 André Gide, *Journal* (Paris: Gallimard, 1951), 1, pp. 691–4.

29 André Germain, 'Le dernier livre de Marcel Proust', *Écrits nouveaux*, 8 (1921), 63–5.
30 Roger Allard, *NRF*, 1 September 1921, 355–7.
31 François Mauriac, 'L'art de Marcel Proust', *La Revue hebdomadaire*, 26 February 1921, 373–6 (Hodson, *Critical Heritage*, pp. 152–3).
32 Allard, '*Sodome et Gomorrhe* ou Marcel Proust moraliste', *NRF*, 1 June 1922, 641–6.
33 René Rousseau, 'Marcel Proust et l'esthétique de l'inconscient', *Le Mercure de France*, 15 January 1922, 361–86.
34 Rivière, 'Marcel Proust et la tradition classique', p. 193, the translation is my own.
35 See Mireille Naturel, ed., *La Réception de Proust à l'étranger* (Illiers-Combray: Institut Marcel Proust International, 2001).

CHAPTER 25

Early critical responses, 1922 to 1950s

Vincent Ferré

Reflections and studies on Proust's early critical reception are (almost) as old as the reception itself: as early as the mid 1920s, critical overviews were published on Proust's success in France. Another specificity has to do with the posthumous publication of most volumes, for the debate surrounding *À la recherche du temps perdu* took place while the last three parts of the *Recherche* were being published: *La Prisonnière* (1923), *Albertine disparue* (1925), *Le Temps retrouvé* (1927), as well as the *Chroniques* volume (collected articles, also published in 1927), collections of letters and the *Correspondance générale* (1930–6). This concomitance explains both the interest and the limits of many articles and books which have followed Proust's death. Moreover, the post-war publication of *Jean Santeuil* (1952) and *Contre Sainte-Beuve* (1954) decisively changed the perception of the birth of his work, and shed new light on early analyses.

It is often said that whilst *À la recherche* is now considered as the masterpiece of modern French literature, Proust was not acknowledged before the 1960s; but a look at the early reception shows how simplistic this conception is. *À la recherche* was a commercial success in 1919, when Proust received the Goncourt Prize for *À l'ombre des jeunes filles*, and critics were unanimous in paying homage to him when he died in November 1922. Nevertheless, his fortune dipped somewhat in France, in the 1920s and 1930s, while Proust was slowly discovered in other countries; after the war, his work came again to the fore, and was widely translated. Proust's early reception might therefore be symbolized by a spiral, combining moments of favour and periods of oblivion or negative critique.

Recognition, controversies and disaffection in France 1922–1940

Just after Proust's death in November 1922, the *NRF* volume *Hommage à Marcel Proust* (1 January 1923), appeared as an exceptional tribute to the writer and gave birth to a consensual critical discourse, accounting for the

191

origin of many topics that seem natural in later criticism. *À la recherche du temps perdu*, especially, is viewed as a unique book and a masterpiece combining psychological analysis (on time and memory) and social observations, sensibility and intelligence; Proust is often compared to Balzac and, especially, Montaigne, by Lucien Daudet and Fernand Gregh, for instance. An important omission is to be noticed: the NRF volume avoids gender issues and homosexuality.

An acceptable doxa is presented to the reader; but also valuable insights, that were to be explored in the following years: the relation to modernism, to space (André Ferré, *Géographie de Marcel Proust*, 1939), to psychoanalysis (Jacques Rivière, *Quelques Progrès dans l'étude du cœur humain*, 1927; Charles Blondel, *La Psychographie de Marcel Proust*, 1932), but also music and metaphysics (Jacques Benoist-Méschin, *La Musique et l'immortalité dans l'œuvre de Marcel Proust*, 1926; Jean Pommier, *La Mystique de Proust*, 1939), aesthetics (Emeric Fiser, *L'Esthétique de Marcel Proust*, 1933), genesis (Albert Feuillerat, *Comment Marcel Proust a composé son roman*, 1934) are tackled by critics in the 1920s and 1930s, as well as stylistics, genre issues and the relation to the modern novel (following Albert Thibaudet's 'Marcel Proust et la tradition française', in the 1923 *NRF* volume). Still, many texts focused on the link between Proust's life and his work, in short essays seldom as interesting as Léon Pierre-Quint's *Marcel Proust: sa vie, son œuvre* (1925), which still merits reading as a historical document.

Proust's importance is shown by the list of authors who wrote on his works during the same period, such as Alain, Barrès, Bataille, Bernanos, Brasillach, Claudel (one of the most hostile critics), Cocteau, Gide, Giraudoux, Larbaud, Mauriac – as well as, in English, Beckett, Conrad, Woolf, and various American writers living in Paris. Most are enthusiastic; some, more or less ambivalent: for instance, Gide's first prejudices are famous, but he then shows a great interest in the *Recherche*, before ultimately expressing criticism about Proust's depiction of homosexuality and his (supposed) hypocrisy. Sartre, for his part, considers the treatment of psychology in *À la recherche* as typical of a bourgeois writer, but is more lenient in his late years; and *L'Être et le néant* acknowledges in 1943 the importance of the analysis on the 'successive plurality of the I's'.[1]

Thus, Proust seemed institutionalized in the early 1920s. His texts are published in anthologies for classrooms, in Benjamin Crémieux's volume on *Le XXe siècle* (1924), and his reputation comes to a peak in 1925 but also remains an object of polemics, concerning his style (sometimes denigrated for its alleged preciosity), the publication of an unfinished *Temps retrouvé* and the numerous typos in the first edition. The pervasive presence of homosexuality and the tone of the last volumes are also criticized, some attacks being based on his letters published at the time. Gradually, by the end of the 1920s, the reception changed, and was not as auspicious as before; then interest increased again in the early 1930s, when the publication of the whole *Recherche* gave a full view of Proust's achievement; but by the end of the 1930s, negative critics prevailed, as Douglas Alden's assessment shows, in *Marcel Proust and His French Critics* (1940).

A slow recognition abroad

The *NRF* volume contained texts written by foreign critics: from Germany (Curtius), Italy (Cecchi), Spain (Ortega), America and Sweden as well as four texts by British critics, one of them being a collective tribute. In the United Kingdom, particularly, among all countries, Proust has been immediately and continuously hailed.[2] His memory was celebrated a few weeks after his death by *Marcel Proust: An English Tribute* (1923), edited by C. K. Scott Moncrieff, whose translation of *À la recherche* was published between 1922 and 1930 – except for *Le Temps retrouvé*, translated by Stephen Hudson (alias Sydney Schiff) and published in 1931. Proust is celebrated as the most accomplished heir of a brilliant French tradition. Generally speaking, critics and commentators (e.g. Woolf and Forster) acclaim Proust's achievement, even though some denounce his style or his egotism, like D. H. Lawrence or Aldous Huxley. Published shortly after Clive Bell's *Proust* (1928), Samuel Beckett's volume (1931) remains one of the most decisive: it contains important reflections on time, characters, habits, music and philosophy (especially through a comparison with Schopenhauer).

In Germany, Curtius's articles in 1922–5 and his *Marcel Proust* (1925) are very influential on German criticism, while Zweig's tribute in 1925 (in Austria) draws the readers' attention to Proust's life. The translation, by Rudolf Schottlaender, of the first part, in 1925 (I. *Der Weg zu Swann*, II. *Im Schatten der jungen Mädchen*, 1926) then 1930 (*Die Herzogin von Guermantes*) immediately predates academic studies, in 1930–7, addressing impressionism and classicism, Bergson, structure and style. Noteworthy among the most prominent critics, articles by Auerbach (1927) and Leo Spitzer (in *Stilstudien*, 1928), by Benjamin ('Zum Bilde Prousts' ['The Image of Proust'], 1929), who also translated *Sodome*, must also be mentioned. But the Nazi regime interrupted the publication of translations, and academic studies were not numerous, the reaction of many intellectuals ranging from indifference to defiance.[3] A similar chronology may be established in

Italy, where the first critical studies devoted to Proust, focusing on aesthetics and psychoanalysis, were published in 1933: Francesco Casnati's *Proust* and Lorenza Maranini's *Proust: Arte e conoscenza*. Early articles had previously paid tribute to Proust, in 1922–5, drawing comparisons with famous writers, French (Montaigne, Bergson) or European (Dostoyevsky), most of these topics being common in other countries. But, according to Carlo Bo, before the 1940s the literary context in Italy was not favourable to Proust: he was not in a position to influence many Italian writers, for whom the question was not so much of a possible revolution of the novel, but of the choice of novel *genre* itself, against 'artistic prose',[4] which prevailed at that period.

Outside Europe, one may think of South America, where a translation by Pedro Salinas was published from 1920 onwards. Critical texts were sometimes written in Europe (Alfonso Reyes, for instance, lived in Madrid until 1924), or published there, like Ortega y Gasset's analysis on time and distance in the NRF volume (1923). But the reception in the United States is less studied. Still, it was not delayed (as it is often said), compared to the UK: *Swann* in English translation was published in 1922, *Jeunes Filles* and *Guermantes* in 1924–5, and (as Elyane Dezon-Jones remarks) the first extract of *À la recherche* translated into English was published not by a British journal, but by an American one (*The Dial*).[5] Nevertheless, by contrast with the UK, American critics paid attention to Proust mostly after his death, when *Sodome* raised a scandal and met success. Then, in 1932, *Le Temps retrouvé* was published in the US in a translation by F. A. Blossom; the competition with Hudson's translation was profitable for Proust.

Besides British criticism, Proust's reception is also mediated by American writers and journalists living in Paris, readers of the *Recherche* in French: Hemingway, Natalie Clifford Barney, Faulkner, Fitzgerald, Gertrude Stein, to name only a few among the writers who wrote on Proust, and admitted his influence or similarities between *À la recherche* and their own works – an admission also later made by Jack Kerouac. Among critical studies, one should mention Joseph Krutch's *Five Masters* (1930) and Edmund Wilson's *Axel's Castle: A Study in the Imaginative Literature of 1870–1930* (1931). They predate the first wave of academic criticism, from 1932 onward,[6] addressing psychology, the arts, society, memory, comparisons with Bergson and Saint-Simon, genesis (Feuillerat, for instance, taught at Yale University, and his book had a profound effect on American criticism). At the end of the decade were published the first critical surveys, like Alden's *Proust and His French Critics* (1940).

Even if most of these books are now obsolete, some remain classics in Proustian studies; moreover, they deserve our attention as foundations of Proustian criticism and as witnesses of the construction of all the clichés that surround Proust's work.

After the war: 1945–1959

Despite Louis Martin-Chauffier ('Proust et le double "Je" de quatre personnes', 1943) and Ramon Fernandez (*Proust*, 1943), the idea then prevailed that Proust's work was anachronistic. But Étiemble's injunction ('Qu'il faut relire Marcel Proust', 1941)[7] was accomplished after the war, thanks both to the great success of André Maurois's *À la recherche de Marcel Proust* (1949), which mixes recollections and analysis, quotes early works by Proust; and to the publication of *Jean Santeuil* (1952) and *Contre Sainte-Beuve* (1954), which played a great part.[8] The same year, the Clarac-Ferré edition of *À la recherche du temps perdu* was published by Gallimard, in the prestigious Bibliothèque de la Pléiade, stimulating Proustian criticism and offering a better basis for translations.

During this period books were published that have become classics in the field, like *Forme et signification* by Jean Rousset (1955, for the first versions), *Le Livre à venir* by Maurice Blanchot (published in 1959, some essays date back to 1954 and take *Jean Santeuil* into account), as well as studies on time (Poulet, *Études sur le temps humain, I*, 1950), psychology (Bonnet, *Le Progrès spirituel dans l'œuvre de Marcel Proust*, 1946–9), space and seclusion (Claude-Edmonde Magny, *Histoire du roman français depuis 1918*, 1950), humour (Donze, *Le Comique dans l'œuvre de Marcel Proust*, 1955; Mansfield, *Le Comique de Marcel Proust*, 1952), style (Louria, *La Convergence stylistique*, 1957; Mouton, *Le Style de Marcel Proust*, 1948), and philosophical readings with Lévinas (*L'Autre dans Proust*, 1947), Delattre (*Proust et Bergson*, 1948) or Newman (*Marcel Proust et l'existentialisme*, 1953); in English: Strauss (*Proust and Literature: The Novelist as Critic*, 1957), on Proust's criticism, and Chernowitz (*Proust and Painting*, 1945). Most of them study topics and issues already analysed in the 1920s and 1930s: there is always something new to discover in Proust's work, even by following (apparently) similar paths that lead further.

As before, writers paid tribute to Proust in novels and fictions, like Claude Simon (as early as 1945 in *Le Tricheur* and *La Corde raide*, 1947) or Nabokov (*Lolita*, 1955; the project of *Ada*, published in 1969, begun in the late 1950s); or, privately, in letters (like Valéry), and explicitly, in essays: Bataille, once more (*La Littérature et le mal*, 1957), Butor (who wrote pages on aesthetic experiments in 1955, later published in *Répertoire I*, 1960), Camus, very laudatory in *L'Homme révolté* (1951), and Sarraute (*L'Ère du soupçon*, 1956) – the advent of the *Nouveau Roman* was favourable to Proust, who gained a new status as the forefather of modern writing.

In other countries too was to be observed a revival, or birth, of interest in his works, as shown by the increasing number of studies and new translation projects. In Italy, Proust was not seen any more (at least not only), as a singular writer, beyond imitation and influence for writers. The number of translations is telling: *À la recherche* was published in Italian between 1946 and 1951 (involving seven translators), simultaneously with *Les Plaisirs et les jours* (1946) and *La Bible d'Amiens* (1946), before *Jean Santeuil* (1953) and a selection of letters (1958); extracts from other works or from the *Recherche* itself are published separately by distinct translators during the same period. This acceleration stimulated critical reactions. A few were hostile: in 1945, Benedetto Croce denounced Proust's 'historical decadentism' (his judgment was based on simplifications regarding Proust and Bergson); but the journal *Letteratura* (1947) offered a tribute to Proust twenty-five years after his death and Giacomo Debenedetti suggested new critical perspectives in his *Saggi critici* (1952), followed by studies on themes (Tita del Valle, 1951), intertextuality, textual genetics (Gianfranco Contini, on *Jean Santeuil*, 1952), philosophy and aesthetics (Elemire Zolla, 1952; Vittorio Mathieu, 1959). The same type of editorial endeavours were launched in Japan, after a previous partial translation of the first volumes (up to *Guermantes I*, in 1935). A full translation was published in 1953–5, preceding two similar enterprises, after 1960, one of them by Kyuichiro Inoue, professor at the university of Tokyo, and active in genetic scholarship from the 1950s onwards.

The situation was not the same in Northern Europe, where translations were late and incomplete, which explains the weak interest by readers before the last decades of the twentieth century. In Sweden, for instance, the first translation (*Swann*, 1930) was not flawless, and only a few studies were published after the war (K. Jaensson, 1944; M. Tuominen, 1949). In Holland, apart from Simon Vestdijk, a writer and poet who produced numerous texts on Proust from the 1930s onward, the critical reception was very limited, sometimes hostile (for religious and political reasons), and the translation of *À la recherche* did not begin before the 1960s. Even in Germany, a complete (and new) translation was published in 1953–7 only (by Eva Rechel-Mertens), after a famous publishing house (Suhrkamp) took up the first (and interrupted) project. In the same period, important studies were published by Jauss (on time, *Zeit and Erinnerung*, 1955) and Adorno (essays in *Noten Zur Literatur*, 1958).

In this respect, the reception in the UK and the US is peculiar, for it remained continuous; in both countries, the number of studies even increased in the 1950s. In the UK, F. C. Green (since *The Mind of Proust*, 1949) and J. M. Cocking (*Proust*, 1956) were two of the most famous scholars. In the US, Proust was more often taught in universities by new 'Proustian specialists', and Proustian studies benefited from important books: Philip Kolb published his PhD in 1948 ('La correspondance de Marcel Proust: chronologie and commentaire critique'), which constitutes the basis of the later publication of separate volumes of letters, before the great project of the *Correspondance* (1970–93). Germaine Brée, Professor in Wisconsin, published in 1955 an English translation of her important essay *Du temps perdu au temps retrouvé* (1950), after a special issue of *Symposium* (1951) and an annotated edition of *Combray* in 1952. Nineteen fifty-nine appears as a climax, as it is the year of the publication (in the UK and the US) of the first volume of George Painter's biography, decisive for studies in English.

Thus, it appears that Proust's recognition as a master of the modern novel is more established than is usually recognized; but also, that the reception of his work is made of accidents, shifts and reversals, according to a rhythm depending on countries and their connections with France. Still, throughout these periods (1922 to the 1940s, the 1940s to the 1960s), Proust has always been seen as an example of French culture, as its finest example or a *terminus ad quem* as Gracq would say. Finally, it is striking that many an early analysis remains stimulating: while they are often underestimated or even forgotten, numerous reviews and books of the first decades of Proustian criticism anticipate a great part of recent studies: readers should be aware of a tendency to amnesia, visible in many contemporary Proustian critics.

Notes

1 J.-P. Sartre, *L'Être et le néant* (Paris: Gallimard, 1976 [1943]), p. 149 (my translation). See Sandra Teroni, 'Nous voilà délivrés de Proust', in J. Brami, ed., *Marcel Proust 8. Lecteurs de Proust au XXe siècle et au début du XXIe* (Caen: Lettres modernes Minard, 2010), p. 117 (and p. 137 for a bibliography on Proust and Sartre).
2 See *Cahiers Marcel Proust II. Études proustiennes IV*, 1982, p. 7. This volume is still authoritative, especially the article by R. Gibson, 'Proust et la critique anglo-saxonne', pp. 11–33.

3 Pascale Fravalo-Tane, *'À la recherche du temps perdu' en France et en Allemagne (1913–1958): Dans une sorte de langue étrangère* (Paris: Honoré Champion, 2008), p. 252.

4 Carlo Bo, introduction to *Alla ricerca del tempo perduto*, quoted by Simonetta Boni, 'La réception de Proust dans les études françaises en Italie', in Mireille Naturel, ed., *La Réception de Proust à l'étranger* (Illiers-Combray: Société des Amis de Marcel Proust et des Amis de Combray, [2002]), p. 116.

5 Elyane Dezon-Jones, 'La réception d'*À la recherche du temps perdu* aux États-Unis', in William C. Carter, ed., *The UAB Marcel Proust Symposium: In Celebration of the 75th Anniversary of 'Swann's Way': 1913–1988*, (Birmingham, AL: Summa, 1989), p. 34.

6 Dezon-Jones, 'La réception', p. 43.

7 René Étiemble, *Hygiène des lettres*, vol. v, *C'est le bouquet* (Paris: Gallimard, 1967), p. 141ff.

8 See Jean-Yves Tadié, *Proust: le dossier* (Paris: Pocket, 1998), p. 186.

CHAPTER 26

Mid-twentieth-century views, 1960s to 1980s
Thomas Baldwin

Proust's *À la recherche du temps perdu* is a privileged object in the fields of philosophy and literary theory, as well as in rather less easily identifiable critical spaces in which literary criticism, political theory, psychoanalysis and visual theory overlap. Proust functions in multifarious ways across and between disciplines, including critical theory, deconstruction, feminism, hermeneutics, Marxism, narratology, structuralism, post-Marxism and post-structuralism. Among prominent philosophers, theorists and literary critics of the 1960s and 1970s, Roland Barthes, Leo Bersani, Maurice Blanchot, Gilles Deleuze, Serge Doubrovsky, Gérard Genette, René Girard, Félix Guattari, Julia Kristeva, Emmanuel Lévinas, Georges Poulet and Jean-Pierre Richard (to name only some of the most influential) have all written at length about Proust. Their understanding of Proust varies widely, but for all of them something more than straightforward exemplarity is at stake: Proust's name is not simply one among others.

It is beyond the scope of this essay to explore each significant engagement with *À la recherche* across two decades of radically shifting critical landscapes. Instead, I shall try to identify some non-totalizing affinities – what Gilles Deleuze, following Proust, calls 'transversals' – between a selection of readings of Proust's work from this period that have endured. Each of these readings provides a different response to the question posed by Deleuze at the very beginning of his *Proust and Signs*, first published in 1964: 'In what does the unity of *À la recherche du temps perdu* consist?'[1]

In *Proustian Space* (1963), the Belgian critic Georges Poulet argues that 'the representation of things' in *À la recherche* is rarely 'total or panoramic';[2] the Proustian universe is 'in pieces' (p. 38). An example of such division is to be found in *Du côté de chez Swann*, where Marcel says that Combray's Guermantes and Méséglise ways are separated by 'one of those distances of the mind which not only keep things apart, but cut them off from one another and put them on different planes' (1: 161; 1, 133). Their

199

demarcation in space and time is absolute.[3] Poulet also suggests that Proust returns to a Cartesian notion of 'duration' (p. 52). In the Proustian world, each individual moment is 'exterior to all others . . ., enclosed within itself' (p. 51). *Contra* Bergson, then, duration is composed of independent moments, each of which is a radically internal fragment; these fragments are unable to communicate with anything outside the walls of what Marcel, in the first and final volumes of *À la recherche*, calls the 'sealed vessels' ('vases clos') in which they are contained.[4] If Proustian duration is Cartesian, Proustian space is broken up to such an extent that it 'resembles that of Leibniz': 'places are islands in space, monads' (p. 33).[5]

In spite of the 'radical originality' (p. 33) of place and moment in the Proustian world, Poulet insists on the Narrator's 'profound need of unity' (p. 87) and identifies in Proust's work 'a continuity . . . at the very heart of discontinuity' (p. 61):[6]

> A figure appears there in profile, in a repeated manner, that of a human being always recognizable, but each time in different conditions . . . So it is that this face, resembling itself in whatever situation it finds itself, can be identified, it may be, in the Proustian novel, with the central consciousness in which everything is reflected; it may be again, with the genius of the author, his omnipresent activity, which, as varied as the episodes of the novel may be, is made to be recognized there, isolated and serially, as their principal unifier. (p. 101)

While Poulet may view *À la recherche* as a structure organized according to a unifying principle, he is no structuralist: by 1963, a 'negation of man' – of 'the dross of speech, of the subject, and of psychology'[7] – and a radical critique of the practice of reading and criticism that relies on aspects of the author's identity to distil meaning from the author's work, were 'essential element[s] of the structuralist paradigm'.[8] In contrast, Poulet seeks an authorial point of departure that will serve as a structural and organizing principle around which the author's work is centred and by which his individuality or 'genius' is defined. The variations and fragmentations of *À la recherche* are thus constrained to the extent that they are understood as an expression of the individual consciousness of its author.

In responding to his own question about the unity of Proust's novel, Deleuze discusses Poulet's analysis. Poulet, he argues, 'upholds in Proust's work the rights of a continuity and of a unity whose very particular original nature he does not attempt to define'.[9] Deleuze rejects Poulet's idea that there is a 'direct means of communication' or of 'totalization' between the isolated fragments of Proust's world (p. 126; translation modified). As Marcel suggests, what we suppose to be our love or our jealousy is never a single, continuous and indivisible passion. It is composed of an infinity of successive loves, of different jealousies, each of which is ephemeral, although by their uninterrupted multiplicity they give us the impression of continuity, the illusion of unity. (1: 448; 1, 366)

While it is made of 'sealed vessels' (p. 126) and its unity is an illusion, the fragmented parts of the Proustian universe are brought into indirect communication by virtue of a system of 'transversals'. Like Poulet, Deleuze views the bits and pieces of *À la recherche* as monadic, but, for Deleuze, there is an important difference between Leibniz's solution to the problem of a communication 'resulting from sealed parts or from what does not communicate' (p. 163) and Proust's. Leibniz's solution is dismissed by Deleuze as a fudge:

Leibniz answers meretriciously that the closed 'monads' all possess the same stock, enveloping and expressing the same world in the infinite series of their predicates, each content to have a region of expression distinct from that of the others, all thus being different viewpoints towards the same world that God causes them to envelop. (p. 163)

In contrast, Proust's system of transversals allows us to pass from one multiple or fragment, understood as a unity in and of itself, to the next. Each of the multiples that makes up the world of *À la recherche* is a unity, but their collective existence within that world does not constitute a unified whole, a 'One'. Multiplicity is thus not reduced to a unity in which each multiple, each 'sealed vessel', is made of – or contains – the same essential stuff:

among all these sealed vessels, there exists a system of communication, though it must not be confused with a direct means of access, nor with a means of totalization. As between the Méséglise Way and the Guermantes Way, the entire work consists in establishing *transversals* that cause us to leap ... from one world to another, without ever reducing the many to the One, without ever gathering the multiple up into a whole, but affirming the original unity of precisely that very multiple, affirming without uniting *all* these irreducible fragments. (p. 126; emphasis in original)[10]

It is tempting to view Deleuze's position here as structuralist.[11] This view is supported by his contention, in the second part of *Proust and Signs* (published in 1970), that the unity of *À la recherche* is located in 'the formal structure of the work of art, insofar as it does not refer to anything else' – an author, for example – 'that can serve as unity' (p. 168). Nevertheless, there is a small but crucial difference between Deleuze's conception of *À la recherche* and a typically structuralist understanding of unity in the work of art. As András Bálint Kovács observes, for structuralism, 'a system is a structure, and a structure is organized according to a unifying principle – understanding and interpreting a system amounts to understanding its unifying principle'.[12] As Deleuze seeks to interpret Marcel's apprenticeship in the reading of signs,[13] his aim is rather different: Proust's work is not organized in accordance with an overarching, transcendent principle that would 'unify the parts, a whole that would totalize the fragments' (p. 163). The only unity at work in *À la recherche* is the unity of each multiple, '*of* this very multiple, *of* this very multiplicity', and these unities are permitted to communicate transversally without suppressing the 'difference or distance' (p. 168; emphasis in original) that obtains between them. The formal structure of *À la recherche* is based on its '*transversal dimension*' (p. 201; emphasis in original). Deleuze's work on Proust's transversals can thus be understood as a movement away from the tenets of structuralism and as a continuation of his attempt, in *Difference and Repetition* (1968), 'to explain what a system is like that does not exclude the one, the same, or the similar, but rather, contains them only as a partial aspect'.[14]

In 1972, two years after the second edition of *Proust and Signs* appeared, Deleuze participated in a round-table discussion on Proust with Roland Barthes, Serge Doubrovsky, Gérard Genette, Jean Ricardou and Jean-Pierre Richard, all of whom, by this time, had published significant essays on Proust's work. Deleuze discusses the 'presence of madness' in *À la recherche* and suggests that the novel is not a 'dress, . . . a cathedral, but a spider web woven before our eyes'.[15] A number of the other round-table participants reflect on the composition of Marcel's mad, arachnid production. Genette, whose *Narrative Discourse: An Essay in Method* was published in the same year and is illustrated throughout with examples from *À la recherche*,[16] identifies 'effects of displacement or delay' at work in the 'amours' between Marcel and his 'mysterious little cousin' (p. 34). These take place in 'Combray' but are only mentioned 'retrospectively much later, when Aunt Léonie's sofa is sold to Rachel's bordello' (p. 34). Given this 'effect of variation', Genette argues, reading Proust's novel requires 'close attention to the chrono-topological disposition of thematic signifiers' (p. 35); the role of the critic, he suggests, is to '*interpret variations*' (p. 36; emphasis in original). Subsequently, Barthes takes issue with Genette's approach to *À la recherche*, arguing that if, 'in analyzing the variations of Proust's work, one seeks a theme, one is entirely within a hermeneutic' (p. 36):

> In music, there is the academic and canonical theme of variation, for example Brahms's variations on a theme by Haydn. The theme is given

first and then ten, twelve, or fifteen variations follow. But we must not forget that in the history of music, there is a great work that pretends to use the 'theme and variations' structure but in fact undoes it: Beethoven's variations on a waltz by Diabelli ... You can see that we are dealing with thirty-three variations without a theme. And there is a theme that is given at the beginning, which is a very silly theme, but one that is given precisely, to some extent, for the sake of derision. I would say that Beethoven's variations here function a little like Proust's work. The theme is diffracted entirely in the variations and there is no longer a varied treatment of a theme. This means that in a way the metaphor ... is destroyed. Or, in any case, the origin of the metaphor is destroyed. (pp. 44–5)

Like Deleuze, Barthes resists the temptation to reduce the variations of Proust's work to a single, transcendental origin or unity. Instead of referring back to an object or 'theme' that would be their ultimate cause, the variations of metaphor in Proust's work set in motion what Paul de Man calls 'an imaging activity that refers to no object in particular'.[17] Similarly, Barthes rejects Genette's argument that the critic's task is to interpret Proust's variations. For Barthes, the critic is not an interpreter, executor or performer of variations that are 'in the text', but an 'operator' of his or her own variations on Proust's work (p. 52). In this role, the critic brings about a 'destructuration of the Proustian text; he or she reacts against the rhetorical structuring (the "outline") that has until now been prevalent in Proust studies' (p. 52). Proust is thus 'unique', Barthes argues, 'to the extent that all he leaves us to do is *rewrite him*, which is the exact contrary of exhausting him' (p. 30; emphasis in original).

Barthes's and Deleuze's work on the unity and variations of Proust's novel provides a key to understanding the modalities of Proust's presence in their respective critical practices. It also sets them apart from their 'Proustian' contemporaries. In his engagements with Proust from the 1950s onwards, Barthes produces a form of rewriting: he 'operates' variations on Proust's text. As Malcolm Bowie observes, 'we could say that Proust's book mattered to Barthes more in its generalized "loomings" than in the copious and artful individual sentences by which other critics have been so readily seduced'.[18] Indeed, Barthes refused to be labelled as a 'Proustian' and produced very few sustained, stand-alone textual analyses of Proust's novel. Although it may be tempting for some to view such critical reticence as symptomatic of an anxiety of influence, it is less the sign of hindrance or compunction within Barthes's critical practice than a precise indication of the ways in which he understands the nature, the 'operations', of critique itself. *À la recherche* acts as a transversal within

Deleuze's œuvre: *Proust and Signs* is the most acute point of a circulation of motifs and concepts drawn from *À la recherche* which traverses Deleuze's work on philosophy (on Nietzsche, for example), on cinema, and on painting (on Francis Bacon), as well as working between Deleuze's thought and writing and that of Félix Guattari, with whom he co-wrote several books. In allowing *À la recherche* to circulate creatively within their own critical economies, both Barthes and Deleuze deliver it from the teleological, instrumentalizing and programmatic discourse of the 'Proustian' who, in the words of Bowie, would 'merely scurr[y] back and forth on the stretched skin of this immense organism [*À la recherche*]'.[19] In so doing, they lever Proust's novel away from standard models of academic criticism, influence and intertextuality.

Notes

1 Gilles Deleuze, *Proust and Signs*, trans. by Richard Howard (London: The Athlone Press, 2000), p. 3; translation modified.

2 Georges Poulet, *Proustian Space*, trans. by Elliott Coleman (Baltimore and London: Johns Hopkins University Press, 1977), p. 37. Further page references are given after quotations in the text.

3 As a number of critics have noted (most notably Deleuze), these paths are reconciled to a certain extent in the final volume of Proust's work: 'between these two high roads a network of transversals was set up' (6: 427; IV, 606).

4 See (1: 161; 1, 133) and (6: 221; IV, 448). For Poulet, Proustian time is 'directly opposed to Bergsonian time' (p. 105). Poulet aligns Proustian time with what Bergson denounces as a 'false duration', namely one whose elements are 'exteriorized, the ones relatively to the others, and aligned, the ones beside the others' (p. 106). For Bergson, duration, or the 'true continuity of our being' (p. 9), is ineffable. It can only be measured if it is translated into the immobile, spatial time of science, whereby it is converted into a succession of distinct parts.

5 For Leibniz, monads are simple substances – simple in that they are not extended. They 'have no windows, by which anything could come in or go out' (Gottfried Wilhelm Leibniz, *Monadology*, trans. by R. Latta (Oxford University Press, 1898), § 7, p. 3).

6 Translation modified.

7 François Dosse, *History of Structuralism: The Rising Sign, 1945–1966*, trans. by Deborah Glassman (Minneapolis: University of Minnesota Press, 1997), p. 51. Translation modified: Glassman translates Dosse's 'négation de l'homme' as 'negation'.

8 Dosse, *History of Structuralism*, p. 51.

9 Deleuze, *Proust and Signs*, p. 184, n. 5. Further page references are given after quotations in the text.

10 Translation modified.

11 Vincent Descombes, for example, refers to Deleuze's book as a '"structural" study' (see *Proust: Philosophy of the Novel*, trans. by Catherine Chance Macksey (Stanford University Press, 1992), p. 33).

12 András Bálint Kovács, 'Notes to a Footnote', in D. N. Rodowick, ed., *Afterimages of Gilles Deleuze's Film Philosophy* (Minneapolis and London: University of Minnesota Press, 2010), pp. 31–45 (p. 37).

13 For a reading of Proust's novel that sets itself up explicitly against Deleuze's, see Julia Kristeva, *Time and Sense: Proust and the Experience of Literature*, trans. by Ross Guberman (New York: Columbia University Press, 1996).

14 Kovács, 'Notes to a Footnote', p. 37. For a different take on the relationship between multiplicity and unity in *À la recherche* (one which focuses in particular on how sense experience contributes to the construction of the novel's imaginary world), see Jean-Pierre Richard, *Proust et le monde sensible* (Paris: Seuil, 1974). Richard argues that 'with Proust, what is disjointed is always also what is in the process of being joined up' (p. 263; my translation).

15 See Gilles Deleuze, 'Proust Round Table', in *Two Regimes of Madness: Texts and Interviews 1975–1995*, trans. by Ames Hodges and Mike Taormina (New York and Los Angeles: Semiotext(e), 2007), pp. 29–60 (p. 33). Further page references are given after quotations in the text.

16 Gérard Genette, *Narrative Discourse: An Essay in Method*, trans. by Jane E. Lewin (Ithaca, NY: Cornell University Press, 1980).

17 Paul de Man, *Blindness and Insight: Essays in the Rhetoric of Contemporary Criticism*, 2nd edn (London: Routledge, 1983), p. 235. Among the first critics to discuss the 'variations' of *À la recherche* was Maurice Blanchot, some eighteen years before the round-table discussion, in 1954. He suggests that the space of *À la recherche* 'had to come close . . . to the essence of the sphere' and that 'his entire book, his language, this style of slow curves, of fluid heaviness, of transparent density, always in movement, wonderfully made to express the infinitely varied rhythm of voluminous gyration, symbolizes the mystery and the thickness of the sphere, its movement of rotation' (Maurice Blanchot, 'The Experience of Proust', in *The Book to Come*, trans. by Charlotte Mandell (Stanford University Press, 2002), pp. 19–37 (p. 33)). See also Leo Bersani's analysis of *À la recherche*'s variations and repetitions in *Marcel Proust: The Fictions of Life and of Art* (Oxford University Press, 1965), especially pp. 177–98.

18 Malcolm Bowie, 'Barthes on Proust', *The Yale Journal of Criticism*, 14/2 (Fall 2001), 513–18 (518).

19 Bowie, 'Barthes on Proust', p. 518.

CHAPTER 27

Late-twentieth- and twenty-first-century responses
Adam Watt

At Proust's death, the sight of the notebooks containing *À la recherche*, standing together near their author's bed, reminded Jean Cocteau of the watches whose ticking continues on the wrists of soldiers slain on the battlefield.[1] Ninety years after Proust's passing, the metronomic ticking continues through the pages he wrote and through the stream of works he still inspires. Books on Proust and the *Recherche* number in their thousands and the flow shows little sign of abating; crucially, though, as this chapter will show, as well as quantity, there is quality. Proust has a broad international readership inside and beyond the academy. In universities, his work is taught at undergraduate and postgraduate level, in parts or as a whole, in relation to cinema and the arts; and within modern languages, comparative literature and gender studies courses.[2] Monographs, comparative critical studies, articles, translations and adaptations continue to appear and critics and practitioners from many disciplines are still drawn to the work, its themes and characters, its Narrator's ideas, the challenges and rewards of its rich and demanding textures. This chapter will consider the primary developments in the most recent phase of Proust criticism, from the publication of the second Bibliothèque de la Pléiade edition of the *Recherche* in 1987–9 to the present day.

To do so is no small undertaking. Just as past time for Proust was never immobile or neatly contained, so his work and the critical engagements it provokes are dynamic, shifting and self-renewing. The text of his novel itself is not static: the three volumes of the first scholarly edition of the *Recherche*, the Pléiade of 1954, amounting to over 3,600 pages, are now dwarfed by the four weighty volumes of the second Pléiade edition, which stretches to over 7,400 pages. This expansion is primarily due to the inclusion of draft material and many (but by no means all) of Proust's preliminary sketches. Since the 1962 acquisition of Proust's notebooks and manuscripts by the Bibliothèque nationale in Paris, scholars have been able better to understand Proust's working methods and how *À la recherche*

206

came into being. Genetic criticism – work based on the scrutiny of Proust's manuscript material, from his preliminary notes and jottings to his abundant additions to the proof sheets for his novel's successive volumes – forms a major part of late-twentieth-century (and ongoing) critical work on Proust. Illuminating early studies that draw heavily on the 'fonds Proust' of the Bibliothèque nationale include Alison Finch's *Proust's Additions* (1977), which maps the manifold ways in which Proust's 'base text' grew organically during the war years and afterwards, and Anthony Pugh's *The Birth of 'À la recherche du temps perdu'* (1987), which studies the crucial creative period of 1908–9. Pugh's expansive *The Growth of 'À la recherche du temps perdu'* (2004) is the most detailed account to date of the materials that make up Proust's novel and its development between 1909 and 1914.

Proust's death before he had completed revising and publishing the *Recherche* renders the status of the 'final' text problematic. The discovery, in 1986, of an alternate, radically shortened version of *Albertine disparue* further troubled the critical waters. Nathalie Mauriac Dyer published this version of the text with Grasset in 1987. Debates in this area, the confrontation of literary and genetic criticism, are developed in an important collection, *Marcel Proust: écrire sans fin* (1996); a detailed account of the late-discovered material and its status can be found in Mauriac Dyer's monograph, *Proust inachevé: le dossier 'Albertine disparue'* (2005). The most recent Pléiade edition of the novel, and all other editions save for Mauriac Dyer's Grasset edition, reproduce the longer, unabridged version. Christine Cano's *Proust's Deadline* (2006) offers an elegant, accessible English-language account of the publishing history of *À la recherche*.

Correspondence and biography

Between 1970 and 1993 were published the twenty-one volumes of Proust's correspondence, which represent an extraordinary store of information about Proust, his contemporaries and their era. Proustian criticism since the 1970s owes a great deal to labours of the editor, Philip Kolb, and of Kazuyoshi Yoshikawa, who directed the Japanese team that prepared the vitally important index to the correspondence. Luc Fraisse has made an invaluable contribution to our understanding of its importance as a mine of information, first in the substantial *Proust au miroir de sa correspondance* (1996), then in the briefer yet still insightful *La Correspondance de Proust: son statut dans l'œuvre, l'histoire de son édition* (1998). Between 1983 and 2000 four volumes of *Selected Letters* were published in English translation.

The correspondence provides a vital source of biographical detail, which nourished a succession of renewed approaches to Proust's biography published, in English and French, throughout the 1990s and beyond, each more expansive than the next. First was Ronald Hayman's almost 600-page *Marcel Proust: A Biography* (1990). This was supplemented by Ghislain de Diesbach's 800-page *Proust* (1991), which was in turn followed in 1994 by Roger Duchêne's *L'Impossible Marcel Proust* (845 pages). The jewel in this crown remains Jean-Yves Tadié's outstanding *Marcel Proust: biographie* (1996). As the general editor of the Pléiade edition of the *Recherche*, few can rival his knowledge of the novel and its author; one who does is William C. Carter, the leading light of twentieth-century Proust scholarship in the United States, whose prize-winning, 900-page *Marcel Proust: A Life* was published in 2000. Carter's work, like Tadié's, is scrupulously researched. Carter's approach is more conventionally linear than Tadié's, and his style a little more discursive. Recently shorter lives have appeared, complementing Tadié and Carter's door-stoppers, notably Edmund White's immensely readable gay life (1999) and Mary Ann Caws' illustrated life (2005), which focuses on the artistic contexts of Proust's literary production. The field was also recently enriched with detailed studies of Proust's father (2003) and his mother (2004). My illustrated, critical life of Proust, drawing substantially on the correspondence and recent scholarship, is published in 2013. A first volume of essays on Proust's closest friends and acquaintances, *Proust et ses amis*, was published in 2010; a second is in preparation.

Edited volumes

Often arising out of conference proceedings, such collections offer a sense of prevailing views and critical trends at a given moment. Such is the case for the important volumes *The UAB Marcel Proust Symposium: In Celebration of the 75th Anniversary of 'Swann's Way'* (1989); *Proust in Perspective: Visions and Revisions* (2002), which arose from the 'Proust 2000' symposium at the University of Illinois; *The Strange M. Proust* (2009), stemming from a 2006 symposium at Princeton; *Le Temps retrouvé Eighty Years After/80 ans après* (2009, from a 2007 University of London conference); *Proust, la mémoire et la literature* (2009), drawing on Antoine Compagnon's Collège de France seminar for 2006–7; *Originalités proustiennes* (2010), arising from a 2009 conference at the Université de Tours; and *Proust face à l'héritage du XIXe siècle* (2012) whose origins were in conferences in Kyoto and Paris in 2010. These richly rewarding collections demonstrate that the scholarship in the field is increasingly international and collaborative. Members of the Équipe Proust research group at the École Normale Supérieure in Paris are drawn from institutions in France, Switzerland, the UK, the USA, Canada and Japan. A major conference recently took place in Brazil; Japanese and Korean (re-)translations are well underway. As the collective title of two recent edited volumes (2007 and 2010) has it, we seem now to be resolutely in an era of *Proust sans frontières*.

The late 1980s and early 1990s

Between 1987 and 1992, among a great many works of criticism published, half a dozen important studies stand out which attest to the diversity of scope and focus within the field and in some ways announce the primary directions of its future development. Malcolm Bowie's *Freud, Proust, and Lacan: Theory as Fiction* (1987) is a powerful work of comparative and connective analysis, which aligns and contrasts three of the century's most innovative and insightful theorists of the human psyche. Published the same year, Vincent Descombes's groundbreaking *Proust: philosophie du roman* opens up the issue of where we might find the author's 'philosophy', arguing persuasively that it is not necessarily in those parts of the novel directly or explicitly concerned with philosophical matters. Peter Collier's *Proust and Venice* (1987) is a study of Proustian aesthetics, whose insights are far more nuanced and wide-reaching than its title might suggest. While Bowie and Descombes illuminate Proust's originality as an analytical thinker, Collier casts light on his powers of artistic synthesis, assimilation and redeployment. Both Bowie and Collier refocus critical attention on *La Prisonnière* and *Albertine disparue*. Two years later, Antoine Compagnon's landmark study *Proust entre deux siècles* (1989) takes as its focus the pivotal, medial volume of the *Recherche*, *Sodome et Gomorrhe*, which for Compagnon typifies the Janus-like nature of Proust's work, writing that is imbued with nineteenth-century aesthetics yet which announces and reaches towards twentieth-century modernity.[3] Another critic who considers Proust in the context of nineteenth-century writers (including Nietzsche, Henry James and Wilde) is Eve Kosofsky Sedgwick, whose *Epistemology of the Closet* (1990) contains an influential chapter on Proust and prepares the ground for subsequent important studies including Elisabeth Ladenson's *Proust's Lesbianism* (1999) and Michael Lucey's *Never Say 'I': Sexuality and the First Person in Colette, Gide and Proust* (2006). Two final works that opened up new directions in Proust criticism are Christie McDonald's *The Proustian Fabric* (1991), a work that attunes our ear to the tensions in the *Recherche* between totality and comprehensiveness on one hand and fragmentation and contingency on the other; and Margaret E. Gray's *Postmodern Proust* (1992), which emphasizes the fractures at the heart of Proust's narrative and its resistance to compartmentalization. All of these works of the late 1980s and early 1990s broaden the reach of scholarly criticism on the *Recherche*, freeing it from the constricting notion of Proust as a snobbish author of an indulgent book 'about' memory and time.

The mid to late 1990s

Julia Kristeva's *Le Temps sensible: Proust et l'expérience littéraire* (1994) is a demanding work, but one which merits the careful attention of students of Proust's novel: Kristeva brings a wide array of learning (above all philosophical and psychoanalytical) to bear on the *Recherche*, focusing attention on the sensory dimension of Proustian temporality and responding directly to the critics who came before her, in particular Gilles Deleuze and Jean-Pierre Richard. Another rewarding study is Jacques Dubois's *Pour Albertine: Proust et le sens du social* (1997), an insightful sociological reading of the *Recherche*, focused above all on the enigmatic Albertine. In 1998 Malcolm Bowie published the finest general study of *À la recherche* available in English, *Proust among the Stars*. Bowie's thematic chapters ('Self', 'Time', 'Art' etc.) are enriched with an extraordinary erudition and by close readings which illuminate and energize the reader in equal measure.[4] In Bowie's wake came a number of excellent monographs dealing with particular thematic or formal areas of Proust's writing. Michael Finn's *Proust, the Body and Literary Form* (1999) investigates the connections between the author's ailments and his literary production. Anne Simon's *Proust ou le réel retrouvé* (2000, reissued 2011) gives a vivid philosophical reading of the *Recherche*, focusing on sensory experience and how it is communicated in ways that prefigure the writing of Merleau-Ponty. Others to appear in 2000 include Nicola Luckhurst's *Science and Structure in Proust's 'À la recherche'*, Margaret Topping's *Proust's Gods* and Ingrid Wassenaar's *Proustian Passions*, all of which bring valuable insights and open up avenues for exploration. While the individual chapters on Proust in more generalist books are too many and various to enumerate, mention should be made of Richard Terdiman's sophisticated reflections on Proust in *Present Past: Modernity and the Memory Crisis* (1993) and Sara Danius's account of Proust's work in her *The Senses of Modernism* (2002).

Twenty-first-century Proust

Alongside these illuminating works in English came important and complementary works in French: most notably Stéphane Chaudier's excellent *La Cathédrale profane: Proust et le langage religieux*; Sophie Duval's *L'Ironie proustienne* (both 2004); and Aude Le Roux-Kieken's *Imaginaire et écriture de la mort dans l'œuvre de Marcel Proust* (2005), all of which have a breadth and depth of reference and sensitivity of approach that make them vital references in the field. Daniel Karlin's *Proust's English* (2005) is a fascinating account of the second language of the *Recherche*, a revealing work of cultural historical significance. William C. Carter's *Proust in Love* (2006) interweaves biographical and literary-critical analyses to offer a portrait of Proustian desire. In France, an edited volume, *Proust et les images: peinture, photographie, cinéma, vidéo*, appeared in 2003, the first of a number of valuable additions to this particular area of research. It was followed the next year by Schmid and Beugnet's rewarding *Proust at the Movies*, which offers expert analysis of Proust's faring on the big screen (including the projects by Visconti and Joseph Losey/Harold Pinter that never made it to production). Eric Karpeles's beautifully produced *Paintings in Proust* (2008) is an invaluable resource which reproduces all of the works of visual art evoked in the novel and should be consulted alongside Kazuyoshi Yoshikawa's *Proust et l'art pictural* (2010). Áine Larkin's *Proust Writing Photography* (2011), Katja Haustein's *Regarding Lost Time: Photography, Identity and Affect in Proust, Benjamin and Barthes* (2012) and a number of articles by Kathrin Yacavone have shaped a reassessment of the place of photography in Proust's aesthetics. The essays collected in Nathalie Aubert's edited volume *Proust and the Visual* (2013) deepen this channel of investigation further still, attesting most positively to the fruits borne by the exploration of Proustian phenomenology.

If Anne Simon's *Proust ou le réel retrouvé* announced an important philosophical turn in twenty-first-century criticism in France, this was soon echoed in the Anglophone domain by Duncan Large's authoritative *Nietzsche and Proust: A Comparative Study* (2001) and Joshua Landy's lively *Philosophy as Fiction: Self, Deception and Knowledge in Proust* (2004), a work which develops a number of concerns explored by Descombes, Bowie and others a generation before. A uniformly rich edited volume, *Proust et la philosophie aujourd'hui* (2008), provides an overview of current research. Most recently, Erika Fülöp, in *Proust, the One, and the Many* (2012) has directed critical thinking about Proust and philosophy both backwards towards Schiller and the German romantics, and forward, like

Martin Hägglund in his bold *Dying for Time: Proust, Woolf, Nabokov* (2012), towards Derrida and Deleuze. My monograph, *Reading in Proust's 'À la recherche': 'le délire de la lecture'* (2009) also draws on these French thinkers, as well as on Freud, offering a reading of the novel that illuminates the privileged but unstable position of interpretive activity in its pages. A special *hors-série* number devoted to Proust of the French *Philosophie Magazine* (January–February 2013) gives an excellent trans-historical survey of the field, providing excerpts of the key critical texts alongside commentary and lengthy citation of the *Recherche*'s 'philosophical' passages. Luc Fraisse's study *L'Éclectisme philosophique de Marcel Proust* (2013) is an outstanding contribution to the field to set alongside his compendious *La Petite Musique du style: Proust et ses sources littéraires* (2011).

Recently, there has been a turn to the socio-historical and the sociological: after the last major works of this sort, Michael Sprinker's Marxist *History and Ideology in Proust* (1994), Catherine Bidou-Zachariasen's *Proust sociologue* and Jacques Dubois's *Pour Albertine* (both 1997), we now have Edward Hughes' important study in cultural history, *Proust, Class and Nation* and Jacqueline Rose's *Proust among the Nations: From Dreyfus to the Middle East* (both 2011). While this latter is a somewhat disparate collection of writings, it nevertheless shows that Proust has a place in intellectual debate well beyond the seminar room. Rose reads Proust alongside and interwoven with Freud, something Jean-Yves Tadié also does with aplomb in his recent essay *Le Lac inconnu: entre Proust et Freud* (2012), which brings a lifetime of living with Proust to a clear-sighted assessment of the novelist's commonalities with Freud (as well as their divergences). Eve Kosofsky Sedgwick's posthumous *The Weather in Proust* (2012) also brings Proust into contact with psychoanalytical theory, although her touchstone is Melanie Klein and not Freud. Sedgwick's late essays, written during her treatment for terminal cancer, bring reflections on Proustian style, aesthetics and morality into contact with Tibetan Buddhism, textile art and queer theory. When reading critics like Hägglund, Rose and Sedgwick at their best, one gets a real and vivifying sense of the almost endless critical and creative adventures to which Proust's work is capable of giving rise. Two recent edited volumes, *Au seuil de la modernité: Proust, literature and the arts*, published in memory of Richard Bales, editor of the excellent *Cambridge Companion to Proust* (2001), and *'When familiar meanings dissolve…': Essays in French Studies in Memory of Malcolm Bowie* (both 2011), whilst marking the loss of major luminaries also attest to the vibrancy and energy of Proust studies today.

Beyond academic criticism, Proust continues to draw interest from the most diverse quarters. An Italian journalist, Lorenza Foschini, recently published *Il cappotto di Proust* (2008), the tale of the collector Jacques Guérin's quest to accumulate Proust's belongings; the book (*Proust's Overcoat* in Eric Karpeles's 2010 translation), has been a major hit. Alain de Botton's popularizing self-help book *How Proust Can Change Your Life* (1997) has sold worldwide in vast quantities. Stéphane Heuet's graphic novel version of the *Recherche* has been translated into more than a dozen languages. Publication began in 1998; the sixth volume appears in 2013: with this, *Du côté de chez Swann* and *À l'ombre* will be complete. Jonah Lehrer has persuasively argued that Proust's writing on memory and affect anticipates the discoveries of modern research into the human brain (*Proust Was a Neuroscientist*, 2007). As interest in cognitive science and the 'neurohumanities' grows, no doubt Proust's place in the critical landscape will continue to shift. What is certain is that a century after *Swann*, Proust's star shows no sign of fading.

Notes

1 See Jean Cocteau, 'De la mesure', in *La Difficulté d'être* [1947] (Monaco: Éditions du Rocher, 1983), pp. 90–1.
2 See Elyane Dezon-Jones and Inge Crosman Wimmers, eds., *Approaches to Teaching Proust's Fiction and Criticism* (New York: MLA Publications, 2003). See 'Further Reading' at the end of this volume for bibliographical information on key texts mentioned in this chapter.
3 A recent study that has developed the work begun by Compagnon is Marion Schmid's excellent *Proust dans la décadence* (2008).
4 Other general approaches include Richard Bales' *Proust: 'À la recherche du temps perdu'* (1995); David Ellison, *A Reader's Guide to Proust's 'In Search of Lost Time'* (2010); and Adam Watt, *The Cambridge Introduction to Marcel Proust* (2011).

CHAPTER 28

Modernism

David Ellison

To read Proust today, some ninety years after his death, is to encounter him enveloped in celebrity, weighed down by reams of critical commentary, domesticated by the wealth of facts and hermeneutical grids with which we can now arm ourselves as we interpret the complexities of his imagined world. Proust has become so well known that it may be difficult for us modern-day readers to imagine just how revolutionary his prose style appeared to the majority of the European reading public during the period ranging from 1913 (when *Du côté de chez Swann* was first published) to 1927 (when *Le Temps retrouvé* finally appeared, five years after the author's death). Proust had difficulty getting published, in part because, like Wagner's tetralogy, *À la recherche du temps perdu* sinned against the accepted order of magnitude for works of art: the sentences were too long, the thoughts too convoluted, the general thematic aims not apparent enough in their wide extension. Put succinctly, what Proust was proposing as a novel was unusual, strange, disquieting. Even the most intelligent of readers found the work hard to classify, impossible to discuss within the given parameters of early-twentieth-century fiction. One such reader, particularly adept at recognizing Proust's genius, was Walter Benjamin, the German-Jewish philosopher and essayist. His description of the *Recherche* is worth quoting, both for its lapidary incisiveness and for the brilliance of its metaphorical formulation. Here are the first sentences of his essay 'The Image of Proust', initially published in 1929:

> The thirteen volumes of Marcel Proust's *À la recherche du temps perdu* are the result of an unconstruable synthesis in which the absorption of a mystic, the art of a prose writer, the verve of a satirist, the erudition of a scholar, and the self-consciousness of a monomaniac have combined in an autobiographical work. It has rightly been said that all great works of literature establish a genre or dissolve one – that they are, in other words, special cases. Among these cases, this is one of the most unfathomable. From its structure, which is at once fiction, autobiography, and commentary, to

214

the syntax of boundless sentences (the Nile of language, which here over-flows and fructifies the plains of truth), everything transcends the norm.[1]

Few writers have expressed more felicitously than Benjamin the various reasons which militate against the efforts a reader or critic might make to insert Proust's work into a given literary movement. Can one say that a text which combines mystical absorption, satire, erudition and mono-maniacal self-consciousness can be called a 'novel' in the usual sense, or are we better off calling it a 'special case' and dispensing with any attempt to include it under some large, all-embracing theoretical or conceptual umbrella? The striking image with which Benjamin concludes his description – which compares Proust's syntax to an overflowing 'Nile of language' – serves as a particularly well expressed warning against the temptation to include a writer possessing such specific and inimitable gifts within a larger literary-historical rubric.

Yet it is only natural for the literary critic to succumb to such a temptation. Just two years after Benjamin wrote 'The Image of Proust', the American critic Edmund Wilson included Proust among six writers who, in his view, could be studied as a group in that their respective writing styles all derived from the theoretical ground and textual practice of French symbolism. Published in 1931, *Axel's Castle: A Study in the Imaginative Literature of 1870–1930*,[2] begins with a chapter on symbolism per se (with special emphasis on the discovery of Edgar Allan Poe by Charles Baudelaire in the movement's early phase), then moves on to individual chapters on W. B. Yeats, Paul Valéry, T. S. Eliot, Marcel Proust, James Joyce and Gertrude Stein. In the concluding chapter, 'Axel and Rimbaud', Wilson moves back from the early-twentieth-century works which he had just examined and establishes a marked contrast between the isolation and withdrawal from society which permeate Villiers de l'Isle-Adam's *Axel* (1890) and Arthur Rimbaud's decision to cease writing poetry after revolu-tionizing it, choosing action in the world over the alchemy of the word.

Yeats, Valéry, Eliot, Proust, Joyce and Stein represent, for Wilson, that strain of literature we would call 'modernist' today, though the critic does not use that term in his book. What characterizes the modernist text is an exceptional degree of self-consciousness, a strong emphasis on the individual over against society, and the capacity to create an imagined world which does not refer directly or mimetically to exterior reality, but calls attention to itself. Although the rhetorical mode of Wilson's analyses possesses a broad range, from technically precise close readings to *ad hominem* attacks and downright grumpiness, few twentieth-century critics have matched him in his sensitivity to modernist innovations – from Yeats's particular use of myth and legend, to Eliot's dramatic sensibility, to Proust's attention to novelistic structure, to Joyce's singular creation of 'a new phase of the human consciousness'[3] in *Ulysses* and those sections of what was to become *Finnegans Wake* which had appeared by 1931. Yet despite his flair for interpreting refined and highly introspective texts, Wilson concludes that modernist literature, with these six writers, has exhausted itself and reached an impasse: 'Axel's world of the private imagination in isolation from the life of society seems to have been exploited as far as for the present is possible. Who can imagine this sort of thing being carried further than Valéry and Proust have done?'[4] Wilson, who had a strongly developed social conscience and who was to compose the widely read treatise on the development of European socialism, *To the Finland Station* (1940), read Proust and the other modernists with less overt admiration than Benjamin; although Wilson possessed a fine ear for modernist textual music, he pointed out, more explicitly and emphatically than other critics, the limits beyond which the self-reflexive, inwardly focused character of modernism could not, or should not, venture.

Although the term 'modernism' is used in Anglo-American intellectual circles more pervasively than in France, the link between modernism and its close linguistic cousin, 'modernity', is obvious and, from the point of view of literary history, not without significance. It is no coincidence that Edmund Wilson places Baudelaire at the origin of the introspective post-Symbolist writings he undertook to analyse in *Axel's Castle.*[5] The author of the innovative and scandalous poetry contained in *Les Fleurs du mal* was also a major literary and cultural critic who espoused the idea that beauty could be found in the present day – in the evanescence of fashion, in the changing styles of architecture, and in the renewal of artistic forms. In an essay ostensibly devoted to the water-colourist and newspaper illustrator Constantin Guys (1802–92) entitled 'Le peintre de la vie moderne', Baudelaire, who is among the first French-language writers to use the term, defines the word *modernité* while imagining M. Guys in his daily artistic peregrinations:

> And so he [Constantin Guys] walks, he runs, he searches. What is he looking for? Certainly this man as I have described him, this solitary individual blessed with an active imagination ... has a higher goal than that of a mere wandering observer [*flâneur*], a more general goal, other than that which present circumstances, fleeting as they are, offer him. He is looking for that something which I hope I may be allowed to call *modernité*; there is no better word to express the idea in question. What he wishes to

do is to extricate from fashion the poetic essence within the historical moment, to pry the eternal from the transitory.[6]

What Baudelaire expresses here will constitute a central core of aesthetic preoccupation for the modernist writers who follow in his wake: how does one represent modern life in its variegated and fluctuating everydayness while at the same time allowing deeper and more essential truths – what Baudelaire calls 'the eternal' – to break through the surface of the writer's fictional world? In works now occupying pride of place in the modernist canon – Joyce's *Ulysses*, Woolf's *To the Lighthouse* and Proust's *Recherche* – there is a strong organizing tension underlying each book's narrative construction: on the one hand, each writer seeks to recreate a highly particularized imagined universe full of physical and psychological detail (Joyce's cacophonous Dublin, Woolf's distant Hebrides and Proust's elegant Parisian salons have become part of our literary patrimony); but on the other, each of them points beyond the literary landscape itself to larger aesthetic and ethical concerns, endowing the narrative spaces they have created with a quasi-geological temporal layering. The Dublin of *Ulysses* through which the father and son figures of Bloom and Stephen Daedalus pass during one single day is at the same time the mirror of the history of Western civilization, from Homer onward; the wind-swept Hebrides, far from being isolated from the horrors of the Great War, become the theatre on which Time itself passes; and the world of wit, of fashion and of social inclusion and exclusion, becomes, at the end of the *Recherche*, merely a stylized stage-set on which writer and reader are compelled to contemplate the prestige of art being threatened by the ravages of human mortality.

It is perhaps no coincidence that Joyce, Woolf and Proust each devised terms and particular modes of writing to express the ways in which the individual human being, despite being caught up in commonplace existence and in the inexorable movement towards death and oblivion, also experiences certain privileged moments which open up (to borrow from Wordsworth) 'intimations of immortality'. In Joyce's early career, these were called 'epiphanies' (the sudden disclosure of one's authentic self); for Woolf, they were 'moments of being' (the revelation of reality coming in a particular moment which temporarily obliterates the usual 'non-being' of one's daily existence); and for Proust, they were the *souvenirs involontaires*, or involuntary remembrances, which emerge from the Narrator's unconscious into his conscious mind one cold and bleak winter's day when, 'dispirited after a dreary day with the prospect of a depressing morrow' (1: 51; 1, 44), he accepts his mother's invitation to drink a cup of tea into which he dips one of those small cakes, to be found in all self-respecting French pastry shops, with the evocative name: petites madeleines. The effect on the Narrator is immediate; the effect on Proust's readers was profound. This particular moment, which begins as follows, has become an icon of modernist literature:

> I raised to my lips a spoonful of the tea in which I had soaked a morsel of the cake. No sooner had the warm liquid mixed with the crumbs touched my palate than a shudder ran through me and I stopped, intent upon the extraordinary thing that was happening to me. An exquisite pleasure had invaded my senses, something isolated, detached, with no suggestion of its origin. And at once the vicissitudes of life had become indifferent to me, its disasters innocuous, its brevity illusory – this new sensation having had on me the effect which love has of filling me with a precious essence; or rather, this essence was not in me, it *was* me. I had ceased now to feel mediocre, contingent, mortal. Whence could it have come to me, this all-powerful joy? I sensed that it was connected with the taste of the tea and the cake, but that it infinitely transcended those savours, could not, indeed, be of the same nature. Whence did it come? What did it mean? How could I seize and apprehend it? (1: 51–2; 1, 44).

With its impressive combination of brevity and dramatic intensity, the scene of the petite madeleine situates the Narrator in a liminal, or threshold, position. As a human being he is subject to 'the vicissitudes of life' – which, in his case, will include progressive disillusionment with the superficiality and cruelty of aristocratic society, much suffering in his loves for Gilberte, the Duchesse de Guermantes and Albertine, and feelings of inadequacy as a budding writer. Yet at the same time, pulling in the opposite direction, is an 'all-powerful joy' which appears to be the sign of something transcendental. Just two pages after the breathless questions – 'Whence did it come? What did it mean? How could I seize and apprehend it?' – the Narrator offers us his memorable response. The impression of something situated beyond the limits assigned to human existence comes from the relational quality of memory itself – its capacity to unify present and past in one synthetic impression, thereby bringing together under one totalizing structure not only the individual's life experiences, but also his consciousness and the power of his imagination. The essence of the past, which cannot be reached by an act of voluntary recall or intellection, is accessible to us all in those rare moments in which we are attuned to the temporal environment in which all human actions bathe. The middle-aged Narrator shortly realizes that the taste of the cake dipped in tea is a euphoric repetition of a childhood experience – the habitual offering of a petite madeleine from his Tante Léonie on Sunday mornings in the provincial town of Combray.

Although the Narrator has by now aged and experienced the disappointments of life, and although he certainly cannot be said to be the same person as the young boy we encounter at the beginning of the novel's chronology (a linear chronology which has been put in abeyance by this particular scene and two others before it), the taste sensation of the little cake dipped in tea, as frail and apparently insignificant as it is, resembles the supporting wall of a vast edifice – the edifice of memory itself:

> But when from a long-distant past nothing subsists, after the people are dead, after the things are broken and scattered, taste and smell alone, more fragile but more enduring, more unsubstantial, more persistent, more faithful, remain poised a long time, like souls, remembering, waiting, hoping, amid the ruins of all the rest; and bear unflinchingly, in the tiny and almost impalpable drop of their essence, the vast structure of recollection. (1: 54; I, 46)

Throughout the *Recherche*, Proust insists upon what one might call, paraphrasing Pascal, the juxtaposed *grandeur* and *misère* of the human condition. Even in those passages of the novel like the one we have just read which possess a triumphant tone, and which seem to promise a form of aesthetic redemption, Proust reminds us of the quotidian realities to which, despite all of our efforts and aspirations, we remain tethered: the human creature is *both* grand and miserable. I think it is with this in mind that we must read the final sentence of the novel in which the Narrator affirms his vocation as writer, remembering not only its beginning and its end, which glorify our expansive temporal destiny, but also its middle, in which we are reminded, gently enough, of the restricted space in which we live, but which we would doubtless prefer to deny:

> If strength were granted me for long enough to accomplish my work, I should not fail, even if the results were to make them resemble monsters, to describe men first and foremost as occupying a place, a very considerable place compared with the restricted one which is allotted to them in space, a place on the contrary prolonged past measure – for simultaneously, like giants plunged into the years, they touch epochs that are immensely far apart, separated by the slow accretion of many, many days – in the dimension of Time. (6: 451; IV, 625)

Notes

1 Walter Benjamin, 'The Image of Proust', in *Illuminations*, trans. by Harry Zohn, ed. Hannah Arendt (London: Pimlico, 1999 [1970]), pp. 197–210 (197).
2 Edmund Wilson, *Axel's Castle: A Study in the Imaginative Literature of 1870 to 1930* (New York: Charles Scribner's Sons, 1931).

3 Wilson, *Axel's Castle*, p. 221.

4 Wilson, *Axel's Castle*, p. 292.

5 Wilson is by no means the only critic to place Baudelaire at the origin of modernism or of modernity. In his *Struktur der modernen Lyrik* (Hamburg: Rowohlt, 1956) [*The Structure of Modern Poetry from the Mid-Nineteenth to the Mid-Twentieth Century* (Evanston, IL: Northwestern University Press, 1974)], Hugo Friedrich, in alluding to 'the poet of modernity', wrote: 'With Baudelaire, French poetry became a matter of concern for all Europe ... Mallarmé admitted that he had begun where Baudelaire had had to leave off. Valéry, nearing the end of his life, traced a direct line of communication from Baudelaire to himself. T. S. Eliot called Baudelaire's work "the greatest example of modern poetry in any language"' (*The Structure of Modern Poetry*, p. 19). In *Mélancolie et opposition: les débuts du modernisme en France* (Paris: Corti, 1987) [*The Writing of Melancholy: Modes of Opposition in Early French Modernism* (The University of Chicago Press, 1993)], Ross Chambers places three French writers of the 1850s – Baudelaire, Flaubert and Nerval – at the forefront of a type of 'oppositional' writing that he characterizes as early modernist. Unlike Wilson, Chambers finds that modernist self-reflexivity can be reconciled with history and with concrete social life. He argues that the modernist literary text opens itself to history 'through the instance of reading presupposed by the text's self-figuration; it is the text's readability that guarantees its interpretive history (or "fortune", one might say) among successive groups of future readers' (*The Writing of Melancholy*, p. 13). And Peter Gay, in what is doubtless the most ambitious recent attempt to write a synthetic history of modernism, has asserted: 'I am casting Charles Baudelaire, in preference to all other heretics, as modernism's first hero' (Peter Gay, *Modernism, The Lure of Heresy: From Baudelaire to Beckett and Beyond* (New York: Norton, 2008), p. 5). According to Gay, the two defining qualities of modernism are 'the lure of heresy' and 'the commitment to a principled self-scrutiny' (pp. 4–5). Although the sheer scope of Gay's work is too vast for him to analyse any particular artist in great detail, the short section he devotes to Proust, in which he compares the 'Intermittences of the Heart' section of the *Recherche* to Lily Briscoe's illumination in *To the Lighthouse*, is well argued and convincing (pp. 208–14).

6 Charles Baudelaire, 'Le peintre de la vie moderne', in *Œuvres complètes*, ed. Claude Pichois, 2 vols. (Paris: Gallimard, 1976), II, p. 696; my translation.

CHAPTER 29

Adaptations/afterlives

Margaret E. Gray

An 1892 photograph portrays an unusually relaxed, clowning Proust strumming a tennis racquet in playful serenade (see Fig. 3). Such an appropriative gesture – such dislocation, manipulation and transformation of tennis racquet into banjo – provides a point of departure for scrutiny of the cultural manipulations and transformations undergone by Proust's work itself. How might we understand the appropriation of his œuvre within popular culture? In this exuberant encounter, what has become of Proust's 'aura': the effect analysed by Walter Benjamin as marker of the singularity of the work of art, of the compelling 'here-and-now-ness' of its unique presence, the immediacy of its power?[1] Benjamin was thinking of visual works of art, in particular, as he argued that it is precisely these elements of singularity and immediacy of the work of art that cannot be mechanically reproduced. For Benjamin, such elements have to do with the work of art's particular embeddedness within a tradition. Yet something has happened to the here-and-nowness of Proust's work; it has been appropriated and manipulated within popular culture, detached from its own tradition and converted into a very different contemporaneity.[2]

Curiously, however, Proust is – in the claim of one reader – 'cooler than you are',[3] having already anticipated and charted the course of such activity. The encounter with popular culture, far from signalling the demise of Proust, renews the Proustian aura, bringing a different 'here-and-now-ness' to the Proustian text. For popular culture's episodic, scattered and idiosyncratic appropriations reveal in its popularized Proust an activity of cultural resistance. Popular culture is everyday culture, and within its everyday Proust thrives a lively resistance that Certeau teaches us to see. Arguing for reading not as passive ingestion, but as a kind of poaching, Certeau suggests that such appropriation acts as resistance to the imposition of massive cultural norms.[4] Whereas we might understand Marcel's long apprenticeship in aesthetics precisely as an effort to absorb the aesthetic 'habitus' – in Bourdieu's term – of the true artist, we find in Marcel's

221

Figure 3. Proust at the tennis courts on boulevard Bineau, 1892

contemporary reader precisely the reverse of such absorption: we find the resistance to such cultural inculcation. For today's reader, then, the *Recherche* provides not only a map for such cultural absorption (the Bourdieu reading), but a map for its resistance (the Certeau reading). It offers not only a map for the cultural codes ultimately mastered by Marcel, but a map for overturning them. In what follows, I study these two maps, and their apparent incompatibility, suggesting that it is through notions of the everyday that such apparent incompatibility may be reconciled.

To start with the Bourdieu reading, we might consult the *Recherche* itself for what it tells us about issues of taste – since taste would seem to provide an important distinction between 'high' culture and popular culture. Indeed, we might read the Proustian Narrator's itinerary as an apprenticeship in taste, a series of lessons shaped by Bourdieu's notion of the 'habitus': the transmission from within a social class of ideas of taste.[5] For instance, in the highly freighted bedtime drama scene, the Narrator's mother reads aloud to him the novel that his grandmother, resolving to provide her grandson a lesson in taste (1: 47–8; 1, 42), had planned to give him for his birthday: George Sand's *François le Champi*. When the Narrator's father ridicules her original choice (Musset's poems, a volume of Rousseau, and Sand's *Indiana*), the grandmother returns to the bookstore, in another town, on a stiflingly hot day – and comes home in such a depleted state as to incite a doctor's scolding. Good taste, we are made to understand, is worth suffering for.

And in her pursuit of good taste, the grandmother has recourse to Swann, that precursor of the Narrator in love and the suffering it entails. Rather than bring herself to sink to the vulgarity of photographs, she consults Swann as to what reproductions of paintings she might give her grandson (1: 46; 1, 43). Swann, as advisor to the grandmother – herself already demanding in her tastes – is therefore positioned, himself, as high priest of taste: a role that becomes all the more poignant in light of Swann's downfall via his love for Odette, whose frantic efforts to mime good taste betray, precisely, her vulgarity. Swann thus delivers, via the grandmother, a lesson in good taste even as he embodies the consequences of betraying it. For the aesthete Swann has become the vulgar husband of the vulgar Odette, the wife who is not welcome, and never received, in Tante Léonie's garden. We understand the depths to which Swann has sunk when he boasts that his wife has received a visit from a minor government official. Any potential promise Swann once had, any artistic possibility, has been betrayed by his weakness: his susceptibility for a woman who is not to his taste, who is not his 'genre'.

Following this lesson, the narrative proceeds with a long, belaboured effort to overcome the danger Swann represents for the Narrator: the danger of ending up like him, through a lapse in taste: a failed, fallen artist.[6] The Narrator's apprenticeship continues, but the instruction is now taken over by successful artists. Among the most important of these lessons – this instruction in the 'habitus', or codes, of artistic taste – is a visit to Elstir's studio in Balbec (2: 478; II, 190). Here, in what the Narrator calls a 'laboratory of creation', Elstir's paintings acquire artistic value not for their subject-matter, not for what is painted but for their chiasmatique technique: seascapes as landscapes, landscapes as seascapes. Art is a matter of how one paints, not of what is painted. This is the lesson, as Bourdieu puts it, of form over function; of the mode of representation over the object of representation.[7]

Another crucial lesson in the Narrator's artistic apprenticeship, of course, is the lesson that is fatal to Bergotte, with a deadliness that ratchets up the stakes for the Narrator. It is a reprise, but a far more stark and pointed one, of the Elstir lesson – as though to make sure the Narrator, and his readers, have understood for good. As the ailing Bergotte studies Vermeer's *View of Delft* at a visiting exhibition, he realizes, too late, that this is how he should have written; he should have made his sentences precious in themselves. Telling himself that the malaise he feels is nothing, a bit of undigested potato, he dies (5: 207–9; III, 692–3). The lesson that costs Bergotte his life, then – the lesson that comes too late – is that artistry inheres in technique, not in the piece of yellow wall itself; in the 'substance' of the sentence, not in what it says. Bergotte's deadly epiphany anticipates the Narrator's crucial and capital discovery that the very material of his œuvre need not necessarily be worthy, heroic; that, indeed, it can be his very life itself, in all its daily banality. The Narrator is able to become an artist only once he discovers his own version of Bergotte's lesson, the lesson of the 'phrase précieuse' – which, for the Narrator, will be the very mundane stuff of his life itself, yet captured within the 'necessary rings' of metaphor.[8]

And it is precisely the everyday, the ordinary, in Proust that popular culture celebrates, thereby honouring – in its own way, to be sure – a lesson learned by his Narrator. Therefore, whereas we might understand Marcel's long apprenticeship in aesthetics as an effort to absorb the 'habitus' of the true artist, the precise lesson of this apprenticeship – in a surprising paradox – implicitly overturns Bourdieu's models of taste and distinction, paving the way for a celebration of popular culture's own vernacular Proust.

Having come as far as we can with Bourdieu and taste, arriving at the uncoupling of subject and form, we are in a position to appreciate – just as the Narrator does at the end of the *Recherche* – the implicit value of the ordinary. To do so, we will move from Bourdieu to Certeau, from the Narrator to his reader, from the absorption of lessons of taste to their resistance. We will be asking, what happens when today's reader picks up Proust? Could any act be more pious, more worshipful, more illustrative of Bourdieu's ideas of cultural absorption, than the reading of such an immortal classic? But if we consult Certeau as to what actually takes place when one reads, we arrive at a very different scenario from the implicit veneration evoked by this scene. Certeau describes a hidden, transgressive, silent, ironic, *other* sort of reading: reading not as rapt absorption, but as poaching. Readers are nomads, poaching in fields they have not written, suggests Certeau.[9] Such illicit appropriation betrays, like bubbles secretly rising from the depths, the indices of a *common* poetics.[10] Intriguingly, Certeau's recurring model in his demonstration of reading as poaching, is Barthes reading Proust into Stendhal, or reading Proust's Normandy apple-trees in bloom into Flaubert. For Barthes himself, such joyfully irreverent reading is 'savoury' in its disregard for chronology.[11] In an essay devoted to the act of reading, Proust's own description of reading-as-poaching hints at precisely such 'désinvolture', or savoury impertinence. Writing that he only feels himself 'live and think' in a room inhabited by other 'profoundly different' lives, a room entered brazenly in which one sits in 'a sort of free promiscuity' upon the settee with 'the life that remains dispersed there,' Proust suggests that one 'play[s] the proprietor' in this room 'filled to overflowing with the souls of others' (*ASB*, 202; *CSB*, 167).

Equipped with models from Certeau, Barthes and Proust himself of savoury, impertinent reading – of reading as poaching – we notice that the transgressive, poaching aspect of reading becomes particularly visible in the encounter of Proust and popular culture. This encounter is dramatized in a cartoon depicting a bed-ridden Proust being told by a cart-pushing vendor that there are no more madeleines, and offered a prune Danish pastry.[12] That the most renowned sweet in all of literary history should be interchangeable with any other; and that the great Proust should be interchangeable with any random customer – as implied by the vendor's calling him a generic 'Jack' – bespeaks a certain 'everyday-ification'. In the infinite exchangeability of elements suggested by an *à la carte* menu, if a madeleine isn't available to inspire a needy writer, something else will do just as well, in the same way that one customer will do just as well as any another. Nowadays, everything, from Proust's madeleine to Proust himself, is exchangeable in commodity culture, in this frenzied *à la carte* levelling of all difference.

The *Recherche*'s deep negotiation with everyday life is particularly rendered, even exploited, in Stéphane Heuet's graphic-novel renditions. Characters that come to us in Proust's text as forbidding, larger-than-life fictional creations, almost monstrous in their power, become, in Heuet's hands, familiar, everyday. The all-powerful, sadistic Françoise is just a plump cook in a white apron. In another emblem of the everydayness brought out by Heuet's interpretation, an illustration of the Balbec boardwalk depicts an elegant *hôtel particulier*: but, we notice, surrounded by scaffolding, and therefore caught in its most mundane, everyday aspect. A final example of the 'everyday-ification' of Proust's text is Heuet's rendition of the madeleine scene itself, where, in an interpretation that has become somewhat infamous, Heuet has the Narrator remark nonchalantly, 'Tiens! Une madeleine!' ['Say! A madeleine!'].[13] What exclamation could more effectively confer such a mundane, quotidian aspect upon what may well be the most famous scene in all of French literature? Heuet's 'Tiens!' only brings out the 'everydayness' generalized across all of Proust's text, beginning with Tante Léonie's fierce attachment to routine, itself matched perhaps only by the Narrator's own. For *Combray* is essentially about habit, as John Porter Houston demonstrates in his study of iterative patterns; where one would expect the singularity of action to call for a perfect tense, the imperfect is used, to convey repetition, habit, everyday routine.[14] And when habit is rarely broken in the 'train-train' of life at Combray, it's to cede to a secondary habit – as in the Saturday lunch that falls an hour earlier than usual, so as to allow Françoise to go to the market. Routine is only breached to make way for a secondary routine.

It is through this exploration of the everyday, the banal, the mundane, that readers – let's call them everyday readers – connect to Proust. And this connection is lengthily developed in what – deliberately mangling grammar to emphasize the colloquial – I call the 'Proust and Me' genre. Demonstrating this unabashedly narcissistic genre's appropriations is Alain de Botton's *How Proust Can Change Your Life*. Botton both charmingly and shamelessly prints a photo of his girlfriend Kate on a beach, emphasizing her resemblance to Albertine, even as he quotes Proust himself as justification: 'En réalité, chaque lecteur est quand il lit le propre lecteur de soi-même' ['In reality every reader is, while he is reading, the reader of his own self'] (IV, 489; 6: 273). In Certeau's terms, we poach and pillage on Proust's territory; we 'play the master' – as Proust himself put it – on his turf, appropriating him to our own purposes.

As a case in point, we might consider the startling differences that distinguish three films based on Proust's *Recherche*. As creakingly wooden as it is lavish, Schlöndorff's version of heritage cinema renders *Un Amour de Swann* as a period piece.[15] A more subtle attempt to render Proustian layers of temporality occurs in the flashbacks and collage of Raoul Ruiz's drama, *Le Temps retrouvé*.[16] The emotional claustrophobia of the Albertine volumes is evoked in the experimental daring and intensity of Chantal Akerman's *La Captive*[17] – where the anachronistic use of mobile phones, for example, only points up the gulfs and chasms that fracture communication between the Narrator and Albertine.

Yet Proust has already out-poached his own poachers in mapping the very moves of their appropriative efforts, in anticipating and defining the vernacular poetics with which he is read by popular culture. In so everyday a gesture as a tennis racquet strummed like a banjo, Proust precisely anticipates popular culture's appropriations. It is for this reason that he is – to borrow the formulation of one of his young readers – 'cooler than you are'. And yet, how could Proust's transformation from scorned text to cool text be more pertinent for a novel teeming with reversals of taste and class distinctions? We recall not only the example of a fallen Swann, but that the greatest of artists, Elstir, proves to be the inane M. Biche of the Verdurin salon. The frantically arriviste Mme Verdurin becomes the Princesse de Guermantes, while Odette, in an ascent only slightly less dramatic following Swann's death, becomes – in her final appearance as a 'rose that has been sterilised' (6: 323; IV, 528) – the mistress of the mildly senile Duc de Guermantes. The novel wreaks zestful havoc with delineations of class and taste. Why should the appropriation of Proust by popular culture then be contrary to what occurs with repeated gusto in the novel itself?

We cannot, then, possibly conclude that Proust is a dusty, obsolete author whose high-modernist masterpiece has as much relevance as ancient history. Instead, Proust remains, to return to the tennis metaphor with which I began, at the top of his game, even a century later. Let us remember that the French 'le tennis' is an appropriation from English, as Daniel Karlin reminds us.[18] Yet the English word 'tennis', Karlin continues, of course itself comes from French, from the interpellation 'tenez' addressed to one's opponent during the 'jeu de paume'.[19] The word 'le tennis' thus re-appropriates from English, back into French, what was originally French – yet with its English side-trip orthographically and phonetically retained. Within this photograph and the activities it depicts, then, we have a dense overlay of corruptions, appropriations and transformations, beginning with the fact that Jeanne Pouquet (who was later to marry Proust's friend Gaston de Caillavet) is standing on a chair: a piece of furniture meant, of course, to be used otherwise. We notice Proust's own joyful pleasure in the scene's most theatrical appropriation of all: turning a tennis racquet into a song, sport into serenade, an everyday game into art. And this transformation of the everyday into art anticipates, of course, the Narrator's subsequent and decisive transformation of the matter of everyday life itself into the art of literature. How could Proust then possibly object to the transformation of his art back into the matter of everyday life, as in popular culture's appropriations? He himself has already just as cheekily, just as impertinently, just as 'coolly', led the way.

Notes

1 Walter Benjamin, 'The Work of Art in the Age of Mechanical Reproduction', in *Illuminations*, trans. by Harry Zohn, ed. Hannah Arendt (London: Pimlico, 1999 [1970]), pp. 211–44.
2 For further analysis of Proust's impact upon popular culture, see Adam Watt's 'Proustian Afterlives', in *The Cambridge Introduction to Marcel Proust* (Cambridge University Press, 2011), pp. 116–22, as well as my own earlier [Margaret E. Gray,] 'Proust, Narrative and Ambivalence in Contemporary Culture', in *Postmodern Proust* (Philadelphia: University of Pennsylvania Press, 1992), pp. 152–76.
3 Katharine Donelson, 'Marcel Proust was Cooler than You Are', review of Alain de Botton, *How Proust Can Change Your Life*, 9 January 2005 http://blogcritics.org/books/article/marcel-proust-was-cooler-than-you.
4 Michel de Certeau, *L'Invention du quotidien: arts de faire*, vol. 1 (Paris: Gallimard, 1980).
5 Pierre Bourdieu, *La Distinction: critique sociale du jugement* (Paris: Éditions de Minuit, 1979).
6 On the 'dangerous' model Swann represents for the Narrator, see Nicola Luckhurst's analysis in the section 'Swann's story' of her chapter, 'Modelling', in *Science and Structure in Proust's 'À la recherche du temps perdu'* (Oxford University Press, 2000), pp. 118–28.
7 Bourdieu, *Distinction*, p. 30.
8 See Malcolm Bowie's eloquent analysis of the little patch of yellow wall's 'layered beauty' in *Proust among the Stars* (London: HarperCollins, 1998), p. 118.
9 Certeau, *L'Invention*, p. 292.
10 Certeau, *L'Invention*, p. 290.
11 Roland Barthes, *Le Plaisir du texte* (Paris: Éditions du Seuil, 1973), pp. 58–9.

12 See Emily Eells's insightful analysis of this cartoon in 'Proust à l'Américaine', in Mireille Naturel, ed., *La Réception de Proust à l'étranger* (Illiers-Combray: Institut Marcel Proust International, 2002), pp. 61–79.

13 Stéphane Heuet, *À la recherche du temps perdu* (adaptation), *Combray* (Paris: Éditions Delcourt, 1998), p. 15.

14 John Porter Houston, 'Theme and Structure in *À la recherche du temps perdu*', *Kentucky Romance Quarterly*, 17 (1970), 209–22.

15 *Swann in Love*. Dir. Volker Schlöndorff. Gaumont, 1984.

16 *Le Temps retrouvé*. Dir. Raoul Ruiz. Gémini Films, 1999.

17 *La Captive*. Dir. Chantal Ackerman. Gémini Films, 2000.

18 Daniel Karlin, *Proust's English* (Oxford University Press, 2005).

19 Karlin, *Proust's English*, p. 139.

CHAPTER 30

Translations

Michael Wood

In 1929 E. M. Forster expressed a faint reservation about C. K. Scott Moncrieff's 'monumental translation' of the first five volumes of *À la recherche du temps perdu* in these terms: 'I was hoping to find Proust easier in English than in French, and do not. All the difficulties of the original are here faithfully reproduced.'[1] In 1981, the year of the publication of his own revision of Scott Moncrieff's work, Terence Kilmartin cited the 'story that discerning Frenchmen preferred to read Marcel Proust in English on the grounds that the prose of *À la recherche du temps perdu* was deeply un-French and heavily influenced by writers such as Ruskin'.[2]

The mythical expectations meet up across more than fifty years. Forster was hoping for, or pretending to hope for, precisely what the discerning Frenchmen claimed to find, and the parties on both sides were not only espousing a theory of translation as clarification but unintentionally shoring up Proust's own claim that 'each artist seems ... to be a native of an unknown country' (5: 290; III, 761).[3] In Proust's view and practice, the artist encounters the reader on this ground, where both may be strangers to themselves ('l'ouvrage de l'écrivain n'est qu'une espèce d'instrument optique qu'il offre au lecteur afin de lui permettre de discerner ce que sans ce livre il n'eût peut-être pas vu en soi-même', IV, 489–90);[4] the myths replace the unknown country with a wish for a known one, certainly foreign but at least in touch with a national spirit in a way the actual text is not.

Many questions about writing and translation crowd together here; about what constitutes failure and success in both realms too. Scott Moncrieff adds his own words and phrases to his versions of Proust's sentences, switches metaphors, inserts allusions and indulges in much elegant variation, so that for *disait*, for example, he will write 'remarked', 'began', 'murmured', 'assured them' etc.[5] Is this why the discerning Frenchmen are happy with this work? Then how could Forster find it faithful to 'all the difficulties of the original'? Could both perceptions be

230

right in some way? They could easily both be wrong, but my suggestion is that the Frenchmen are half-right and that Forster, if we allow him a little leeway for overstatement, is almost entirely right. Scott Moncrieff made Proust's texts his own, and in many ways, as critics have said, tended 'to the purple and the precious' where Proust's style is 'quite free of preciosity, archaism or self-conscious elegance'.[6] But he did not make Proust simpler or less foreign, he shifted him into a second unknown country, into the artful, decadent English-speaking world that he discovered when he looked so long and so fondly through Proust's optical instrument.

Scott Moncrieff's translations began with *Swann's Way*, which appeared in 1922, the year of Proust's death, when three volumes of the whole novel still remained to be published in French. *Within a Budding Grove* (1924), *The Guermantes Way* (1925), *Cities of the Plain* (1927), *The Captive* (1929) and *The Sweet Cheat Gone* (1930) followed in steady order. The translator died in 1930, and the last volume of *À la recherche* was translated in England (as *Time Regained*, 1931) by Sydney Schiff, who wrote under the name of Stephen Hudson, and in America (as *The Past Recaptured*, 1932) by Frederick A. Blossom. A later version (1970) by Andreas Mayor came to be regarded as the completion of Scott Moncrieff's work.

This work, in various editions, was much read and admired 'almost as a masterpiece in it own right', as Kilmartin cautiously said.[7] As late as 1958 Pamela Hansford Johnson, the author of a series of brilliant 'reconstructions' of Proust, was still calling it a 'miracle'.[8] It has its staunch defenders even now, but the appeal of a new translation grew over time, largely because the claim that Scott Moncrieff belonged to Proust's own era and wrote in its idiom became a liability rather than a source of authority. The translator's language, it seemed, had dated in a way Proust's hadn't; either Scott Moncrieff belonged to an age just before that of Proust, as translators so often predate their sources stylistically, or Proust belonged to an unknown time, much as he was the native of an unknown country. Shirley Hazzard offers a very good account of this situation and this altering mood.[9]

The first major response to the idea of a new translation was Kilmartin's 'reworking', as he called it, of Scott Moncrieff's (and Mayor's) version. There was a 'need to revise the existing translation' because it was based on a 'notoriously imperfect' French edition. English-speaking readers were to have a text that corresponded to the first scholarly Pléiade text of *À la recherche* (1954). This need 'also provided an opportunity of correcting mistakes and misinterpretations in Scott Moncrieff's version'.[10] The same need, and a similar opportunity, arose with the publication of the second

Pléiade edition of the novel in French (1987–9), and D. J. Enright, who had worked with Kilmartin on his reworking, now revised the revision for a translation finally called *In Search of Lost Time* (1992). Kilmartin had died in 1991.

The final change of title had been one Kilmartin had wanted to make in 1981, but he had yielded to the publisher's desire to keep the old one. The two options in themselves define in miniature many aspects of the debate about translating Proust. *Remembrance of Things Past* is allusive, literary, evocative. It puts Proust in the best (Shakespearean) company – the reference is to the opening of Sonnet 30:

> When to the sessions of sweet silent thought
> I summon up remembrance of things past.

However, the eloquent title actually contradicts one of the major claims of Proust's novel: that what we consciously summon up as remembrance is not memory, only a sort of mummified replacement of what is gone. *In Search of Lost Time* is literal and functional, but can't do anything about the double meaning of *perdu*, and misses the slightly technical aspect of research in *recherche*. 'Search' in its way is as romantic as remembrance, and I am not sure that lost time means anything if it isn't also felt to be wasted, in need of redemption.

Kilmartin is less polite about Scott Moncrieff's version in his *Grand Street* essay than in his 'Note on the Translation'. He lists a number of howlers in the Scott Moncrieff work, and reminds us that the translator's French was 'far from perfect' – as we can see from the wonderful school-boyish rendering of 'Il y a combien de temps' ('how long ago'), as 'how many times'. He still says however that 'it is extraordinary how successful Scott Moncrieff was'. 'It is when one considers the alternatives that one warms to Scott Moncrieff's inventions.'[11] As Kilmartin justly remarks, 'it is only too easy for the latecomer to assume the *beau rôle*'[12] – indeed it may seem to us, in the light of many quite different cases, translations of Rilke for example, that the belated *beau rôle* is all but irresistible to most people.

It is not the role assumed by Christopher Prendergast and his team of translators for the new version of 2002, and it is interesting to see how close Prendergast is in his way to Kilmartin. If Proust's style for Kilmartin is 'essentially natural and unaffected', for Prendergast it is a 'robustly hewn form of writing'.[13] The target in both of these phrases is the decadent Proust who emerges in Scott Moncrieff's flowery unrevised version, 'a purveyor of high-grade cultural narcotics', in Prendergast's words.[14] There is more than translation at stake here. The objection is to the picture of the old Proust of the English (and French) imagination, devotee of the religion of art and a firm if desperate believer in redemption, in the secure finding, however late, of what has been lost. This picture has taken a bit of a battering over the years, from Leo Bersani, Malcolm Bowie and Prendergast himself, and of course it misses and mystifies too much of Proust's achievement. It needs to be said, though, as these critics do indeed say, that Proust himself invented the old Proust, and was his first acolyte so to speak; the beauty of the critical situation is that he also invented, and had done from the very beginning, the new, sceptical Proust, the ironic doubter who allows us to give the other one a hard time. Whether even the sceptical Proust can exactly be called 'natural and unaffected' or hews 'robustly' at his writing is a question for another day.[15]

The translation of which Prendergast is the general editor is also called *In Search of Lost Time*, and its individual volumes have the following names and translators: *The Way by Swann's* (Lydia Davis); *In the Shadow of Young Girls in Flower* (James Grieve); *The Guermantes Way* (Mark Traherne); *Sodom and Gomorrah* (John Sturrock); *The Prisoner* (Carol Clark); *The Fugitive* (Peter Collier); *Finding Time Again* (Ian Patterson). Clearly these versions are in dialogue with (and sometimes are identical to) the Scott Moncrieff/Kilmartin text, but they are new work, not any sort of revision; and the different translators have made different kinds of decisions. The whole set is carefully edited, that is, but it is not standardized. It is entertaining to imagine the quarrels, amounting perhaps to a small novel, that lie behind this sentence telling us that if there are 'issues on which, in the interests of consistency, editorial intervention has been necessary to cut the Gordian knot of passionately held differences of philosophical outlook, there are other areas in which the intrinsically heterogeneous nature of a team-translation has been allowed to express itself more freely'.[16]

The suggestion is not that these different English Prousts add up to a perfect picture of the writer; rather that the method actually multiplies Proust in an interesting way, both reflects his own multiplicity and compounds it, 'heightens the chances of bringing into focus the stylistic variety we encounter as we move from one volume to the next'.[17]

'No one has monopoly powers over the "correct"', Prendergast says, and the reminder is useful in more than one way.[18] In a first sense it means everyone can make mistakes, and even the new translation has a few errors of its own. There is the translation of 'laque' as lake rather than lacquer; the appearance of an occultist in the place of an oculist (this is probably the uncorrected contribution of a spell-checking programme rather than a human agent).[19] There is a salutary reminder that it is always possible not only to miss Proust's meaning but invert it: the death which is said in French to take up early residence with a dying person arrives late in English.[20]

The second sense of Prendergast's proposition assumes its full strength, however, if we take a basic accuracy for granted, or at least are happy to keep dealing with it case by case. The notion of fidelity has dogged translation since antiquity, and it certainly means more than correctness – it's hard to plead for infidelity as a virtue. But it has the immense drawback of presuming the existence of a stationary original text, always faithful to itself. Different versions, in this view, would come closer or not to the model, the dream of perfection being a translation just like its source, in the spirit of Borges's map of the universe that is the same size as the universe. But the original text of any work that matters changes over time. It creates new readings, which in turn alter the text itself, make old simplifications unavailable, close off roads of interpretation that have come to seem short or narrow or too hospitable to disreputable traffic, and open longer, wider and kindlier ones. Readers change over time too, bring their own history to the text, which responds to that new history, that new context. The words of Proust remain, unchanging now even if he kept changing them till he died; the script is unalterable, as the priest tells Josef K in *The Trial*; but the meanings, within certain grammatical and lexical limits, are alive and variable, difference in interpretation is endless in one sense *because* the words are the same.

Thus in comparing translations we are not – or do not have to be – thinking about improvement or who is winning some sort of competition. The otherwise impeccable Shirley Hazzard was quite wrong to say that Scott Moncrieff's translation of Proust could be challenged only if it is 'conspicuously bettered'.[21] Every translation has its own mode of tuning and once we are beyond gross errors, we can come to our own conclusions about the music. We may prefer the directness of the new version, and I do, but such a preference can itself be interpreted. And even within such a preference we may feel that Patterson's 'till the cows come home'[22] is a bit too slangy for *à perte de vue* (IV, 461), even if Kilmartin/Enright's 'until the crack of doom' (6: 237) (or indeed Scott Moncrieff's 'till doomsday') seems rather violent.[23] We may think that the literal 'abdication' and 'renunciation' (6: 244; IV, 465) carry longer and richer associations than 'surrendering of authority' and 'withdrawal'.[24] We might even enjoy Scott Moncrieff's 'You're as strong as the Pont Neuf',[25] which no doubt rests on a misunderstanding of a familiar locution (II, 884), more than Kilmartin's idiomatic 'You're as sound as a bell' (3: 691), or Mark Traherne's hearty 'You're in strapping shape.'[26] There is much more to be said along these lines, but it will all confirm Prendergast's claim. Translators, as readers and like readers, make interpretive choices, which can be attacked and defended on many grounds, literary, historical and philosophical; but we shall rarely be able to adjudicate the contest by a simple appeal to the notion of getting things right.

National languages play a part in these choices and their effects, since varying linguistic structures create and take away particular possibilities for all writers not just for Proust. Here is a simple sentence: 'Chez le prêtre comme chez l'aliéniste, il y a toujours quelque chose du juge d'instruction' (11, 635). If we wish to render *aliéniste* in Spanish for example, as Pedro Salinas did, the first translator of *À la recherche*, who arrived at the task even earlier than Scott Moncrieff, publishing *Por el Camino de Swann* in 1920, we do not have to look far: *alienista* will do very well.[27] Scott Moncrieff[28] (and Kilmartin and Enright, 3: 391) settle for 'alienist', but I'm not sure English-speaking readers are likely to know at once what this is, and Traherne has 'specialist in mental disorders'.[29] The person who was really in luck over this term, however, was Walter Benjamin, who with his friend Franz Hessel translated *À l'ombre des jeunes filles* and *Le Côté de Guermantes*. The German word is the magnificent *Irrenarzt*, doctor of the mad, or very literally doctor of those who stray.[30] Even Proust didn't have the benefit of this vivid word-picture.

Similar considerations arise with syntax. Proust writes 'Comme la souffrance va plus loin en psychologie que la psychologie!' (IV, 3). Scott Moncrieff and Kilmartin have 'How much further does anguish penetrate in psychology than psychology itself' (5: 477). Collier has 'How much more sharply suffering probes the psyche than does psychology.'[31] We can leave aside for the moment the refusal of both translators to let Proust's double use of the same word perform its task on its own, and concentrate on the form of the exclamation. There is no way of avoiding the qualification of the 'how' in English (much further, much more sharply) but the French, precisely and elegantly, has only the 'how'.

This is partly to say that what we miss or need to add in English is the same as with almost any translation where the original is full of play with its own language, we fall short of our own sense of 'the detailed pleasures' of the writing, in Patterson's words, 'its poetic features, alliterations, anagrams and paragrams'.[32] Very broadly, though, Proust's French welcomes translation, because it rests so much on reproducible elements, like elaborate argument, logical surprise, unlikely comparisons, an impeccable if elastic grammar. Proust's ironies, for example, are conceptual or narrative, not tonal – whereas in many English and German writers irony is *all* a matter of tone. This is not to say the task of translating Proust is easy, only that it may be hard for a reason we do not expect: there are, most of the time, too many good possibilities rather than too few.

In spite of Forster's fine joke about Proust's sentences – the principal verb, he said, was a like a 'wounded partridge' that scarcely seemed worth all the trouble of the hunt – it is possible to maintain their structure and timing in another language, and when we have kept these elements, we shall already find ourselves worrying less about what we have lost, or wasted.

A comparative look at a famous passage may help here. At one point in the novel the Narrator catches sight of his grandmother without her seeing him, so that for a moment she is no relative of his and he is no one, just the equivalent of a photographer come to take a picture. We see at once why the timing is essential, why the object of the sentence has to come right at the end, and why the delaying epithets are almost but not quite too many or too much.

> Et, comme un malade qui ne s'était pas regardé depuis longtemps, et composant à tout moment le visage qu'il ne voit pas d'après l'image idéale qu'il porte de soi-même dans sa pensée, recule en apercevant dans une glace, au milieu d'une figure aride et déserte, l'exhaussement oblique et rose d'un nez gigantesque comme une pyramide d'Égypte, moi pour qui ma grand-mère c'était encore moi-même, moi qui ne l'avais jamais vue que dans mon âme, toujours à la même place du passé, à travers la transparence des souvenirs contigus et superposés, tout d'un coup, dans notre salon qui faisait partie d'un monde nouveau, celui du temps, celui où vivent les étrangers dont on dit 'il vieillit bien', pour la première fois et seulement pour un instant, car elle disparut bien vite, j'aperçus sur le canapé, sous la lampe, rouge, lourde et vulgaire, malade, rêvassant, promenant au-dessus d'un livre des yeux un peu fous, une vieille femme accablée que je ne connaissais pas. (II, 439–40)

Here are the relevant versions.

> And, as a sick man who for long has not looked at his own reflexion, and has kept his memory of the face that he never sees refreshed from the ideal image of himself that he carries in his mind, recoils on catching sight in the glass, in the middle of an arid waste of cheek, of the sloping red structure of a nose as huge as one of the pyramids of Egypt, I, for whom my grand-mother was still myself, I who had never seen her save in my own soul, always in the same place in the past, through the transparent sheets of contiguous, overlapping memories, suddenly in our drawing-room which

formed part of a new world, that of time, that in which dwell the strangers of whom we say 'He's begun to age a good deal', for the first time and for a moment only, since she vanished at once, I saw, sitting on the sofa, beneath the lamp, red-faced, heavy and common, sick, lost in thought, following the lines of a book with eyes that seemed hardly sane, a dejected old woman whom I did not know.[33]

And – like a sick man who, not having looked at his own reflexion for a long time, and regularly composing the features which he never sees in accordance with the ideal image of himself that he carries in his mind, recoils on catching sight in the glass, in the middle of an arid desert of a face, of the sloping pink protuberance of a nose as huge as one of the pyramids of Egypt – I, for whom my grandmother was still myself, I who had never seen her save in my own soul, always in the same place in the past, through the transparency of contiguous and overlapping memories, suddenly, in our drawing-room which formed part of a new world, that of time, that which is inhabited by the strangers of whom we say "He's begun to age a good deal", for the first time and for a moment only, since she vanished very quickly, I saw, sitting on the sofa beneath the lamp, red-faced, heavy and vulgar, sick, vacant, letting her slightly crazed eyes wander over a book, a dejected old woman whom I did not know.[34]

And – like a sick man who, not having looked at his own reflexion for a long time, and regularly composing the features which he never sees in accordance with the ideal image of himself that he carries in his mind, recoils on catching sight in the glass, in the middle of an arid desert of a face, of the sloping pink protuberance of a nose as huge as one of the pyramids of Egypt – I, for whom my grandmother was still myself, I who had never seen her save in my own soul, always in the same place in the past, through the transparency of contiguous and overlapping memories, suddenly, in our drawing-room which formed part of a new world, that of Time, that which is inhabited by the strangers of whom we say 'He's begun to age a good deal', for the first time and for a moment only, since she vanished very quickly, I saw, sitting on the sofa beneath the lamp, red-faced, heavy and vulgar, sick, day-dreaming, letting her slightly crazed eyes wander over a book, an overburdened old woman whom I did not know.[35]

And, like a sick man who has not looked in a mirror for a long time and who constantly composes the set of features he never sees in accordance with the ideal image of the face he carries in his mind, then recoils when he catches sight in a mirror of a monumental red nose, slanting out of the arid desert of his face like an Egyptian pyramid, I, for whom my grandmother was still myself, I who had only ever seen her with my soul, always at the same point in the past, through the transparency of contiguous and overlapping memories, suddenly, in our drawing-room which had now become part of a new world, the world of Time, inhabited by strangers we describe as 'ageing well', for the first time and for a mere second, since she vanished almost immediately, I saw, sitting there on the sofa beneath the lamp, red-faced, heavy and vulgar, ill, her mind in a daze, the slightly crazed eyes wandering over a book, a crushed old woman whom I did not know.[36]

So erging es mir denn wie einem Kranken, der sich lange nicht mehr gesehn und jederzeit das Gesicht, das er nicht sah, nach dem Idealbilde, das er vom eigenen Ich in sich trägt, gestaltet hat: er schreckt zurück, wenn er im Spiegel mitten aus einem dürren öden Antlitz schräg und rosa wie eine ägyptische Pyramide eine gigantische Nase steigen sieht. Für mich war meine Großmutter noch – ich selbst, ich, der sie immer nur in meiner Seele gesehn, immer an derselben Stelle der Vergangenheit, durch die Transparenz angrenzender und übergellagerter Erinnerungen, und nun sah ich plötzlich in unserm Salon, der ein Teil der neuen Welt bildete, der Welt der Zeit, der Welt, in der die Fremden leben, von denen man sagt 'Er wird recht alt', nun sah ich zum ersten Male und nur für einen Augenblick, denn ganz schnell verschwand sie wieder, auf dem Kanapee unter der Lampe rot, schlaff, gewöhnlich, krank, dösend, mit etwas irren Augen über ein Buch gleitend, eine gedrückte Frau, die ich nicht kannte.[37]

Benjamin and Hessel split the sentence into two after the simile of the nose and the pyramid, and repeat the main subject and verb of the original sentence ('nun sah ich …' 'nun sah ich …') for clarity. The meaning of the sentence becomes more immediately available, but the sense of continuity between simile and proposition – the sick man and the Narrator both surprised by alienating glimpses of the familiar – is lost. This translation, like the others, carefully maintains the rhythm of the close of the passage, the patient delaying of the arrival of the verb's object.

All the English versions keep the single sentence as one. All the translators have a good time with the simile about the nose and the desert. There is genuine disagreement about the phrase 'il vieillit bien': does it mean ageing well or ageing a lot? And two particular words provoke a wide range of choices. 'Rêvassant' and 'accablé' produce 'lost in thought' and 'dejected'; 'vacant and dejected'; 'day-dreaming' and 'overburdened'; 'her mind in a daze' and 'crushed'; 'dösend' and 'gedrückte'. Benjamin and Hessel, out of a chivalry that Proust would have appreciated but not endorsed, cannot bring themselves to call the grandmother old. She is simply a Frau whom the Narrator does not know.

The differences among the translations are interesting but their convergences are perhaps more interesting still, since they remind us that in each case we are reading Proust. Each succeeds to a considerable degree in catching the complex shifts of register and the unmistakable pathos of a remarkable passage.

Notes

1 E. M. Forster, 'Proust', reprinted in *Abinger Harvest and England's Pleasant Land* (London: Andre Deutsch, 1996), p. 92.

2 Terence Kilmartin, 'Translating Proust', *Grand Street*, 1:1 (1981), 134.

3 Christopher Prendergast cites this line in his 'General Editor's Preface' to the recent Penguin translation: see *The Way by Swann's* (London: Allen Lane, 2002, p. xx). By an irony not at all irrelevant to questions of translation, the cited version is the same as Scott Moncrieff's and rather different from the one offered by Carol Clark in the edition of which Prendergast is the editor. Clark makes the artist a 'great artist', and 'a citizen of a unknown homeland'. See *The Prisoner and the Fugitive* (London: Allen Lane, 2002), p. 235.

4 The available English translations are very close to each other here: 'The writer's work is merely a kind of optical instrument, which he offers to the reader to enable him to discern what, without this book, he would perhaps never have perceived in himself', *Remembrance of Things Past*, III, trans. by Andreas Mayor and Terence Kilmartin (London: Penguin, 1983) p. 949; the same is reproduced in the Vintage edition of *Time Regained*, trans. by Andreas Mayor and Terence Kilmartin, rev. by D. J. Enright (6: 273); the US edition is *Time Regained* (New York: Modern Library, 1999), p. 322. Cf. the recent Penguin: 'The writer's work is only a kind of optical instrument which he offers the reader to enable him to discern what without this book he might not perhaps have seen in himself', *Finding Time Again*, trans. by Ian Patterson (London: Allen Lane, 2002), p. 220.

5 These examples appear in Lydia Davis's introduction to *The Way by Swann's*, p. xxxiii.

6 Terence Kilmartin, 'Note on the Translation', in Marcel Proust, *Remembrance of Things Past* I (London: Penguin, 1983), p. xi.

7 Kilmartin, 'Note on the Translation', p. ix.

8 Pamela Hansford Johnson, *Six Proust Reconstructions* (London: Macmillan, 1958), p. ix.

9 See *The Proust Project*, ed. André Aciman (New York: Farrar, Straus and Giroux, 2004), pp. 174–81.

10 Kilmartin, 'Note on the Translation', p. xi.

11 Kilmartin, 'Translating Proust', pp. 137, 140, 145.

12 Kilmartin, 'Note on the Translation', p. xi.

13 Kilmartin, 'Note on the Translation', p. xi. Prendergast, 'General Editor's Preface', p. viii.

14 Prendergast, 'General Editor's Preface', pp. vii–viii.

15 And one addressed in Prendergast's monograph, *Mirages and Mad Beliefs: Proust the Skeptic* (Princeton University Press, 2013).

16 Prendergast, 'General Editor's Preface', p. xvii.

17 Prendergast, 'General Editor's Preface', p. xvii.

18 Prendergast, 'General Editor's Preface', p. xi.

19 *Du côté de chez Swann* (I, 170); *The Way by Swann's*, p. 173. *Le Côté de Guermantes* (II, 623); *The Guermantes Way*, trans. by Mark Traherne, (London: Allen Lane, 2002), p. 325.

20 'Mais il est rare que ces grandes maladies ... n'élisent pas pendant long-temps domicile chez le malade avant de le tuer' (II, 612); 'But these serious illnesses ... seldom take up residence in a sick person for long before they kill him'. *The Guermantes Way*, trans. Traherne, p. 314.

21 *The Proust Project*, p. 176.

22 *Finding Time Again*, p. 191.

23 *Remembrance of Things Past*, II, p. 1003.

24 *Finding Time Again*, p. 195. Scott Moncrieff has 'abdication' and the 'habit of postponing', *Remembrance of Things Past*, II, pp. 1006–7.

25 *Remembrance of Things Past*, I, p. 1141.

26 *The Guermantes Way*, p. 597.

27 Marcel Proust, *En Busca del Tiempo Perdido*, I, trans. by Pedro Salinas and José María Quiroga Plá (Barcelona: Janes, 1952), p. 1306.

28 *Remembrance of Things Past*, I, p. 959.

29 *The Guermantes Way*, p. 338.

30 Walter Benjamin, *Schriften*, Supplement III (Frankfurt: Suhrkamp, 1987), p. 335.

31 *The Prisoner and the Fugitive* (London: Allen Lane, 2002), p. 387. To be absolutely precise, Scott Moncrieff has 'farther' rather than 'further'.

32 *Finding Time Again*, p. xii.

33 Scott Moncrieff, *Remembrance of Things Past*, I, p. 815.

34 Scott Moncrieff/Kilmartin, *Remembrance of Things Past*, II, pp. 142–3.

35 Scott Moncrieff/Kilmartin/Enright, *In Search of Lost Time*, 3: 156–7.

36 *The Guermantes Way* (Traherne), p. 138.

37 Benjamin, *Schriften*, pp. 135–6.

Further reading

Unless otherwise stated, sources in French are published in Paris. Translations are included where they are available. For reasons of space, entries for Chapters 24 to 30 only include sources not already listed for other chapters.

1. Life

Carter, W. C., *Marcel Proust: A Life* (New Haven and London: Yale University Press, 2000).
   Proust in Love (New Haven and London: Yale University Press, 2006).
Tadié, J.-Y., *Marcel Proust. Biographie* (Gallimard, 1996); trans. by E. Cameron, *Marcel Proust: A Biography* (Harmondsworth: Penguin, 2000).
Watt, A., *Marcel Proust* 'Critical Lives' (London: Reaktion, 2013).
White, E., *Proust* (London: Weidenfeld & Nicolson, 1999).

2. Correspondence

Duchêne, R., 'L'homosexualité dans les lettres de Marcel Proust', in A. Magnan, ed., *Expériences limites de l'épistolaire* (Champion, 1993), pp. 59–73.
Fraisse, L., *La Correspondance de Proust: son statut dans l'œuvre, l'histoire de son édition* (Les Belles Lettres, 1998).
   Proust au miroir de sa correspondance (SEDES, 1996).
Kolb, P., *La Correspondance de Marcel Proust: chronologie et commentaire critique* (Urbana: University of Illinois Press, 1949).
Mauriac Dyer, N., A. Rivière and P.-E. Robert, eds., *Robert Proust et la Nouvelle Revue Française: les années perdues de la 'Recherche' (1922–1931)* (Gallimard, 1999).
Proust, M., *Lettres (1879–1922)*, ed. by F. Leriche, K. Kolb and V. Greene (Plon, 2004).
Robitaille, M., 'Études sur la correspondance de Marcel Proust: une synthèse', *Bulletin Marcel Proust*, 46 (1996), 109–27.
   Proust épistolier (Presses de l'Université de Montréal, 2003).
Westerwelle, K., ed., *Marcel Proust und die Korrespondenz* (Berlin: Insel, 2010).

3. Finding a form: *Les Plaisirs et les jours* to *Contre Sainte-Beuve*

Cocking, J. M., *Proust: Collected Essays on the Writer and His Art* (Cambridge University Press, 1982).

Melmoux-Montaubin, M.-F., *L'Écrivain-journaliste au XIXᵉ siècle: un mutant des lettres* (Saint-Étienne: Éditions des Cahiers intempestifs, 2003).

Milly, J., *Les Pastiches de Proust* (Armand Colin, 1970).

Proust, M., *Le Carnet de 1908*, ed. by P. Kolb (Gallimard, 1976).

Watt, A., *Reading in Proust's 'À la recherche': 'le délire de la lecture'* (Oxford University Press, 2009).

4. Finding a voice: from Ruskin to the *Pastiches*

Borrel, A., ed., *Marcel Proust: écrits de jeunesse 1887–1895* (Illiers-Combray: Institut Marcel Proust international, 1991).

Eagles, S., *After Ruskin: The Social and Political Legacies of a Victorian Prophet, 1870–1920* (Oxford University Press, 2011).

Eells, E., *Proust's Cup of Tea: Homoeroticism and Victorian Culture* (Aldershot and Burlington: Ashgate, 2002).

Ellison, D., *The Reading of Proust* (Oxford: Blackwell, 1984).

Gamble, C., *Proust as Interpreter of Ruskin: The Seven Lamps of Translation* (Birmingham, AL: Summa Publications, 2002).

La Sizeranne, R. de, *Ruskin et la religion de la beauté* (Hachette, 1897); trans. Countess of Galloway, *Ruskin and the Religion of Beauty* (London: George Allen, 1899).

Milly, J., ed., *Marcel Proust, L'Affaire Lemoine. Pastiches* (Geneva: Slatkine Reprints, 1994).

Ruskin, J., *La Bible d'Amiens*, preface, translation and notes by Marcel Proust, ed. by Y.-M. Ergal (Bartillat, 2007).

Sésame et les lys, preface, translation and notes by Marcel Proust, ed. by A. Compagnon (Brussels: Éditions Complexe, 1987).

Searls, D., ed., foreword by E. Karpeles, *Marcel Proust and John Ruskin: On Reading* (London: Hesperus, 2011).

5. Composition and publication of *À la recherche du temps perdu*

a. *Manuscripts available online*

http://gallica.bnf.fr (easy access via www.item.ens.fr/index.php?id=578147).
http://gallica.bnf.fr/dossiers/html/dossiers/Proust.

b. *Manuscript editions*

Albertine disparue, édition originale de la dernière version revue par l'auteur, ed. by N. Mauriac and É. Wolff (Grasset, 1987).

Albertine disparue, édition intégrale, ed. by J. Milly (Champion, 1992); *Albertine disparue* (11e partie de *Sodome et Gomorrhe III*) (Garnier Flammarion, 2003).
'Bricquebec'. *Prototype d'À l'ombre des jeunes filles en fleurs*, ed. by R. Bales (Oxford: Clarendon Press, 1989).
Cahiers 1 à 75 de la Bibliothèque nationale de France, ed. by N. Mauriac Dyer *et al.*, eds., (BnF, Brepols, 2008–). Cahiers 26, 53, 54 and 71 have appeared to date (2013).
Carnets, ed. by F. Callu and A. Compagnon (Gallimard, 2002).

c. Periodicals and collective volumes

Bulletin d'informations proustiennes [*BIP*], Presses de l'École normale supérieure (1975–1998), Éditions rue d'Ulm (1999–).
Bulletin d'informations proustiennes, 9 (1979): Inventories of the ten *Contre Sainte-Beuve* cahiers, by B. Brun, C. Quémar, E. des Portes and K. Yoshikawa.
Études proustiennes, Cahiers Marcel Proust nouvelle série (Gallimard, 1973–87).
Marcel Proust, La Revue des Lettres modernes, Minard (1992–).
Warning, R., and J. Milly, eds., *Marcel Proust: écrire sans fin* (CNRS Éditions, 1996).
Mauriac Dyer, N., and K. Yoshikawa, eds., *Proust aux brouillons* (Turnhout: Brepols, 'Le Champ proustien', 2011).
Proust 1913, Genesis, 36 (2013), ed. by N. Mauriac Dyer.

d. Monographs

Mauriac Dyer, N., *Proust inachevé: le dossier 'Albertine disparue'* (Champion, 2005).
Milly, J., *Proust dans le texte et l'avant-texte* (Flammarion, 1985).
Quaranta, J.-M., *Le Génie de Proust, genèse de l'esthétique de la Recherche, de 'Jean Santeuil' à la madeleine et au 'Temps retrouvé'* (Champion, 2011).
Pugh, A. R., *The Birth of 'À la recherche du temps perdu'* (Lexington: French Forum, 1987)
   The Growth of 'À la recherche du temps perdu': A Chronological Examination of Proust's Manuscripts from 1909 to 1914, 2 vols. (University of Toronto Press, 2004).
Schmid, M., *Processes of Literary Creation: Flaubert and Proust* (Oxford: Legenda, 1998).
Winton [Finch], A., *Proust's Additions. The Making of 'À la recherche du temps perdu'*, 2 vols. (Cambridge University Press, 1977).

6. Proust's reading

Foschini, L., *Proust's Overcoat*, trans. by Eric Karpeles (New York: Ecco, 2010).
Lambilliotte, J., 'La bibliothèque de Marcel Proust: de la lecture à l'écriture', *Bulletin d'informations proustiennes*, 30 (1999), 81–9.

Mauriac Dyer, N. and D. Ferrer, 'Défense de Flaubert 1919–1922', *Bulletin d'informations proustiennes*, 30 (1999), 29–48.
'L'exemplaire annoté de *La Chartreuse de Parme*', *Bulletin d'informations proustiennes*, 35 (2005), 9–17.
Picon, J., *Passion Proust, l'album d'une vie* (Textuel, 1999).

7. Decadence and the fin de siècle

Aubert, N., ed., *Proust and the Visual* (Cardiff: University of Wales Press, 2013).
Compagnon, A., *Proust entre deux siècles* (Seuil, 1989).
Hohl, R., 'Die *Recherche* und der Post-Impressionismus', in *Proustiana XXI* (Frankfurt am Main and Leipzig: Insel, 2001), 67–84.
Proust, M., *Écrits de jeunesse, 1887–1895* (Illiers-Combray: Institut Marcel Proust International, 1991).
Schmid, M., *Proust dans la décadence* (Champion, 2008).
Thompson, H., 'Decadence', in W. Burgwinkle, N. Hammond and E. Wilson, eds., *The Cambridge History of French Literature* (Cambridge University Press, 2011), pp. 541–8.
Weir, D., *Decadence and the Making of Modernism* (Amherst: University of Massachusetts Press, 1995).

8. Paris and the avant-garde

Aubert, N., ed., *Proust and the Visual* (Cardiff: University of Wales Press, 2013).
Azérad, H., 'Parisian Literary Fields: James Joyce and Pierre Reverdy's *Theory of the Image*', *Modern Language Review*, 103 (2008), 665–81.
Bauman, Z., *Modernity and Ambivalence* (Cambridge: Polity Press, 1991).
Bobillot, J.-P., 'Proust et la poésie de son temps: ironies, résonances, incompatibilités', *Bulletin d'informations proustiennes*, 41 (2011), 35–54.
Bürger, P., *Theory of the Avant-Garde*, trans. by Michael Shaw (Minneapolis: University of Minnesota Press, 1984).
Calinescu, M., *Faces of Modernity* (Bloomington: Indiana University Press, 1977).
Cottington, D., *Cubism and Its Histories* (Manchester University Press, 2004).
Danius, S., *The Senses of Modernism: Technology, Perception, and Aesthetics* (Ithaca, NY: Cornell University Press, 2002).
Fauchereau, S., *Hommes et mouvements du XXe siècle* (Éditions Cercle d'Art, 2005).
Fraisse, L., 'Il y a plusieurs manières d'être avant-garde: Proust et le cubisme', in Pascal Dethurens, ed., *Peinture et Littérature au XXème siècle* (Presses universitaires de Strasbourg, 2007), pp. 173–87.
Jenny, L., *La Fin de l'intériorité* (Presses universitaires de France, 2002).
Keller, L., 'Proust au-delà de l'impressionnisme', in Sophie Bertho, ed., *Proust et ses peintres* (Amsterdam: Rodopi, 2000), pp. 57–70.
Kern, S., *The Modernist Novel* (Cambridge University Press, 2011).

Lewis, P., *The Cambridge Introduction to Modernism* (Cambridge University Press, 2007).

Poggi, C., *Inventing Futurism* (Princeton University Press, 2009).

Rabaté, J.-M., *1913: The Cradle of Modernism* (Oxford: Blackwell, 2007).

Savy, N., 'Jeune roman, jeune peinture', in J.-Y. Tadié, ed., *Marcel Proust: l'écriture et les arts*. (Réunion des musées nationaux, 1999), pp. 55–65.

Schuerewegen, F., 'Proust est-il dadaïste? (à propos d'un mystère non encore élucidé de l'histoire littéraire)', *Marcel Proust Aujourd'hui*, 5 (2007), 137–160.

Sheppard, R., *Modernism, Dada, Post-Modernism* (Evanston, IL: Northwestern University Press, 2000).

9. The novelistic tradition

Bouillaguet, A., *Proust lecteur de Balzac et de Flaubert: l'imitation cryptée* (Champion, 2000).

Compagnon, A., *Proust entre deux siècles* (Seuil, 1989); trans. by R. E. Goodkin, *Proust between Two Centuries* (New York: Columbia University Press, 1992).

ed., *Proust, la mémoire et la littérature* (Odile Jacob, 2009).

Fraisse, L., *La Petite Musique du style: Proust et ses sources littéraires* (Garnier, 2011).

Tadié, J.-Y., *Proust et le roman* (Gallimard, 1971; reprinted 1986).

10. Philosophy

Beckett, S., *Proust and Three Dialogues with Georges Duthuit* (London: John Calder, 1965).

Carbone, M. and E. Sparvoli, eds., *Proust et la philosophie aujourd'hui* (Pisa: Edizioni ETS, 2008).

Danius, S., 'The Aesthetics of the Windshield: Proust and the Modernist Rhetoric of Speed', *Modernism/Modernity*, 8 (2001), 100–26.

Descombes, V., *Proust: philosophie du roman* (Minuit, 1987); trans. by C. Chance Macksey, *Proust: Philosophy of the Novel* (Stanford University Press, 1992).

Landy, J., *Philosophy as Fiction: Self, Deception and Knowledge in Proust* (Oxford University Press, 2004).

Large, D., *Nietzsche and Proust: A Comparative Study* (Oxford University Press, 2001).

Henry, A., *Marcel Proust, théories pour une esthétique* (Klincksieck, 1981).

'Proust du côté de Schopenhauer', in A. Henry, ed., *Schopenhauer et la création littéraire en Europe* (Klincksieck, 1989), pp. 149–64.

11. Painting

Aubert, N., ed., *Proust and the Visual* (Cardiff: University of Wales Press, 2013).

Butor, M., *Les Œuvres d'art imaginaires chez Proust* (University of London, Athlone Press, 1964).

Karpeles, E., *Paintings in Proust: A Visual Companion to 'In Search of Lost Time'* (London: Thames & Hudson, 2008).

Marcel Proust: L'Écriture et les arts. Exhibition catalogue, dir. Jean-Yves Tadié (Gallimard/Bibliothèque nationale de France/Réunion des musées nationaux, 1999).

Monnin-Hornung, J., *Proust et la peinture* (Geneva: Librairie Droz, 1951).

Townsend, G., *Proust's Imaginary Museum: Reproduction and Reproductions in 'À la recherche du temps perdu'* (Oxford, Bern: Peter Lang, 2008).

Wakefield, D. F., 'Proust and the Visual Arts', *The Burlington Magazine*, vol. CXII, 806 (1970), 291–6.

Yoshikawa, K., *Proust et l'art pictural* (Champion, 2010).

12. Music

Benoist-Méchin, J., *Retour à Marcel Proust* (Pierre Amiot, 1957).

Carbone, M., 'Composing Vinteuil: Proust's unheard music', *RES: Anthropology and Aesthetics*, 48 (2005), 163–5.

An Unprecedented Deformation: Marcel Proust and the Sensible Ideas (New York: State University of New York Press, 2010).

Costil, P., 'La construction musicale de la *Recherche du temps perdu*', *Bulletin des Amis de Marcel Proust et des Amis de Combray*, 8 (1958), 469–89; and 9 (1959), 83–110.

Coueroy, A., 'Music in the Work of Marcel Proust', *The Musical Quarterly*, 12 (1926), 132–51.

Matoré, G., and I. Mecz, *Musique et structure romanesque dans la 'Recherche du temps perdu'* (Klincksieck, 1972).

Milly, J., *La Phrase de Proust – des phrases de Bergotte aux phrases de Vinteuil* (Larousse, 1975).

Nattiez, J.-J., *Proust musicien* (Christian Bourgois, 1984); trans. by D. Puffett, *Proust as Musician* (Cambridge University Press, 1989).

Newark, C., *Opera in the Novel from Balzac to Proust* (Cambridge University Press, 2011).

Pauset, E.-N., *Marcel Proust et Gustav Mahler: créateurs parallèles* (L'Harmattan, 2007).

Piroué, G., *Proust et la musique du devenir* (Denoël, 1960).

Shattuck, R., 'Making Time: A Study of Stravinsky, Proust and Sartre', *The Kenyon Review* 25 (1963), 248–63.

Yoshikawa, K., 'Vinteuil ou la genèse du Septuor', *Cahiers Marcel Proust* 9. *Études proustiennes* III (Gallimard, 1979), 289–347.

13. Theatre and dance

Bolens, G., *Le Style des gestes: corporéité et kinésie dans le récit littéraire* (Lausanne: Éditions BHMS, 2008).

Hanna, J. L., *Dance, Sex and Gender: Signs of Identity, Dominance, Defiance, and Desire* (University of Chicago Press, 1988).

Hemmings, F. W. J., *The Theatre Industry in Nineteenth-Century France* (Cambridge University Press, 2006).

Magill, M. M., 'Pas de pas de deux pour Proust: l'absence de la danse dans *À la recherche du temps perdu*', *Dalhousie French Studies*, 53 (2000), 49–55.

Pritchard, J., ed., *Diaghilev and the Golden Age of the Ballets Russes 1909–1929* (London: V&A Publishing, 2010).

Schaller, P., 'Theatre in Proust – the Fourth Art', in 'Proust et le théâtre', *Marcel Proust aujourd'hui*, 4 (2006), 51–70.

Townsend, J., *The Choreography of Modernism in France: La Danseuse, 1830–1930* (Oxford: Legenda, 2008).

14. Freud and psychoanalysis

Baudry, J.-L., *Freud, Proust et l'autre* (Éditions de minuit, 1984).

Bizub, E., *Proust et le moi divisé: 'La Recherche', creuset de la psychologie expérimentale (1874–1914)* (Geneva: Droz, 2006).

Bowie, M., *Freud, Proust and Lacan: Theory as Fiction* (Cambridge University Press, 1987).

Deschamps, N., 'Critique psychanalytique', in A. Bouillaguet and B. G. Rogers, eds., *Dictionnaire Marcel Proust* (Champion, 2004), pp. 268–71.

Fernandez, D., *L'Arbre jusqu'aux racines, psychanalyse et création* (Grasset, 1992).

Haustein, K., 'Proust's Emotional Cavities: Vision and Affect in *À la recherche du temps perdu*', *French Studies*, 63 (2009), 161–73.

Landy, J., 'Proust among the Psychologists', *Philosophy and Literature*, 35 (2011), 375–87.

Mijolla, A. de, *Freud et la France 1885–1945* (Presses universitaires de France, 2010).

Panzac, D., *Le Docteur Adrien Proust: père méconnu, précurseur oublié* (L'Harmattan, 2003).

Roudinesco, É., 'Freud et Proust: un parallèle impressionniste', www.cifpr.fr/+Freud-et-Proust-parallele+, 12 June 2012.

Tadié, J.-Y., *Le Lac inconnu: entre Proust et Freud* (Gallimard, 2012).

15. Sexuality

Eells, E., *Proust's Cup of Tea: Homoeroticism and Victorian Culture* (Aldershot: Ashgate, 2002).

Ladenson, E., *Proust's Lesbianism* (Ithaca, NY and London: Cornell University Press, 1999).

Laqueur, T., *Solitary Sex: A Cultural History of Masturbation* (New York: Zone Books, 2003).

Lejeune, P., 'Écriture et sexualité', *Europe*, 49 (1971), 113–43.

Lucey, M., *Never Say I: Sexuality and the First Person in Colette, Gide, and Proust* (Durham, NC: Duke University Press, 2006).

Sedgwick, E. K., *Epistemology of the Closet* (Berkeley: University of California Press, 1990).

Further reading

16. Health and medicine

Béhar, S., *L'Univers médical de Proust* (Gallimard, 1970).
Bragg, L. and W. Sayers, 'Proust's Prescription: Sickness as the Pre-Condition for Writing', *Literature and Medicine*, 19.2 (2000), 165–81.
Finn, M. R., *Proust, the Body and Literary Form* (Cambridge University Press, 1999/2006).
Fladenmüller, F., 'Le Nerveux Narrateur dans *À la recherche du temps perdu*', *Bulletin d'informations proustiennes*, 17 (1986), 35–42.
Holdinet, R. S. G., 'Proust et la médecine', *Marcel Proust aujourd'hui*, 5 (2007), 217–35.
Miguet, M., 'La neurasthénie entre science et fiction', *Bulletin Marcel Proust*, 40 (1990), 28–42.
Soupault, R., *Marcel Proust du côté de la médecine* (Gallimard, 1967).
Strauss, B., *The Maladies of Proust: Doctors and Disease in his Life and Work* (New York: Holmes and Meier, 1980).
Yoshida, J., 'Proust et la maladie nerveuse', *La Revue des lettres modernes: histoire des idées et des littératures*, 1067–72 (1992), 101–19.

17. Technology and science

Bizub, E., *Proust et le moi divisé: 'La Recherche', creuset de la psychologie expérimentale (1874–1914)* (Geneva: Droz, 2006).
Danius, S., *The Senses of Modernism: Technology, Perception, and Aesthetics* (Ithaca, NY: Cornell University Press, 2002).
Finn, M. R., *Proust, the Body and Literary Form* (Cambridge University Press, 1999).
Kern, S., *The Culture of Time and Space: 1880–1918* (Cambridge, MA and London: Harvard University Press, 2003 [1983]).
Luckhurst, N., *Science and Structure in Proust's 'À la recherche du temps perdu'* (Oxford: Clarendon Press, 2000).
Scribner, C., Jr, 'Scientific Imagery in Proust', *Proceedings of the American Philosophical Society*, 134 (1990), 243–308.
Shattuck, R., *Proust's Binoculars* (London: Chatto & Windus, 1964).
Thiher, A., *Fiction Refracts Science: Modernist Writers from Proust to Borges* (Columbia: University of Missouri Press, 2005).
  Fiction Rivals Science: The French Novel from Balzac to Proust (Columbia: University of Missouri Press, 2001).
Vannucci, F., *Marcel Proust à la recherche des sciences* (Monaco: Rocher, 2005).

18. Religion

Autret, J., *L'Influence de Ruskin sur la vie, les idées et l'œuvre de Marcel Proust* (Geneva: Droz, 1955).
Bales, R., *Proust and the Middle Ages* (Geneva: Droz, 1975).

Diamant, N., 'Judaism, Homosexuality and Other Sign Systems in *À la recherche du temps perdu*', *Romanic Review*, 82 (1989), 179–92.

Fraisse, L., *L'Œuvre cathédrale: Proust et l'architecture médiévale* (Corti, 1990).

Hassine, J., 'L'écriture des allégories de l'Église et de la Synagogue dans l'œuvre de Marcel Proust', *Bulletin d'informations proustiennes*, 39 (2009), 135–54.

Ésotérisme et écriture dans l'œuvre de Proust (Minard, 1990).

Marranisme et hébraïsme dans l'œuvre de Proust (Minard, 1994).

Hughes, E. J., *Marcel Proust: A Study in the Quality of Awareness* (Cambridge University Press, 1983).

Mingelgrün, A., *Thèmes et structures bibliques dans l'œuvre de Marcel Proust: étude stylistique de quelques interférences* (Lausanne: L'Âge d'homme, 1978).

Recanati, J., *Profils juifs de Marcel Proust* (Buchet/Chastel, 1979).

Rivers, J. E., *Proust and the Art of Love: The Aesthetics of Sexuality in the Life, Time and Arts of Marcel Proust* (New York: Columbia University Press, 1981).

Walker, S. F., 'The Name of the Madeleine: Signs and Symbols of the Mass in Proust's *In Search of Lost Time*', *Religion and the Arts*, 7.4 (2003), 389–411.

Zenou, G., 'Proust et la judéité', *Europe: Revue Littéraire Mensuelle*, 705–6 (1988), 157–64.

19. Travel

Alcorn, C., 'Cars, Trains, Planes and Proust', *Nineteenth-Century French Studies*, 14.1–2 (1985–6), 153–61.

Bales, R., 'The Loneliness of the Long-Distance Narrator: The Inscription of Travel in Proust and W. G. Sebald', in J. Conroy, ed., *Cross-Cultural Travel: Papers from the Royal Irish Academy Symposium on Literature and Travel* (New York: Peter Lang, 2003), pp. 507–12.

Bray, P. M., *Novel Selves: Mapping the Subject in Stendhal, Nerval and Proust* (Cambridge, MA: Harvard University Press, 2005).

Brendon, P., *Thomas Cook: 150 Years of Popular Tourism* (London: Martin Secker & Warburg, 1992).

Collier, P., *Proust and Venice* (Cambridge University Press, 1989).

Cornette, J., 'The *Recherche* as "tout-monde": Toward a Francophone Proust', *Contemporary French and Francophone Studies*, 9.1 (2005), 87–95.

Hunter, F. R., 'Tourism and Empire: The Thomas Cook & Son Enterprise on the Nile, 1868–1914', *Middle Eastern Studies*, 40.5 (2004), 28–54.

Jordan, J., 'Proust's Narrator: Travels in the Space–Time Continuum', in N. Harkness and M. Schmid, eds., *Au seuil de la modernité: Proust, Literature and the Arts. Essays in Memory of Richard Bales* (Oxford: Peter Lang, 2011), pp. 151–64.

Megay, J., 'Le thème du voyage dans l'œuvre de Marcel Proust', in F. C. Amelinckx and J. N. Megay, eds., *Travel, Quest, and Pilgrimage as a Literary Theme: Studies in Honor of Reino Virtanen* (Lincoln, NE: Society of Spanish and Spanish-American Studies, 1978), pp. 221–30.

Siegel, J., *Haunted Museum: Longing, Travel and the Art–Romance Tradition* (Princeton University Press, 2005).

Urbain, J.-D., 'Les catanautes des cryptocombes: des iconoclastes de l'Ailleurs', *Nottingham French Studies, 'Errances urbaines'* special issue, ed. Jean-Xavier Ridon, 39.1 (2000), 7–16.

'"I travel therefore I am": the "Nomad Mind" and the Spirit of Travel', trans. by C. Forsdick, *Studies in Travel Writing*, 4 (2000), 141–64.

20. Journalism

Assouline, P., ed., *Autour de 'La Recherche': Lettres* (Éditions Complexe, 1988).

Albert, P., *Histoire de la presse* (Presses universitaires de France, 1970).

Blandin, C., *Le Figaro: deux siècles d'histoire* (Armand Colin, 2007).

Cano, C., 'Gide, Proust, and the Nouvelle Revue française', *Romance Quarterly*, 50 (2003), 33–42.

'Proust and the Wartime Press', in A. Watt, ed., *'Le Temps retrouvé' Eighty Years After/80 ans après: Critical Essays/Essais critiques* (Oxford: Peter Lang, 2009), pp. 133–40.

Finn, M. R., *Proust, the Body and Literary Form* (Cambridge University Press, 1999).

Quint, P.-L., *Marcel Proust: sa vie, son œuvre* (Éditions du Sagittaire, 1925).

Sandre, Y., 'Proust chroniqueur', *Revue d'histoire littéraire de la France, special issue 'Marcel Proust'*, 71 (1971), 771–90.

Whitington, T., *The Syllables of Time: Proust and the History of Reading* (Oxford: Legenda, 2009), ch. III: 'The French Press in *À la recherche*', pp. 39–50.

21. Politics and class

Bidou-Zachariasen, C., *Proust sociologue: de la maison aristocratique au salon bourgeois* (Descartes & Cie, 1997).

Bowie, M., *Proust among the Stars* (London: HarperCollins, 1998).

Chaudier, S., *Proust et le langage religieux: la cathédrale profane* (Honoré Champion, 2004).

Descombes, V., *Proust: philosophie du roman* (Minuit, 1987); trans. by C. Chance Macksey, *Proust: Philosophy of the Novel* (Stanford University Press, 1992).

Dubois, J., *Pour Albertine: Proust et le sens du social* (Seuil, 1997).

Grandsaigne, J. de, *L'Espace combraysien: monde de l'enfance et structure sociale dans l'œuvre de Proust* (Minard, 1981).

Hughes, E. J., 'Proust and Social Spaces', in R. Bales, ed., *The Cambridge Companion to Proust* (Cambridge University Press, 2001), pp. 151–67.

Proust, Class, and Nation (Oxford University Press, 2011).

Revel, J.-F., *Sur Proust* (Grasset, 1987 (1960)).

Schmid, M., 'Ideology and Discourse in Proust: The Making of "Monsieur de Charlus pendant la guerre"', *Modern Language Review*, 94/4 (1999), 961–77.

Sprinker, M., *History and Ideology in Proust: 'À la recherche du temps perdu' and the Third French Republic* (Cambridge University Press, 1994).

Tadié, J.-Y., *Marcel Proust: Biographie* (Gallimard, NRF Biographies, 1996).

22. The Dreyfus Affair

Chêne, J., E. Aberdam and D. Aberdam, eds., *Comment devient-on dreyfusard?* (L'Harmattan, 1997).

Harris, R., *Dreyfus: Politics, Emotion, and the Scandal of the Century* (New York: Metropolitan Books, 2010).

Hassine, J., *Marranisme et Hébraïsme dans l'œuvre de Proust* (Minard, 1994).

Murakami, Y., 'L'Affaire Dreyfus dans l'œuvre de Proust' (doctoral thesis, Université de Paris–Sorbonne, 2012).

Schmid, M., 'The Jewish Question in *À la recherche du temps perdu* in the Light of Discourses of Race', *Neophilologus*, 83 (1999), 33–49.

Sprinker, M., *History and Ideology in Proust: 'À la recherche du temps perdu' and the Third French Republic* (Cambridge University Press, 1994).

Tadié, J.-Y., *Marcel Proust: Biographie* (Gallimard, NRF Biographies, 1996).

Wilson, S., *Ideology and Experience: Antisemitism in France at the Time of the Dreyfus Affair* (East Brunswick, NJ: Associated University Presses, 1982).

23. The First World War

The webpage of the ITEM Équipe Proust 2010–11 seminar, *'À la recherche du temps perdu*, roman de la guerre', gives a comprehensive reading list. See www.item.ens.fr/index.php?id=577710.

Cano, C. M., 'Proust and the Wartime Press', in A. Watt, ed., *'Le Temps retrouvé' Eighty Years After/80 ans après: Critical Essays/Essais critiques* (Oxford: Peter Lang, 2009), pp. 133–40.

Compagnon, A., *'La Recherche du temps perdu* de Marcel Proust,' in P. Nora, ed., *Les Lieux de mémoire* [1984–92], 'Quarto' edition, 3 vols., III 'Les France' (Gallimard, 1997), pp. 3835–69.

Dubois, J., 'Proust et le temps des embusqués,' in P. Schoentjes, ed., *La Grande Guerre: un siècle de fiction romanesque* (Geneva: Droz, 2008), pp. 205–25.

Hughes, E. J., 'Cataclysm at One Remove,' in E. Dezon-Jones, ed., *Approaches to Teaching Proust's Fiction and Criticism* (New York: MLA, 2003), pp. 38–43.

Proust, Class, and Nation (Oxford University Press, 2011).

Ifri, P., 'La première guerre mondiale dans la *Recherche* et la correspondance: un parallèle', *Bulletin Marcel Proust*, 62 (2012), 19–30.

Rieuneau, M., 'La guerre dans *Le Temps retrouvé*', in *Guerre et révolutions dans le roman français de 1919 à 1939* (Klincksieck, 1974), pp. 112–33.

Schmid, M., 'Ideology and Discourse in Proust: The Making of "Monsieur de Charlus pendant la guerre"', *Modern Language Review*, 94/4 (1999), 961–77.

Sprinker, M., *History and Ideology in Proust: 'À la recherche du temps perdu' and the Third French Republic* (Cambridge University Press, 1994).

24. Critical reception during Proust's lifetime

Most of the newspapers and periodicals, which are seminal to Proust's critical reception during his lifetime and have been cited in this chapter can be accessed via Gallica, the excellent digital portal of the Bibliothèque nationale de France: http://gallica.bnf.fr.

Ahlstedt, E., *La Pudeur en crise: un aspect de l'accueil d' 'À la recherche du temps perdu' de Marcel Proust (1913–1930)* (Touzot, 1985).

Alden, D., *Marcel Proust and His French Critics* (New York: Russell & Russell, 1940).

Cano, C. M., *Proust's Deadline* (Urbana and Chicago: University of Illinois Press, 2006).

Fravalo-Tane, P., *'À la recherche du temps perdu' en France et en Allemagne (1913–1958): 'Dans une sorte de langue étrangère. . .'* (Champion, 2008).

Hodson, L., ed., *Marcel Proust: The Critical Heritage* (London: Routledge, 1989).

Naturel, M., ed., *La Réception de Proust à l'étranger* (Illiers-Combray: Institut Marcel Proust International, 2001).

Tadié, J.-Y., *Lectures de Proust* (Armand Colin, 1971).

25. Early critical responses, 1922 to 1950s

Alden, D., *Marcel Proust and His French Critics* (New York: Russell & Russell, 1940).

Benjamin, W., 'The Image of Proust', in *Illuminations*, trans. by H. Zohn, ed. by H. Arendt (London: Pimlico, 1999 [1970]), pp. 197–210.

Blanchot, M., *Le livre à venir* (Gallimard, 1959); *The Book to Come*, trans. by C. Mandell (Stanford University Press, 2002).

Dezon-Jones, E., 'La réception d'*À la recherche du temps perdu* aux États-Unis', in W. C. Carter, ed., *The UAB Marcel Proust Symposium: In Celebration of the 75th Anniversary of 'Swann's Way': 1913–1988*, (Birmingham, AL: Summa Publications, 1989), pp. 31–48.

Fravalo-Tane, P., *'À la recherche du temps perdu' en France et en Allemagne (1913–1958): 'Dans une sorte de langue étrangère. . .'* (Champion, 2008).

Hommage à Marcel Proust, 1871–1922, *Nouvelle Revue française* (1923).

Maurois, A., *À la recherche de Marcel Proust* (Paris, 1949); *The Quest for Proust*, trans. by G. Hopkins (Harmondsworth: Penguin, 1962).

Rivière, J., *Quelques progrès dans l'étude du cœur humain*, *Études proustiennes*, *Cahiers Marcel Proust*, n.s. 13 (Gallimard, 1985 [1927]).

Rousset, J., *Forme et signification: essai sur les structures littéraires de Corneille à Claudel* (José Corti, 1963).

Scott Moncrieff, C. K., ed., *Marcel Proust: An English Tribute* (London: Chatto & Windus, 1923).

Spitzer, L., 'Le style de Marcel Proust', in *Études de style* (NRF, 1970 [first German publication 1928]).

Teroni, S., 'Nous voilà délivrés de Proust', in J. Brami, ed., *Marcel Proust 8: lecteurs de Proust au XXe siècle et au début du XXIe* (Caen: Lettres modernes Minard, 2010).

Wilson, E., 'Marcel Proust', in *Axel's Castle: A Study in the Imaginative Literature of 1870–1930* (London: Collins Fontana, 1979 [1931]), pp. 111–54.

26. Mid-twentieth-century views, 1960s to 1980s

Bersani, L., *Marcel Proust: The Fictions of Life and of Art* (Oxford University Press, 1965).

Blanchot, M., 'L'expérience de Proust', in *Le livre à venir* (Gallimard, 1959), pp. 19–37; 'The Experience of Proust', in *The Book to Come*, trans. by C. Mandell (Stanford University Press, 2002), pp. 19–37.

Bowie, M., 'Barthes on Proust', *The Yale Journal of Criticism*, 14/2 (2001), 513–18.

Deleuze, G., *Proust et les signes* (Presses universitaires de France, 1964; fourth edn, rev. 1970); *Proust and Signs*, trans. by R. Howard (London: The Athlone Press, 2000).

'Proust Round Table', in *Two Regimes of Madness: Texts and Interviews 1975–1995*, trans. by A. Hodges and M. Taormina (New York and Los Angeles: Semiotext(e), 2007), pp. 29–60.

Man, P. de, *Blindness and Insight: Essays in the Rhetoric of Contemporary Criticism*, 2nd edn (London: Routledge, 1983).

Dosse, F., *History of Structuralism: The Rising Sign, 1945–1966*, trans. by D. Glassman (Minneapolis: University of Minnesota Press, 1997).

Genette, G., 'Discours du récit', in *Figures III* (Seuil, 1972), pp. 65–282; *Narrative Discourse: An Essay in Method*, trans. by J. E. Lewin (Ithaca, NY: Cornell University Press, 1980).

Kristeva, J., *Le Temps sensible: Proust et l'expérience littéraire* (Gallimard 'Folio Essais', 2000 [1994]); *Time and Sense: Proust and the Experience of Literature*, trans. by R. Guberman (New York: Columbia University Press, 1996).

Poulet, G., *L'Espace proustien* (Gallimard, 1963); *Proustian Space*, trans. by E. Coleman (Baltimore and London: Johns Hopkins University Press, 1977).

'Proust', in *Études sur le temps humain* (Plon, 1952), pp. 400–38.

Richard, J.-P., *Proust et le monde sensible* (Seuil, 1974).

27. Late-twentieth- and twenty-first-century responses

Benhaïm, A., ed., *The Strange M. Proust* (Oxford: Legenda, 2009).

Beugnet, M., and M. Schmid, *Proust at the Movies* (Aldershot: Ashgate, 2004).

Brun, B., M. Oguro and K. Yoshikawa, eds., *Marcel Proust 6: Proust sans frontières 1* (Caen: Lettres modernes Minard, 2007).

eds., *Marcel Proust 7: Proust sans frontières 2* (Caen: Lettres modernes Minard, 2009).

Carter, W. C., *Marcel Proust: A Life* (New Haven, CT, and London: Yale University Press, 2000).

ed., *The UAB Marcel Proust Symposium: In Celebration of the 75th Anniversary of 'Swann's Way'* (Birmingham, AL: Summa, 1989).

Caws, M. A., *Marcel Proust* (New York and London: Overlook Duckworth, 2003).

Chardin, P., ed., *Originalités proustiennes* (Éditions Kimé, 2010).

Cléder, J. and J.-P. Montier, eds., *Proust et les images, peinture, photographie, cinéma, vidéo* (Presses Universitaires de Rennes, 2003).

Compagnon, A., ed., *Proust, la mémoire et la littérature* (Odile Jacob, 2009).

Duval, S., *L'Ironie proustienne: la vision stéréoscopique* (Champion, 2004).

Ellison, D., *A Reader's Guide to Proust's 'In Search of Lost Time'* (Cambridge University Press, 2010).

Fraisse, L., *L'Éclectisme philosophique de Marcel Proust* (Presses université Paris–Sorbonne, 2013).

Gray, M., *Postmodern Proust* (Philadelphia: University of Pennsylvania Press, 1992).

Hägglund, Martin, *Dying for Time: Proust, Woolf, Nabokov* (Cambridge, MA: Harvard University Press, 2012).

Harkness, N. and M. Schmid, eds., *Au seuil de la modernité: Proust, literature and the arts. Essays in Memory of Richard Bales* (Oxford and Bern: Peter Lang, 2011).

Haustein, K., *Regarding Lost Time: Photography, Identity and Affect in Proust, Benjamin and Barthes* (Oxford: Legenda, 2012).

Karlin, D., *Proust's English* (Oxford University Press, 2005).

Kotin, A. and K. Kolb, eds., *Proust in Perspective: Visions and Revisions* (Urbana, University of Illinois Press, 2002).

Larkin, Á., *Proust Writing Photography: Fixing the Fugitive in 'À la recherche du temps perdu'* (Oxford: Legenda, 2011).

Lehrer, J., *Proust Was a Neuroscientist* (Boston and New York: Houghton Mifflin, 2007).

Le Roux-Kieken, A. *Imaginaire et écriture de la mort dans l'œuvre de Marcel Proust* (Champion, 2005).

Mauriac Dyer, N., K. Yoshikawa and P.-E. Robert, eds., *Proust face à l'héritage du XIXe siècle: tradition et métamorphose* (Presses Sorbonne-Nouvelle, 2012).

McDonald, C., *The Proustian Fabric: Associations of Memory* (Lincoln and London: University of Nebraska Press, 1991).

Rose, J., *Proust among the Nations: From Dreyfus to the Middle East* (University of Chicago Press, 2012).

Sedgwick, E. Kosofsky, *The Weather in Proust* (Durham, NC: Duke University Press, 2012).

Segal, N. and G. Rye, eds., *'When familiar meanings dissolve…': Essays in French Studies in Memory of Malcolm Bowie* (Oxford, Bern: Peter Lang, 2011).

Simon, A., *Proust ou le réel retrouvé* (Presses universitaires de France, 2000; new edn, Champion, 2010).

Watt, A., *The Cambridge Introduction to Marcel Proust* (Cambridge University Press, 2011).
  ed., *'Le Temps retrouvé' Eighty Years After: Critical Essays/Essais critiques* (Oxford, Bern: Peter Lang, 2009).
White, E., *Proust* (London: Weidenfeld & Nicolson, 1999).

28. Modernism

Benjamin, W., 'The Image of Proust', in *Illuminations*, trans. by H. Zohn, ed. by H. Arendt (London: Pimlico, 1999 [1970]), pp. 197–210.
Chambers, R., *Mélancolie et opposition: les débuts du modernisme en France* (José Corti, 1987); *The Writing of Melancholy: Modes of Opposition in Early French Modernism*, trans. by M. Seidman Trouille (University of Chicago Press, 1993).
Friedrich, H., *Struktur der modernen Lyrik* (Hamburg: Rowohlt, 1956); *The Structure of Modern Poetry from the Mid-Nineteenth to the Mid-Twentieth Century*, trans. by J. Neugrsochel (Evanston, IL: Northwestern University Press, 1974).
Gay, P., *Modernism, The Lure of Heresy: From Baudelaire to Beckett and Beyond* (New York: Norton, 2008).
Wilson, E., *Axel's Castle: A Study in the Imaginative Literature of 1870–1930* (London: Collins Fontana, 1979 [1931]).

29. Adaptations/afterlives

Barthes, R., *Le Plaisir du texte* (Seuil, 1973).
Benjamin, W., 'The Work of Art in the Age of Mechanical Reproduction', in *Illuminations*, trans. by H. Zohn, ed. by H. Arendt (London: Pimlico, 1999 [1970]), pp. 211–44.
Bourdieu, P., *La Distinction: critique sociale du jugement* (Minuit, 1979).
Certeau, M. de, *L'Invention du quotidien: arts de faire*, vol. 1 (Gallimard, 1980).
Houston, J. P., 'Theme and Structure in *À la recherche du temps perdu*', *Kentucky Romance Quarterly*, 17 (1970), 209–22.
Naturel, M., ed., *La Réception de Proust à l'étranger* (Illiers-Combray: Institut Marcel Proust International, 2002).

30. Translations

Aciman, A., ed., *The Proust Project* (New York: Farrar, Straus and Giroux, 2004).
Johnson, P. Hansford, *Six Proust Reconstructions* (London: Macmillan, 1958).
Kilmartin, T., 'Translating Proust', *Grand Street*, 1:1 (1981), 134–46.
Prendergast, C., *Mirages and Mad Beliefs: Proust the Skeptic* (Princeton University Press, 2013).

Index

256